Praise for

reconceptualizing early childhood care & education

"Today when the disenchantment with the dominant discourses within the field of early childhood education is pervasive, this is a timely and important book. The editors, as the leading-edge of the reconceptualizing early childhood education movement since the early 1990s, have here assembled researchers who have been influential in contesting the normalizing and universalizing processes of the mainstream discourses within the field, as well as in creating a space for new critical theories and paradigmatic positions that welcome complexity, diversity, uncertainty as well as wonder."

—Gunilla Dahlberg, Professor Emerita, Stockholm University, Sweden

"The authors draw on twenty years of research and scholarship on reconceptualizing early childhood education to push us to intensify our struggles for equity, justice, inclusion, redistributive economics and social politics. With stories and voices that are both discomfiting and inspirational, they ask hard questions about how it could be and how we can use our imaginations and our activisms to make it better for all children."

—Mara Sapon-Shevin, Professor of Inclusive Education, Faculty Member,
Disabilities Studies, Women's Studies, Programs in the Analysis
and Resolution of Conflicts, Syracuse University

reconceptualizing early childhood care & education

Rethinking Childhood

Gaile S. Cannella
General Editor

Vol. 50

The Rethinking Childhood series is part of the Peter Lang Education list.
Every volume is peer reviewed and meets
the highest quality standards for content and production.

PETER LANG
New York • Washington, D.C./Baltimore • Bern
Frankfurt • Berlin • Brussels • Vienna • Oxford

reconceptualizing early childhood care & education • A READER

Critical Questions, New Imaginaries and Social Activism

Marianne N. Bloch, Beth Blue Swadener, and Gaile S. Cannella,
EDITORS

PETER LANG
New York • Washington, D.C./Baltimore • Bern
Frankfurt • Berlin • Brussels • Vienna • Oxford

Library of Congress Cataloging-in-Publication Data

Reconceptualizing early childhood care and education:
critical questions, new imaginaries and social activism: a reader /
edited by Marianne N. Bloch, Beth Blue Swadener, Gaile S. Cannella.
pages cm. — (Rethinking childhood; v. 50)
Includes bibliographical references.
1. Early childhood education—Social aspects. 2. Social justice—Study and teaching.
I. Bloch, Marianne N. II. Swadener, Beth Blue. III. Cannella, Gaile Sloan.
LB1139.23.R4   372.21—dc23   2013042279
ISBN 978-1-4331-2366-5 (hardcover)
ISBN 978-1-4331-2365-8 (paperback)
ISBN 978-1-4539-1237-9 (e-book)
ISSN 1086-7155

Bibliographic information published by **Die Deutsche Nationalbibliothek.**
Die Deutsche Nationalbibliothek lists this publication in the "Deutsche
Nationalbibliografie"; detailed bibliographic data is available
on the Internet at http://dnb.d-nb.de/.

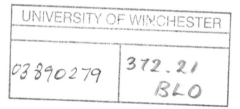
Cover art: *Child Musician* by Francis X. Nnaggenda

Photo credit: Daniel Swadener

The paper in this book meets the guidelines for permanence and durability
of the Committee on Production Guidelines for Book Longevity
of the Council of Library Resources.

© 2014 Peter Lang Publishing, Inc., New York
29 Broadway, 18th floor, New York, NY 10006
www.peterlang.com

Printed in the United States of America

Contents

Acknowledgments

We're delighted to be the 50th volume in the *Rethinking Childhood* series started by our friends and colleagues in Rethinking and Reconceptualizing Early Childhood Education (RECE), and original series editors: Janice Jipson and Joe Kincheloe. While Jan was unable to contribute to this current volume, her publications, and work on the initial *Rethinking Childhood* series remains so very critical. She is also a founding member of RECE, and co-hosted two of its conferences. We also want to acknowledge the continuing contribution of our volume co-editor, and the current series editor of *Rethinking Childhood*, Gaile S. Cannella, who supported the publication of *Reconceptualizing Early Care and Education: Foundational Debates, New Imaginaries, and Social Activism in the Peter Lang Rethinking Childhood* book series.

This volume reflects more than two decades of scholarship and dialogue focused on reconceptualizing research, practice, and policy related to early childhood. We acknowledge the role that the Reconceptualizing Early Childhood Education (RECE) conferences played over the past 21 years. We also would like to acknowledge the many people who have influenced our work in what is now a large global network. For all three of us, readings, critical scholarship, policy discussions, and work have informed this volume. As we've done our individual and collective work, dialogues and debates with a global network of scholars/teachers/policymakers and members of different global and local cultural communities have played a very influential role in helping us to continue to ask: Why and why not?

This global network, including those in and out of academic contexts, has provided an environment for challenges. It has also provided each of us a space for sharing our work, questions, and diverse imaginaries. We especially thank all of the contributing authors for raising critical issues and sharing their newest work and thinking.

In addition, we want to thank Christopher Myers, managing director of Peter Lang, who was responsive and helpful as well as our excellent copyeditor, Linda Henry. We also appreciated working closely with book series editor and book co-editor Gaile S. Cannella and production editor Bernadette Shade. We benefited greatly from the assistance of Nathalia Biscarra in formatting and reference checking, and Dr. Ruth Peach, a colleague and friend, in helping us prepare the final manuscript for submission. Finally, we deeply appreciate the support and patience of those who assisted us throughout the book editing process. In particular, we want to acknowledge Peter Bloch, Daniel Swadener, and Bert Cannella who have been patient and supportive during our many projects; this one and others could never have happened without that sharing of interests, and respect for each other's work.

While we have worked together before, we have never co-edited a book together. What fun! We also have become grandmothers within the past seven years. So to our grandchildren—Jordan, 5 years; Evan, 2 years; Liam, 8 years; Chloe, 4 years; Violet, 4 years; and Sophie, 1 year; and to other people's children throughout the world—we hope our small efforts to work toward peace and social justice, and toward continued acknowledgment of your rights, knowledge, and experiences bear fruit, some day soon.

Introduction

Exploring Reconceptualist Histories and Possibilities

Marianne N. Bloch, Beth Blue Swadener, and Gaile S. Cannella

The primary purpose of this book, as a volume in the Peter Lang series Rethinking Childhoods, is to show new directions in ways of understanding and imagining childhoods, rethinking early education and child care, as well as thinking about ways in which scholars in diverse fields are engaging in action and activisms related to childhood, early education, and child care. Each chapter in this volume consists of a newly written or revised contribution by leading authors working across the fields of critical childhood studies, early childhood education/care, and/or reconceptualizing early childhood education/care. Authors were asked to write chapters because the editors (Bloch, Swadener, and Cannella in collaborative discussions) felt each could contribute distinctly new and innovative ways to dialogue, dream, and envision childhood studies, including how early education and child care theory, policy, pedagogy, and curriculum might be re-imagined. While many authors contributed, no volume could contain the many others whose work, knowledge, and voices might have been included.

We especially want to acknowledge the past and continuing scholarly influences of Sally Lubeck, Liane Mozère, Jeanette Rhedding-Jones, and Leslie Williams, who all passed away in the past decade. Liane Mozère, who wrote a chapter for this book, passed away while it was in press. All four have been friends and colleagues with each of us, and with many writing in this volume. Their germinal work has been important in so many ways to dialogues, publications, critical policy analysis, and mentorship of a new generation of scholars. In addition, Sally and Jeanette hosted the Reconceptualizing Early Childhood Education Conference; Sally at the University of Michigan–Ann Arbor (U.S.) in 1993, and Jeanette at the Oslo University College in Oslo (Norway) in 2004. Leslie served as the editor of the Teachers College Press Early Childhood Education Series, one of the first in the U.S. to support critical, reconceptualist scholarship. Liane brought her intellectual knowledge and spirit to our discussions of, especially, French philosophers whom she had worked with since the 1960s. We, and many others, miss their continuing wisdom, scholarship, laughter, and friendship. Our book is dedicated to their memory and their contributions to our collective dialogues and work.

The volume's title, *Reconceptualizing Early Childhood Care and Education: Critical Questions, Diverse Imaginaries, and Social Activism,* is comprised of three major sections, beginning with "Foundational Debates and Critical Questions." The second section is titled "Diverse Imaginaries," for which authors were invited to bring in new issues, theoretical frames, critical questions, and to imagine new possibilities. The third and final section is titled "Social Action/Activism(s)," for which we selected authors who are engaged in "direct" ways to connect theory/research and critical social action and activism. Authors were given latitude to develop their chapters to reflect older debates and persistent issues, as well as newer ways to envision doing action/activism, or imaginaries of what could be, opening new spaces for thinking and action within childhood studies, as well as the reconceptualization of early education and child care. Our hope is that this volume brings together diverse contemporary perspectives on a global "movement," to critique, rethink, and reimagine early childhood and childhood studies in ways that encourage deeper analysis, new ways to reason and to act. Many chapters, though not all, embed a way of looking for equitable, socially just ways to consider children in local as well as global spaces (concepts) and places (constructed geographical spaces. Contributors were invited especially because their ideas, we thought, would shed light on old and new questions, ideas, and action/activist opportunities; nonetheless, the authors write from the spaces they know—Canada, Australia, New Zealand, the United Kingdom, France, and Sweden, East Asia, Chile, and the U.S. Again, more diverse dialogues and discussions can come from these chapters, and in a next publication. This book was meant to highlight conversations and debates between more senior authors and newer authors within and across chapters. In addition, we intentionally mixed, especially, the second and third sections to highlight different ways of thinking, doing, and imagining.

Background and Rationale

From the late 1970s and into the mid-1980s, critically oriented psychologists, sociologists, and cultural anthropologists interested in early education and child care were asking questions about the narrow perspectives of the dominant empirical research in child development/ECE in research in the United States and in Great Britain, Australia, Northern, Western, and East-Central Europe, Latin America, Asia, and Africa. Others were involved in research that allowed us to recognize the value of qualitative/ethnographic research, and the diversity of childhood cultural contexts in which children lived and grew (e.g., Whiting & Whiting, 1975; Tobin, Wu, & Davidson, 1989; also see Mallory & New, 1994; Rogoff, 2003). Some were beginning to form a group examining the sociology of childhood (e.g., Jenks, 1982; James, Jenks, & Prout, 1998.) While many anthropological studies of childhood helped illuminate the narrow view "child development" promulgated as universal "truth" in Western contexts at the same time, writers critiqued the "representation of 'others'" (e.g., Marcus & Fischer, 1986) that is part of the history of anthropology, sociology, and psychology. While the 1970s and 1980s provided a foundation for many critiques of the role of science in determining what is legitimated as "truth," the role of power relations (political/economic/social) in development and education (for a few examples, see Apple, 1978/2012; David, 1980; Pinar, 1975; Popkewitz,

1987, 1991) and the politics of cultural/racial/gendered identities, inclusions and exclusions, also became critically important in discussions (e.g., Ellsworth, 1989; Sleeter & Grant, 1987) as well as in many political and educational research and actions.

In the U.S., especially, theory, research, policy, and curriculum were organized around positivist methods and, as Kessler and Swadener (1992; Swadener & Kessler, 1991) suggested, most research was descriptive, focusing on what "is" rather than what might or ought to be. In early research in the U.S. by Bloch (1987); Hatch (1995); Lubeck (1985); Polakow-Suransky (1982); Tobin, Wu, and Davidson (1989); Silin (1987); and Ayers (1989); as well as many others, represented in a special issue of *Early Education and Development* (Swadener & Kessler, 1991) or in the volume edited by Kessler and Swadener (1992), alternative methodologies, often qualitative and interpretive, as well as a variety of critical theories were used. These diverse contributions examined a variety of issues related to early education and child care policy (e.g., Bloch, 1987; Lubeck, 1985; Polakow-Suransky, 1982), pedagogy and curriculum (Silin, 1987; Ayers, 1989; Kessler & Swadener, 1992), and the ways in which dominant modes of inquiry and thought limited the types of questions that might be asked or the "evidence" found that propelled policy in early education and child care (Bloch 1992; Hatch, 1995; Swadener & Lubeck, 1995; Mallory & New, 1994). They illustrated the importance of new ways of doing research, the contributions of different theoretical frameworks, and the questions and practices in need of interrogation, or illumination.

In 1991, the first Reconceptualizing Early Childhood Education (RECE) Conference was held; the 20th was held in 2012 in the United States at Pennsylvania State University, and the 21st (just prior to this volume's publication) was held at Kenyatta University in Nairobi, Kenya. The RECE Conference turning 20 was one of the instigators for this new volume, as we grappled with persistent questions and issues, including the following: What foundational arguments and debates influenced the development and continuation of the reconceptualist 'movement' and its annual conferences? What are new imaginaries in our collective teaching, pedagogies, political action, and research? In what ways were the initial ideas of "reform and change" realized, and in which ways are we still "waiting for the revolution"? (see Michael O'Loughlin's chapter and title, this volume). Have we tried to engage in different actions/activisms over the years—with some success? In which ways has there been a renarrativized or deterritorialized notion of universal developmental psychology or child development as a foundational way to construct childhood, children, and curriculum, given that this was an initial important debate? In which ways and for which reasons might there have been little apparent shift in reasoning, action, or conduct? These questions motivated the development of this book, and the ways in which we selected representative authors, the foregrounding we gave for their thinking prior to writing, and the publication of the volume itself.

Foundational Writings and Issues

Along with those already discussed, this volume focuses on initial critiques and debates that provided a foundation for the diversity that emerged as part of the rethinking and reconceptualist writings from the late 1970s onward in Great Britain, Canada, Australia, and in the U.S., at least. While some critiques drew from critical theories originally coming from the German Frankfurt School, others drew from continental philosophers' deconstructions of discursive language and practices. Others drew from feminist, postcolonial, decolonizing, liberatory pedagogical, political-economic, historical, sociological, philosophical, and/or anthropological/cultural studies lenses. We have tried to include representative writers from the early periods of critique, as well as newer contributors whom, we hope, add questions or forms of diversity/being that were unimagined in the work of two to three decades ago.

Among many early critical childhood researchers, we want to highlight the early and influential work of scholars like Miriam David (1980), Valerie Walkerdine (e.g., 1984/2005), Erica Burman (1994), and Bronwyn Davies (1982, 1989), all of whom have published influential volumes critiquing constructions of "child," child care, and pedagogy through a variety of critical, poststructural, and feminist theoretical lenses. Valerie Polakow, whose work is published in this volume, in *The Erosion of Childhood* (Polakow-Suransky, 1982) provided early U.S.-based critiques of the dominance of child development as a foundation of truth about children, using phenomenological and existential theory and research to shed light on poverty, the existential lives of low income families, and "other" people's children in what Polakow named "the Other America" (Polakow, 1993, p. 200). Gaile Cannella's (1997) *Deconstructing Early Childhood Education* and Gunilla Dahlberg, Peter Moss, and Allen Pence's (1999/2007) *Beyond Quality: Early Education and Child Care in Post-Modernity* were then and remain highly influential volumes that have illustrated how and why interrogating taken for granted concepts and practices is important. These, collectively, have been influential in the rethinking or reconceptualizing of early childhood education, child care "quality," and the concepts of development and childhood itself.

A variety of conference venues, including conferences of the Council on Anthropology of Education, which focused on anthropological studies of children in and out of school, and the Bergamo Conference in the U.S. that focused on curriculum theory, were influential for many of us in the U.S., early on, and throughout the years. RECE from 1991 onward, and the Critical Perspectives in Early Childhood Education Special Interest Group at the American Education Research Association (which began in 1999) also offered spaces for new debates and challenges. These different meeting spaces and places allowed for an informal, multidisciplinary, and multitheoretical space/place for discussions and a space to try on "new ideas" and to grow in specific, dynamic, and unpredictable ways as we began to move both globally and locally. Through these different discussions and meetings, a variety of publication opportunities grew, which further allowed the discussions to grow: the Peter Lang series focused on Rethinking Childhood in which this book is published (edited at first by Joe Kincheloe and Jan Jipson, and now by Gaile Cannella), several books published in Teachers College Press' Early Education; two Routledge series, Contesting Early Childhood and Changing Images of Early Childhood (the first co-edited by Gunilla Dahlberg and Peter Moss; the second by Nicolla Yelland); as well as the Palgrave Macmillan series Critical Cultural Studies of Childhood (co-edited initially by Bloch, Swadener, and Cannella). These new opportunities provided important windows for new discussions and the formation of a global network of scholars and scholarship.

In contrast, while there have been fewer refereed journals over these years with a focus on critical theoretical perspectives in early education and child care, or childhood studies, the online journal *Contemporary Issues in Early Childhood* or *CIEC*, the *Journal of Early Childhood Research*, as well as several newer journals (*Global Childhoods, International Journal of Critical Childhood Policy Studies*) gave space for the growing discussions and publication of open-access "peer-reviewed" theoretical arguments and research. As this is an important space for wider readership, and required for promotion at many higher education institutions, the continuing scarcity of refereed journal possibilities has been an ongoing issue.

This volume reintroduces some of the initial debates and questions raised during what we have termed the foundational period for critiques and questions (see Section I chapters by Bloch, Kessler, Hatch, Silin, and O'Loughlin, especially on these issues), and reflection on the aims, objectives, strategic successes/failures, as well as new issues and openings as we imagine the future. In the volume, we and many leading researchers and writers in the various fields mentioned, from multiple countries, examine several strands of research and key themes discussed in the areas of critical childhood studies, critical theories of curriculum and pedagogy related to childhood, pedagogy, theory, policy, and research. In addition, we include initial debates and critiques as well as authors' new perspectives envisioned by authors within each contribution, but especially in the different sections focusing on "diverse imaginaries," and "social action and activism." Many of the contributions aim to open further dialogue, and to facilitate discussion and debate, to tell stories about research—tales from the field, and to talk "research stories" about what some refer to as the "reconceptualist" early childhood education movement. Others use different terms to recognize the general importance of critical childhood studies scholarship, policy analysis, new important theoretical frameworks and social and political action and activism in the fields of childhood studies, education, curriculum theory and research, social actions related to global and local childhoods, as well as social and environmental justice that includes attention to global and local economic inequalities, power relations, and complex ways of understanding and acting.

Whether critical perspectives, rethinking, or reconceptualizing, the aims of the contributing scholars have been to open up alternatives for theory, research, policy, and practice in the fields of early education and child care, to deconstruct the importance of child development, or a narrowed individualistic perspective on ways of examining children, and childhood itself, and to decolonize Western research and the "science of knowledge" on/about/with children and families (see, for one highly readable example, Rhedding-Jones, 2005). The chapters highlight the contributors' own and others' contributions, while also leaving space for additions, discussion, and continuing critical dialogue. Moving backward and forward allows movement that is unpredictable, nonlinear, and rhizomatic (Deleuze & Guattari, 1987). Drawing on various theoretical frameworks (critical, postmodern, feminism/gender studies, queer theory, posthumanist, decolonizing, postcolonialisms), the contributions to the volume continue the tradition of interrogating and asking questions of what is constructed as "normal"; the authors also continue their work toward the use of new critical qualitative methodologies and critical policy analyses.

Autobiography and Activism

For many of us, to engage in the varied work we've done over five, ten, 30, or more years, focused on critiquing constructions of the "normal," has also been useful, transformative, and personally/professionally important—though at times also dangerous, risky, and certainly lonely. But the critiques that began in the 1970s, 1980s, and 1990s also require continuing reflection and critique: What were (and are) the aims, successes, barriers, and contributions of this work? But it is critical also to ask what, currently, are the macro-politics and micro-politics of our work, especially within the frameworks of global hypercapitalism, neoliberal economic policies, and a massive return to "gender wars" against women, children, early education/child care teaching and teachers, and families? We look at macro-politics as well as the minor politics of our writing, actions, politics, and daily work (Dahlberg & Moss, 2005; see also the chapter in this volume by Polakow and the chapter by Nagasawa, Peters, & Swadener). How do or could our strategic alliances and actions work in different ways toward various notions of inclusion, social justice, greater equity, redistributive economics and social politics for young children, their families, and teachers/caregivers (note these questions by Grieshaber & McArdle in their chapter)? In which directions might specific strategic actions move us further in fighting, resisting, or renarrativizing how truth is understood in relation to children, families, and "good education and care"?

We also collectively examine ethical perspectives that might be envisioned—including, at the least, an ethics and responsibility toward children's care/education, not only in the richer, Western nations and the economically/socially richer communities within them, but globally and locally as we collaborate with and sometimes act for the other. As we continue to battle from a marginal space within the context of increasing notions of the standardized child, childhood, curriculum, teacher, and parent, what are our current visions for new actions/ imaginaries? We reinforce the importance of the space of critical reflection and activism within an increasingly punitive political and economic global context that narrows possibilities, especially for poor children and their families around the world.

What are our continuing responsibilities? Where have we excluded while intending to include, whether topic, political movement, or pedagogical/curricular moment? Currently as we face continuing assaults from global capitalism, and renewed efforts to standardize bad practices in the name of quality "Education for All" (or No Child Left Behind, or Race to the Top, or assessments of young children, or continued lack of focus on childhood inequities, lack of rights, global perpetuations of bad pedagogies and practices, continuations of deficit discourses, to name a few), what might be our responses or ways of acting together over the next year, five years, or 20 years? What is the range of activities or endeavors that we might consider as we move toward an imagined "future"?

Have there been stories that have been possible to tell, that otherwise might have been omitted or excluded from collective knowledge? How have truth, knowledge, and power relations been affected—if at all? Have the individual and collective voices, ideas, and writings been heard; are we talking to ourselves, or are we talking and writing into ever-narrowing discursively confined spaces? Where are the openings, new lines of flight? Where is the serpent lurking, closing down barely envisioned spaces or possibilities (Dahlberg & Bloch, 2006)?

In this collection, we explore how different narratives have been allowed to continue and new narratives have emerged that constrain new possibilities for children/families/education and children's care. Various contributors discuss how our collective actions and/or new alliances might be used in new ways toward new ways of thinking and action. Again, can we speak truth to power in alternative ways as a collective voice, or through individual and collective contingent social actions (see Steinberg & Cannella, 2012; Swadener, Lundy, Habashi, & Blanchet-Cohen, 2013)? The authors in this volume look backward and forward at the same time. As suggested earlier, the book is neither comprehensive nor fully inclusive, but rather a compilation of what the contributors each wanted to emphasize related to their past and present work and actions. The book presents ideas from a variety of actors that will broaden and continue these critical reflections and the dialogue provoked from the initial questions and critiques posted in the 1980s and early 1990s moving us toward cultural reasoning systems and policies of "the present." While the content of the volume is nonlinear, moving backward and forward—with attention to key questions and debates within and across different groups that examine early education and child care—diverse theoretical, philosophical, and political/economic frames are used to do so. As editors, we hope to provoke new critiques, actions, conduct, and possibilities, while continuing to highlight the value of a diversity of perspectives for asking new questions, seeing things differently, and for new alliances or networks around different topics to emerge.

Through studies of "standards" to examinations of universal care that is far from universally accessible, from recognizing the continuing effect of neoliberal and cultural politics on and in the education of children to acknowledging the colonization of minds, methods, and voices, along with the possibilities constructed by new forms of critical analysis—we hope to continue political, economic, and educational challenges/practices that would move toward increased social/environmental justice and equity. By adding older voices with newer voices in contributions in and across sections, we hope for a variety of new insights even as each reader interacts with the text.

When we began to imagine this project, we posed the following questions:

1. Why is developmental theory and quantitative/positivist research still dominant and dominating notions of truth in early childhood research, policy, pedagogy, curriculum, and theory? If not developmental theory and research, which other ways of thinking and acting can we envision or imagine? Are there any responses to the Developmentally Inappropriate Practice/Developmentally Appropriate Practice (DIP/DAP) prescriptions?

2. Are there collective or individual ideas within the different contributions that involve notions of individual/collective actions or activisms at different local, regional, and global levels that represent new possibilities? Can we see or create new ways to deterritorialize, or rupture, or create new openings that are outside what is taken as natural or normal?

3. In which ways has our work opened up new dialogues and ways to think about subjectivities, identities, a multiplicity of diversities? In which ways has the rethinking of childhood studies, child care, and early education using a variety of critical, feminist, poststructural, and decolonizing theories aimed at enhancing inclusion of different knowledge systems? Have we found new ways to be inclusive of many new ideas and practices, and pushed for more equitable and inclusionary policies and practices (e.g., see, for example, MacNaughton, 2003)? But have we also been exclusive, marginalizing, and, perhaps, in-the-margins at the same time?

4. Which new approaches to theory, research, and methodology have been generated, and which new challenges are raised by contributors? In which ways, if any, has the aim to decolonize methods/methodologies/Indigenous epistemologies helped, and/or been co-opted, by new discourses of colonization, new governing forces and knowledge systems?

5. In which ways do contributors add to ways to think about subjectivity, performance, desire, and pleasure within early education and care? How has psychoanalysis and the body helped in illuminating the child, the teacher, the curriculum, as bodies (docile,

bodies without organs, performing or embodying diverse situated identities and subjectivities)?

6. Where are children in our discourses (is research on or about them, or with them)?
7. How do diverse theoretical and methodological frameworks add to our individual and collective intellectual work; in which ways have we also moved into a post-reconceptualist (Malewski, 2010) space, in which it is necessary to follow:

ethical commitments [to] the range of possibilities…. That there be spaces for traditionalists, empiricists, and developmentalist discourses regardless of the extent to which such ideas need to be challenged…(but is it) important that such work be displaced so as to break up sedimentary conjunctions, epistemological dominance, to open spaces where a thousand theories and stories are made and unmade, where alternative feasible readings proliferate. (Malewski, 2010, xiii)?

8. Within this, we have not lost our focus on young children, their care and education; critical policy and critical advocacy remain central to the challenges we still face. In which ways do our policies and practices still focus on pedagogies of inclusion/exclusion; in which ways do the politics of accessibility/disabilities/minority/majority voices/spaces/geographies frame our actions and practices?
9. In which ways has work represented over the years helped to resolve critical curriculum and policy studies related to (early) childhood, given globalizing capital and neoliberal narrowing of possibilities, a space where in the U.S., for example, developmentally appropriate practice(s) (DAPs, see Mallory & New, 1994) now almost seem "good" by comparison with other "standardized" and more didactic approaches to teaching?
10. What are different and diverse imaginaries about children and childhood as pleasure and desire? How has popular media and global and local practices surrounding children "in danger" been addressed, analyzed, or constructed/deconstructed through our actions?
11. While early childhood education and child care are gaining attention in global policy, in which ways might we imagine new ways to do research, to write, to envision curriculum, or critiques leading to new social actions and activisms?

In this volume, we represent a "post-reconceptualist" notion of a diversity of theories/methodologies—as well as diverse imaginaries for new pedagogical spaces, social justice action and activisms, peace, and hope. We want to be inclusive of the majority of children on the planet who do not live in the geographies and cultural spaces of the "rich." In diverse ways, the authors challenge everyone to develop a sense of planetary kindness, an ethics of collective care for the "other" that avoids the construction of "others" (whether those who are younger or otherwise), and a posthumanist agenda that moves beyond privileging the self-identified human (or adult) toward an ethical practice that addresses the relational (including nonhuman and even nonliving) environment that surrounds us all, as well as environmental justice and possibilities for all aspects of our being.

This Reader

While addressing all these questions is beyond the scope of our introduction, they do represent many of the themes in the diverse contributions authors have made to the volume. Nonetheless, there are several ways to think about the contributions—by section, and by themes or questions asked/responses given, as well as new debates and challenges. In the following sections, we highlight important issues raised in this volume by different contributors.

Foundational Debates and Questions

Almost every chapter in the first section of the book raises some points about the initial debates and challenges that scholars brought to a rethinking or a reconceptualizing of early education/child care theory, research/methods, policies, and curricular/pedagogical practices. Across the majority of chapters, the initial debates about the reliance on psychology and child development (developmental psychology) as a way to guide research, theory, policy, and what was considered to be "best practices" or high quality in curriculum is mentioned.

In "Interrogating the Reconceptualization of Early Care and Education (RECE)—20 Years Along," Marianne Bloch presents a history of the "movement" from her perspective, suggesting initial purposes, historical background, and new discursive contexts/texts that maintain or change beliefs, politics and policies, and pedagogical opportunities and openings.

Shirley Kessler's chapter, "Reconceptualizing the Early Childhood Curriculum: An Unaddressed Topic," draws on reconceptualist curriculum theory and critical historical perspectives, repeating the question: What values are embedded in the early childhood curriculum? Kessler provides a challenging argument that there are many ways in which values are foundational to curriculum choices and content, and that these issues have still not been discussed. As a critical curriculum historian in early education, her foundational arguments (Kessler, 1991; Kessler & Swadener, 1992; Swadener & Kessler, 1991) related to what counts and who decides, leave us with a reminder of persistent questions that must be responded to with a reinvigorated urgency.

Amos Hatch's chapter, "Reconceptualizing Early Childhood Research," highlights foundational questions that began a movement away from positivist inquiry, what some call "quantitative" research in early education and child care research. He discusses important classic ethnographic and qualitative research, and suggests that in the past decade the renewed call for good scientific educational research (National Research Council, 2002) did damage to early childhood/child care research, as well as other qualitative research. From his position as past editor of significant qualitative journals and books, he suggests renewed attention to important, rigorous, but qualitative research in our field, a request that has been repeated in different ways by a range of scholars (Steinberg & Cannella, 2012; Lather, 2010; Lincoln & Cannella, 2004).

The chapters by Jonathon Silin, Michael O'Loughlin, and Richard Johnson remind the reader of each of the author's early work, as well as the scholarship of many others, critiquing the dependence in early childhood education and care on child development. These critiques resulted in debates between those who constructed notions of developmentally appropriate practices in the early 1990s (see, especially, Jipson, 1991, for critique) and those who were concerned with the hegemony of such constructs. Each of the three authors reminds us that there has been little change for the better, even little hope that "the revolution" might cause change. Jonathan Silin, in "Through a Queer Lens: Recuperative Longings and the Reconceptualizing Past," and Michael O'Loughlin in "Still Waiting for the Revolution" both acknowledge the counter-discourses of "standards," "testing," and "push-down curriculum" that have created reactionary positions that support "developmentally appropriate curriculum." In both cases, the authors use personal stories in their work and in their writing to help us reexamine the importance of narrative in conjunction with our subjective experiences of "history." Both invite early childhood researchers and practitioners to ask new questions and to continue diverse ways of rethinking, acting, and reacting.

In "Disciplining 'Safe' Bodies in a Global Era of Child Panic: Implementing Techniques for Disciplining the Self," Richard Johnson contrasts his old and new work directed at nurture, touch, and care in the curriculum. Using diverse theoretical framings related to sexuality, the body, and desire, he re/questions the construction of gender, the notions of nurturing relationships, and who decides what/who/when touch in early childhood programs can occur as exhibited in an intensified surveillance of teachers, especially those who are identified as males. The author believes that the formation of the subjective self in relation to others, to desire, and to love and care with/for young children and their teachers is at stake, at least within the legal surveillance system in the U.S.

Representing the intersection between policy and curriculum, in "Social Justice, Risk, and Imaginaries," Susan Grieshaber and Felicity McArdle propose that the original focus on social justice and equity that many of us felt our work embodied has not been realized. Further, they suggest that at global, national, and regional levels, inequalities in caregiver/teacher wages in a field characterized as (women's) gendered work, unequal access to reasonable child care or preschool programs for many of the world's children, and the particular aspects of class, gender, and racial policy and pedagogical practice all need urgent attention and action. From the point of view of Sue Grieshaber's work as editor of the *Contemporary Issues in Early Childhood* journal published in Australia, staying in place is not an alternative. Addressing social justice is a risk, but a necessary one that requires redirection.

Liane Mozère's chapter titled "What About Learning?" draws on her long-term association with Gilles Deleuze and Félix Guattari to suggest that we neither "know" children nor childhoods. From French philosophy, and her diverse studies of children and families in immigrant and diverse cultural/class settings in France, she illustrates the possibilities of imagining children's movements and thoughts otherwise—opening ourselves to new encounters and new childhoods that current discourses constrain. In her short piece, she brings us into a new realm of encounters with others and with constructions, and beliefs about, learning. Using her own experiences, she illustrates learning as an unpredictable, political, changing act. She describes learning (and education) as both amorous and fatal, placing both death and life at stake. This work provides a form of mentoring that helps the reader see rhizomatic lines of flight for pedagogical, theoretical, and research becomings.

Finally, in "New Imaginaries Related to Authors' Scholarly Work and Praxis *Ki te Whai ao, Ki te ao Marama*," Cheryl Rau and Jenny Ritchie describe the decolonizing work they have practiced in New Zealand. Their work in collaboration with Maori scholars, activists, and communities of teachers and families provides a window into what could be imagined. Further, this work constructs positions from which conceptualizations of what might be done can be generated. Also included is a discussion of the ways that counter narratives and macro/micro-politics facilitate or prevent movement, new flows, and more socially and environmentally just education and care.

Diverse Imaginaries

As we explore the possibilities for the future as grounded in diverse imaginaries and multiplicity, the authors in the second section generate new directions for their own work, for research in the field, and even for childhood counter politics and public policy. To varying degrees, the chapters illustrate multiple directions through which the personal and professional are entangled, possibilities for future lives and work as conceptualized through as yet unthought notions of grace, love, and spirituality (that does not emphasize patriarchal religion), and expansions of scholarship and conceptualizations/performances of childhood using the work of boundary bending/breaking/busting scholars like Butler, Haraway, and Deleuze, as well as theories like posthumanism as applied to childhood.

In her work that focuses on "children's common world relations," Affrica Taylor labels her approach as collectivist (rather than individualist), and positioned within a more-than-human (rather than exclusively humanist) framework. She stresses that children are always already enmeshed within the "common worlds" that they inherit and inhabit along with a whole host of human and nonhuman others. As a geographer, Taylor focuses on children's "emplacement" within these common worlds, as well as the ways in which we think about children's entangled relations with the nonhuman, "natural" world.

Relatedly, in their chapter "Posthumanist Imaginaries for Decolonizing Early Childhood Praxis," Veronica Pacini-Katchabaw and Fikile Nxumalo provide an account of the potential of posthumanist perspectives for "decolonizing" early childhood education practices. Working at the intersection of postcolonial, Indigenous, and posthumanist literatures, the authors engage with the following question: How can we conceive a politics for troubling colonialisms in which human individuals are not necessarily the central players, but players among nonhuman others? The chapter explores human and nonhuman entanglements to generate decolonizing early childhood practices providing three examples of reconceptualist practice.

In "Radical Theories of Presence in Early Childhood Imaginaries," Chelsea Bailey draws on stories from recent work in China to examine how the unfamiliar exposes the uncertain, and how this uncertainty can lead us quite suddenly to a breakdown out of which the potential for tenderness arises. Rather than being a simple cross-cultural tale of difference and its failures and misunderstandings in the present, Bailey uses the lessons offered by these stories of lateral discontinuity to map a route to tenderness, a best version of what could possibly come next. The heart of this essay considers what happens after Western narratives of certainty have ceased to function and entertains possibilities for how the next chapter of what we currently call "childhood" could be written.

Inspired by authors like bell hooks to write "Black and Chicana Feminisms: Journeys Toward Spirituality," Michelle Salazar Pèrez and Cinthya Saavedra describe their attempts at enacting feminisms within the intersection of their own personal and professional lives. The work provides stories of the often undocumented insight into the theoretical and methodological influence of such feminisms on research. Traditionally marginalized feminisms are considered sights for the construction of unthought possibilities for childhood/s inquiry.

Alejandro Azocar begins the chapter that focuses on poststructural storytelling by positing major questions: Can an early childhood educational researcher be a storyteller? Can both roles be fused in one? What could the result be: educational research or literary excerpts? He argues that a hybridization of early childhood educational research is possible and, in fact, should be encouraged in present-day postmodernist times where the complex life of the immigrant child, the bilingual child, or the disabled child, to name a few, needs to be told to a larger audience. Azocar demonstrates that researchers need to question the push for normality that surrounds the child's experience, especially the child who happens to be "different" from the mainstream.

Questioning of the "normal" is exactly what present-day storytelling can achieve in the academic realm of early childhood education.

Drawing on critical perspectives in "Revisiting Risk/Re-Thinking Resilience: Fighting to Live vs. Failing to Thrive," Travis Wright contemplates the advantages and limitations of current discussions of resilience by presenting three case examples emerging from ongoing research, one focused on the demands of respect in the preschool classroom, the other exploring the risk and resilience associated with various preschool masculinities, and the third focused on the behaviors of maltreated children in the preschool classroom. Wright notes that under conditions of poverty, trauma, and/or high stress, what might be a source of strength in one part of a child's or family's life may be a source of risk in another. Similarly, across individuals, what might be protective for some may be destructive for others. Further, attention is paid to how discussions of resilience may be reflecting stereotypical notions of race, class, and gender.

Denise Proud and Cynthia à Beckett present their friendship that spans three decades as an example of the way strong bonds grow through shared understandings of working with young children in early childhood settings in their chapter that focuses on "imagining love and grace." Whether there are differences or similarities in the various life circumstances of diverse early childhood educators, sharing the early childhood education/care experience is discussed as a relational starting point, a meeting place for connections to begin. The authors argue that working with young children is a position of grace (explaining what they consider to be the definition of "grace"), and further raising the question as to whether we fall from grace when we no longer work with those who are younger. In many ways they echo both Johnson's and Bailey's call for relationality and ethics toward self and others in larger communities of care.

In "Bring Back the Asylum: Reimagining Inclusion in the Presence of Others," Gail Boldt and Joseph Valente use the concept of asylum as discussed from the 1930s to the 1990s to consider the concept of place. They advance critical disability studies by asserting that to matter, the concept of place (and the asylum illustration) must be formed through the commitment to what it means to consider the presence of all participants living together in shared experience. The authors use the concept to assist in examining recent research at an inclusive French preschool, L'Ecole Gulliver, that unconditionally admits (subject to space) all children regardless of the nature or severity of their disability or chronic illness.

Liselott Olsson and Ebba Theorell describe a component of the Magic of Language research project (Dahlberg & Olsson, 2009) in "Affective/Effective Reading and Writing Through Real Virtualities in a Digitized Society." The project is funded by the Swedish Research Council with the purpose of exploring preschool children's relations to didactic tools for language, reading, and writing. Preliminary work confirms earlier findings that preschool children are immersed in, and great users of, all sorts of digital devices. Most important, the children approach digital devices through a *productive* representational linguistic logic. These experimentations demonstrate that even the very youngest children are very familiar (and skilled) with digital devices.

Finally, in "Learning From the Margins: Early Childhood Imaginaries, 'Normal Science,' and the Case for a Radical Reconceptualization of Research and Practice," Mathias Urban discusses what appears to be a paradigm shift in recent European Union policies toward young children. At the center of Urban's interrogation lies a critical inquiry into a mainstream research-policy-practice complex that privileges "normal science." The following is asked: Who benefits, who speaks, and who is silenced? Making the case for a radical paradigm shift very different from that proposed by the European Union, the chapter aims at identifying and questioning the narratives that are employed to justify policies and practices focusing on young children, and on early childhood education and care in particular. The questioning, the author argues, opens a space for possible and necessary counter-discourses and renarrativization.

Social Action/Activisms

Chapters in this section bring together multiple theories and approaches to critical activism and raise policy and practice issues. The section begins with "Critical Qualitative Research and Rethinking Academic Activism in Childhood Studies" by Gaile Cannella. The purpose of the chapter is to provide an exploratory outline for the use of critical social science, especially critical qualitative research, as an instrument for the construction of critical academic activism in early childhood studies (and other fields). The author notes that many scholars have worked as activists locally and globally for their entire careers; as critical academic forms of activism are generated, this work provides a range of possibilities for thought/action and should at all points be acknowledged. Using the work of Foucault as illustrative (and specifically related to the neoliberal condition), the outline is presented to serve as either a framework for those who feel that they need a form of solid grounding for beginning critical activist scholarship, or as a position from which to construct critical lines of flight for those who would continue (and increase the transformative power of) their own critical work.

In her chapter, "None for You: Children's Capabilities and Rights in Profoundly Unequal Times," Valerie Polakow calls for intensified, focused, collective attention to children in poverty. The chapter examines what it means to be a poor child in the second decade of the 21st century in the United States and engages several critical questions, including "how do children see their own lifeworlds that are bounded by poverty, inequality, and social and educational exclusion?" She also examines ways in which children cope with their daily lives of poverty and hardship, and how they assume active, rather than passive, roles in strategically marshaling resources, demonstrating that these issues have been under-researched. In the poverty policy literature, children are typically constructed as passive recipients of support or stigma. How children and adolescents confront poverty and the violation of their rights is vital to document as part of a growing literature on children's rights and capabilities.

In "The Costs of Putting Quality Firsts: Neoliberalism, (Ine)quality, (Un)affordability, and (In)accessibility?" Mark Nagasawa, Lacey Peters, and Beth Blue Swadener draw from a Gramscian analysis, combined with contemporary theories to look at the contradictory nature (common-sense/good-sense/bad-sense) of neoliberal policies in early childhood education. These policies include the current emphasis on quality—while neglecting accessibility, affordability, and cultural relevance to families and children. A case is made for direct engagement with community and policy shapers and makers to not just critique the "bad-sense" but to build on the moments or elements of "good-sense" in current early childhood systems and programs/initiatives.

Kylie Smith and Sheralyn Campbell's chapter, "Social Activism: The Risky Business of Early Childhood Educators in Neoliberal Australian Classrooms," focuses attention on teacher education and critical action research in relation to policy as approaches toward action and activism. Despite their illustrations of collective work with regional and national early-education-curriculum framework makers, they suggest change is easier at local levels than at larger levels. Within the new Australian Government Early Learning Framework (Australian Government, 2012), discourses and openness to new theoretical frameworks have been included; but regional and local school policies constrain or restrain teachers and programs from understanding what to use and why to adopt change, and little on-the-ground training has helped this. In addition, government at different levels continuously requires new standards, as in the U.S., Great Britain, and Canada, and has taken on new methods of assessment for early childhood programs, and for teachers. Therefore, the authors propose that suggested changes on paper fail to equate with change—thus far. Despite these discouraging signs, local critical action research with (not on) teachers suggests greater promise for understanding and reconstruction of what it might mean to teach toward equity and social justice, and is illustrated in the chapter.

In "(Im)possibilities of Reinvention of Palestinian Early Childhood Education," Janette Habashi analyzes the roles and issues with early education and care for non-governmental organizations (NGOs) on the West Bank. She draws from her experiences working with mothers and early childhood teachers on a collaborative project that has grown into an NGO—A Child's Cup Full (ACCF). Her chapter articulates the progress and the steps taken to understand the role of NGOs in early childhood education in the occupied Palestinian Territories (oPT) and the lessons learned while conceptualizing ACCF's plan for Palestinian early childhood education in the Jenin Refugee Camp. To facilitate the achievement of such a dream, it is essential to scrutinize the Palestinian historical, structural, and political context that might or might not make it possible to realize this path, especially relating to the challenges of NGOs' external/internal funding and early childhood curricula. She argues that the contextualization and interrelation of these elements are cornerstones for ACCF to envision an example of the reinvention of early childhood education in the oPT, whereby the community is not contingent on external funding and therefore has a voice in the discussion of the curricula and local programming.

I-Fang Lee and Nicola Yelland draw from a larger project on global childhoods for their chapter, "The Global Childhoods Project: Complexities of Learning and Living With a Biliterate and Trilingual Literacy Policy." The project has an overall aim to explore contemporary childhoods in Asia and is a collaboration involving academics and teachers from Hong Kong, Japan, Korea, Malaysia, Taiwan, and Thailand who have come together to interrogate Asian childhoods in the 21st century. In the first instance, a focus has been on beginning to understand children's literacy learning and practices in their own cultural contexts. Seeking to understand contemporary Asian childhoods and children's lifeworlds (both learning and living experiences), analyses and discussions aim to move beyond the simple dichotomies of Western/non-Western binary constructions of childhoods and appropriate/inappropriate pedagogical practices in an attempt to reconceptualize aspects of childhoods in the era of globalization. The authors describe how they used an ethnographic approach in an attempt to understand Hong Kong children's contemporary literacy learning in the context of a biliterate and trilingual education policy in a nonprofit kindergarten in Hong Kong. Lee and Yelland critically analyze the paradoxical moments of children's lives within systems that are requiring a universal construction of best pedagogical practices in the era of globalization.

A Closing and an Invitation to Read and to Interact In/With This Book

Each chapter in the book asks important new questions, provides additional critique, and calls for new forms of critical action. In the end, we hope the volume is not seen as "history" in that such a history could be another story for another day (see, for example, discussions of cultural history in Popkewitz, Franklin, & Pereyra, 2001). Rather, we would like the book to be read as a collection of new and re-energized responses to an old call for *what could be*.

References

Apple, M. (1978/2012). *Ideology and the curriculum* (3rd ed.) London: Routledge.

Australian Government. (2012). Early Years Learning Framework, National Quality Framework for Early Childhood Education and Care. http://deewr.gov.au/early-years-learning-framework

Ayers, W. (1989). *The good preschool teacher*. New York: Teachers College Press.

Bloch, M. N. (1987). Becoming scientific and professional: An historical perspective on the aims and effects of early childhood education. In T. S. Popkewitz (Ed.), *The formation of school subjects* (pp. 25–62). London: Falmer.

Bloch, M. N. (1992). Critical perspectives on the historical relationship between child development and early childhood education research. In S. Kessler & E. B. Swadener (Eds.), *Reconceptualizing the early childhood curriculum: Beginning the dialogue* (pp. 3–20). New York: Teachers College Press.

Burman, E. (1994). *Deconstructing developmental psychology*. New York: Routledge.

Cannella, G. S. (1997). *Deconstructing early childhood education*. New York: Peter Lang.

Dahlberg, G., & Bloch, M. N. (2006). Is the power to see and visualize always the power to control? In T. S. Popkewitz, K. Petersso, U. Olsson, & J. Kowalczyk (Eds.), *The future is not what it appears to be: Pedagogy, genealogy, and political epistemology* (pp. 105–123). Stockholm: HLS Förlag.

Dahlberg, G., & Moss, P. (2005). *Ethics and politics in early childhood education*. London: RoutledgeFalmer.

Dahlberg, G., Moss, P., & Pence, A. (1999/2007). *Beyond quality in early childhood education and care: Languages of evaluation* (2nd ed.). London: Routledge.

Dahlberg, G., & Olsson, L. M. (2009), *The magic of language – Young children's relation to language, reading and writing*. (Research proposal addressed to the Swedish Research Council).

David, M. E. (1980). *The state, the family, and education*. Radical Social Policy Series, Vol. 80. London: Routledge & Kegan Paul.

Davies, B. (1982). *Life in the classroom and playground: The accounts of primary school children*. London: Routledge & Kegan Paul.

Davies, B. (1989). *Frogs and snails and feminist tales: Preschool children and gender*. St. Leonards, Australia: Allen & Unwin.

Deleuze, G., & Guattari, F. (1987). *A thousand plateaus: Capitalism and schizophrenia*. Minneapolis: University of Minnesota Press.

Ellsworth, E. (1989). Why doesn't this feel empowering?: Working through the repressive myth of critical pedagogy. *Harvard Education Review, 59*(3), 297–325.

Hatch, A. (Ed.). (1995). *Qualitative research in early childhood settings*. New York: Praeger.

James, A., Jenks, C., & Prout, A. (1998). *Theorizing childhood*. New York: Teachers College Press.

Jenks, C. (1982). *The sociology of childhood: Essential readings*. London: Batsford.

Jipson, J. (1991). Developmentally appropriate practice: Culture, curriculum and connections. Early Education and Development, 2, 120–136.

Kessler, S. (1991). Alternative perspectives on early childhood education. *Early Childhood Research Quarterly, 6,* 183–197.

Kessler, S., & Swadener, E. B. (Eds.). (1992). *Reconceptualizing the early childhood curriculum: Beginning the dialogue*. New York: Teachers College Press.

Lather, P. (2010). *Engaging SCIENCE policy: From the side of the messy*. New York: Peter Lang.

Lincoln, Y., & Cannella, G. S. (2004). Qualitative research, power, and the radical right. *Qualitative Inquiry, 10*(2), 175–201.

Lubeck, S. (1985). *The sandbox society*. New York: Falmer.

MacNaughton, G. (2003). *Shaping early childhood: Learners, curriculum, and contexts*. Maidenhead, England: Open University Press.

Malewski, E. (2010). Preface and Introduction: Proliferating curriculum. In E. Malewski (Ed.), *Curriculum studies handbook: The next moment* (pp. xi–41). New York: Routledge.

Mallory, B., & New, R. (Eds.). (1994). *Diversity and developmentally appropriate practices: Challenges for early childhood education*. New York: Teachers College Press.

Marcus, G., & Fischer, M. (1986). *Anthropology as cultural critique: An experimental moment in the human sciences*. Chicago: University of Chicago Press.

National Research Council. (2002). *Scientific research in education* (Committee on Scientific Principles for Education Research, R. Shavelson, & L. Town [Eds.]). Center for Education, Division of Behavioral and Social Sciences and Education. Washington, DC: National Academy Press.

Pinar, W. F. (Ed.). (1975). *Curriculum theorizing: The reconconceptualists*. New York: McCutcheon.

Polakow, V. (1993). *Lives on the edge: Single mothers and their children in the other America*. Chicago: University of Chicago Press.

Polakow-Suransky, V. (1982). *The erosion of childhood*. Chicago: University of Chicago Press.

Popkewitz, T. S. (1987). *The formation of school subjects*. London: Falmer Press.

Popkewitz, T. S. (1991). *The political sociology of educational reform: Power-knowledge in teaching, teacher education, and research*. New York: Teachers College Press.

Popkewitz, T. S., Franklin, B. M., & Pereyra, M. (Eds.). (2001). *Cultural history and education*. New York: Routledge Press.

Rhedding-Jones, J. (2005). *What is research?: Methodological practices and new approaches*. Oslo, Norway: Universitetsforlaget AS.

Rogoff, B. (2003). *The cultural nature of human development*. New York: Oxford University Press.

Silin, J. (1987). The early childhood educator's knowledge base: A reconsideration. In L. G. Katz (Ed.), *Current topics in early childhood education* (pp. 17–31). Norwood, NJ: Ablex.

Sleeter, C., & Grant, C. (1987). An analysis of multicultural research in the United States. *Harvard Education Review, 57*(4), 421–445.

Steinberg, S. R., & Cannella, G. S. (Eds.). (2012). *Critical qualitative research reader*. New York: Peter Lang.

Swadener, B. B., & Lubeck, S. (Eds.). (1995). *Children and families "at promise": Deconstructing the discourse of "at risk."* New York: SUNY Press.

Swadener, B. B., Lundy, L., Habashi, J., & Blanchet-Cohen, N. (Eds.). (2013). *Children's rights and education: International perspectives*. New York: Peter Lang.

Swadener, E. B., & Kessler, S. A. (1991). Reconceptualizing early childhood education: An introduction. *Early Education and Development, 2*(2), 85–94.

Tobin, J., Wu, D. Y. H., & Davidson, D. H. (1989). *Preschool in three cultures*. New Haven: Yale University Press.

Walkerdine, V. (1984/2005). Developmental psychology and child-centered pedagogy. In J. Henriques, W. Holloway, C. Urwin, C. Venn, & V. Walkerdine (Eds.), *Changing the subject: Psychology, social regulation and subjectivity* (pp. 153–202). London & New York: Routledge (first published by Methuen, 1984).

Whiting, B. B., & Whiting, J. (1975). *Children of six cultures*. Cambridge, MA: Harvard University Press.

SECTION I

Foundational Debates and Continuing Questions

ONE

Interrogating Reconceptualizing Early Care and Education (RECE)—20 Years Along

Marianne N. Bloch[1]

While some of the history of the first Reconceptualizing Early Childhood Education (RECE) Conference was initiated in 1991 as a tentative start for new discussions, critique, and presentation of then-marginalized approaches to research, theory, policy, and pedagogy, it was hardly the beginning of these debates, nor, of course, is it the end—as this volume illustrates well. In this chapter, I present a form of history of the RECE Conference, illustrate some of the key questions we asked, and, finally, continue to ask questions and interrogate where we've "been" and where we might move. Thus, this is a history that draws upon my memories and reflections, as well as events that, though incompletely discussed or illustrated, I have constructed as important.

A framework for reading this chapter: histories are not linear, nor are they "truth" (Foucault, 1980). They involve memories and forgettings, intentional and without seeming intention. In addition, following Scott (1991) and Butler (1993, 2004) "experience" as well as identity(es) are contingently situated and related or performed in the discursive moment in which "experience" or storytelling (in this case) happens. As I narrate this story, therefore, please see the narrative as non-linear, with ruptures, and that different discursive moments may account in ways I or "we" (then and now) think, act, and write.

Brief Overview of RECE's Early Days/Years

Therefore, drawing from my memories (and forgettings), I try to represent the work of other critical theorists in education and curriculum studies at different moments. My narrative begins with disciplinary, theoretical/methodological backgrounds of the early participants.

My Memories: As suggested in the introduction to this book, the attendees at the first few RECE conferences had different theoretical roots, diverse disciplinary affiliations and backgrounds in research. There was also a desire to stimulate new discussions, new research approaches and to search for more equitable policies and pedagogical practices in early care and education at a material level with families, teachers, and children. We/they were also primarily academic researchers and teachers focusing on curriculum, early- and elementary-level teacher education, and most of us were doing graduate education and research. Some of us were engaged in what we thought to be the initial debates about the dominance of psychology and child development "truths" about children and childhood. Many of us were concerned about the dominance of positivist research in determining what knowledge was considered valid and reliable about children, their families, and how good "quality" teaching and curriculum for young children was culturally, socially, historically, and philosophically constructed. We represented somewhat different disciplinary backgrounds, some with emphasis in anthropology, many with developmental psychology/ child development backgrounds, some sociologists, others interested in critical curriculum theory, some coming with backgrounds in feminist/gender studies; some with historical, philosophical, or psychoanalytic interests and experience. We all shared an interest in early education and child care.

The dominance of psychology, child development and positivist, largely quantitatively oriented "Science" that was based on logical-empiricist or empirical-analytical principles had emerged in the United States particularly in the beginning of the 20th century (Bloch, 1991, 1992; Burman, 1994; Cannella, 1997; Rose, 1989/1999). In various publications from the mid-1980s onward, there had been questions about the dominance of psychology and child development as well as "empirical-analytic" or positivist research in early childhood education (ECE) and the ways in which these discourses of developmental psychology and positivist research paradigms governed ECE and child care and teacher education, as well as research on and with teachers, parents, and children (Bloch, 1987; David, 1980; Polakow Suransky, 1983; Polakow, 1992; Silin, 1987; Walkerdine, 1984). In addition, as suggested in the introductory chapter, many early-education-oriented researchers were beginning to draw from critical curriculum theorists and the Frankfurt School of Critical Theory to question taken-for-granted approaches to curriculum development in education; Jonathan Silin (1987) asked whose knowledge should count in the curriculum? What knowledge is most valued for young children? Bernard Spodek (1980) also asked whether developmental psychology was the only framework that should guide the early childhood curriculum; what content matters in the curriculum, and who should decide? Others suggested that common, taken-for-granted precepts in ECE such as Piagetian theory or a child-centered curriculum may reproduce inequalities rather than provide a liberal space for learning (Walkerdine, 1984; O'Loughlin, 1992). King (1982) described how play and work reproduced class inequalities within the kindergarten curriculum, while Gracey (1975) called kindergarten academic boot camp by illustrating how the curriculum focused on regimented behavior such as learning to line up and be quiet and know who (the teacher) was in charge. David (1980) drew on critical feminist and neo-Marxist theory to examine the relation among the state, parenting, and education. Rather than focusing on "maternal involvement" in school as a neutral good, she suggested that maternal rather than paternal involvement was expected as part of women's assignment to childrearing as their primary state productive labor.

Valerie Suransky Polakow's (Suransky, 1983/Polakow, 1992) initial critique of our concepts of childhood and child development were also focused on gender and class inequalities and were published in *The Erosion of Childhood*. Lubeck (1985) in *The Sandbox Society* showed through ethnographies of children in low-income Head Start and middle-class preschools how class (and to some extent race) relates to curriculum and pedagogical practices for young children in the United States. Tobin, Wu, and Davidson (1989) in *Preschool in Three Cultures* illustrated how qualitative research and ethnography cross-nationally could be used to see things in ways other than the traditional positivist research had shown to date.[2] Again, by 1989, Ayers' *The Good Preschool Teacher* (1989) and Davies' (1989) *Frogs and Snails and Feminist Tales* had been published and continued to illuminate the importance of critical, poststructural, feminist perspectives and how qualitative research could show how teachers' and children's experiences varied by class and gender and how the experiences of teachers and children could and should be represented in research. Attendance and joint discussions at the Bergamo Conference for Curriculum Theory and the Council on Anthropology and Education, as well as at the American Education Research Association meetings, helped us (all from the United States at that time) recognize a desire for a new conference, modeled especially after the informality and critical discussions of the Bergamo Conference as well as at the Anthropology and Education conference meetings, but with an emphasis on early education and child care.

The Reconceptualists

The foundations for the RECE Conference were varied. An early purpose of the RECE conference was simply to have a space to present academic research drawing on disciplines and theoretical and methodological frameworks that were marginalized within the broader field of academic ECE conferences and publications. From this amorphous intellectual desire, "we"[3] formed other desires and made room for the pleasure of meeting in small conferences together to talk, think, and reinforce critical pedagogical and policy action. We wanted a "safe" space to engage in critiques of dominant paradigms, methodologies, policies, and pedagogical practices and to explore new theories and their meaning or implications for our research. We also wanted to support younger colleagues by forming a network in which we could learn from each other and support each other in our individual work. We used the RECE forum as a way to open up spaces to new ideas with a social justice and equity framework that drew from the diverse critical theories we were using.

The term "reconceptualizing" the curriculum, however, came from key curriculum theorists who had used that specific term initially to critique traditional studies of curriculum (e.g., see Pinar, 1975a, 1975b) with chapters or references to work by Huebner, Schubert, Pinar, Apple, Grumet, Miller, and Greene among others where they drew on this phrase or title initially. According to Kessler (1991) and Kessler and Swadener (1992b), Pinar's (1975a) edited volume called for the reconceptualization of curriculum studies in education and his critique of the Tyler Rationale (e.g., especially see Kliebard, 1975, for this argument) with its focus on objectives, lesson plans, and prescribed evaluation of outcomes and testing, and this formed a foundation for their critique of early childhood theory and curriculum. In addition, Kessler and Swadener (1992b) focused on other critical curriculum theory questions, which Shirley Kessler's chapter in this volume repeats again—20 years later: What knowledge counts? Whose knowledge is represented in the curriculum, and whose is excluded? How do we decide what is valuable to teach? How does the reproduction of an exclusionary or privileged and incomplete knowledge relate to power and the reproduction or production of inequalities?

By 1990, a small group initiated the first RECE conference, and the call for "reconceptualization" of early childhood curriculum and critical childhood studies more broadly. Amos Hatch, in a separate conference, focused on Qualitative Research in Early Education in 1989 that illustrated exceptional qualitative/ethnographic research focused on early education and child care, most done in the United States. This group, represented by those in the edited volume by Hatch (1995), and new significant research by Graue (1993), and Leavitt and Powers (1994), joined in the effort to reconceptualize early education research—illustrating new theories and methodologies, and pushing for recognition of nonpositivist research in the broader field of early education research.

In 1991 the first conference was held at the University of Wisconsin–Madison, using the title "reconceptualizing early childhood education." The word "reconceptualizing" early childhood education (RECE) designated the very specific history within critical curriculum studies in the United States at the time. The push to examine power relations and structures that reproduced or produced inequities within schooling, early education, and child care settings and within broader social institutions affiliated with education and care came from this foundational background. Those in attendance drew from feminist, critical, and poststructural theories, and did research in sociology, psychology, anthropology, political economy, history, and philosophy. The word "reconceptualist," therefore, was particular and specific to discussions at a specific time and place, drawing first from the published work and scholarly debates in Swadener and Kessler (1991).

Trying to Rupture Theory, Methodology, Curriculum, and Policies in Early Childhood Education: 1991–1997

Primary themes in the first years of RECE were critiques of the universal claims about childhood made by the dominant discourses of developmental psychology and the pedagogical framework that informed notions of "quality education" in the widely used Developmentally Appropriate Practice (DAP) guidelines (Bredekamp, 1987; Bredekamp & Copple, 1997; Kessler, 1991). In the U.S., these dominated concepts of "best quality" in early education/care programs; by the mid-1990s, these ideas were spreading elsewhere (e.g., see Dahlberg, Moss, & Pence, 2007).

As suggested earlier, critiques also focused on the privileging of positivist research/theory/methodologies as "best evidence" and the use of and importance of different types of qualitative research methodologies, as well as critical, poststructural, and feminist theories and methodologies in research (Ayers, 1989; Bloch, 1992; Burman, 1994; Cannella, 1997; Davies, 1989; Graue, 1993; Hatch, 1995; Kessler & Swadener, 1992a; Leavitt & Powers, 1994; Lubeck, 1994; Mallory & New, 1994; Silin, 1995).

Other work in the early conferences focused on exclusions and reproductions of class/gender/racial/age/ability inequities based on the centuries-long assimilationist/colonizing forms of education that prevailed (Bloch, 1987; Cannella, 1997; Polakow, 1993). We focused on the need for more attention to multilingual/multicultural and a social reconstructionist/social-justice-oriented early childhood education and the politics of early childhood education.

While far from inclusive, several well-known examples of this 1990s work include: *Deconstructing Early Childhood Education: Social Justice and Revolution* (Cannella, 1997); *Language, Culture, and Power* (Soto, 1996); *The Politics of Early Education* (Soto, 2000); *Lives on the Edge: Single Mothers and Their Children in the Other America* (Polakow, 1993); *Children and Families "At Promise": Deconstructing the Discourse of "At Risk"* (Swadener & Lubeck, 1995); and *Sex, Death, and the Education of Children: Our Passion for Ignorance in the Age of AIDS* (Silin, 1995). Different attendees at the early RECE conferences also focused on cross-national policy (Cannella & Kincheloe, 2002; Swadener & Bloch, 1997), different ways to understand inclusions and exclusions in pedagogies around sexuality and cultural identities (Greishaber & Cannella, 2001; Silin, 1995; Tobin, 1997), and deconstructing the concept and evaluation of "quality" (Dahlberg et al., 2007).

Rupturing Dominant Discourses in Theory/Research/Pedagogies/Policy in the Early 21st Century: Again—Scientific Rigor, Standards, and the Universal Child

Since the mid-1990s, new themes and different approaches to research have emerged rhizomatically (Deleuze & Guattari, 1987) within, around, and before and after different conferences related to groups and ideas from those who had been and from those who were not part of earlier discussions. Continuing critiques by sociologists of childhood from the new sociology of childhood researchers (e.g., James, Jenks, & Prout, 1998; Jenkins, 1998) as well as continuing work by Valerie Walkerdine (e.g., 1998), Joe Tobin and colleagues (2000) pushed at the borders of foundational arguments about the truth and constructed knowledge base in early education and child development. Despite this, growing neoliberal counter-discourses calling for "scientific rigor" and "evidence-based" (read this as: largely quantitative, positivist/empirical; non-qualitative) in the social sciences and in education held many critiques at bay, or reinstated them in the "margins." Most critique, now related to a new constellation of discursive events, were now (again) against mainstream policy, pedagogy, research, and teacher education. This, however, was not only true in early education/child care fields, but also within educational research more broadly (see Cannella & Viruru, 2004; Steinberg & Cannella, 2012). Critical scholarship, critical qualitative research and policy analyses were increasingly done, and of interest to many, but still marginal in terms of funding, and still rarely published in "high-status" early education and child care journals, necessary for tenure and promotion for many junior faculty.

Nonetheless, calls for more critique *with political action* (for example, Soto, 2000), inclusion of more diverse groups (more teachers especially, more diverse representation of different cultural groups, and less attention to "minority world" research and researchers—see Pence & Hix-Small, 2009) were important in RECE conferences and publications. Themes that more actively use decolonizing/anti-colonial perspectives in research were made. More of the RECE and critical ECE researchers moved toward a call for more marginalized voices to be heard in curriculum, including a focus on children's voices and experiences (e.g., Soto & Swadener, 2005; Mutua & Swadener, 2005; Polakow, 2007; Tobin, 1997, 2000) and more feminist, poststructural, and postcolonial and decolonizing theoretical framings of research (e.g., Rhedding-Jones, 2005). In conferences held at the University of Hawaii–Manoa (1997), the Queensland University of

Technology (2000), Bank Street College, NYU, and Teacher's College, Columbia (2001), at Arizona State University (2003), at the University of Waikato (2006), at the RECE conference held in Palestine (2008), and at the 2013 conference at Kenyatta University in Nairobi, Kenya, a focus on the global and local and recognition of indigenous knowledge and decolonizing research have been strong and important parts of debates and discussions. Perhaps because of the growing international group of presenters, even the pattern of holding RECE in the United States every two years (as it was founded in the U.S.) has been quite legitimately questioned. These questions raised new questions—whose voices are heard in most reconceptualist publications? How can diverse global and local critiques, theories, knowledge bases, policies, and pedagogical practices be included (Brougere & Vandenbroeck, 2007; Cannella, Swadener, Che, 2007).

By the late 2000s, these conferences, individual presentations, new publications, and appropriate self-critique were leading to new approaches to research, greater experimentation with poststructural and postcolonial/decolonizing, feminist/gender/queer studies, and posthumanist research than had been represented in the early years of the conferences (e.g., Blaise, 2005; Bloch, Holmlund, Moqvist, & Popkewitz, 2003; Cannella & Viruru, 2004; MacNaughton, 2003, 2005; Mutua & Swadener, 2005; Pacini-Ketchabaw, 2010; Taylor, 2013).

In 2004, in Oslo, Norway, the theme focused on language and power. In more recent years, Dahlberg, Moss, and Pence's (2007) work, drawing on both Foucault and Deleuze and Guattari's theoretical work with the rhizome, has been used to discuss a continued critique of the neoliberal naturalness of discourses of "quality," the circulation of discourses of efficiencies, privatization, standards, and outcomes-based assessments. The call for new macro- and micro-political analyses of programs and pedagogies in early childhood care and education, and an ethics of listening to the other (Dahlberg & Moss, 2005) spurred new research that focused on different ways of working with teachers and children, new pedagogical openings (Ryan & Grieshaber, 2005; Lenz-Taguchi, 2009; Olsson, 2009). These ideas, represented in diverse research, publications, and experimentation with new pedagogies in teaching have led to even greater attention toward critical action research in classroom pedagogies, opening up new spaces for children's and teacher's thinking in conferences and in some teacher preparation programs and curriculum texts. Nonetheless, increasingly, and despite the prominence of some of these authors, researchers, and teacher educators, teacher education and curriculum seems to continue to be dominated by the (re)new(ed) emphases on developmental approaches (DAP as now represented by Copple & Bredekamp, 2009), literacy, math, and science, and universal assessments and standards.

But whose voices and knowledge count? Whose values are embedded in what we think is appropriate curriculum, and for whom? Critical questions and some responses are illustrated in Soto and Swadener (2005), Mutua and Swadener (2005), and in the critically significant work of the Maori/non-Maori researchers participating in the development and continued critique of the *Te Whariki* early childhood curriculum (originally published in 1997; Ritchie & Rau, 2007, 2009). These ideas have moved some toward a new approach (rupture[4]) in thinking. The focus on the politics involved in decolonizing/doing anti-colonial and posthumanist, environmental research (Pacini-Katchabow, 2010; Taylor, 2013) that has allowed for the imagining of the "natures" of child with/in his/their ecological and cultural context has added powerful dimensions to possibilities for curriculum theory and pedagogy.

From a different theoretical framework, continual examinations of childhood voice, subjectivity, and *imagining children otherwise* (e.g., O'Loughlin & Johnson, 2010) also facilitated the intertwining of Lacanian and other psychoanalytic theorizing to be used in resistance of what some perceived as overly constraining structural and poststructural theories that overlooked self and subject. The reduction of the subjective self to discursive or structural constraints and analyses is also an important part of Jonathan Silin's continuing research and writing (e.g., see Silin, 1995, and his contribution in this volume).

RECE Turns Almost Twenty and Some of Us Are Getting Old(er)

Reform That Aims to Rupture Thinking and Action

In revisiting some of the early goals, values, and purposes of RECE, I ask what thinking or actions did we "cut open," rupture, or change? Which of the initial purposes, goals, and values seem to have been "achieved" even partially, while others appear to remain locked into place by new forms of dominant discourses, and/or to be rhizomatically shifting in unpredictable ways? For example, in the 1990s, we (speaking from my memories and reconstruction) hoped to "dismantle," or find alternatives to:

> discourses of *child development, developmental psychology,* and *educational psychology,* discourses of the child as *innocent, developing (primitive innocent unknowing) child to developed (mature sophisticated rational/logical thinking) child/adult.* (My memories, italics used for emphasis)

Yet recently, in a talk I gave at the 18th RECE Conference in Georgia (October 2010), I stated:

> In the USA, the majority of state standards for early learning remain tied to child development ages/stages and research as a dominant guide for teachers and teacher educators, as well as for state and federal policies about which information represents "best knowledge" about children. (Bloch, 2010, also see Bloch & Kim, 2012)

In addition, best practices in pedagogy are still tied to "Developmentally Appropriate Practice" guidelines, in much the same way they were (or more so) in 1991 and 1992 when the RECE conferences (held respectively in Madison, Wisconsin, and in Chicago, Illinois) first critiqued these. Yet, key and mainstream researchers are writing to keep critiques available; more linkages and network alliances may be necessary *for new times, for renarrating, and reterritorializing discourses and reasoning of the present* (see, for example, Cannella, in press; Ryan & Grieshaber, 2004, 2005).

In the 1990s, we hoped to break open:

> Discourses of *disciplinary expertise* within the psychological sciences—especially child development, developmental psychology, and educational psychology—*with a call to open up spaces to interdisciplinary and multidisciplinary studies of childhood* (e.g., the fields of sociology of childhood studies, anthropological studies of childhood and education, historical studies of early education and child care). Discourses related to rigorous "evidence"-based, experimental design, and positivist/logical-empiricist *assumptions about what research is best, and produces legitimate truth.* In contrast, we wanted to open up new spaces for examining early education/ child care as *a critical theoretical space—drawing on the emerging work in critical structural and poststructural theories, including diverse feminist theories and gender/sexuality/queer studies.* (My memories, italics used for emphasis)

Indeed, the RECE network focused a great deal of attention on opening up to new ways of doing research, different ways of thinking about "best evidence" or what some now call the "gold standard" of educational research (randomized and/or quasi-experimental design, rigorous, cause-and-effect studies, taking off from the natural science model of research, positivist, statistical, objective, replicable, and generalizable searches for truth).

Our "discourse communities" (Kittler & Meteer, 1992) have been special to those of us who attend (Tobin, 2007), but also isolated from many—with some intentionality in so doing. This intentional decision to keep the conference small may have limited its ability to be heard by others. Having it be larger, however, may have led toward the politics of co-optation, as some argued, and made it less intellectually fruitful.

The publications and discussions that have emerged suggest some success at diversifying theory/methodologies and a move toward what Malewski (2010) calls "post-reconceptualist recognition of the diverse approaches. Moreover, despite the small number of those in RECE at any given conference, the diverse perspectives and international backgrounds of those attending RECE have pushed individuals toward new methodologies and ideas, new theories, different ways to read and use theoretical frameworks in our work, and certainly opened us up toward different ideas about policy, pedagogical practices and research methodology. The RECE network, over the years has published work—for some of us still new—on decolonizing research, polyvocality in research, studying children's or parent's voices, using critical ethnographic, narrative, life history, critical and poststructural action research, strands of feminist theory laced with different methodologies (collaborative/teacher, parent, children as researched and researching), various forms of critical discourse analyses (e.g., MacLure, 2003), and, as suggested, diverse qualitative theory/methodologies (e.g., Rhedding-Jones, 2005; Steinberg & Cannella, 2012). We have pushed each other, answering the initial calls for "difference" in regimes of truth, different traditions of research, allowing different knowledge formation, policy ideas, and political action to take place (see diverse contributions in this volume).

In the 1990s, we also hoped to:

> Develop a social network of researchers and teacher educators and graduate students as a very important early goal (drawing on Bloch, 1992); a longer-term goal was to increase the number of faculty hires with a reconceptualizing ECE or critical/poststructural and feminist theoretical background and ECE background and interest in research at universities across the nation (first described explicitly in Bloch, 1992). This was important in terms of not wanting to continue to reproduce dominant discourses in teacher training and research. We wanted to be open to new paradigms of research, multidisciplinary research beyond the psychological sciences and child development, and, especially, to allow for critical theoretical research that would enable different ways of thinking and acting related to "dominant" or "normative" pedagogy and policy in ECE and child care. (My memories and words; italics used for emphasis)

Over the past 20 years, we have certainly created new spaces for publications, conferences, and networks of support. Many young graduate students have been hired at major universities in the U.S. and elsewhere—despite the fact that their research may still be considered "different" or "abnormal." Nevertheless, it has still been difficult for many new lecturers and assistant professors without tenure to publish in peer-reviewed journals, at least in the U.S. Along with the Australian on-line journal *Contemporary Issues in Early Childhood* (*CIEC*), new journals are appearing that open up spaces for conversation and critique. The *International Journal on Critical Policy Studies of Childhood* and *Global Childhoods* have emerged as sites for publishing and discussion; they are also open access and globally available.

Last, but I'm certain not least, over these past 20 years, our initial goals included the following questions: Whose voices were privileged or excluded; which values, knowledge, and truths guided curriculum choices in ECE; what and whose theories and knowledge were included in, as one example, the U.S.-published "Developmentally Appropriate Practice" guidelines (Bredekamp, 1987; Bredekamp & Copple, 1997; Copple & Bredekamp, 2009); what and which theories framed constructions of childhood as well as "best" policies and pedagogical practices for children, teachers, and families? Here, in light of tightening discourses of standardization and testing of young children, increasing push-down of academics into the preschool years, and relentless assessment of "quality" of programs that, if lucky, rely on NAEYC Developmentally Appropriate Standards criteria, the RECE discussions have had, in my experience and review (e.g., Bloch & Kim, 2012; Perez & Lee, in press), limited impact.

The response to our initial aims and purposes, and the values we espoused in our search for what and whose values count in the curriculum have been important and yet small at the same time. Since at least the 1980s when global and neoliberal/conservative policies in education and research have resulted in more emphasis on testing, standardized curricula, and even universal standardized childhoods, the research, writing, and openings of new ideas in teacher education that have occurred have been both discouraging and encouraging (and/but). In New Zealand, the *Te Whariki* curriculum and new assessment tools provide an example for many of us that shifts and ruptures can occur. In Australia's new Early Years Learning Framework (Australian Government, 2013), there are subtle shifts in wording that provide a lens into the important work Australian early childhood educators have been able to do in these past years—through being at the "table" for policy development, they have, with difficulty and perseverance, begun to make important changes in the framework policy documents (e.g., Sumsion, Barnes, Cheeseman, Harrison, Kennedy, & Stonehouse, 2009; Phelan & Sumsion, 2008). In the recent Australian Government Early Years Learning Framework (Australian Government, 2013), we see a statement of values about what we should care for, which ethical commitments are important, responding perhaps to Shirley Kessler's call for examining "What knowledge counts, who decides" (Kessler & Swadener, 1992a; Kessler, this volume). In Canada (Early Learning Advisory Group, 2008), Sweden, and in the OECD documents (e.g., *Starting Strong: Early Childhood Education and Care*, Organisation for Economic Cooperation and Development, 2001), we see a movement in the curriculum frameworks of postmodern theory as one of the guiding theories for the written documents. In many cases, critical researchers, many who participate in RECE as well as other critically oriented research, teaching, and writing, have helped to frame and insert these changes in government documents (Dahlberg & Moss, 2005; Sumsion et al., 2009).

These are important changes—in language, in the policy discourses that have begun to rupture, shift, and open up new possibilities for thinking and action. But, as suggested earlier, in the United States and elsewhere, we still see little change, small ruptures in politics, some changes that are, in my opinion (and of many others in this book), worse than what we initially worked against in the 1980s and 1990s. We can attribute some of this to increasing globalization, new counter-balancing networks of "control" and "discipline" (Deleuze, 1995; Dahlberg & Bloch, 2006), as well as new ways of "governing our souls," as Nikolas Rose (1989/1999) has so aptly phrased things. I would counter that our network society (Castells, 2009/2011) and alliances could act more strategically, more micro-politically (see Dahlberg & Moss, 2005), and with greater action/activism to open new spaces and recognize rhizomatic possibilities that are opening every day in local and global arenas. While some things have been done, so very many things appear to be worsening, for so many families and young children across the globe; important, and more challenging fights lay ahead.

Selected References

Australian Government. (2013). *Early Years Learning Framework, National Quality Framework for Early Childhood Education and Care.* http://deewr.gov.au/early-years-learning-framework

Ayers, W. (1989). *The good preschool teacher.* New York: Teachers College Press.

Blaise, M. (2005). *Playing it straight: Uncovering gender discourse in the early childhood classroom.* London: Routledge.

Bloch, M. N. (1987). Becoming scientific and professional: An historical perspective on the aims and effects of early childhood education. In T. S. Popkewitz (Ed.), *The formation of school subjects* (pp. 25–62). London: Falmer.

Bloch, M. N. (1991). Critical science and the history of child development's influence on early education research. *Early Education and Development, 2*(2), 95–97.

Bloch, M. N. (1992). Critical perspectives on the historical relationship between child development and early childhood education research. In S. Kessler & E. B. Swadener (Eds.), *Reconceptualizing the early childhood curriculum: Beginning the dialogue* (pp. 3–20). New York: Teachers College Press.

Bloch, M. N. (2010). Languages of power: Which ideas are governing current programmatic and curricular policies for programs for 3–4 year olds in the USA? Paper presented at the 18th International Reconceptualizing Early Childhood Education Conference, Dalton, Georgia (U.S.).

Bloch, M. N., Holmlund, K., Moqvist, I., & Popkewitz, T. S. (Eds.). (2003). *Governing children, families, and education: Restructuring the welfare state.* New York: Palgrave.

Bloch, M. N., & Kim, K. (2012). Governing young children's learning through educational reform: A poststructural analysis of discourses of best practice, standards, and quality. In S. Steinberg & G. S. Cannella (Eds.), *Critical qualitative research reader* (pp. 257–275). New York: Peter Lang.

Bloch, M. N. (2013). Reconceptualizing theory/Policy/curriculum/pedagogy in early child (care and) éducation : Reconceptualizing early childhood éducation (RECE) 1991–2012. *In the International Journal for Equity and Innovation in Early Childhood.*

Bredekamp, S. (1987). *Developmentally appropriate practices in early childhood education.* Washington, DC: National Association for the Education of Young Children.

Bredekamp, S., & Copple, C. (1997). *Developmentally appropriate practices in early childhood programs* (2nd ed.). Washington, DC: National Association for the Education of Young Children.

Brougere, G., & Vandenbroeck, M. (2007). *Repenser l'education des jeunes enfants.* London: Peter Lang.

Burman, E. (1994). *Deconstructing developmental psychology.* New York: Routledge.

Butler, J. (1993). *Bodies that matter: On the discursive limits of "Sex."* London: Routledge.

Butler, J. (2004). *Undoing gender.* New York: Routledge.

Cannella, G. S. (1997). *Deconstructing early childhood education: Social justice and revolution.* New York: Peter Lang.

Cannella, G. S. (In press). [Special issue]. *International Review of Qualitative Research.*

Cannella, G. S., & Kincheloe, J. (2002). *Kidworld: Childhood studies, global perspectives and education.* New York: Peter Lang.

Cannella, G. S., Swadener, B. B., & Che, Y. (2007). Reconceptualizing early childhood education. In R. New (Ed.), *International encyclopedia of early childhood education* (Vol. 4). Westport, CT: Praeger.

Cannella, G., & Viruru, R. (2004). *Childhood and postcolonization: Power, education, and contemporary practice.* New York: RoutledgeFalmer.

Castells, M. (2009/2011). *The rise of the network society. The Information Age: Economy, society, and culture* (Vol. 1). New York: Wiley-Blackwell.

Copple, C., & Bredekamp, S. (Eds.). (2009). *Developmentally appropriate practice in early childhood programs: Serving children from birth through age 8* (3rd ed.). Washington, DC: National Association for the Education of Young Children.

Dahlberg, G., & Bloch, M. N. (2006). Is the power to see and visualize always the power to control? In T. S. Popkewitz, K. Petersson, U. Olsson, & J. Kowalczyk (Eds.), *The future is not what it appears to be: Pedagogy, genealogy, and political epistemology* (pp. 105–123). Stockholm: HLS Förlag.

Dahlberg, G., & Moss, P. (2005). *Ethics and politics in early childhood education.* London: RoutledgeFalmer.

Dahlberg, G., Moss, P., & Pence, A. (2007). *Beyond quality in early childhood education and care: Languages of evaluation* (2nd ed.). London: Routledge.

David, M. E. (1980). *The state, the family, and education* (Radical Social Policy Series, Vol. 80). London: Routledge & Kegan Paul.

Davies, B. (1989). *Frogs and snails and feminist tales: Preschool children and gender.* St. Leonards, Australia: Allen & Unwin.

Deleuze, G. (1995). A postscript to societies for control. In G. Deleuze (Ed.), *Negotiations: 1972–1990* (pp. 177–182). New York: Columbia University Press.

Deleuze, G., & Guattari, F. (1987). *A thousand plateaus: Capitalism and schizophrenia.* Minneapolis: University of Minnesota Press.

Early Learning Advisory Group. (2008). *British Columbia early learning framework.* British Columbia, Canada: Ministry of Health and Ministry of Children and Family Development. http://www.bced.gov.bc.ca/early_learning/pdfs/early_learning_framework.pdf

Foucault, M. (1980). *Power/knowledge: Selected interviews and writings 1972–1977,* trans. C. Gordon. New York: Pantheon.

Gracey, H. (1975). Learning the student role: Kindergarten as academic bootcamp. In H. R. Stub (Ed.), *The sociology of education: A source book* (3rd ed.). (pp. 82–95). Homewood, IL: Dorsey.

Graue, E. M. (1993). *Ready for what? Constructing meanings of readiness for kindergarten.* Albany: SUNY Press.

Greishaber, S., & Cannella, G. (2001). *Embracing identities in early childhood education: Diversity and possibilities.* New York: Teachers College Press.

Hatch, A. (Ed.). (1995). *Qualitative research in early childhood settings.* New York: Praeger.

James, A., Jenks, C., & Prout, A. (1998). *Theorizing childhood.* New York: Teachers College Press.

Jenkins, H. (Ed.). (1998). *The children's culture reader.* New York: NYU Press.

Kessler, S. (1991). Alternative perspectives on early childhood education. *Early Childhood Research Quarterly, 6,* 183–197.

Kessler, S., & Swadener, E. B. (Eds.). (1992a). *Reconceptualizing the early childhood curriculum: Beginning the dialogue.* New York: Teachers College Press.

Kessler, S., & Swadener, E. B. (1992b). Introduction: Reconceptualizing curriculum. In S. Kessler & E. B. Swadener (Eds.), *Reconceptualizing the early childhood curriculum: Beginning the dialogue* (pp. xiii–xxviii). New York: Teachers College Press.

King, N. (1982). Work and play in the classroom. *Sociology of Education, 46,* 110–113.

Kittler, F. A., & Meteer, M. (1992). *Discourse networks, 1800/1900.* Stanford, CA: Stanford University Press.

Kliebard, H. (1975). Reappraisal: The Tyler rationale. In W. Pinar (Ed.), *Curriculum theorizing: The reconceptualists* (pp. 70–83). Berkeley, CA: McCutchan.

Leavitt, R., & Powers, M. (1994). *Emotions in infant and toddler daycare.* New York: SUNY Press.

Lenz-Taguchi, H. (2009). *Going beyond the theory/practice divide in early childhood.* London: Routledge.

Lubeck, S. (1985). *The sandbox society.* New York: Falmer.

Lubeck, S. (1994). The politics of developmentally appropriate practice: Exploring issues of culture, class, and curriculum. In B. Mallory & R. New (Eds.), *Diversity and developmentally appropriate practice(s)* (pp. 17–43). New York: Teachers College Press.

MacLure, M. (2003). *Discourse in educational and social research.* Buckingham, U.K.: Open University Press.

MacNaughton, G. (2003). *Shaping early childhood education.* Maidenhead, U.K.: Open University Press.

MacNaughton, G. (2005). *Doing Foucault in early childhood studies.* London: RoutledgeFalmer.

Malewski, E. (2010). Introduction: Proliferating curriculum. *Curriculum studies handbook: The next moment* (pp. 1–41). New York: Routledge.

Mallory, B., & New, R. (Eds.). (1994). *Diversity and developmentally appropriate practices: Challenges for early childhood education.* New York: Teachers College Press.

Mutua, K., & Swadener, B. B. (Eds.). (2005). *Decolonizing research: Critical personal narratives.* New York: SUNY Press.

O'Loughlin, M. (1992). Rethinking science education: Beyond Piagetian constructivism toward a sociocultural model of teaching and learning. *Journal of Research in Science Teaching, 29*(8), 791–820.

O'Loughlin, M., & Johnson, R. T. (Eds.). (2010). *Imagining children otherwise: Theoretical and critical perspectives of childhood subjectivity.* New York: Peter Lang.

Olsson, L. M. (2009). *Movement and experimentation in young children's learning.* London: Routledge.

Organisation for Economic Cooperation and Development. (2001). *Starting strong: Early childhood education and care.* Paris, France: OECD.

Pacini-Ketchabaw, V. (Ed.). (2010). *Flows, rhythms, and intensities of early childhood education curriculum.* New York: Peter Lang.

Pence, A., & Hix-Small, A. (2009). Global children in the shadow of the global child. *International Critical Childhood Studies Journal, 2*(2), 75–91.

Perez, M., & Lee, I. F. (Ed.). (In press). [Special issue]. *International Journal of Critical Childhood Policy Studies.*

Phelan, A. M., & Sumsion, J. (Eds.). (2008). *Critical readings in teacher education: Provoking absences.* Rotterdam: Sense.

Pinar, W. F. (Ed.). (1975a). *Curriculum theorizing: The reconconceptualists.* New York: McCutcheon.

Pinar, W. F. (1975b). Currere: Toward reconceptualization. In W. F. Pinar (Ed.), *Curriculum theorizing: The recon-conceptualists* (pp. 396–414). New York: McCutcheon.

Polakow, V. (1992). *The erosion of childhood*. Chicago: University of Chicago Press.

Polakow, V. (1993). *Lives on the edge: Single mothers and their children in the other America*. Chicago: University of Chicago Press.

Polakow, V. (2007). *Who cares for our children? The child care crisis in the other America*: New York: Teachers College Press.

Rhedding-Jones, J. (2005). *What is research? Methodological practices and new approaches*. Norway: Universitetsforlager.

Ritchie, J., & Rau, C. (2007). Ma wai nga hua? "Participation" in early childhood in Aotearoa/New Zealand. *International Journal of Educational Policy, Research and Practice: Reconceptualizing Childhood Studies, 8*(1), 101–116.

Ritchie, J., & Rau, C. (2009). Ma wai nga hua? "Participation" in early childhood in Aotearoa/New Zealand. *International Critical Childhood Policy Studies, 2*(1), 93–108.

Rose, N. (1989/1999). *Governing our soul: The shaping of the private self*. London: Free Association Books.

Ryan. S., & Grieshaber, S. (2004). It's more than child development: Critical theories, research, and teaching young children. *Young Children: Journal of the National Association for the Education of Young Children, 59*(6), 44–52.

Ryan, S., & Grieshaber, S. J. (Eds.). (2005). *Practical transformations and transformational practices: Globalization, postmodernism, and early childhood education* (Advances in Early Education and Day Care, Vol. 14). Netherlands, Amsterdam: Elsevier JAI.

Scott, J. W. (1991). The evidence of experience. *Critical Inquiry, 17*(4), 773–797.

Silin, J. (1987). The early childhood educator's knowledge base: A reconsideration. In L. G. Katz (Ed.), *Current topics in early childhood education* (pp. 17–31). Norwood, NJ: Ablex.

Silin, J. (1995). *Sex, death, and the education of children: Our passion for ignorance in the age of AIDS*. New York: Teachers College Press.

Soto, L. D. (1996). *Language, culture, and power*. Albany: SUNY Press.

Soto, L. D. (2000). *The politics of early education*. Albany: SUNY Press.

Soto, L. D., & Swadener, B. B. (2005). *Power and voice in research with children*. New York: Peter Lang.

Spodek, B. (1980). The kindergarten: A retrospective and contemporary view. In L. Katz (Ed.), *Current topics in early education* (Vol. 4; pp. 173–191). Norwood, NJ: Ablex.

Steinberg, S. R., & Cannella, G. S. (Eds.). (2012). *Critical qualitative research reader*. New York: Peter Lang.

Sumsion, J., Barnes, S., Cheeseman, S., Harrison, L., Kennedy, A. M., & Stonehouse, A. (2009). Insider perspectives on developing "Belonging, being and becoming: The early years learning framework for Australia." *Australasian Journal of Early Childhood, 34*(4), 4–13.

Suransky, V. (1983). *The erosion of childhood*. Chicago: University of Chicago Press.

Swadener, E. B., & Bloch, M. N. (Thematic issue eds.). (1997). International perspectives in early childhood education. *Early Education and Development, 8*(3), Psychology Press.

Swadener, E. B., & Kessler, S. (Thematic issue eds.). (1991). Reconceptualizing early childhood education. *Early Education and Development, 2*(2), Psychology Press.

Swadener, E. B., & Lubeck, S. (Eds.). (1995). *Children and families "at promise": Deconstructing the discourse of "at risk."* New York: SUNY Press.

Taylor, A. (2013). *Reconfiguring the natures of childhood*. London: Routledge, Chapman, & Hall.

Tobin, J. (1997). *Making a place for pleasure in early childhood education*. New Haven, CT: Yale University Press.

Tobin, J. & Colleagues (2000). *"Good guys don't wear hats": Children talk about the media*. New York: Teachers College Press.

Tobin, J. (2007). Rôle de la théorie dans le mouvement: Reconceptualiser l'éducation de la petite enfance. In G. Brougere & M. Vandenbroeck (Eds.), *Repenser l'éducation des jeunes enfants* (pp. 19–48). London: Peter Lang.

Tobin, J., Wu, D. Y. H., & Davidson, D. H. (1989). *Preschool in three cultures*. New Haven, CT: Yale University Press.

Walkerdine, V. (1984). Developmental psychology and child-centered pedagogy. In J. Henriques, W. Holloway, C. Urwin, C. Venn, & V. Walkerdine (Eds.), *Changing the subject: Psychology, social regulation and subjectivity* (pp. 153–202). London & New York: Routledge (first published by Methuen, 1984).

Walkerdine, V. (1998). *Daddy's girl: Young girls and popular culture*. Cambridge, MA: Harvard University Press.

Yelland, N. (Ed.). (2005). *Critical issues in early childhood education*. Maidenhead, England: Open University Press.

Notes

1. This chapter is a shortened version of a keynote presentation at the Centre for Equity and Innovation in Early Childhood annual conference held at the University of Melbourne, Australia, in November 2011. This article is a shortened and adapted version of: Bloch, M. N. (2013). Reconceptualizing theory/policy/curriculum/pedagogy in early child (care and) éducation: Reconceptualizing early childhood éducation (RECE) 1991–2012. In the *International Journal of Equity and Innovation in Early Childhood*, vol. 11, No. 1, 2013, (pp. 65–85).
2. A conference sponsored by Amos Hatch (1989) focused on qualitative research in ECE in the U.S. (see Hatch, 1995).
3. The use of "we" is a metaphor for my own portrayal of what I remember, and what I have never known, or forgotten. Given that there is no one correct representation, my memories and my forgettings and exclusions are part of my understandings of shared memories and a collective historical narrative. Of the initial people at the 1991 RECE conference, Beth Swadener, Shirley Kessler, Sally Lubeck, Joe Tobin, Jan Jipson, Daniel Walsh, Bernard Spodek, Gary Price, Chelsea Bailey, Beth Graue, and I had been instrumental in formulating the idea of the conference. It was hosted at University of Wisconsin–Madison in 1991 because much of the early work had initiated with the faculty and alumni of the critical-theory-oriented Department of Curriculum and Instruction. A list of those who attended the first conference is available upon request.
4. Rupture is used in a very significant way in Foucauldian histories of the present, or genealogical work; it signals a significant break in discourse—one that isn't evident "in the present" of this 20-year examination; so I use the word "lightly" but with significance here.

Reconceptualizing the Early Childhood Curriculum: An Unaddressed Topic

Shirley A. Kessler

Many years ago, I was intrigued by comments made by Herbert Kliebard during a graduate seminar at the University of Wisconsin (Kliebard, 1980). He said, "Curriculum making is utopia building," and "all curriculum is made with a view of the future in mind, a utopian vision." I take these remarks to mean that when we plan a curriculum we have a vision in mind of what we want the future to look like. Additionally, we have a vision of what we want the children we teach to become. While I wrote earlier about "utopian visions" (Kessler, 1991; Kessler & Swadener, 1992), I did not elaborate or further articulate what this idea might mean for the early childhood curriculum and, henceforth, set aside any further research and writing that addresses this important question with regard to curriculum planning. Then, I and others called for a reconceptualization of early childhood education, but not a reconceptualized curriculum. In this chapter I want to return to the question of what a reconceptualized curriculum in early childhood might entail by focusing on four questions curriculum planners must address:[1]

What vision of the future and the "good life" guides curriculum planning in early childhood?
What should be taught and what is the justification for decisions made?
Who is taught; that is, do all students receive the same curriculum?
What is the relationship between teaching and the curriculum?

Responses to these questions should lead to further discussions among reconceptualists and others and begin a dialogue about what is meant by a reconceptualized approach to early childhood curriculum planning and the ways in which an alternative curriculum might be enacted.

What Vision of the Future Guides Curriculum Planning in Early Childhood?

Those of us who suggest or plan programs for children must ask ourselves: *What* vision of the future guides our thinking about the curriculum we plan for young children, and *whose* vision prevails? Froebel expressed an idealistic view of kindergarten education when he stated that the purpose of the kindergarten was to "lead man to [an understanding of] the inner law of Divine Unity…attained through nourishing good tendencies and learned through symbols" (Weber, 1984, p. 43). William T. Harris, then superintendent of schools in St. Louis, wholeheartedly supported Froebel's kindergarten to promote social harmony as well as educational goals: "Society would benefit by providing rational kindergarten training…. Poor children would be kept out of the streets where they developed evil associations; rich children would be kept out of the hands of unskilled servants who ruined them through self-indulgence" (Weber, 1969, p. 29). Margaret Naumburg, a socialist, was critical of what she saw as a "herd psychology" promoted in schools that required conformity to social norms. She founded the Walden School in 1915 during the Progressive Era, where the curriculum was based on creative self-expression that she thought led to strong individuals and diversity of thought. She claimed, "Without the expansion of many-sided individuals, there can be no vital and varied social group" (Naumburg, 1928, p. 122) and/or the expression of alternative perspectives necessary for social progress. Much more recently, Bill Ayers (2013) called for the president to rethink his ideas regarding education and instead promote a system that does not treat education as a commodity. Ayers' utopian vision was a strong, vibrant democracy, but he saw the current school reform movement as anathema to a democratic form of government, as it advocates such practices as "reducing education to a single narrow metric that claims to recognize an educated person through a test score." Recently, I learned about a private school in New York called The IDEAL School of Manhattan that states unequivocally on its website its utopian vision: The school "is an inclusion school dedicated to creating a diverse community that affirms and accepts the full identities of all people, while inspiring academic excellence, creative leadership, and a desire to build a more just and equitable world" (2013).

Another vision could resemble, for example, President Roosevelt's four freedoms, where freedom of speech and freedom of worship were joined by two additional freedoms: freedom from want and freedom from fear (Roosevelt, 1941). What role would education play in the realization of these four freedoms? President Obama's view of the future as stated in his 2013 State of Union address is a future where a "smart" government can foster a prosperous middle class, economic opportunity, a cleaner environment, and health care for all; in essence, a future "where government works on behalf of the many." Also in his vision, "doors of opportunity are available to every child" by making "high-quality preschool available to every single child in America" (2013). What implications for curriculum planning follow from this view of the future? Obviously, the visions expressed previously are those of privileged individuals and not those of the working poor or individuals from differing religious, cultural, racial, or ethnic backgrounds. We must seek to understand and include views of individuals from these groups, and others, as we develop a reconceptualized early childhood curriculum.

Clearly, one's utopian vision is solidly grounded in one's personal values and political ideology. I believe we must ask ourselves how one's vision relates to the early childhood curriculum that one plans and enacts. In addition, we must ask ourselves whose vision of the future should prevail when we plan programs for young children. Both questions raise issues of power and influence on the curriculum. A discussion of these questions should attract all early childhood educators, not just the reconceptualists.

What Should We Teach in the Early Childhood Curriculum?

This question is fundamental to curriculum planning and follows from one's utopian vision. As I argued earlier, "curriculum decisions are based on beliefs about what school leaders think is important to know and what the child and the community need" (Kessler, 1991). Obviously, not everything one would like can be taught in the early childhood curriculum, so choices must be made. Kliebard maintained in his 1980 seminar that "certain things are drawn from the culture to influence teaching." Ralph Tyler (1949) recommended that objectives for the curriculum (the "things") be selected from an examination of the child's needs, the needs of society, and subject-matter experts. These objectives were to be passed through a philosophical screen to determine their compatibility with local schools' philosophies, as well as through a psychological screen to determine their compatibility with children's developmental levels. Kliebard's critique is brilliant: One's philosophy precedes the selection of content, as well as the determination of the needs of society and the needs of the child. For example, he argued, the interests of students are not legitimate until they are compared with what is desirable. Likewise, the recommendations from subject-matter experts and from studies of contemporary life are similarly value laden (Kliebard, 1975). Nevertheless, Tyler's approach to curriculum planning is very attractive to many educators. This so-called "rational approach" has had much influence on curriculum planning: it is logical and does not deal with the messy business of talking about values and priorities where difference would no doubt emerge and conflict ensue.

Critical perspectives on the selection of knowledge to be included in the curriculum claim that knowledge is not neutral, but is socially constructed by influential groups, varies in status, and is distributed unequally (Kessler, 1991; Kessler & Swadener, 1992). Jan Jipson and Nicholas Paley (1991) highlighted the concept of the "selective tradition" in teachers' choices of literature to use in their classrooms. They wrote, "Books are not ideologically neutral; that is, they both reflect and convey certain sorts of sociocultural values, beliefs and attitudes to their readers...teachers 'select' for or against...certain...cultural values in their classrooms" (p. 148). In their study of 55 teachers' choices of literature to use in their classroom, they found that only 15% of the rationales given for choosing particular books included race, gender, and ethnicity as factors that were considered. The extent to which such practices exist today is an open question.

Further, if critical theorists are correct, curriculum knowledge is not determined by minority groups or the poor and hence may have little relevance to them. Lack of meaning associated with "official knowledge" among poor and minority students can help explain their low scores on tests. William Pinar (1975) addressed the importance of examining the meaning the curriculum holds for individuals by introducing the concept of "currere," turning the noun, "curriculum," into a verb. "Currere, historically rooted in the field of curriculum in existentialism, phenomenology, and psychoanalysis, is the study of educational experience" (Pinar, 1975, p. 400).

Nancy King (1992) provided an example of currere in kindergarten. Many teachers believe in the importance of play to promote the development of creativity, intentional behavior, concept development, language development, social interaction, and so on. However, as Nancy King's early research indicates, children learn attitudes toward work and play by the way teachers structure the environment. Children in this study did not regard all kinds of planned play activities as "play," only those activities that were freely chosen and not held to any standard.

Today, many early childhood educators teach the traditional school curriculum that focuses on skills, such as reading readiness and concepts of quantity and numeration, among others, in answering the question of what to teach. One school in DuPage County, Illinois, where I live, posted its objectives for kindergartners that include: "Makes predictions based on illustrations"; "Isolates beginning and ending sounds in words"; and can perform "Addition of two groups using manipulatives" (Schafer Elementary, 2013). I don't think the objectives for kindergarten education in this school represent an isolated case. Further, this orientation toward curriculum is evident in preschool education as well. A friend of mine said she had to look hard to find a play-based preschool program for her daughter; most parents in her cohort group wanted an academically oriented educational experience for their child.

Bredekamp's (1987) work that addressed the inappropriate "academic" curriculum in early childhood classrooms has had little influence on current practice despite her authorship of a strong position paper (1987) published by the nation's largest association of early childhood educators, a publication that many refer to as DAP, that called for practices (a curriculum) more in tune with children's developmental level. (Curriculum theorists believe that when you change the methods to teach a particular concept or skill, you essentially change the curriculum, a view that will be highlighted in a later section of this chapter.) Nor have 20 years of our work as reconceptualists had any influence on the curriculum in schools in DuPage County, Illinois, and probably elsewhere, as indicated by posted objectives. It is significant that Bredekamp (1991) later claimed that the DAP document was written to counter the pressure educators felt for the skills-oriented curriculum and indicated that this response was in part a political one. Is the DAP publication, therefore, a political document? Does it advance a particular view of what is good? To what extent are all curriculums essentially political documents? As Mary Hauser and I wrote earlier (Kessler & Hauser, 2000):

> Early childhood educators are not accustomed to viewing the curriculum politically…. [But] in order to educate its young members, individuals in a particular social group must collaborate to ensure that their children are educated in such a way so as to perpetuate the interests of that particular collective…. [which] leads to different perspectives as to how education should be accomplished. Furthermore, it is natural for individuals to form alliances with those who share their views in an attempt to influence others to see this project as they do and to exert pressure on others in order to accomplish their agenda which is rationalized as the best way to proceed. (pp. 60–61)

We must ask ourselves why, today, have basic skills been selected for emphasis in early childhood? What political forces are at play that foster this curriculum orientation?

In addition, some (most?) rationales for early childhood education provide evidence for a "preparation for the future" orientation. For example, another nearby early childhood program, the Jefferson Early Childhood Center for preschoolers in DuPage County, Illinois, proclaimed its purpose was to "offer a dynamic and fun learning environment to help prepare your child for a successful kindergarten experience" (Jefferson Preschool Registration, 2013). This "preparation for the future" orientation was best expressed almost a century ago by Franklin Bobbitt who wrote the first book on curriculum (Bobbitt, 1918). To Bobbitt, the purpose of education was to prepare students for adult life. Further, he stated, "human life…consists in the performance of specific activities. Education that prepares for life is one that prepares… for those specific activities" (p. 42). This so-called scientific approach to curriculum planning meant that educators would study "scientifically" the world of work to decide what skills needed to be mastered to meet the needs of the then-current workforce; those skills would become the objectives of the curriculum. Bobbitt's "utopian vision" assumed a stratified society where those engaged in menial labor would be educated to have the right attitude about their work so that they would realize the importance of their endeavors for the good of the collective and thereby not only accept but appreciate their place in society. I doubt if early childhood educators today want to educate their students for a future where social class is assumed and individuals must find their place within it. Yet, aren't we doing just that? Preparing a child for his/her future begs the question of what kind of future? Do curriculum planners today see the future as relatively static, in need of little modification? Who are these planners and what is their relationship to a curriculum based on preparation for the future as they see it?

Some educators have added to the previously-mentioned versions of the early childhood curriculum by articulating and promoting the "anti-bias curriculum" intending to promote understanding, tolerance, and appreciation of people who are "different" (Derman-Sparks & The A.B.C. Task Force, 1989). Early on, the emphasis was on the sexual, racial, and cultural differences among children that should be addressed in order to promote understanding of others and social equality in the classroom and beyond. Jonathan Silin (1995) added to these categories by raising sexual orientation as an important distinction among groups whose members need to be understood and who should be treated fairly in school and beyond. The anti-bias curriculum can likewise be viewed as a political document.

Those educators who value an anti-bias curriculum are promoting a social-reconstructionist orientation toward curriculum, articulating the belief that the school curriculum should address social problems, particularly social and economic inequality, and become an agent of social change. The social-reconstructionist orientation toward curriculum has a long history, and was most clearly articulated by George S. Counts in 1932 in a well-known piece titled *Dare the Schools Build a New Social Order?* (Counts, 1932/1978). In this work and other writings, Counts set forth his belief that the role of schools was to correct the ills of society. Writing during the Great Depression, Counts' main criticism was directed at the economic system: "Unless the democratic tradition is able to organize and conduct a successful attack on the economic system, its complete destruction is inevitable" (p. 41). Counts believed schools could bring about change by formulating an ideal American society, communicating that ideal to students, and encouraging them to use the ideal as a standard for judging their own and other societies.

Building on Counts' ideas, Harold Rugg (Kliebard, 1986) wrote a set of social studies textbooks beginning with the identification of 300 important problems facing American society that became the backbone of a new social studies curriculum.[2] Rugg's textbook series was short-lived (1929–early 1940s), arguably due to his focus on the weaknesses of capitalism, his leaning toward collectivist views, and additionally, his support of the labor movement, ideas that were viciously attacked by social conservatives then and now. Rugg's curriculum was clearly making a political statement.

This example of the realization of a social reconstructionist orientation in a well-developed curriculum has much to teach us. Those of us who want the curriculum to address social problems are very much constrained by the social values and mores currently held by the majority culture and its support of privilege and power. If we go too far in criticizing unjust governmental and economic policies and practices that contribute to social inequality, we risk ferocious attacks on our work and eventually, I believe, we could become irrelevant and forgotten, like Counts and Rugg. Likewise, Froebel's curriculum disappeared from use when it was outlawed after the revolution of 1848 in Germany, when liberal thought "favoring the natural rights of man, individual freedom, and humanitarian and democratic ideals" (Weber, 1984, p. 34) was defeated and a return to authoritarianism prevailed. Addressing opposition to his ideas, Froebel lamented, "I only wanted to train up *free, thinking, independent* men" (Brubacher, 1947, p. 622; emphases in original). Wrote Brubacher, "[T]he governmental bureaucracy was not mistaken in the idea that schools imbued with Froebel's pedagogy could not be contained within the existing social order but must necessarily revolutionize it" (Brubacher, 1947, p. 622).[3] As an aside, the failure of the 1848 revolution in Germany led to the immigration of Carl Schurz, a leader of the failed revolution, and his wife, Margareth, to the United States and eventually to Watertown, Wisconsin, where Margareth, who studied with Froebel, opened the first kindergarten in this country.

Margaret Naumburg gave up trying to promote individualism and creative ways of learning school subjects. In an interview I had the privilege to hear, she later stated that "The whole system should be bombed" (Hamilton & Hamilton, 1971). In contrast, the goals of The IDEAL School of Manhattan have not been challenged, no doubt because it is a private organization.

The recommendations of curriculum planners for an anti-bias curriculum for young children can address some issues, such as fair treatment in the classroom for all, but cannot change structural factors that support the status quo. Those of us who believe that schools should address social problems would do well to understand that our prescriptions for practice could be overly ambitious. We must ask ourselves if the programs we are developing or the research we are conducting have any chance of being implemented or influencing the field. Bredekamp's (1987) work represents a failed attempt to influence the curriculum by issuing prescriptions for practice based on the beliefs of professional early childhood educators. What forces worked against the acceptance of DAP? Are we out of touch with the realities of early childhood education as it exists today? We must ask ourselves if the articulation of a curriculum that enhances social and economic equality is the best way to bring about a reconceptualized early childhood curriculum.[4]

Who Is Taught?

This question addresses the issue of the ways in which children are organized and/or grouped for instruction. The most common way to group students for instruction is by age. Kindergartners are typically 5 years old; first graders are usually 6. The question arises, should 5-year-olds be excluded from kindergarten because their birthdays fall after a certain cutoff date? Is it fair that my great-nephew, age 4, cannot participate in a classroom of other

4-year-olds simply because he misses the cut-off date by a few days? Whose interests are served by this approach to grouping children for instruction?

Furthermore, criteria based on other demographics have come into play. Income level might determine eligibility for a particular program, such as Head Start, or when some school districts charge an additional fee for children to attend preschool. For example, one preschool program in Wheaton, Illinois, charges parents $235 per month for their child to attend a half-day program (Jefferson Preschool Registration, 2013), a cost that represents a substantial addition to the family budget of the average worker whose wage has grown little since the 1960s (Krugman, 2013). Neighborhoods, likewise, serve as a way children are organized for instruction. Children in poor neighborhoods attend local schools where they have traditionally performed poorly on achievement tests. Recent studies indicated that family income is now seen as the largest determining factor in student achievement, larger than the educational level of parents (Reardon, 2011).

Another common practice in many classrooms is to group children by ability. The NEA is against ability grouping (NEA Resolutions, 1998, 2005), but their resolutions seem to have had little effect on current practice. District 200 in the county in which I live has a program for gifted students. Critical theorists would view such grouping practices as examples of high-status knowledge (academic knowledge) made available to a rather elite group and thus distributed unequally. The rationale for ability grouping must be examined. Is such grouping fair? Is it based on reliable measures of ability? Is it linguistically and culturally sensitive? Whose interests are served by the practice of grouping children by ability?

Another criterion used to group children in early childhood classrooms is "readiness." The early work of Elizabeth Graue (1992) illustrated the way in which this concept is socially constructed in two different schools by teachers and community members. The concepts varied widely, with socially constructed and shared definitions enabling some parents to have a greater voice in determining meanings of "readiness for kindergarten" in their child's school, whereas parents with less cultural capital left decisions about their child's readiness up to the school. Thus, readiness is not seen as a characteristic of children, but a construct developed by members of influential groups; a claim made by critical theorists of the curriculum that in Graue's study had important implications for the curriculum taught to children seen as "ready" and those seen as "not ready." Graue's later work (2006) maintains that readiness is an ethical responsibility we all have for our children, one that "encompasses coordinated systems of early care and education and receptive schools" (p. 43).[5]

What Is the Relationship Between the Curriculum and Teaching?

Earlier, I stated that Kliebard claimed that the items or content selected from the culture (literacy, problem solving, and the like) were intended to influence teaching. This concept is important because it sets forth the assumption that teachers influenced what was taught. They were seen as active participants, not robots teaching uncritically the prescribed content. In fact, conceptions of curriculum, such as the "curriculum-in-use," the "enacted curriculum," the "emergent curriculum," the "hidden curriculum," and/or the "experienced curriculum" were developed to account for the variations between what teachers planned, what they actually taught, and what students learned.

Many factors influence teachers' decisions about what to teach. In fact, in one study, teachers rated 28 "influences" that they considered in their decisions about what to teach, including students' ability. Shavelson and Stern (1981) found that "students' achievement level and 'participation' are significant influences in teachers' planning and the decisions they make even while in the act of teaching." However, teachers' stated beliefs about teaching may not be evident in the enacted curriculum. Wen and Elicker (2011) studied the relationship between teachers' beliefs about developmentally appropriate practices and their classroom interactions with children and found that there was little correlation between teachers' stated beliefs and the curriculum-in-use. Other factors such as the way in which teachers structured the environment and interacted verbally and nonverbally with students taught a curriculum—in this case, cultural values and attitudes—of which teachers were not aware (Lubeck, 1985); this is an example of what Phillip Jackson (1968) called the "hidden curriculum."

Furthermore, while teachers today may be less able to make decisions about what to teach due to the influence of state standards on the curriculum and the influence of achievement tests in reinforcing the teaching of those standards, the methods teachers choose when teaching standard content influence the curriculum-in-use, or the experienced curriculum. I found that the teaching methods employed in one kindergarten classroom, what we would call "developmentally appropriate," enabled children to be more influential, as defined in this study; but the result was a curriculum-in-use that enabled boys to be more influential than girls and reinforced gendered roles (Kessler, 1989). Here, boys had an edge in determining the experienced curriculum, an outcome the teacher did not intend, and I believe would have been horrified to learn. Likewise, the curriculum in one Head Start classroom (Kessler & Hauser, 2000) led to similar results. The teaching methods determined by the program adopted a "hands-off" approach to the teachers' role during free play. Left on their own, girls reinforced gendered roles; the curriculum-in-use led to outcomes or children's experiences not planned by the teachers or programs. Further, observations of some children in this classroom indicated ways in which they resisted teachers' attempts to redirect their play to accomplish academic goals by ignoring teachers' suggestions, and thus creating experiences for themselves that countered teachers' priorities for learning.

Conclusion

What is the takeaway from a focus on the four questions posed at the start of this chapter? I believe we must first acknowledge the extreme complexity of the school curriculum. Selection of content is influenced by the world views or utopian visions of educators and school leaders right from the start, a vision that is largely influenced by one's political ideology. The selection of content and the ways in which children are grouped for instruction are undoubtedly influenced by the political interests of educators. Finally, complexity is enhanced by teachers' interpretation of curriculum content, the methods chosen to teach that content, and students' ability to influence teachers and the curriculum. As we plan curricula that represent our version of the good life, we must first realize that it may undergo many translations and/or transformations before and during its implementation and be experienced by students differently. Also important, though not dealt with in this chapter, is the necessity to understand the school as a bureaucratic organization, where today the top-down nature of decision making about what to teach leaves less room for teachers and children to influence what is taught. In addition, powerful groups that develop state standards and evaluation procedures must be examined for their personal and political investment in the curriculum they advocate.

However, we cannot simply study children and the process of schooling and develop new programs, although important understandings can result from such efforts.[6] Research, though well intended, or position papers such as DAP, have little chance of leading to reconceptualized early childhood curriculum unless we become politically active. We might form a forceful interest group ourselves and advocate, after much deliberation, for the utopian vision we might all share and a school curriculum that would support such a vision.

Postmodern theories have made a great contribution to our thinking about education when they warn us about the hegemonic possibilities of communal deliberation that evolves into a meta-narrative that excludes the voices of others in particular situations. Our search for a shared vision of the good life must include an analysis of "the particular" as well as "the general," a dialectical relationship, if you will: "the sense that the local can illuminate the more general, and that the global can heighten our sensitivity to the more particular" (Beyer & Liston, 1992, p. 375). In addition, political action requires some form of communal identity that does not have to lead to a rejection of outside interests. Further, the awareness that knowledge is personal and contextualized should not lead us to reject all knowledge claims, per se (Beyer & Liston, 1992).

Deliberations in the moral realm, including the representation of particular voices, as well as theoretical ideas as to what is "right" and "good," are a necessary prelude to effective action necessary for social and educational change. Moral deliberation and political action provide the only means for changing early childhood education to reflect what I believe we agree would be an emancipatory pedagogy, promoting justice and fairness and a vision of the future that has potential for improving our democracy and the world. An endeavor such as this contains within it the possibility of developing a reconceptualized early childhood curriculum.

References

Ayers, W. (2013, January 10). Mr. President, education is a human right, not a product. *Truth Out*. Retrieved from http://truth-out.org/opinion/item/13813-bill-ayers-a-letter-to-the-president

Beyer, L., & Liston, D. (1992). Discourse or moral action? Critique of postmodernism. *Educational Theory, 42*(4), 371–393.

Bobbitt, F. (1918). *The curriculum*. New York: Houghton Mifflin.

Bredekamp, S. (Ed.). (1987). *Developmentally appropriate practice in early childhood programs serving children from birth through age 8*. Washington, DC: National Association for the Education of Young Children.

Bredekamp, S. (1991). Redeveloping early childhood education: A response to Kessler. *Early Childhood Research Quarterly, 6*, 199–209.

Brubacher, J. S. (1947). *A history of the problems of education*. New York: McGraw-Hill.

Counts, G. S. (1932/1978). *Dare the schools build a new social order?* Carbondale: Southern Illinois University Press.

Derman-Sparks, L., & The A.B.C. Task Force. (1989). *Anti-bias curriculum: Tools for empowering young children*. Washington, DC: National Association for the Education of Young Children.

Fichte, J. G. (1968). Address to the German nation. Trans. R. F. Jones & G. H. Turnbull. Eds., and Revised G. A. Kelly, New York: Harper Row.

Graue, E. (1992). Meanings of readiness and the kindergarten experience. In S. Kessler & B. Swadener (Eds.), *Reconceptualizing the early childhood curriculum: Beginning the dialogue* (pp. 62–90). New York: Teachers College Press.

Graue, E. (2006). The answer is readiness. Now what is the question? *Early Education and Development, 17*(1), 43–56.

Hamilton, J., & Hamilton, M., (1971). Interview with Margaret and Zinberg, February 6, 1971. New York.

Henkin, R. (1998). *Who's invited to share? Using literacy to teach for equity and social justice*. New York: Heinemann.

IDEAL School of Manhattan. (2013). *Statement of philosophy*. Retrieved from http://www.theidealschool.org

Jackson, P. W. (1968). *Life in classrooms*. New York: Holt, Rinehart & Winston.

Jacobs, D. T. (Four Arrows), & Mann, B. (2013). *Teaching truly: A curriculum to indigenize mainstream education.* New York: Peter Lang.

Jefferson Preschool Registration. (2013). Retrieved from http://www.cusd200.org/hawthorne/cwp/view.asp?A=3&Q=3

Jipson J., & Paley, N. (1991, October). The selective tradition in teachers' choice of children's literature: Does it exist in the elementary classroom? *English Education,* Vol. 23, 148–159.

Kessler, S. (1989). Boys' and girls' effect on the kindergarten curriculum. *Early Childhood Research Quarterly,* 4(3), 479–503.

Kessler, S. (1991). Alternative perspectives on early childhood education. *Early Childhood Research Quarterly,* 6, 183–197.

Kessler, S., & Hauser, M. (2000). Critical pedagogy and the politics of play. In L. D. Soto (Ed.), *The politics of early childhood education* (pp. 59–71). New York: Peter Lang.

Kessler, S., & Swadener, B. (Eds.). (1992). *Reconceptualizing early childhood education: Beginning the dialogue.* New York: Teachers College Press.

King, N. (1992). The impact of context on the play of young children. In S. Kessler & B. Swadener (Eds.), *Reconceptualizing early childhood education: Beginning the dialogue* (pp. 43–61). New York: Teachers College Press.

Kliebard, H. (1975). Reappraisal: The Tyler rationale. In W. Pinar (Ed.), *Curriculum theorizing: The reconceptualists* (pp. 70–83). Berkeley: McCutchan.

Kliebard, H. (1980). Graduate Seminar (Notes taken by Shirley Kessler).

Kliebard, H. (1986). *The struggle for the American curriculum 1893–1958.* Boston, MA: Routledge & Kegan Paul.

Krugman, P. (2013, June 23). Greg Mankiw forgets 'we are a much more unequal society now.' *Huffington Post.* Retrieved from http://www.huffingtonpost.com/2013/06/23/paul-krugman-greg-mankiw_n_3486784.html

Lubeck, S. (1985). *Sandbox society: Early education in black and white America.* Philadelphia: Falmer.

Naumburg, M. (1928). *The child and the world.* New York: Harcourt, Brace & Co.

NEA Resolutions. (ccaBss-16, 1998, 2005). Retrieved from http://www.nea.org/bare/print.html?content=/bare/16899.htm

Obama, B. (2013, February 12). *The 2013 State of the Union.* Retrieved from www.whitehouse.gov/state-of-the-union-2013

Pinar, W. F. (1975). Currere: Toward reconceptualization. In W. F. Pinar (Ed.). *Curriculum theorizing: The reconceptualists* (pp. 396–414). Berkeley: McCutchan.

Reardon, S. (2011). *Whither opportunity? Rising inequality, schools, and children's life chances.* New York: Russell Sage Foundation.

Roosevelt, F. D. (1941, January 6). *The Four Freedoms: The 1941 State of the Union.* Retrieved from www.american rhetoric.com/speeches/fdrthefourfreedoms.htm

Schafer Elementary Curriculum, Grade K. (June 15, 2013). Retrieved from http://www.d45.dupage.k12.il.us/schafer/sc-curriculum-schafer-main/first-step

Shavelson, R. J., & Stern, P. (1981). Research on teachers' pedagogical thoughts, judgements, decisions, and behaviors. *Review of Educational Research,* 51, 455–498.

Silin, J. (1995). *Sex, death, and the education of children: Our passion for ignorance in the age of AIDS.* New York: Teachers College Press.

Tyler, R. (1949). *Basic principles of curriculum and instruction.* Chicago: University of Chicago Press.

Weber, E. (1969). *The kindergarten.* New York: Teachers College Press.

Weber, E. (1984). *Ideas influencing early childhood education: A theoretical analysis.* New York: Teachers College Press.

Wen, X., & Elicker, J. (2011). Early childhood teachers' curriculum beliefs: Are they consistent with observed classroom practices? *Early Education and Development,* 22(6), 945–969.

Notes

1. Kliebard (1980) stated four questions should be addressed by curriculum planners: What is taught? Who is taught? What is the influence of the curriculum over time? How is the curriculum organized and integrated? I included two of these questions in this discussion.

2. For example, one volume included a description of the disparity between the rich and the poor. Another volume considered the atrocities of the slave trade. One might imagine a series of textbooks today focusing on problems of income inequality and the unscrupulous practices of major banks in contributing to the economic downturn we are currently experiencing.

3. In contrast to Froebel's curriculum, Johann Fichte, German philosopher, set forth an alternative view of educational goals in several lectures he gave in Berlin beginning in 1806 (Fichte: Addresses to the German Nation, 1968, New York: Harper & Row). Fichte was a major figure espousing a German form of idealism at the University of Jenna when Froebel was a student there. Fichte proclaimed the need to recover and strengthen a true German identity through education, an identity that was

shattered by the French occupation under Napoleon. Students were to be molded into a "corporate body" (p. 12) where the selfish interests of the individual were to be subordinated to the idea of the community (p. 150).

4. One way is to integrate social justice themes into current educational programs, as do the anti-bias curriculum, the teaching of literacy that Roxanne Henkin (1998) describes, and the guidelines set forth for integrating themes and methods found in Indigenous cultures into K–12 education (Jacobs & Mann, 2013).

5. Ability/disability also determines eligibility for some programs within schools. Gender likewise is a means for selection.

6. Classroom research has great potential for achieving a more complete understanding of schooling; though time consuming, laborious, and replete with the need to address traditional issues like establishing validity and reliability, interrogating our own interests, gaining access, etc., we must do this hard work.

THREE

Reconceptualizing Early Childhood Research

J. Amos Hatch

From its genesis, the reconceptualizing early childhood education (RECE) ethos has had strong connections to parallel movements within the broader scholarly community, including movements that challenge the dominant discourse of positivist science. In this chapter, I trace some of the evolvement of that parallel development, highlighting some of the prominent debates concerning early childhood research that have occurred from the 1980s to the present. As I discuss each movement, I include references to publications by RECE authors that exemplify scholarship linked to the debates of that period. I conclude with a call for a renewed commitment to generating high-quality scholarly inquiry that continues to reconceptualize the field.

Paradigm Conflicts

It is not a coincidence that the beginnings of the RECE movement coincide with ferment for rethinking the ways that research is done within the educational research community and the scholarly community at large. During the 1980s and 1990s, "paradigm wars" raged in the pages of *Educational Researcher* and other top education journals and in the hallways and meeting rooms at the most important educational research conferences. Qualitative researchers argued that their approaches to conceptualizing, implementing, and writing up educational research provided valuable insights into understanding educational phenomena that were unavailable via traditional statistically based studies. Quantitative researchers countered that qualitative work did not have standing as legitimate science because it did not meet requirements for reliability, validity, and generalizability that define traditional approaches to inquiry. After years of battling back and forth, the upshot was a kind of uneasy peace. One author described the trajectory of the conflict as a move from "distain to détente" (Rist, 1977), with both sides apparently finding value in the other side's potential contributions.

Doctoral programs of the day were beginning to offer qualitative methods courses often based in anthropology and sociology departments. Advanced graduate students in education, including early childhood types, began to explore applications of qualitative work to their fields, and doctoral dissertations utilizing qualitative research approaches started to appear. I was one of those who fought for the qualitative side during the paradigm wars and completed an early qualitative dissertation in early childhood education. In 1989, I was invited to guest edit with Richard Wisniewski a special issue of the newly founded *International Journal of Qualitative Studies in Education* (*QSE*) on the topic of early childhood qualitative research. To attract papers for the special issue, I organized a conference that was held at the University of Tennessee in September of that year, and many of the pioneers of qualitative research in the early childhood education field were in attendance and became acquainted at that event. The conference led to the special issue of *QSE* (Hatch & Wisniewski, 1990) and later to the publication of an edited book (Hatch, 1995). Many of the participants in the Tennessee conference were important players in the formation of the reconceptualizing early childhood education group that held its first meetings in 1991.

During this early period, RECE participants produced book-length reports of research that made significant contributions to the emergence of qualitative inquiry as legitimate research in early childhood. Some of these were Sally Lubeck's (1985) *Sandbox Society: Early Education in Black and White America*; Bill Ayers' (1989) *The Good Preschool Teacher: Six Teachers Reflect on their Lives*; Joe Tobin, David Wu, and Dana Davidson's (1989) *Preschool in Three Cultures: Japan, China and the United States*; and Beth Graue's (1993) *Ready for What? Constructing Meanings of Readiness for Kindergarten*.

Crisis of Representation

At the same time that qualitative researchers were making headway in having their work accepted as legitimate by the larger scholarly community, serious questions about qualitative researchers' ability to capture the lived experience of others arose within their own ranks. Critics argued that it was difficult or impossible for qualitative researchers to accurately and fairly represent the lives of the participants in their studies (Geertz, 1988). They pointed out that the complexities involved in making distinctions between lives as lived, lives as experienced, and lives as told are highly problematic for qualitative researchers (Bruner, 1984). They noted that the complexity is compounded when researchers bring their own cultural and theoretical lenses to interpreting the actions and words of others (Clifford & Marcus, 1986). Further, based on deconstructivist perspectives (e.g., Derrida, 1973), critics argued that "language, in both its written and spoken forms, is always inherently unstable, in flux, and made up of the traces of other signs and symbolic statements. Hence, there can never be a clear, unambiguous statement of anything" (Denzin, 1989, p. 14). Given these issues and the additional problems of writing up qualitative findings within the confines of discourse structures that circumscribe how scholars communicate in text (Emihovich, 1995), this crisis of representation generated genuine angst within the qualitative research community.

Early childhood reconceptualists were vitally interested in the theoretical underpinnings of what many have termed a crisis of representation (Marcus & Fischer, 1999). From their earliest meetings, the reconceptualists presented papers and held formal and informal discussions about the ideas of postmodern, poststructuralist, critical, and feminist scholars whose work powerfully shaped how the crisis of representation played out. One of the attractions of RECE meetings was the opportunity to write, think, and talk about implications for research, theory, and practice of scholarship that was never mentioned at mainstream early childhood conferences. I have vivid memories of sitting over lunch or in sessions exploring the ideas of thinkers such as Derrida, Foucault, Racour, Freire, Butler, and many others. The crisis of representation was part of a larger critique of all of the assumptions that drive modernist ways of generating and using knowledge.

Many RECE conference attendees have made important contributions to critiquing and reconceptualizing the theoretical underpinnings of early childhood research of all stripes. Examples of published work of this type include Elizabeth Graue and Daniel Walsh's (1998) *Studying Children in Context: Theories, Methods, and Ethics*; Jan Jipson's (2000) "The Stealing of Wonderful Ideas: The Politics of Early Childhood Research"; Gaile Cannella and Joe Kincheloe's (2002) *Kidworld: Childhood Studies, Global Perspectives and Education*; and Lourdes Diaz Soto and Beth Swadener's (2005) *Power and Voice in Research With Children*.

Genre Bending

Denzin and Lincoln (2005) characterize one of the major shifts in qualitative research as a kind of "genre diaspora" (p. 18), arguing that the lines that separated traditional forms of qualitative inquiry were blurred during this period. In addition, lines of separation between individual social sciences were erased. Even lines that have historically separated science from the arts and humanities were challenged. As a result, qualitative researchers were freed to adapt theoretical perspectives from a wide variety of disciplines, to create hybridized data collection and analysis strategies, and to write up their findings in forms that were previously the purview of novelists, journalists, or historians.

At conferences and in their publications, researchers from the RECE group have been in the forefront of genre-blurring efforts in early childhood research. From the earliest meetings, RECE conference participants have experimented with alternative forms of communicating the outcomes of their inquiry, including the use of multimedia, poetry, theater, music, and dance. Their written scholarship has included the application of theories and methods developed in fields as diverse as social psychology, cognitive anthropology, identity politics, literary criticism, cultural studies, queer studies, critical theory, women's studies, black studies, and performance studies, most of which represent blurred genres in their own right.

Robin Leavitt's (1994) *Power and Emotion in Infant-Toddler Day Care* is a salient example of utilizing theoretical perspectives as diverse as symbolic interactionism, critical theory, and feminism to examine early childhood social phenomena. Other examples of published work that utilizes elements of genre bending include Mary Hauser and Jan Jipson's (1998) edited collection *Intersections: Feminisms/Early Childhoods*; Shirley Kessler and Mary Hauser's (2000) "Critical Pedagogy and the Politics of Play"; David Fernie, Bronwyn Davies, Rebecca Kantor, and Paula McMurray's (1993) "Becoming a Person in the Preschool: Creating Integrated Gender, School Culture, and Peer Culture Positionings"; and the application of queer theory in several chapters of Joe Tobin's (1997) edited book *Making a Place for Pleasure in Early Childhood Education.*

Post-Everything Inquiry

At the 1998 RECE Conference held at the University of Hawaii, I presented a paper entitled "Introducing Postmodern Thought in a Thoroughly Modern University." The paper was later published in a book edited by Lourdes Diaz Soto (2000), which included papers by many early childhood reconceptualists. In the concluding sections of my chapter for the edited book (Hatch, 2000), I asked several questions, including, "Where are we going when we make the postmodern turn?"; "What comes after a post-everything world?"; and "What would a postmodern text look like, anyway?" (pp. 189–190). These questions crystallize the complexity and paradoxical nature of doing and interpreting research that pays serious attention to postmodern thought.

RECE scholars have boldly engaged the complexity and paradoxes associated with doing early childhood research in and about our postmodern world. Adopting theoretical and methodological stances from postpositivism to poststructuralism and postcolonialism, RECE researchers have troubled taken-for-granted conceptions that have dominated how the early childhood field has traditionally thought about what young children are like, what they can do, and what kinds of experiences they need. In addition, these postmodern frameworks have given researchers alternative lenses for considering social, psychological, and political phenomena that impact all aspects of early childhood.

Among RECE scholars, Joe Tobin (1995) was among the first to apply poststructuralist perspectives to research in early childhood education. His books and book chapters (e.g., Tobin, 1997, 2000; Grace & Tobin, 1997) stand as powerful exemplars of the place of postmodern thought in early childhood research. Other important examples of "post-everything" research analyses in early childhood include Glenda Mac Naughton's (2005) *Doing Foucault in Early Childhood Studies: Applying Post-Structural Ideas*; and edited books by Sharon Ryan and Sue Grieshaber (2005), *Practical Transformations and Transformational Practices: Globalization, Postmodernism, and Early Childhood Education*; Kagenga Mutua and Beth Swadener (2004), *Decolonizing Research in Cross-Cultural Contexts: Critical Personal Narratives*; and Marianne Bloch and colleagues' (2006) *The Child in the World/The World in the Child: Education and the Configuration of a Universal, Modern, and Globalized Childhood.*

Legislated Positivism

My view is that alternative forms of research in the field of education, including early childhood studies, have suffered significantly from the (re)elevation of "scientifically based" research approaches to the status of "normal science" since the turn of the 21st century. Kuhn (1970) famously argued that the history of science is characterized by the rise and fall of competing paradigms. When one paradigm's assumptions about how the world is or is not ordered (ontology), what can be known (epistemology), and how it can be known (methodology) disrupt and replace another paradigm's metaphysical assumptions, the practices of the new paradigm become normal science. For Kuhn, these paradigm shifts occur based on the relevant community of scholars' reaction to the give-and-take arguments of the competing paradigmatic camps. I have made the case that as part of a broader movement "back to modernity," the positivist research paradigm, under the banner of "scientifically based research," has been reestablished as normal science in education, moving early childhood research approaches that are not grounded in positivist assumptions to less-than-normal status (Hatch, 2007).

The positivist research paradigm assumes an objective universe that has order independent of human perceptions. The overarching goal of positivist science is to uncover facts and laws that explain how the world works. Early in the 21st century, in an effort to ensure that positivist assumptions were applied to educational research, conservative forces established panels and wrote legislation that defined "scientifically based" research based on models developed in the fields of medicine and experimental psychology. The *Report From the National Reading Panel* (2000) and *Scientific Research in Education* (National Research Council, 2002) set the stage for the infusion of their definitions of scientifically based scholarship into the No Child Left Behind (NCLB) legislation. NCLB codified statistically based, double-blind studies with large numbers of subjects as the only "science" that would be recognized when federal research dollars were allocated or funding for educational programs was approved. Qualitative studies in early childhood and across the education spectrum were effectively stigmatized as not worthy of consideration as educational policies, programs, and practices were developed and implemented.

Chonika Coleman-King and I recently completed a handbook chapter on "Conducting Early Childhood Qualitative Research in the 21st Century" (Hatch & Coleman-King, in press). In order to gauge the trajectory of early childhood qualitative studies over the recent past, we charted the publication of qualitative articles for the preceding decade in *Early Childhood Research Quarterly* (*ECRQ*), the journal that is ranked highest among early childhood journals by Journal Citation Reports (ISI Web of Knowledge, n.d.). Of 315 research articles published in *ECRQ* over this ten-year period, we found that only 13 qualitative research reports (4.1%) and nine mixed-methods reports (2.9%) were included. Looking at the most recent three years, of 112 research articles published in *ECRQ*, only two were identified as qualitative studies and two as mixed methods (1.8% each). This crude analysis matches my perception and the testimony of many of my colleagues that it is increasingly difficult to publish early childhood qualitative research in top-tier journals. I take this phenomenon to be directly linked to the elevation of research based on positivist assumptions to the status of "scientifically based" and the concomitant relegation of research approaches of any other type to the sidelines of early childhood inquiry.

Conclusions

In some ways, it feels like early childhood research has come full circle. Conservative and neoliberal forces in society and in educational research have done their best to marginalize alternative forms of scholarly inquiry that had become more "acceptable" over the past 40 years. While this marginalization is disappointing and frustrating, it reinforces the need to continue fighting the good fight. I have argued that scholars who have been pushed to the side of the educational research road should take the offensive:

> Let's re-engage in the paradigm wars. Let's defend ourselves against those who would impose their modern notions of science on us by exposing the flaws in what they call scientifically

based research. Let's mount a strong offense by generating qualitative studies that are so powerful they cannot be dismissed. (Hatch, 2006, p. 405)

Critique is at the core of what early childhood reconceptualists do and how they think. Focusing
that critique on the methods, findings, and applications of scientifically based research should
be an ongoing priority for reconceptualist scholars.

Even more important, reconceptualizing early childhood researchers should redouble their
efforts to design, implement, and publish high-quality studies that demonstrate the efficacy
of alternative forms of inquiry in our field. Much of the work cited in this chapter has had an
impact beyond reconceptualist circles, and such work needs to be continued and expanded.
Even though it is difficult to publish work that does not meet the criteria of scientifically based
research in the current sociopolitical climate, the need for reconceptualized scholarship that is
so powerful it cannot be ignored has never been more acute.

References

Ayers, W. (1989). *The good preschool teacher: Six teachers reflect on their lives.* New York: Teachers College Press.

Bloch, M. N., Kennedy, D., Lightfoot, T., & Weyenberg, D. (Eds.). (2006). *The child in the world/the world in
the child: Education and the configuration of a universal, modern, and globalized childhood.* New York: Palgrave
Macmillan.

Bruner, E. M. (1984). The opening up of anthropology. In E. M. Bruner (Ed.), *Text, play, and story: The construction
and reconstruction of self and society* (pp. 1–18). Washington, DC: American Ethnological Society.

Cannella, G. S., & Kincheloe, J. L. (Eds.). (2002). *Kidworld: Childhood studies, global perspectives and education.*
New York: Peter Lang.

Clifford, J., & Marcus, G. E. (Eds.). (1986). *Writing culture: The poetics and politics of ethnography.* Berkeley: University of California Press.

Denzin, N. K. (1989). *Interpretive biography.* Newbury Park, CA: Sage.

Denzin, N. K., & Lincoln, Y. S. (2005). Introduction: The discipline and practice of qualitative research. In N. K.
Denzin & Y. S. Lincoln (Eds.), *Handbook of qualitative research* (3rd ed.; pp. 1–32). Thousand Oaks, CA: Sage.

Derrida, J. (1973). *Speech and phenomena.* Evanston, IL: Northwestern University Press.

Emihovich, C. (1995). Distancing passion: Narratives in social science. In J. A. Hatch & R. Wisniewski (Eds.), *Life
history and narrative* (pp. 37–48). Bristol, PA: Falmer.

Fernie, D. E., Davies, B., Kantor, R., & McMurray, P. (1993). Becoming a person in the preschool: Creating integrated gender, school culture, and peer culture positionings. *International Journal of Qualitative Studies in
Education, 6*(2), 95–110.

Geertz, C. (1988). *Works and lives: The anthropologist as author.* Stanford, CA: Stanford University Press.

Grace, D. J., & Tobin, J. J. (1997). Carnival in the classroom: Elementary students making videos. In J. J. Tobin
(Ed.), *Making a place for pleasure in early childhood education* (pp. 159–187). New Haven, CT: Yale University
Press.

Graue, M. E. (1993). *Ready for what? Constructing meanings of readiness for kindergarten.* Albany: SUNY Press.

Graue, M. E., & Walsh, D. J. (1998). *Studying children in context: Theories, methods, and ethics.* Thousand Oaks,
CA: Sage.

Hatch, J. A. (Ed.). (1995). *Qualitative research in early childhood settings.* Westport, CT: Praeger.

Hatch, J. A. (2000). Introducing postmodern thought in a thoroughly modern university. In L. D. Soto (Ed.), *The
politics of early childhood education* (pp. 179–196). New York: Peter Lang.

Hatch, J. A. (2006). Qualitative studies in the era of scientifically-based research: Musings of a former *QSE* editor.
International Journal of Qualitative Studies in Education, 19, 401–405.

Hatch, J. A. (2007). Back to modernity: Early childhood qualitative research in the 21st century. In J. A. Hatch
(Ed.), *Early childhood qualitative research* (pp. 7–24). New York: Routledge.

Hatch, J. A., & Coleman-King, C. (In press). Conducting early childhood qualitative research in the 21st century.
In O. N. Saracho (Ed.), *Handbook of research methods in early childhood education* (pp. 1–54). Charlotte, NC:
Information Age Publishing.

Hatch, J. A., & Wisniewski, R. (Eds.). (1990). Qualitative research in early childhood settings [Special issue]. *International Journal of Qualitative Studies in Education, 3,* 209–302.

Hauser, M., & Jipson, J. A. (Eds.). (1998). *Intersections: Feminisms/early childhoods.* New York: Peter Lang.

ISI Web of Knowledge. (n. d.) Journal Citation Reports. http://workinfo.com/products-tools/analytical/jet/

Jipson, J. (2000). The stealing of wonderful ideas: The politics of early childhood research. In L. D. Soto (Ed.), *The politics of early childhood education* (pp. 167–177). New York: Peter Lang.

Kessler, S. A., & Hauser, M. (2000). Critical pedagogy and the politics of play. In L. D. Soto (Ed.), *The politics of early childhood education* (pp. 59–71). New York: Peter Lang.

Kuhn, T. S. (1970). *The structure of scientific revolutions.* Chicago: University of Chicago Press.

Leavitt, R. L. (1994). *Power and emotion in infant-toddler day care.* Albany: SUNY Press.

Lubeck, S. (1985). *Sandbox society: Early education in black and white America.* London: Falmer.

Marcus, G. E., & Fischer, M. M. (1999). *Anthropology as cultural critique: An experimental moment in the human sciences.* Chicago: University of Chicago Press.

Mac Naughton, G. (2005). *Doing Foucault in early childhood studies: Applying post-structural ideas.* New York: Routledge.

Mutua, K., & Swadener, B. B. (2004). *Decolonizing research in cross-cultural contexts: Critical personal narratives.* Albany: SUNY Press.

National Reading Panel. (2000). *Report from the National Reading Panel.* Washington, DC: National Institute for Child Health and Development.

National Research Council. (2002). *Scientific research in education.* Washington, DC: National Academy Press.

Rist, R. C. (1977). On the relations among educational research paradigms: From disdain to détente. *Anthropology & Education Quarterly, 8*(2), 42–49.

Ryan, S., & Grieshaber, S. (2005). *Practical transformations and transformational practices: Globalization, postmodernism, and early childhood education.* Amsterdam: Elsevier.

Soto, L. D. (Ed.). (2000). *The politics of early childhood education.* New York: Peter Lang.

Soto, L. D., & Swadener, B. B. (2005). *Power and voice in research with children.* New York: Peter Lang.

Tobin, J. J. (1995). Post-structural research in early childhood education. In J. A. Hatch (Ed.), *Qualitative research in early childhood settings* (pp. 223–244). Westport, CT: Praeger Publishers.

Tobin, J. J. (Ed.). (1997). *Making a place for pleasure in early childhood education.* New Haven, CT: Yale University Press.

Tobin, J. J. (2000). *Good guys don't wear hats: Children's talk about the media.* Chicago: University of Chicago Press.

Tobin, J. J., Wu, D. Y., & Davidson, D. H. (1989). *Preschool in three cultures: Japan, China and the United States.* New Haven, CT: Yale University Press.

FOUR

Through a Queer Lens: Recuperative Longings and the Reconceptualizing Past

Jonathan Silin

The invitation to contribute to this volume appeared in my in-box as something of a surprise. For the last decade, I've been writing about topics—aging, grief, and the displacements of time—that would, at first blush, have little to do with early childhood imaginaries. But it also arrived at a moment when I've been making a practice of saying "yes" to who and what shows up, letting go of my usual circumspection about taking on new assignments. Soon enough I realized that two events were also conspiring to rekindle my interest in both the past and future of the field. They would ultimately come to weave their way through this chapter. For one, a recent trip to San Francisco prompted me to reflect on the ways that social amnesia shapes our understanding of activist movements and our ability to draw on their histories to imagine the future otherwise. For another, the 20th anniversary of Reconceptualizing Early Childhood Education (RECE), in which I was an early and energetic participant, had prompted me to consider how, if at all, this particular movement might have succeeded in reframing the theory and practice of early education.

The birth of the reconceptualizing movement was attended by growing numbers of early childhood educators who, in the late 1980s, felt estranged by the growing conservatism of the field. Identifying early childhood as theoretically barren and socially irrelevant, we sought to resuscitate what we perceived as a moribund field by storming the epistemological barricades established by the National Association for the Education of Young Children (NAEYC), engaging in a new theoretical promiscuity, and making our work responsive to the social and political realities of late industrialized society.

Today, early childhood education is again an endangered field. Then, intellectual stagnation and an entrenched leadership inside the field allowed little room for change and innovation. Now the threats are coming from outside: the demand for an increasingly academic curriculum by politicians and policymakers, the insistence on easily quantified and measurable results, and the incorporation of early childhood classrooms into elementary schools. These trends, which belie the special qualities of young children and all that can be learned from them, make the future of the field as a discrete arena of theory and practice uncertain.

The 20th anniversary of RECE (2012) was an opportunity to identify the themes that characterized its first years and to suggest how this history might shine a light forward in these dark times for early childhood educators. It is also an opportunity to reflect more broadly on how social change movements are remembered and how this remembering functions to serve some interests and thwart others.

My curiosity about the uses to which we put the past was sparked this past winter when my partner, David, and I visited San Francisco, a city that we both know and love. Upon our arrival, we were surprised by how much the Castro, the iconic gay village, had changed. Most striking on our frequent neighborhood walks: the absence of gay men. The streets, once thick with handsome, bearded men in 501s, plaid shirts, and leather jackets, who smiled so easily and eagerly, seemed deserted. For us then, it was as if everyone knew you, and you unquestionably knew them. Now there are few such acknowledgments of public camaraderie and shared experience.

We meet Stephen, a close friend and long-time Castro resident, in the once popular Cafe Flore. No need to stand in the middle of the terrace anxiously looking from table to table for a place to squeeze in among groups of chatting friends catching a few rays of precious afternoon sun. There are plenty of seats, most of the tables occupied by solitary men and women, gaze fixed on laptop or smart phone screens. Life happens online, virtual communities and cyber connections taking their place alongside brick-and-mortar neighborhoods and face-to-face interactions. Stephen explains that young men from elsewhere can no longer afford the rents in the newly gentrified Castro. They alight in different parts of the city and make only occasional visits to this and other neighborhoods once replete with queer life.

David and I adjust to these new realities brought about by economic and social trends combined with the long-term impact of AIDS. We acknowledge that not all gay people felt as welcome in the Castro as we once did and that for some, cyber connections are more liberating than alienating, opening previously unthought possibilities for creating and sustaining queer lives. We also tell each other that vibrant urban centers are constantly changing and take heart in the fact that lesbians and gay men feel comfortable living everywhere rather than congregating in concentrated communities.

Our conversations are filled too with talk about individuals gone missing—Michael the Zen practitioner, Eric the teacher, Maurice the political strategist—all activists of my stripe or another. Their memories elicit within me the exhilaration that came with resisting social norms as we sought new ways of living together, and ultimately, the crazy courage necessary to fight the medical and political establishments in the face of AIDS. They are about individuals and they are about the ideas of social transformation embodied in their unique lives. On this particular trip, at this moment in history, I reexperience the loss of an entire way of life.

Now when I pass the Hartford Street Zen Centre, where I lived while crafting what was to be a seminal article on AIDS and education for the Teachers College Record (Silin, 1987), I take heart in the story of how a small, struggling spiritual community temporarily transformed itself into the Mitre Hospice during the worst of the epidemic. With much goodwill and very little professional assistance, with some practitioners turned patients and others caregivers, the community responded when many larger institutions did not. For me, the building—returned to its former use, spruced up with fresh paint, new signs, and schedules for regular practice periods—has become emblematic of successful grassroots initiatives and organizing.

While the current political climate has supported stunning successes for gay people—marriage, military service, family rights—reflecting a conservative and normalizing social agenda, the commitment to more inventive, imaginative, and relational possibilities that shaped the early gay movement has largely been erased (Halberstam, 2011; Schulman, 2012). So too have the critical successes of our AIDS organizing: the rethinking of double-blind drug trials, the creation of innovative home care options, the growth of harm reduction programs (Weber & Weissman's *We Were Here*, 2011; Cogan & David's *How to Survive a Plague*, 2012).

In discussing this concern about the hidden history of AIDS activism, indeed of gay life before AIDS, I am reminded that many of my female graduate students take for granted the opportunities available to them now only because of determined struggles of earlier generations of women with which they are largely unfamiliar. They do not identify as feminists. They do not understand the need for sustained vigilance to retain and expand the rights that have been achieved.

I think here of another unremembered past as well: that of the pedagogical progressives in the first half of the 20th century. Again, my students assume that any environment that is humane, that takes for its rationale developmental psychology and the rhetoric of "the whole child," is consistent with the progressive cause, but progressive educators wanted something more: a curriculum that focuses on the workings of the social world, the effort to right social wrongs, to allow time and space for participatory democracy in the classroom (Counts, 1932/1978; Krakowsky, 2010; Vascellaro, 2011). The radical political ideas of our educational foremothers and fathers are now hidden from view, papered over by an ethic of individualized instruction and care. The sharp social critique that propelled the reformers to explore the world with their students has been lost to scientific studies of the child that were more palatable to government funders in the 1960s (Silin, 1992), buried in the 21st century under stacks of tests and core curricula that are touted as producing more competitive workers for the new global economy.

How are we to understand these various forms of social amnesia? Whose interests are served, and whose interests are constrained? And, are there lessons for early childhood educators in these stories about the pitfalls and promise of collective memory?

As a gay liberationist, AIDS advocate, and progressive teacher, I know that social change is both a top-down and bottom-up process. Most frequently, it is the former that is highlighted in texts we are given to teach and the latter that is shortchanged. The charismatic leader is always more glamorous than the work of picket lines and protest movements. Without images of grassroots activism, it is easy to believe individuals and marginalized groups have no agency, no ability to tell their story and to effect change.

Here I want to argue that if memory arranges itself around imaginative reconstructions of the past, reconstructions that suit our present needs and validate the world view we wish to perpetuate, then an intentional investigation into what is forgotten and what is remembered can become a source of reparative interpretations as well, a recuperative project for imagining the future otherwise. This is to resist the nostalgia that mistakes the present for an imperfect, failed copy of the past and to appreciate the fluid, political nature of collective memory.

In my work with new teachers, I have argued that childhood memories can become a rich resource for pedagogical understanding (Silin, 2000). More recently, I have drawn on the experience of becoming a photographic archivist to describe the work of building curriculum and community in the classroom (Silin, in press), and I've written about the ways that painful individual losses often have within them the potential for generative acts, for moments of creative self-renewal (Silin, 2013). Trolling the streets of San Francisco last winter, I recognized that collective losses may hold similar opportunities. Reviewing the history of AIDS, Castiglia and Reed (2012) argue:

> Loss is not synonymous with silence or absence or defeat; loss can be a starting point, an invocation, an inspiration, a rallying cry. Necessity, it is said, is the mother of invention, and needs are never greater than in times of loss. (p. 26)

They go on to suggest that memories—"suspended between responsibility for the spectacular realness of the past and collective inventiveness of the present"—can fund contemporary activism. This is to say that hidden histories can be mined for aspirational images to guide the present. What was it that AIDS activists dreamed and achieved? How did early gay liberationists imagine their work, and how did they live their lives? How did politics and pedagogy come together for progressive educators in the classrooms they inhabited and the schools they built?

Especially in this era of evidence-based learning, when everything pedagogical must be recorded and remembered, I do not want my curiosity about the past to be mistaken for yet another project to fix history and to ensure an unensurable certainty about what was and what might be. In the classroom I continue to argue the pleasures and generative possibilities of forgetting (Silin, 2005). Lost in the present, unshackled by the past, children can play and create with the intensity and abandon that allows them to imagine the new and unrehearsed (Doty, 2010; Halberstam, 2011). When students of any age surrender, by choice or circumstance, the coherence of the familiar, they may be at a loss, the world kaleidoscopically fragmented. At the same time, it is the willingness to explore this very fragmentation that holds the promise of a viable future (Silin, 2013).

Here, however, I am curious about how our partially achieved forgetting allows the past to haunt us and limit our hopes for the future. I do not refer to the kind of psychodynamic haunting that Judith Butler (1997) takes up in describing the heterosexual culture of melancholy in which we are constrained to lose our loving attachment to the same-sex parent and disavow it even as possibility. Then, the loss is unacknowledged and it haunts us exactly because it is unnamed and therefore, ungrievable. Rather, I refer to losses that are recoverable, within the zone of "proximal development" if you will, not ones that are buried so deeply within us and within the culture that they cannot be recuperated. I am after what can be reasonably recognized as opposed to that which would require a new insight of an entirely different order.

Such projects of recognition are supported by recent modifications in the theoretical apparatus of queer time. Initially impelled by a sense of imminent mortality, queer theorists valorized the present as the moment in which past and future can be most fully understood and realized. Impelled as well to examine the meaning of time in lives often unscripted by traditional models of family life, the nurture of children and generational succession, queer theorists rejected a middle-class logic of "reproductive temporality." This logic, they pointed out, was future oriented, assuming a progression from immaturity to maturity and from dangerous, ungovernable desires to safe, stable, and properly disciplined lives (Halberstam, 2005). In contrast, queer time was understood to be nonlinear, discontinuous, and disruptive of the orderly progress assured by traditional temporal rationalities. It was and is rich in possibilities for reconsidering the complexity of lived lives and the scholarship that might comment on them (Dinshaw, 1999).

Recent attempts to recuperate the GLBTQ past, in theory and political practice, might be read as a response, a corrective if you will, to the ideas about queer time that first appeared in the wake of AIDS. Now there is a renewed interest in how the past not only lives in the present, but also how it might best be mined to fund the future. Archives of fact and figures, emotions and affects, and words and images, are valued resources for identifying the way forward as well as for illuminating the road already taken (Cvetkovich, 2003). This is the past imagined more expansively, not as determinative of or constraining the present, but as a place for generating ideas about an unrealized future.

In retrospect, the inaugural desire to imagine a temporality that more accurately reflected the phenomenological realities of GLBTQ people who inhabited the social margins, who would never achieve "heterosexual maturity," and whose lives might only be accounted for in unruly narratives (Stockton, 2009), was not so very different from the goal of early childhood reconceptualists who critiqued stage theories of development in the 1980s (Silin, 1995). We too sought to resist the normalizing effects of linear modes of reasoning that identified some people—notably children, queers, and women—as undeveloped, lacking in "adult" attributes. We too sought to recognize expanded opportunities for pleasure and modalities for respectfully representing lived experience.

Taking my lead from those who look to the past for its aspirational potential, I propose for consideration three ideas that characterized RECE in its first decade and a way to understand these in the context of cultural work more generally.

Making a Place for Pleasure in Early Childhood Education

I baldly appropriate the title of Joe Tobin's edited volume (1997) to identify the first big theme in early reconceptualizing discourse: transforming the field into a site of pleasure for adults as well as children. Despite its radical roots in the late 19th and early 20th centuries, by the 1980s, early childhood had become a conservative field concerned with protecting vulnerable children from imagined threats—interior and exterior—to the child, the former lurking in and amongst unsettling emotions and desires and the latter contained in difficult knowledge or predatory individuals. Echoing this protectiveness toward children, many early childhood educators shielded themselves as well from new social and literary theories that threatened the developmental canon upon which they relied.

My own and other contributions to the Tobin volume sought to bring new theoretical apparatuses to bear on what was and wasn't happening in early childhood classrooms (Silin, 1997). As a group we advocated a curriculum that trusts children, eschews intensified forms of surveillance, and embraces the child as a desiring, often transgressive agent. Consistent with the belief in childhood competency was the commitment to the socially relevant classroom, a place where the child's existing "funds of knowledge" were to be welcomed, deployed, and expanded. Rather than sanitize the curriculum, reconceptualists sought a more complex, dare I say "real," representation of the world that would reflect the children's lived experiences. Explorations of difficult topics and the emotional discomfort they may bring in their wake encourage children to value multiple perspectives, to tolerate uncertainty, and to recognize that some questions defy final answers.

Equally important, and perhaps even more radical, was the RECE commitment to a field where adults too might find pleasure and explore desire. The classic early childhood watchwords—"only in the best interests of the child"—did not leave space for the adult as an agentive presence in the classroom, let alone in research and in writing. Reconceptualists deconstructed images of the facilitative female who lived and worked to support the growth of others, most often assumed to be boys, and the potentially predatory image of the male teacher whose intentions were always in question.

Desire makes us, child and adult, vulnerable. It is a potential source of danger as well as pleasure, risk as well as reward. Educators who encouraged children to strike out in new directions in order to learn and grow wanted no less for themselves. This is to say that we were willing to acknowledge our unknowingness in order to enjoy new fields of play. This exploration of postmodern, postcolonial, feminist, and queer theory changed not only what we said, but how we said it, the questions we asked and the strategies we took up to answer them.

We were a theoretically promiscuous group, tired of safe scholarship, and willing to engage many partners in what amounted to little more than one-night stands while seeking our place in a larger world of cultural endeavors. Willy-nilly, this curiosity about other disciplines and modes of theorizing implied a complete role reversal for early childhood educators. Immersing ourselves in new ways of thinking and willing to be surprised by theory, we were willing to own our uncertainty and the provisional nature of our knowing (Gallop, 2002). At the same time, we increasingly understood that young children entered the schoolhouse door already knowledgeable, competent, and capable in ways that belied earlier concerns about needing to protect their innocence and purity from the intrusions of unwonted information and ideas.

Advocating for Lives on the Edge

People came to the reconceptualizing movement with very different histories and needs. Those who primarily sought intellectual stimulation came from work situations in which they were long isolated, frequently the only early childhood instructor on a college faculty, or newly minted PhDs experiencing the stressful transition from being part of a lively, challenging cohort of early childhood doctoral candidates to being alone in a department focused on elementary or secondary education. Among those seeking intellectual community were also scholars who had already moved into previously unexplored realms and desired forums for pushing their thinking further afield.

On early RECE program committees there was often disagreement between those who would accept proposals that reflected best practices but were under-theorized or did not expand the boundaries of our thinking and those who championed proposals that brought forward new ideas or theories previously unexplored in relationship to early childhood education.

RECE also attracted scholar-activists whose primary interest was in building a movement immediately responsive to lives lived on the edge, as Valerie Polakow (1993) described the struggles of single mothers and children surviving in deep poverty. They were eager to engage in projects of direct action that would influence legislative decision making and public policy. The goal was to assure that all families had access to essential practical and social supports to enable their children to survive and thrive. These reconceptualists advocated for protection of the young but in the interests of social equity rather than in the interests of cognitive or emotional immaturity as traditionalists argued.

Wanting to seize opportunities as they presented themselves at each conference to engage with the struggles of local early childhood educators, scholar-activists also brought a keen desire to include people working in other countries. They understood that the RECE Conference could offer critical support and legitimation, theoretical and practical, for social justice efforts around the world, and they grappled with the constraints of time and money that made such participation more challenging.

These distinct, not necessarily antithetical projects—storming the epistemological barricades erected by early childhood traditionalists and focusing on direct action and public policy—sometimes pulled conference planners and participants in different directions. Needless to say, the desire to be practically relevant and immediately responsive to the issues facing teachers and families, as well as the desire to engage in new conversations about our theoretical grounding lived within individuals as well. And, rather miraculously, RECE has managed to accommodate the productive tension resulting from these diverse commitments.

Speaking Truth to Power

I attended my first RECE conference in 1992 after having completed a decade as an AIDS educator and advocate and with a certain weariness with respect to questions of strategy and tactics. In my experience, speaking truth to power through public protest, political advocacy, and critical journalism sometimes brought important successes. In other situations, a more effective strategy was to turn our collective backs to power in order to create small, innovative services and educational initiatives that government and private foundations did not immediately understand.

At the RECE Conference in Chicago, I was immediately aware of a similar kind of strategic challenge faced by reconceptualists. At the time, NAEYC, with its full-time staff in Washington, more than 43,000 individual members and 300 affiliate groups, an annual conference that attracted upwards of 20,000 people, and a full roster of publications including *Young Children*, the most widely read journal in the field, seemed an immovable force blocking change. There were some among us who directed our attention to getting NAEYC to see things otherwise, and there were some, including myself, who took the position that our limited resources would best be utilized in creating interesting events, pursuing a different kind of scholarship, that would ultimately attract new adherents. In time, we reasoned, NAEYC would of its own accord come calling.

Although Sue Bredekamp, editor of the first NAEYC position paper on developmentally appropriate practice published in 1986, accepted an invitation to participate in a conference "conversation," she clearly had not come calling of her own accord nor was she interested in real dialogue. An exact description of the format of this meeting fails me, however my memory of the angry, frustrated emotions generated at the time are all too clear. Our effort to speak truth to power was something of a catastrophe although, as often happens in such situations, a visible opponent in view did strengthen our resolve.

To be clear, there are no villains or saints in this story but people with very different political and social perspectives. In reality, many were active in both RECE and NAEYC, produced fine publications for the latter, and argued that only through participation can you wield influence and promote change. At the same time, NAEYC itself was far from a monolith. There were many who participated in a range of organizational projects—Millie Almy, Barbara Biber,

Bernard Spodak—and who also held strong social commitments and more generous intellectual visions that belied NAEYC's public positions. With its singular focus on clearing new ground, RECE did not acknowledge the contributions or build alliances with those who held minority positions within NAEYC.

From my own perspective, the NAEYC agenda in the 1980s and 1990s—professionalization of the field through career ladders, certifications, and institutionalization of a scientific knowledge base—felt wrong-headed, and the possibility of a productive, public dialogue was foreclosed by the organization's intractability. Implicit in the absolutist manner in which NAEYC held on to the developmental canon was an unspoken fear that without this body of knowledge, a field that was viewed by many as little more than organized child minding would be increasingly marginalized. As in other fields with an overwhelmingly female workforce, such as nursing and social work, salaries would remain extraordinarily low, benefits few and far between, and its professional status problematic. The identification of early childhood education and developmental theory was so complete in these years that NAEYC president Bettye Caldwell (1984) could confidently proclaim: "Our field represents the applied side of the basic science of child development" (p. 53).

In contrast, with a more open disposition toward shifts in other disciplines, reconceptualists were ready to ask: What, if anything, makes early childhood a discrete field of theory and practice? How permeable can we become to other disciplines without losing our identity, and would such a loss be a bad thing? Ironically, these questions of disciplinary coherence are now being forced upon us from the outside by the increasing downward pressures for academically oriented programs that are in turn leading to new certification regulations that minimize, even erase, the utility of distinct early childhood qualifications.

Undoubtedly, there are many ideas other than the three I have identified here—making a place for pleasure, advocating for lives lived on the edge, and speaking truth to power—that catalyzed RECE during its formative years. In trying to tell our story, to find an overarching narrative, a through-line that holds it together, I am struck by the heuristic power of adapting Melanie Klein's distinction between a paranoid/schizoid position and a depressive position to describe critical reading practices. Eve Sedgwick (2003) explains that, originally posited by Klein as a "characteristic posture that the ego takes up with respect to its object" (p. 128), these positions may also be interpolated as different ways of knowing and contrasting interests in what is known. The paranoid/schizoid position leads to strong, universalizing theories that eschew surprises, the potential humiliation that may come with exposure, and more free-ranging exploration of the world, whereas the depressive position leads to a loosely connected web of local theories that enjoy contingency and offer reparative readings to restore relationships. The former, built on the "hermeneutics of suspicion," is grounded in a search for certainty, propositional knowledge, and the avoidance of error, while the latter seeks to maximize pleasure and care of the self while opening an ethics of possibility based in fuller recognition of the other.

In Klein's formulation, positions are not linear developments, the one closing down the other, but rather tendencies that co-exist within every adult's stance toward the world. The schizoid/paranoid position is one in which we seek to avoid pain through remaining hypervigilant to potential sources of danger. In the depressive mode, no longer prompted solely by fear and anxiety, we are better able to receive comfort and nourishment from more coherent identifications with objects once understood as threatening and vengeful. Open to a broader range of emotions, including the reparative pleasures that come with such positive identifications, we are also less fearful of surprises and mistakes. Reflecting this depressive position in theory making, for example, Joseph Litvak invites us to "take the terror out of error" and to make mistakes, "sexy, creative, even cognitively powerful" (Sedgwick, 2003, p. 147).

In brief, I read our desire to open the field of early childhood to a much broader range of theories and styles of theory making as an attempt to move from a schizoid/paranoid position to a depressive one. Rather than defend the developmental canon, rather than rely on scientific "truths" that promise certainty, legitimacy, and as NAEYC leaders claimed, higher salaries for underpaid workers through professionalization, we sought to embrace a more playful, dare I say pleasurable, stance toward theorizing the world of children and classrooms. Over and against the rigidity of the NAEYC position grounded in claims to the "truth" value of developmentalism, we sought a more flexible, inclusive approach to what counts as salient knowledge to educating young children. We used a Foucauldian language to query our own work: How does this knowledge function in the world? What does this knowledge do and not do? Who benefits and who loses by its instantiation into early childhood practices?

I do not suggest that we were always successful at asking, let alone answering, these questions. I do suspect, however, that we were more successful in shifting our theorizing than in changing our own practices or those more widely employed in early childhood classrooms. In my more Zen moments, I think that perhaps our singular accomplishment was just that: to make theorizing a form of practice in a field that had become theoretically barren and epistemologically bankrupt. No small accomplishment and one that I can only hope still thrives across the chapters of this volume.

References

Butler, J. (1997). *The psychic life of power*. Stanford: Stanford University Press.

Caldwell, B. (1984). Growth and development. *Young Children, 39*(6), 53–56.

Castiglia, C., & Reed, C. (2012). *If memory serves: Gay men, AIDS, and the promise of the queer past*. Minneapolis: University of Minnesota Press.

Cogan, D. (Producer), & David, F. (Director). (2012). *How to survive a plague* [Motion picture]. United States: Sundance Selects.

Counts, G. (1932/1978). *Dare the schools build a new social order?* Carbondale: Southern Illinois University Press.

Cvetkovich, A. (2003). *An archive of feelings: Trauma, sexuality, and lesbian public cultures*. Durham, NC: Duke University Press.

Dinshaw, C. (1999). *Getting medieval*. Durham, NC: Duke University Press.

Doty, M. (2010). *The art of description: World into words*. Minneapolis, MN: Graywolf.

Gallop, J. (2002). *Anecdotal theory*. Durham, NC: Duke University Press.

Halberstam, J. (2005). *In a queer time & place: Transgender bodies, subcultural lives*. New York: New York University Press.

Halberstam, J. (2011). *The queer art of failure*. Durham, NC: Duke University Press.

Krakowsky, L. (2010). *Leonard Covello: A study of progressive leadership and community empowerment*. (Occasional Paper No. 24). New York: Bank Street College of Education.

Polakow, V. (1993). *Lives on the edge: Single mothers and their children in the other America*. Chicago: University of Chicago Press.

Schulman, S. (2012). *The gentrification of the mind: Witness to a lost imagination*. Berkeley: University of California Press.

Sedgwick, E. (2003). *Touching feeling: Affect, pedagogy, performativity*. Durham, NC: Duke University Press.

Silin, J. (1987). The language of aids: Public fears, pedagogical responsibilities. *Teachers College Record, 89*(1), 3–19.

Silin, J. (1992). New subjects, familiar roles: Progressive legacies in the postmodern world. In F. Pignatelli & W. Pflaum (Eds.), *Celebrating diverse voices: Progressive education and equity* (pp. 221–241). Newbury Park, CA: Corwin.

Silin, J. (1995). *Sex, death, and the education of children: Our passion for ignorance in the age of AIDS.* New York: Teachers College Press.

Silin, J. (1997). The pervert in the classroom. In J. Tobin (Ed.), *Making a place for pleasure in early childhood education* (pp. 214–235). New Haven: Yale University Press.

Silin, J. (2000). Real children and imagined homelands: Preparing to teach in today's world. In N. Nager & E. K. Shapiro (Eds.), *Revisiting a progressive pedagogy* (pp. 257–275). Albany: SUNY Press.

Silin, J. (2005). Who can speak?: Silence, voice and pedagogy. In N. Yelland (Ed.), *Critical issues in early childhood education* (pp. 81–95). Maidenhead, Berkshire, U.K.: Open University Press.

Silin, J. (2013). At a loss: Scared and excited. *Contemporary Issues in Early Childhood, 14*(1), 16–23.

Silin, J. (In press). The teacher as archivist. *Studies in Gender and Sexuality.*

Stockton, K. (2009). *The queer child, or growing sideways in the twentieth century.* Durham, NC: Duke University Press.

Tobin, J. (Ed.). (1997). *Making a place for pleasure in early childhood education.* New Haven, CT: Yale University Press.

Vascellaro, S. (2011). *Out of the classroom and into the world.* New York: The New Press.

Weber, B., & Weissman, D. (Directors). (2011). *We were here* [Motion Picture]. United States: Red Flag Releasing.

FIVE

Still Waiting for the Revolution

Michael O'Loughlin

Much remains to be done to undo societal prejudices against children. While organizations such as Reconceptualizing Early Childhood Education (RECE) have agitated for change in specific areas, the health of the overall ecological infrastructure of contemporary childhood in the U.S. is very troubling. The passing of Maurice Sendak (1928–2012) reminds me how ephemeral our passions and accomplishments are and causes me to worry that the accomplishments of RECE and the many talented individuals who comprise it, too, may be fleeting. Reflecting back on the inaugural RECE meeting at the University of Wisconsin–Madison in 1991 evokes in me memories of nurturance, hope, possibility, and a perpetual wish for more. Is it possible to thread a movement from such moments? Have we stormed the epistemological barricades? What can a life's work of child therapy and child pedagogy, teacher education, and writing preserve? In a world of predatory capitalism, ruthless mechanical notions of accountability, and disinterest in the existential and liberatory potential of care and education, for what might we be remembered? Our humanitarian and critical impulses give me optimism, and the reactionary politics of all power structures give me pause. I find the tenaciousness of normative developmental models of childhood discouraging. Has our RECE movement had any lasting influence on policy and practices? Do we have the capacity to stand up to the retrogressive influences that seek to roll back the gains in our field? I fear I'm still waiting for the revolution.

In this chapter I will chart the course of a journey that began with my early critiques of early childhood education, ripostes that were sometimes tinged with the sharpness and impatience of my relative youth. I will contrast that with my position today—one edged by my concern about legacy and the passing on of an ethic of care and a language of critique to future scholars and practitioners. In seeking to rupture the tenacious hold of developmental normativity, bolstered nowadays by foreclosing tropes such as "evidence-based practice," I will present my current conceptualization of the possibilities of childhood through what I have begun to call "a psychoanalysis of the social"—an approach that combines psychoanalytic notions of valuing emotions, imagination, and the possibility of the unconscious with lessons from intergenerational trauma theory that offer profound insights into the role of ancestry, spirituality, history, culture, and difference in our coming to be as subjects. I will argue that we must find a way to add greater political muscle to the urgent case for a more liberatory imaginary for future generations of children.

Compulsory Retrospection

Compulsory retrospection is tricky stuff. As a younger person I thought and wrote like… well…like a younger person. I had faith at that point that we could charge the epistemological barricades, and in some respects we did. The infusion of queer theory, postcolonial theory, and critical qualitative research into the discourses of early childhood education, and indeed the establishment and remarkable continuance of the RECE Conference for more than 20 years, offers extraordinary testimony to our capacity for change and to our ability to work in relative solidarity to keep an idea going. As I have grown older, I think perhaps what has changed most for me is that I have considerably less interest in just winning an argument or scoring rhetorical points, and more interest in seeding a movement. I am interested in living a philosophy of life and seeking to spread that word to those who may have a receptivity to the human values that I believe in, and, by putting my ideas out there, contributing at a minimum to keeping alive the possibilities of being, becoming, imagining, and acting, for future children.

Vivian Paley devoted her life to understanding the importance of storytelling and fantasy in the lives of the children in her kindergarten classes. Her 2005 book, *A Child's Work: The Importance of Fantasy Play*, offers a troubling view of where the schooling of young children is headed when the nurturance of imagination and the provision of a space for the working through of feelings is no longer of consequence. Instead, predictability and reliability offer a safer and more sanitary path for teachers:

> What an astonishing invention is this activity we call fantasy play. Are we really willing to let it disappear from our schools and kindergartens? "I'm not inclined to encourage fantasy play any more if my teachers can't handle it," a preschool director admitted recently. "If the teachers are worried about what's coming out, especially with the fours and fives, everyone is better off if we stick to lesson plans and projects."
>
> "Has the play changed that much?" I ask.
>
> "The teachers think so. Maybe it's the increased tension since 9/11. Children do seem less prepared, more at risk. We're on safer ground with a somewhat academic curriculum. It's more dependable." (p. 7)

As Paley notes, expectations for young children have become so instrumental and fixed that "The potential for surprise is largely gone." "We no longer wonder," she continues, "'Who are you?' but instead decide quickly 'What can we do to fix you?'" (2005, p. 47)

As I leaf back through my own contributions to the early RECE debates,[1] I notice a salient binary ethos in the argument: us versus them. RECE versus the National Association for the Education of Young Children (NAEYC). RECE versus Developmentally Appropriate Practice (DAP). RECE versus oppressive and retrogressive pedagogy. RECE versus sell-outs and hold-outs. I now realize that binaries are unhelpful because they bind us in a dialectic that provokes resistance and may inhibit change; and also by virtue of our opposition, we may unwittingly reify and confer legitimacy on the status quo that we seek to supplant. A third path is needed.

Leaving that aside, however, I am struck by how relatively constant my concerns have been. The arguments of my more youthful self still resonate deeply with me, but I think I have made progress in two ways. First, by becoming a child therapist and psychoanalyst, and having now seen children in therapy for close to 10,000 hours, I have become more attuned to the experience of being with children, and this has grounded my ideas immeasurably. Second, I learned to think psychoanalytically. I have identified a liberatory lineage in psychoanalysis going all the way back to Freud's Free Clinics,[2] and I have found a way, through what I call a "psychoanalysis of the social," to argue that not only does psychoanalysis have useful insights to offer into the emotional foundation of children's lived experiences, but that it has potential, through speaking to a sociohistorically defined unconscious, to address the ancestral, cultural, and historical formation of the child and thereby to contribute to liberatory pedagogical practices. I should note too—and here the writings of Deborah Britzman, Gail Boldt, Jonathan Silin, and Peter Taubman are illustrative[3]—that one does not need to be formally trained either as a psychologist, therapist, or psychoanalyst to claim a space in the psychoanalytic world or to use critical psychoanalytic concepts. When I put out a call recently for chapters for a book that would speak to childhood and schooling from psychoanalytic perspectives, I received enough material to produce two books with 33 chapters, written by passionate child advocates from a variety of professions.[4] This gives me cause for optimism.

Nowhere to Grow?

Five-year-old Errol's[5] parents were puzzled. He absolutely refused to have a party to celebrate his birthday. He was adamant that he was not growing up and that he would never turn 6. More seriously, 10-year-old Dave wore the belt of his pants cinched a few notches too tight in order to maintain an image of slightness, and each year when his mother took him shopping for back-to-school clothes he insisted on clothes that were at least two sizes too small. One day, in my consulting office, he drew a womb-like image with a tiny stick figure, perhaps two centimeters long, inside. He drew a speech bubble and an arrow pointing to the figure within the womb. Then he wrote the legend "I'm hear" [sic] in the bubble. He labeled the picture, poignantly, "The boy who wouldn't grow up."

In *The Queer Child* (2009), Kathryn Stockton speaks of the child who, faced with normative, linear, heterosexist notions of advancement, simply has "nowhere to grow" (p. 3). As Stockton notes, if growing up inevitably means encountering continual trouble or permanent misrecognition, some children will recognize that if they wish to follow a path that includes any vestige of their own desires, they have little choice but to seek an alternative sideways path forward. Do we have any room in our thinking for such sideways paths? Is "developmental delay," with all of its connotations of pathology, retardation, and deficit, the only alternative to growing up?

Stockton points to the queerness of notions of childhood that preclude consideration of "sex, aggression, secrets, closets, or any sense of what police call 'a past,'" thus revealing the core notion of the normative child as innocent and walled off, a child who "on its path to normativity, seems safe to us and whom we therefore safeguard at all costs" (2009, p. 30). As Bruhm and Hurley note in *Curiouser: On the Queerness of Children* (2004), childhood innocence is imbued with notions of asexuality and incipient heterosexuality. "The figure of the queer child," Bruhm and Hurley state, "is that which doesn't quite conform to the wished-for way that children are supposed to be in terms of gender and sexual roles" (p. x). The conundrum of the child, inserted discursively into a retrospective normative role of innocence that is deeply invested with adult fears, anxieties, and projections of innocence, not to mention socially normative scripts about class, race, and gender (cf. Bernstein, 2011), is to either sacrifice desire on the altar of parental and societal notions of normative expectation, or else run into the brick wall of developmental arrest and thus be viewed as delayed, deviant, or oppositional. These kinds of interpellative processes are onerous and alienating for all children, as they seek to keep children cordoned within the realm of thinkable ways of being and within the realm of bourgeois aspiration and social hierarchy through the suppression of any aberrant or nonmaterial desire. They are all the more catastrophic for the queer child—the child who by definition may embody homosexual identifications, transgender identifications, racial identifications, or any other interests that bourgeois society might regard as uppity, perverse, aberrant, deviant, or dangerous to the bourgeois status quo. What then of the dilemma facing a transgender child such as Ludo in the movie *Ma Vie en Rose* (Berliner, 1999), who faces a willfully misunderstanding family and community? Or what of Willie, the gay protagonist in the movie *The Hanging Garden* (Fitzgerald, 1996) whose mother seeks to straighten him through a visit to a hooker, and whose attempts to eat his way out of heterosexual progression and spurned homosexual love leads to an impasse that brings him precipitously close to catastrophe? Or what of Billy, the main character in *Billy Elliot* (Daldry, 2001), who seeks to pursue his desire to be a ballet dancer despite the vehement condemnation of his working-class patriarchal homophobic father and brother, the envy of his gay friend Michael, and his own attempt to bob and weave around the societal expectation that his interest in ballet inevitably means that he is a poof? Is it possible for a child to push through this pain to a place of desire and possibility?

The Troubled State of Early Education in the United States Today

In my early work, I was interested in challenging specific facets of the epistemology underpinning developmental psychology and early childhood pedagogy. Gradually I came to understand that the problem was larger. Since then I have attempted to articulate one dimension of an alternative epistemological understanding of the notion of childhood and the paths by which children might negotiate themselves to positions of desire and a capacity to question both the paths of their individual life trajectories and the collective paths that are offered by post-industrial societies that seem willing to market technological progress and material consumption as the solution to the meaning of life. In doing so I have no illusion that the theory of embodied and embedded subjectivity that I offer here is, on its own, the answer to what ails our society. My hope is that those of us who share a rejection of the core epistemological principles of normative childhood, linear development, and prescriptive pedagogies, often artfully disguised as student-centered and humane education, might take seriously the need to articulate a comprehensive critical alternative vision to the status quo.

My central critique of RECE is that we have failed to coalesce around a comprehensive, critically progressive, located, and multidimensional understanding of childhood experience, and hence of the multiple ways in which particular children—each of whom is queer in their own way—may seek opportunities to think, imagine, and experience their own critical possibilities for becoming. I am very concerned with the decidedly anti-child drift of current educational practices and policies.

With a few notable exceptions, for the most part the discourses of child development, classroom management, early childhood education, special education, school psychology, and school counseling have constructed notions of children and schooling that are often behaviorist, instrumental, and symptom focused. In the educational arena, curriculum too often focuses on rote acquisition of knowledge; discipline is conceptualized as compliance (Kohn, 1996/2006) and symptoms such as anger, school resistance, oppositionality, etc. are pathologized and reacted to out of context. Children's special needs are often conceptualized instrumentally, and children with complex psychological symptoms or complex social backgrounds are delimited, depersonalized, or simply removed (Books, 1998/2006; Polakow, 1998; Polakow-Suransky, 2000). While this has been true of North America for some time, the biologization and pathologization of psychic distress in children as behavior to be medicated and eliminated, is spreading across the world.

For a quarter century, I've been teaching a course called "The Emotional Lives of Children and the Possibility of Classroom as Community" to teachers and psychologists. I also teach courses on child development, child therapy, and classroom management, all focusing on the emotional quality of children's lives, and on the complexities of transference relationships between children and the adults who care for them. I have found students to be receptive to the person-centered and psychodynamic perspectives we study through fiction, memoir, film, and academic texts, and my students are invariably puzzled that these perspectives rarely form part of the core principles of their preparation. Why are so few psychologists, social workers, and teachers introduced, for example, to the writings of Donald Winnicott, Margaret Mahler, Maud Mannoni, Louise Kaplan, or Selma Fraiberg? "What if, instead of manualized therapy and scripted pedagogy, we assisted professionals in using their talents and gifts to work *obliquely* with children (cf. O'Loughlin & Merchant, 2012) so that our services to children speak to desire and imagination instead of demanding rigid conformity and stifling uniformity?" (O'Loughlin, 2013c, p. 2).

The reductiveness of outcomes-based and supposedly evidence-based methodologies has crept up into university preparation in the United States, primarily through the influence of accreditation processes that have increasingly constricted the space in which either philosophical ideals, imagination, or emotion can be discussed (cf. Biesta, 2007). Our critical voices are diminutive indeed in the face of an alliance between postcapitalist and neoconservative ideologies, coupled with a strain of anti-intellectualism, all thinly disguised in an ethos of school reform and a desire to mold children into becoming willing participants in a culture of material consumption, teaching them to fit in with corporate business practices, and perhaps even teaching children to accept the necessity for their own eventual unemployability in a ruthless global market economy.

With this in mind, looking at my early papers I enumerate the following concerns that were at the forefront of my mind 20 years ago. I invite you to consider how well they have been addressed within the reconceptualizing movement, specifically within RECE itself, as well as within mainstream early childhood policies and practices in the United States. If these concerns continue to be relevant today, that raises troubling questions about our capacity to effect substantive change in the field. With respect to early childhood education, back then I argued that:

- Despite a veneer of student-centered and discovery-oriented learning, the meaning-making capacities of children are denied, and the teleology of early childhood curriculum is impositional, bourgeois, and culturally exclusive.
- Ancestral, historical, social, cultural, and local contexts of meaning-making are denied.
- Learning is conceptualized as a mentalistic or intrapsychic process as opposed to being viewed as sociohistorically constituted and fundamentally social in form.
- Child growth is conceptualized as linear and founded on hierarchical assumptions from a decontextualized and universalized developmental psychology. This epistemological hegemony prevails despite the pioneering work of Valerie Walkerdine and her colleagues as presented in the seminal work *Changing the Subject* (Henriques, Hollway, Urwin, Venn, & Walkerdine, 1984), and subsequent works (e.g., Burman, 1994; Walkerdine, 1984, 1987, 1990, 2002, 2004) challenging that paradigm.
- Early childhood education fails to speak of children in genuinely socioculturally inclusive and plural ways.
- Notions of curriculum and learning in early childhood education fail to acknowledge the mind as socioculturally and discursively located and as dialectical in operation.
- Early childhood education uses the concept "development" uncritically. If development is at all useful as a concept, should we not consider it as ecosocial, nonlinear, nonhierarchical, opportunistic, and locally and contextually situated?
- Education is not conceptualized within larger systems of power and ideology. The workings of power and inequality in the relations between language, culture, and schooling, and in models of practice and in modes of research inquiry are not problematized or interrogated critically.
- Early childhood education theory, policy, and practice occur within larger political and policy contexts, often contexts that do not privilege equity, justice, and opportunity. While espousing critique, progressive early childhood education professors are also beneficiaries of the privileging systems that perpetuate the status quo and generate cultural capital and career status [as I am doing right now by writing this chapter] while promulgating critique from a safe distance.

In critiquing Developmentally Appropriate Practice (DAP; Bredekamp, 1987), the practice philosophy promulgated by the National Association for the Education of Young Children and keystone of the NAEYC accreditation process for early education, I offered the following additional critiques:

- The rhetoric of certainty and progressive linearity embodied in the DAP prescriptions is problematic. How do we presume to know what is good for all children in all contexts? What happens if our prescriptions for children are inherently normative and unsuited to particular children in particular locales and contexts? What would locally generated critical constructivist—as opposed to positivist—curriculum practices look like?
- DAP is founded on the narrow epistemological foundation of Piagetian notions of knowledge and a linear, hierarchical understanding of human development and is

therefore inherently unsuited to a critical, open, inclusive, grounded curriculum process.

- Appropriate for whom? Why propose a "one size fits all" model? How can a culturally responsive or locally grounded pedagogy be conceptualized within a generic "one size fits all" model? Doesn't the use of the term "appropriate" betray the inherent normativity of the enterprise and the hegemonic epistemological assumptions underlying the curriculum prescriptions that are advanced as precepts of best practice?
- Where is the space in DAP for emancipatory or critically located pedagogy? What is the ultimate goal of the kind of pedagogy formulation DAP embodies? Who benefits?

A Third Way: The Emergence of Childhood Subjectivity Discursively

As I noted earlier, in *Changing the Subject* (1984) Henriques and his colleagues not only challenged hierarchical, normative, and essentialist understandings of the experience of childhood, but, using postmodern and postcolonial theory, they began to articulate a complex understanding of the coming to be of human subjectivity. In *The Subject of Childhood* (2009a), drawing on the work of Rex and Wendy Stainton-Rogers (1992), I suggested that notions of childhood are, to use their term, "manufactured." "Childhood," with its accompanying notions of naturalness and innocence, is a discursive creation that is designed to serve certain ideological functions. The difficulty with unreflexive early childhood pedagogies and curriculum practices, however humanely presented, is that they are built upon a foundation of hegemonic discursive assumptions and ideological and epistemological tenets that go unexamined.

With respect to ideology, what if the underlying foundations of the field are built around notions of commodification; that is, the artful construction of childhood subjectivity to prepare a child for a specific niche in society? Schools and nursery schools, after all, are instruments of socialization for society. The robust and acrimonious debates that occur around the content of textbooks, as well as the never-ending battle over mechanisms of evaluation, reveal the ideological battles for the hearts and minds of children. How can teachers and schools act as if they operate in a benevolent and humanistic vacuum in the middle of such a maelstrom? What are the implications for teachers if indeed most children in U.S. public schools are "schooled to order" as David Nasaw (1981) suggested in the book of the same title? Such considerations also extend of course to norms of sexual identity and the banishment of queerness, and indeed to the restriction of children's capacities to use their imaginations. What if a child were to think the unthinkable? Is there space—or even time—in our nursery schools and elementary schools for such a possibility? And if there is not, what happens to the possibility of education for freedom?

The concept of subjectivity, therefore, offers a way out of the binary in which the child is conceived as an intrapsychic "developing" entity, and the external world acts on the child. Employing the more situated term "subjectivity" allows us to consider that rather than a homunculus that preexists action or interaction with the world, the becoming child is subjectively constructed through immersion in the world. Althusser (1971) captured this notion in his articulation of processes of interpellation. "Subjectivity" as a central concept, therefore, allows us to become interested in the ways in which children become who they need to become by making use of the cultural and symbolic resources put at their disposal.

A particular value of thinking about childhood in terms of evolving subjectivity, therefore, is that it brings to the fore the dilemma of the conflict between socialization and the possibilities of becoming a free subject. As Judith Butler noted in *The Psychic Life of Power* (1997), becoming a subject necessarily requires becoming subject to prevailing discursive practices. Considering the pressure for assimilation and the insidious workings of interpellation inherent in processes of socialization such as child-rearing, education, normative race, class and gender socialization, and induction into religious and political thought, what chance is there for a particular child to pursue queer or sideways paths toward becoming and desire? Adopting subjectivity as a central organizing principle offers the opportunity to pose important political questions about the role of early childhood educators as guardians of the status quo with respect to gender, race, class, and ideological norms.

These uncomfortable questions are at the heart of what Paulo Freire (1969, 1970) termed "education as the practice of freedom." Might it be possible for teachers of young children to think of their work as being about resisting some of the interpellative processes that are placed on children in order to allow them, as Rich Johnson and I expressed elsewhere, to "imagine themselves otherwise" (O'Loughlin & Johnson, 2010)?

I conclude my first chapter of *The Subject of Childhood* with a modest suggestion that self-reflexive autobiographical inquiry may offer a starting point in developing questioning capabilities in young teachers who might then go on to nurture similar capacities for questioning and for reflection on desire and possibility in the children with whom they work:

> I think what bothers me most about the grand narratives of childhood that are so endemic to conventional wisdom about children and pedagogy is the determinism of the child's life path. Where is there room for questions? How is the child to ever develop imaginative possibilities and experience desire if all of life is hemmed in with the ever-increasing demand of teachers, parents, pediatricians, pastors and others? If we, the adults who conceptualize childhood and schooling, cannot enter into dialogue with our own child selves, and if we cannot break out of the narrow pathways of our own experience, what hope is there for emancipatory, opportunistic, or imaginative dreaming among the children of our future? (2009a, p. 26)

On Possible Lines of Rupture: Troubling Spectrality and Genealogical Filiation

In the conventional view, the epistemological story lines are simple. Children are born with anticipated futures, poised to grow up to claim a space in society. The educational conundrum is not about what they need to know to become well-functioning adults, because society has already specified the curriculum paths for their lives within certain race-, gender-, and class-bound parameters. The sole remaining ideological question is whether the socialization should be done in Dickensian fashion, using harsh pedagogical techniques, or whether we can create softer modes of induction that create a less jarring entry into culture for the child. Early childhood education, with its focus on student-centeredness and "discovery" learning approaches, espouses the latter strategy. These are, however, distinctions only in kind. As noted earlier, the normative and assimilative intent of the enterprise is unchanged and the ontological assumptions of the system are a given.

Conventional normative socialization is premised, therefore, on the ontological notion that what counts is official knowledge. Yet, as Adam Phillips (1998) reminds us, Freud and other early psychoanalysts were fascinated with the child's refusal of official knowledge and with her preoccupation with illicit knowing, particularly about the realm of sexuality and sex play. With a few notable exceptions (e.g., Dyson, 1993, 1997, 2003; Tobin, 1997), the unofficial worlds of childhood are typically ignored by researchers. It seems that we practice the taboo that we also preach to children!

In *Specters of Marx* (1994), Derrida proposed replacing ontology with "hauntology," a way of thinking that shakes up the linearity of time; that allows for spectral memory and preoccupations; and that recognizes the delayed occurrence of meaning for an event that has occurred in earlier time. Applied to the world of a child, this formulation allows for the recognition that children have dynamic pasts. They not only grow up inserted into narrative strands and preexisting discursive practices, but there are many spectral qualities to the child's experience based on intergenerationally transmitted unnamable knowledges and experiences, and based on the notion of après coup, where events that have occurred earlier only retroactively acquire significance. In addition, spectral knowing pushes the dimensions of knowing into new arenas, including ancestral, spiritual, and historical knowledges and realms of fantasy and the uncanny that are excluded by formal ontological understandings of knowledge as static, event-filled, and informational, and of child growth and development as teleological and normative. Such spectral knowledges occasionally burst into the open with unruly zest. What kinds of questioning might be possible for a child if we welcomed these unruly guests to the table?

What distinguishes this notion of inheritance and genealogical filiation (cf. Apfelbaum, 2002) is the dynamic nature of the pasts that are imaginable, and the potential, given optimal pedagogical or child-rearing conditions, for a particular child to explore gaps, fissures, points of rupture, and openings to multiple ways of experiencing and entering into possible subjectivity. Students of hauntology, scholars of indigenous epistemologies and practices, and scholars who analyze sociohistorical aspects of experience[6] have all contributed to specifying the architecture of the cryptic spaces in which such knowledge resides and pointing out the straitjacket in which growth is placed if the dynamic and spectral origins of experience are delimited, discarded, or ignored.

In *Trauma Trails*, Judy Atkinson (2002), exploring the limit case of the catastrophic consequences of the abuses of the Stolen Generations for Australian Aboriginal Peoples, conceptualizes the relative consequences of growing up with or without access to ancestral, historical, and familial ties in terms of notions of lore and lorelessness. Lacking access to lore and to the narrative threads linking present and past times, lacking continuity with ancestors and sprits, and lacking a capacity to be in dreamtime, has caused aboriginal people to experience severe dislocation and an inability to dream. While this conceptualization has special relevance for historically marginalized groups, it should not be thought of so narrowly. What is at issue here is a form of dreaming, namely our capacity to imagine our children embedded in large webs of different types of epistemologies, filiations, and lineages, arranged on multiple planes and at multiple levels. The marvelous opportunity for any child to discover the multiple possible arcs of their own growth is brutally crushed if we ignore these epistemological dimensions and reduce growth to teleological and normative development, and if we continue to define education as reductionist socialization.

Coda: Troubling Pedagogy

How might this conceptualization of subjectivity translate into pedagogical actions? The most fundamental commitment is to the question of the child. Can we permit the child to reach for a place of desire? In my work as a therapist with children, I see my primary attributes as an acutely attuned receptivity to the child's emotions, and a capacity to resist obfuscating a child's truth-seeking with comforting platitudes. In addition I struggle to "do nothing"; that is, to express as little desire as possible in order to create a facilitative space where either the child's desire emerges, or the inhibitions to the child's desire become evident and can be named (O'Loughlin & Merchant, 2012). I have described in some detail elsewhere the elements of an evocative pedagogy that is designed to address the child's unconscious, as well as the notion of a regenerative curriculum that is built around the idea that pedagogy ought to be about assisting children in creating social linkages between their current being/becoming and spectral, ancestral, and unnamable aspects of their own subjectivity (O'Loughlin, 2009a, 2010, 2013d, 2013e). I recently summarized the process this way:

> Turning then to pedagogy, a social-historical psychoanalytic approach calls for subjectivization as a primary goal. Pedagogy ought to provide opportunities for an intensive engagement with spoken and unspoken experience, with history, lore, ancestry, and imagination so that each child can enter into a dynamic relationship with the ruptures and gaps of the past, and with multiple possible futures. A minimal condition of depth pedagogy, therefore, is the reclamation of narrative threads and the location of children as subjects in history—people with genealogical filiations, narrative continuity, and a possibility for becoming that is informed by, but not constrained by, ancestral, historical, and familial legacies. Each child possesses a latent culturally constituted unconscious that embodies ancestral history and ways of being, as well as inherited traumas due to displacements, wars, genocides, familial trauma, and other forms of unspoken and unmetabolized suffering. Ought not a teacher be prepared to tap into these resources to help children better understand their locations in history?
>
> From a pedagogical perspective, in addition to creating an inviting intersubjective and emotionally secure dialogical space, teachers "should" understand how to evoke the unconscious in children through their own evocative presences. A teacher with a passion for myth, storytelling, drama, memory, and the wisdom of elders will draw these evocative knowledges into the classroom, and will elicit evocative responses from students that allow students to experience their own inner knowledges as namable and addressable. (O'Loughlin, 2009a, pp. 40–41)

Davoine and Gaudillière (2004) speak of the analyst primarily as an "annalist"; that is, a receiver of story and a chronicler of journeys in progress. What a privilege it is for a teacher-annalist to accompany children a piece of the way on their journey into becoming.

References

Althusser, L. (1971). Ideology and ideological state apparatuses (Notes towards an investigation). In L. Althusser, *Lenin and philosophy and other essays*. New York: Monthly Review Press.

Apfelbaum, E. (2002). Uprooted communities, silenced cultures and the need for legacy. In V. Walkerdine (Ed.), *Challenging subjects: Critical psychology for a new millennium*. New York: Palgrave.

Atkinson, J. (2002). *Trauma trails, recreating song lines: The transgenerational effects of trauma in Indigenous Australia*. North Melbourne, Australia: Spinifex Press.

Berliner, A. (1999). (Director). *Ma vie en rose* [Motion picture]. Belgium: Sony Pictures Classics.

Bernstein, R. (2011). *Racial innocence: Performing American childhood from slavery to civil rights.* New York: New York University Press.

Biesta, G. (2007). Why "what works" won't work: Evidence-based practice and the democratic deficit in educational research. *Educational Theory, 57,* 1, 1–22.

Boldt, G. (2006). *Love's return: Psychoanalytic essays on childhood, teaching, and learning.* New York: Routledge.

Books, S. (Ed.). (1998/2006). *Invisible children in the society and its schools.* Hillsdale, NJ: Erlbaum.

Bredekamp, S. (1987). *Developmentally appropriate practice in early childhood programs serving children from birth through age 8.* Washington, DC: National Association for the Education of Young Children.

Britzman, D. (2009). *The very thought of education: Psychoanalysis and the impossible professions.* Albany, NY: SUNY Press.

Britzman, D. (2010). *Freud and education.* New York: Routledge.

Bruhm, S., & Hurley, N. (2004). *Curiouser: On the queerness of children.* Minneapolis: University of Minnesota Press.

Burman, E. (1994). *Deconstructing developmental psychology.* London: Routledge.

Butler, J. (1997). *The psychic life of power.* New York: Routledge.

Daldry, S. (Director). (2001). *Billy Elliot.* [Motion picture]. United States: Universal Studios.

Davoine, F., & Gaudillière, J. M. (2004). *History beyond trauma.* New York: Other Press.

Derrida, J. (1994). *Specters of Marx: The state of the debt, the work of mourning, and the new international.* New York: Routledge.

Dyson, A. H. (1993). *The social worlds of children learning to write in an urban primary school.* New York: Teachers College Press.

Dyson, A. H. (1997). *Writing superheroes: Contemporary childhood, popular culture and classroom literacy.* New York: Teachers College Press.

Dyson, A. H. (2003). *The brothers and sisters learn to write: Popular literacies in childhood, school and cultures.* New York: Teachers College Press.

Fitzgrald, T. (Director). (1996). *The hanging garden.* [Motion picture]. Canada: MGM.

Freire, P. (1969). *Education for critical consciousness.* New York: Continuum.

Freire, P. (1970). *Pedagogy of the oppressed.* New York: Continuum.

Henriques, J., Hollway, W., Urwin, C., Venn, C., & Walkerdine, V. (1984). *Changing the subject: Psychology, social regulation, and subjectivity.* London: Methuen.

Kohn, A. (1996/2006). *Beyond discipline: From compliance to community.* Alexandria, VA: Association for Supervision and Curriculum Development.

Nasaw, D. (1981). *Schooled to order: A social history of public schooling in the United States.* New York: Oxford University Press.

O'Loughlin, M. (1991, October). Rethinking early childhood education: A sociocultural perspective. In J. Jipson (Chair), *Deconstructing constructivism.* Paper presented at the 1st conference on Reconceptualizing Research in Early Childhood Education, *Loosening the ties that bind.* University of Wisconsin–Madison.

O'Loughlin, M. (1992, September). Appropriate for whom? A critique of the culture and class bias underlying developmentally appropriate practice in early childhood education. Paper presented at the 2nd conference on Reconceptualizing Early Childhood: *Reclaiming the progressive agenda in early childhood education,* Chicago, IL.

O'Loughlin, M. (1993, April). Developing a rationale for emancipatory knowledge construction: Five questions for constructivists. In F. Peterman (Organizer), *Restructuring constructivism: A conversation about constructivism, teacher education, and the classroom ecology.* Symposium presented at the 66th annual meeting of the National Association for Research in Science Teaching, Atlanta, GA.

O'Loughlin, M. (1994a, September). On the virtues of disobedience: The possibilities of the margin as a site of radical change in schools and universities. Paper presented at the 4th interdisciplinary conference, Reconceptualizing Early Childhood Education: Research, theory, and practice, Durham, NH.

O'Loughlin, M. (1994b, September). Making the case for culturally relevant pedagogy. Paper presented at the 4th interdisciplinary conference, Reconceptualizing Early Childhood Education: Research, theory, and practice, Durham, NH.

O'Loughlin, M. (1995, May). Six propositions concerning children, their growth, and the language we use to describe them. In M. O'Loughlin (Organizer), *If not child development, then what?: Exploring the possibilities of dialogic and sociocultural theories for our understanding of the growth and education of children in communities and schools.* Presented at the 5th interdisciplinary conference, Reconceptualizing Early Childhood Education: Research, theory, and practice, Santa Rosa, CA.

O'Loughlin, M. (2001, October). The subject of psychoanalysis: Thoughts on subjectivity, subjection, and a role for psychoanalysis in articulating liberatory understandings of the possible lives of children. Presented at the 10th annual conference, Reconceptualizing Early Childhood Education: Research, theory, and practice, New York.

O'Loughlin, M. (2003, January). Strangers to ourselves: The decolonizing potential of the displacement, loss, and "homelessness" of migrant experiences. In M. O'Loughlin (Organizer), *"On being homeless": The decolonizing possibilities of displaced lives and fractured subjectivities.* Presented at the 11th annual conference, Reconceptualizing Early Childhood Education: Research, theory, and practice, Tempe, AZ.

O'Loughlin, M. (2004, May). Through a glass darkly: Troubling memories of loss, desire, belonging, and lack, then and now. In M. O'Loughlin [Organizer], *Oh me, oh my! Troubling shame, loss and phantasy in childhood.* Presented at the 12th annual conference, Reconceptualizing Early Childhood Education: Research, theory, and practice, Oslo, Norway.

O'Loughlin, M. (2005, October). Constructing a liveable subjectivity: Hauntology as the basis of a pedagogy for young children. In M. O'Loughlin (Organizer), *When language is the subject: On the spoken and unspoken in children's coming to be.* Presented at the 13th annual conference, Reconceptualizing Early Childhood Education: Research, theory, and practice, Madison, WI.

O'Loughlin, M. (2006, November). Recreating the social link between children and their histories: Revisiting ghosts in the nursery and exploring the power of story as a decolonizing strategy. In M. O'Loughlin & R. Johnson (Organizers), *Troubling decolonization: The radical (?) potential of a pedagogy of disorder for young children.* Symposium conducted at the 14th annual conference, Reconceptualizing Early Childhood Education: Research, theory, and practice, Rotorua, New Zealand.

O'Loughlin, M. (2008). Radical hope or death by a thousand cuts? The future for Indigenous Australians. *Arena Journal, 29/30,* 175–202.

O'Loughlin, M. (2009a). *The subject of childhood.* New York: Peter Lang.

O'Loughlin, M. (2009b). An analysis of collective trauma among Indigenous Australians and a suggestion for intervention. *Australasian Psychiatry, 17,* 33–36.

O'Loughlin, M. (2010). Ghostly presences in children's lives: Toward a psychoanalysis of the social. In M. O'Loughlin & R. Johnson (Eds.), *Imagining children otherwise: Theoretical and critical perspectives on childhood subjectivity.* New York: Peter Lang.

O'Loughlin, M. (2012). Trauma trails from Ireland's Great Hunger: A psychoanalytic inquiry. In B. Willock, R. Curtis, & L. Bohm, (Eds.), *Loneliness and longing: Psychoanalytic reflections.* New York: Routledge.

O'Loughlin, M. (Ed.). (2013a). *Psychodynamic perspectives on working with children, families and schools.* Lanham, MD: Jason Aronson.

O'Loughlin, M. (Ed.). (2013b). *The uses of psychoanalysis in working with children's emotional lives.* Lanham, MD: Jason Aronson.

O'Loughlin, M. (Ed.). (2013c). Introduction. In M. O'Loughlin (Ed.), *Psychodynamic perspectives on working with children, families and schools.* Lanham, MD: Jason Aronson.

O'Loughlin, M. (2013d). Reclaiming genealogy, memory and history: The psychodynamic potential for reparative therapy in contemporary South Africa. In C. Smith, G. Lobban, & M. O'Loughlin (Eds.), *Psychodynamic psychotherapy in contemporary South Africa: Contexts, theories, and applications.* Johannesburg, SA: Wits University Press.

O'Loughlin, M. (Ed.). (2013e). The uses of psychoanalysis. In M. O'Loughlin (Ed.), *The uses of psychoanalysis in working with children's emotional lives.* Lanham, MD: Jason Aronson.

O'Loughlin, M., & Johnson, R. (Eds.). (2010). *Imagining children otherwise: Theoretical and critical perspectives on childhood subjectivity.* New York: Peter Lang.

O'Loughlin, M., & Merchant, A. (2012, June). Working obliquely with children. *Journal of Infant, Child & Adolescent Psychotherapy, 11,* 149–159.

Paley, V. (2005). *A child's work: The importance of fantasy play.* Chicago: University of Chicago Press.

Phillips, A. (1998*). The beast in the nursery: On curiosity and other appetites.* New York: Vintage.

Polakow, V. (1998). Homeless children and their families: The discards of the postmodern 1990s. In S. Books (Ed.) *Invisible children in the society and schools.* Mahwah, NJ: Erlbaum.

Polakow-Suransky, S. (2000). America's least wanted: Zero-tolerance policies and the fate of expelled students. In Polakow, S. (Ed.), *The public assault on America's children: Poverty, violence, and juvenile injustice* (pp. 101–129). New York: Teachers College Press.

Silin, J. (1995). *Sex, death, and the education of children: Our passion for ignorance in the age of AIDS.* New York: Teachers College Press.

Stainton-Rogers, R., & Stainton-Rogers, W. (1992). *Stories of childhood: Shifting agendas of child concern.* Toronto: University of Toronto Press.

Stockton, K. B. (2009). *The queer child: On growing sideways in the twentieth century.* Durham, NC: Duke University Press.

Taubman, P. (2011). *Disavowed knowledge: Psychoanalysis, education, and teaching.* New York: Routledge.

Tobin, J. (Ed.). (1997). *Making a place for pleasure in early childhood education*. New Haven, CT: Yale University Press.

Walkerdine, V. (1984). Developmental psychology and the child-centered pedagogy: The insertion of Piaget's theory into early education. In J. Henriques et al., (Eds.), *Changing the subject: Psychology, social regulation and subjectivity* (pp. 152–202). London: Methuen.

Walkerdine, V. (1987). *Surveillance, subjectivity and struggle: Lessons from pedagogic and domestic practices*. Minneapolis: University of Minnesota Press.

Walkerdine, V. (1990). *Schoolgirl fictions*. London: Routledge.

Walkerdine, V. (Ed.). (2002). *Challenging subjects: Critical psychology for the new millennium*. London: Palgrave.

Walkerdine, V. (2004). Developmental psychology and the study of childhood. In M. Kehily, (Ed.), *An introduction to childhood studies* (pp. 96–107). Maidenhead: Open University Press.

Notes

1. The development of my thought can be followed through a series of papers presented at RECE conferences (O'Loughlin, 1991, 1992, 1993, 1994a, 1994b, 1995, 2001, 2003, 2004, 2005, 2006). Many of these unpublished papers may be downloaded from my website at: http://michaeloloughlinphd.com/my-recent-writings/rece-archive-papers/. The arguments are also summarized in my book *The Subject of Childhood* (2009a).
2. For further discussion of the liberatory possibilities of psychoanalysis, please see O'Loughlin (2010).
3. See, for example, Britzman (2009, 2010), Boldt (2006), Silin (1995), and Taubman (2011).
4. The books are *Psychodynamic Perspectives on Working with Children, Families and Schools* and *The Uses of Psychoanalysis in Working with Children's Emotional Lives* (O'Loughlin, 2013a, 2013b).
5. Patient names have been changed and identifying details disguised to protect identity.
6. Due to space constraints, supporting citations are not provided here. However, for discussion, see O'Loughlin, 2008, 2009b, 2010, 2012, 2013d. A comprehensive bibliography to accompany this chapter may be downloaded from my website: http://michaeloloughlinphd.com/my-recent-writings/rece-archive-papers/

Disciplining "Safe" Bodies in a Global Era of Child Panic: Implementing Techniques for Disciplining the Self

Richard T. Johnson

One thing about the body, then, is that it is a contested terrain, both theoretically and in representation. (Holliday & Hassard, 2001, p. 7)

Our identities as caring providers and dedicated caregivers have been questioned and altered in the recent past as schools and other professional organizations (re)define our relationships with children and with ourselves. In his critique of schooling practices almost 20 years ago, Michael O'Loughlin notes the overwhelmingly static nature of teachers in public education as he identifies them as "functionaries assisting in the preservation of a larger system of knowledge and culture" while they keep themselves firmly embedded as a "mechanism in the naturalization of the status quo" (1995, p. 107). He goes on to illustrate how "State bureaucrats and local school boards hand down decisions about the regulation of curriculum, via testing requirements, textbook selection, and state and local policies, and teachers effectively become the distributors of the spectacles through which children come to see all aspects of their society" (1995, p. 107). When I look at current popular literature, I readily witness most of those same issues today, some 187 years after O'Loughlin's critique. For example, when I look at myself and other early childhood educators and caregivers of young children, I continue my ongoing critical considerations (i.e., O'Loughlin's "Daring the Imagination") of my body's newfound, altered status as a teacher and/or coach of children and youth today. I readily realize that "I've attained active placement in a subjugated position(s) whereby my body, identity, and sense of being has been conquered, re-written and re-composed, dominated under the control of another" (Johnson, 2013, p. 11).

Phillipson and Fisher (1999) illustrated how the "dailyness" of looking influences our viewing of images and the fluidity within which we take in these images. They discuss how "'dailyness' is suffocated by an excess of representation, a superfluity of images which pose no question about themselves or their emergence" (p. 129). This perspective rings so true when I continuously view the risk-based policies and procedures that my student teachers abide by as they implement no-touch policies or are forced to incorporate scripted lesson plan formats into their daily practices and when I view my colleagues in our College of Education incorporating scripted assessment rubric formats into their semester-long (i.e., syllabus) practices.

Stories From the Field

Just as the family became an "instrument, a point of application, in the monitoring of a larger group (the population)" (Baker, 1998, p. 131), so too do families of professionals (i.e., child-care workers, preschool teachers, social workers, teachers, principals, and academics) expertly manage individuals. With efficient management, certain kinds of normalization are always possible. As I've witnessed from much of my previous research and site-supervisor practicum experiences with students, teachers, and children, a seemingly simple way around many of the "no-touch" issues in the classroom is through risk management (Johnson, 2000, 2012, 2013). This is illustrated in this following example where an undergraduate preservice teacher education student notes that he will closely follow these "tips" during future classroom interactions with students. As a teacher, he reports he will:

1. Never be alone with a student, male or female, without another teacher or other students around.
2. Never initiate touching a student in any manner unless they indicate in an overt manner that they don't mind it. For example, a student who initiates touching you on the shoulder or arm, or offers a hug, is indicating that he/she does not mind those displays of affection or attention. Of course, certain touching is never appropriate... you should never touch "areas where a bathing suit covers you."
3. Never cover up the window on the classroom door. It prohibits administrators and other teachers from looking in, and unless you have something to hide, it's not necessary.
4. Keep the classroom door open as much as possible.
5. Send the child to the nurse if he/she has a problem (such as soiling his or pants, etc.). If there are other problems in clothing sensitive areas (e.g., belt buckle and pants zipper), elicit the help of a fellow teacher, preferably one of the opposite sex, regardless of the presence of other children.
6. Always hug from the side; avoid frontal hugs whenever possible.
7. Legally, keep a critical incident file for every student.

In another related example, several years ago in the United States, National Public Radio (NPR) included a special within their daily *Morning Edition* newscast titled, "Day Care Center Goes to Extremes to Protect Reputation." It described a childcare center in the United States that implemented a no-touch policy that basically says (according to the director):

"It's against our policy to pick up the kids. It's against our policy to hold them on your lap." The no-touch policy is more to protect the center than the children. In the business of day care, she explains, reputation is everything, and reputation is fragile. It would be too easy, she says, for one innocent hug or playful piggyback ride to be misinterpreted. "The picking-up thing, I don't allow, because that's one of those issues where you have, you know, the direct physical contact, body to body, that could be misconstrued, so I—I stop it there." (National Public Radio, 1994)

The issues that arise in the previous story are quite prevalent today (Piper, 2010; Piper & Stronach, 2008). When I reflect on my experiences of coaching my children in soccer the past 18 years, I readily visualize the previously-mentioned no-touch issues, which assists in my further understanding of my identity as a caregiver/coach in today's times (Johnson, 2011a). Continuous photo-therapeutic reflection of my personal interactions with children clearly speaks to me about how my body today truly does not fit in with coaching and caregiving as those fields are currently being redefined. My body, which had strong emotional, social, and physical connections with young children (as recalled by seeing these pictures and images), has been (mis)appropriated and weakened by others, by myself, and by popular discourses in teaching and professional development practices in education and sports management. This (mis)appropriation has influenced my subjectivity so much that it is no longer recognizable by me and others (Johnson, 2013, 2011b).

Rather than entertain any deep intellectualization of no-touch, we're more apt to run away from it, purposely plead ignorance, and refuse to face it. We can only face it if we can mask it within a protective risk-based stance that guards us and makes both us (adults) and the children safe. Our protective stance is embedded in a discourse named and institutionalized as "risk management." A brief review of several online risk-management professional education opportunities assists in this initial critique.

The first example is a course, RiskAware® for Managed Care, offered by MedRisk®. The goal of the course is to assist physicians in handling liabilities associated with managed care. As advertised, when this course is completed participants will:

Distinguish characteristics of five types of managed care organizations.
Recognize how the doctor–patient relationship is formed and terminated in managed care.
Be able to reconcile sources of interpersonal conflict in managed care settings.
Know how to handle potential liabilities associated with cost containment.
Be able to apply defensible charting techniques to their own documentation practices.
Understand how their liability is determined when they participate in managed care. (www.medrisk.com)

In the next example, the Risk Management and Insurance Department at the University of Iowa identifies itself as a unit organized to minimize the risk of financial loss to the university through the identification and analysis of risk, implementation of loss control programs, and contractual transfer or other risk reduction or financing techniques. The Risk Management and Insurance Department administers insurance and self-insurance programs covering property and liability risks, including buildings, equipment, fine art, vehicles, fidelity, liability claims, and disaster response planning (www.uiowa.edu/~fusrm/index.html).

A&E Groups, whose slogan professes it will "Shield your employees, shield your company," is a company that seeks to alleviate "the weight of losses from workplace and school violence, accidents, employee theft, Workers' Compensation fraud, and sexual harassment litigation, all of which amount to billions of dollars each year in lost revenue, inventory, and personnel." A&E reveals that serious problems can "drain your profits, drive away productive employees, *and expose your company or educational institution to serious legal trouble and costly civil suits*" (emphasis theirs). As protection against these perils, A&E provides the following types of interactive training services and preventative maintenance programs to increase workplace and school safety, enhance staff morale, reduce loss, and improve staff retention:

1. A comprehensive workplace protection program for business teaches employees and management how to work together to shield your company from problems such as theft, violence, or sexual harassment.
2. A school violence prevention program trains your students, parents, and teachers to recognize and react to the early warning signs of alienation, harassment, and threatening behaviors that can lead to school violence.
3. A sexual harassment prevention program, which A&E Groups notes is a specialization area for their company as they are "developing comprehensive sexual harassment prevention programs for companies and organizations throughout the United States," meant to "Protect your students, protect your school." (www.aegroups.com)

Each of the companies named here and the thousands like them elsewhere provides risk-management consultancy services to a broad range of industries worldwide. In today's world, a company like Risk Solutions prides itself on providing balance in a volatile world, 1999 http://www.intrisksolutions.com.

In her recent theoretical paper on risk management and culture, Tamasailau Suaalii, a researcher at the University of Auckland, personalized her own research by interrogating the "insidious nature of risk and risk management" and the ways that this discourse is redistributing risk, knowingly shifting it from state to self through various forms of governmentality (Suaalii, 1999). Given the previous examples, it is not difficult to anticipate here how this redistribution of risk works, especially when one is forced to sit through mandatory in-service sessions, and engage at some level, easy-to-use professional development models that claim to help you manage risks:

1. Handle potential liabilities;
2. Apply defensible charting techniques to their own documentation practices;
3. Recognize how the doctor–patient relationship is formed and terminated in managed care;
4. Expose your company or educational institution to serious legal trouble and costly civil suits;
5. Shield your employees, shield your company;
6. In responding to the dramatic increase in sexual harassment claims and litigation;
7. The mission of risk management is to minimize the risk of financial loss through the identification and analysis of risk;
8. Providing balance in a volatile world (The Conservative Foundation, 1985)

As Suaalii (1999) speculates, this formal redistribution of risk repositions the individual (i.e., the teacher or the social worker) with new surveillance skills and she/he is now afforded refined techniques of "self- and social observation and judgment made possible through modern measurements—allow[ing] self-examination and self-limitation to seem normal" (Wagener, 1998, p. 150). If I'm taught to "handle liabilities, apply defensible charting techniques, minimize risk through identification and analysis, and consider the volatile world," how can I not be engaged in and further embody these various forms of governmentality? In fact I've now used "risk management" as an issue of my very first lecture to preservice teachers as I alert them about what to expect (Douglas, 1995; *Economist*, 1993; Ferudi, 1994; Fryer, 1993), and beg them to contest and fight against it or maybe more smartly, get out of the education field, now.

The quality of the lives of our children and their teachers is diminished through regimes of risk management/social control like no-touch. Certainly as a group of people who provide a wide range of services for young children, early childhood educators, social workers, child protective service specialists, teachers, caregivers, administrators, academics, and parents have passively sat back and knowingly allowed much to be done and said to and about us, especially related to no-touch. Collectively, we have been ignorant of intellectualizing and theorizing many of the critical, underlying issues evident throughout the collected research cited in this chapter.

Dangerous Desire

Just as I did as a teacher in the early 1980s (Johnson, 2000), representatives of many of the groups that serve children in various capacities today are allowing their collective identities to be created, to be *marked,* by moral panic (Jones, Bailey, & Santos, 2013). The growing popularity of no-touch policies such as no male diaper changing in child care, not allowing children to sit on caregiver laps, no hugging children on campus, and teaching caregivers how to appropriately touch/not touch children in their care, demonstrate this phenomenon. The relatively rare occurrence of sexual abuse in schools (in the United States, reported to occur in as few as 1% of all reported child sexual abuse cases in all schools, not just early education settings) should not define what we can and cannot do with the young children we serve as teachers and administrators (Contratto, 1986; Kitzinger, 1997).

As a field we must balance the likelihood of child abuse in our centers with the costs to our profession of our overzealous prevention (Adler, 1994; Green, 1998; Terzian, 1997). What is gained by our continued support of no-touch policies in early childhood education? Children are becoming more distrustful of adults, especially teachers; we continue to betray young children (and what we know about good early childhood practices) as we submit them to a variety of inappropriate sexual abuse curricula; caregivers are leaving the childcare profession en masse; potential talented male caregivers are looking elsewhere for employment opportunities; directors are likely to spend more money on liability than on teacher salaries; and misinformed legislators funnel millions of dollars into prevention programs that could otherwise be spent on educating our young in more effective ways (Johnson, 2000).

This reveals how far-reaching our practical and theoretical search must be in further understanding risk and risk awareness and in seeking to present alternative ways of thinking about the institutionalization, care, and teaching of young children (Howitt, 1993; Jóhannesson, 1998; Rose, 1990). Instead of simply dismissing no-touch as only a moral panic, I can instead interrogate why no-touch influenced me and other teachers and groups in particular ways at particular times (Johnson, 1997). This interrogation might then give rise to further questions and lead us to critique, as Stephens (1993) notes:

Other widespread public resonances as serious moral discourses on our time, and we might work towards developing the theoretical and methodological frameworks that would allow us to interpret the different kinds of truths embedded within contemporary discourses on threatened children. (p. 251)

Within this interrogation Stephens also pleads with us to consider how much we have thought about how no-touch affects the way children connect to one another, to care-givers and teachers, to familial cultural traditions, to local places, and to electronically mediated worlds that parents know little about.

I'm always keen for stories of no-touch, and I'm now not surprised at how often they appear and reappear. I was having coffee recently and quickly glimpsed the words "without touching her" on the cover of one of the many magazines (*Details*, 1999) available in this particular shop. Words like "touch" readily catch my now well-trained eyes; surveillance does work! I glanced through the article, and although this particular magazine story was basically a how-to article about seducing your adult partner, part of it actually relates to my own interests in no-touch, though not in seductive ways. The second paragraph reads:

> Touch yourself in a place that she would want to be touched, says clinical psychologist Judy Kuriansky, Ph.D. "You're suggesting you want to touch her. Soon you'll find her touching herself in those places, and the synchronicity creates a type of mirror, a subconscious connection." (p. 114)

I'm sharing this partly tongue-in-cheek (humor has helped me deal with the amazing ludicrousness of no-touch) and partly because it is profoundly related to the way(s) we're progressing with no-touch policies. When I try to imagine the classroom of the future, a classroom that will surely have less touch in it than even today, I can actually envision where this information would be helpful to me as the kids would see me hugging myself (like I want to hug them, to console), tousling my head of hair, see me stroking my shoulder (like I want to rub their shoulder to acknowledge their presence) or see me patting myself on the back. Heeding the professional advice of this article, this mimicry might in fact be creating a "subconscious connection" that no-touch policies instantly disallow.

When I look back, I'm amazed at how quickly we've become "disciplined…'socialized' into the [no-touch] culture, such that one is both enabled and also, in a quite specific sense, 'made safe'" (Green, 1998, p. 184). Remember my earlier soccer coaching story, about my skepticism over the introduction of the "child advocate" in relationship to "safe havens" for children? Let me briefly conclude that story here. In further discussions at that particular coaches' meeting, when I pushed the group slightly, I then found out the far-reaching extent of the policy, a policy that I was told will soon disallow adult males from coaching their female children without a female assistant coach. Again, all in the name of protection!

In this era of no-touch, I'm shocked with what body(s) I am left with, for now. Do my male-ness, my desire to teach and nurture young children, provide and mark me with a dangerous, normalized body? Although I don't want to believe this to be true, other discourses clearly say it is so. It is what I, what we, do with those "other" discourses that can lead us, in some emancipatory fashion, out of the disciplinary regime we find ourselves unintellectually trapped within. Our critical interrogation of the "techniques by which the [our] lives, thoughts, and desires…have become microscopically examined and strategically regulated" (Wagener, 1998, p. 150) can assist us in moving out of the dark place we now find ourselves.

Renaming Ourselves

I leave off slightly in despair as I consider the power of no no-touch, while continuing to theorize my/our place in all of this. In his critique of prisons, Foucault said that "This is a functional reduction of the body. But it is also an insertion of this body-segment in a whole ensemble over which it is articulated. The soldier whose body has been trained to function part by part for particular operations must in turn form an element in a mechanism at another level" (1977, p. 164). As a collective group of people who are concerned about and care for children, through our ignorance and silence, our most popular selective disciplinary techniques to date, we've "exercised a power of normalization" over each other and the children we serve, "allow[ing] for both the construction and maintenance of disciplinary power: while we observed and judged the lives, thoughts, actions, and souls of children" (Wagener, 1998, p. 157).

So ingrained is this power of no-touch, as a point of investigation and regulation, it has reorganized, restricted, and intensified relations with other institutions. The "reorganization, restriction, and intensification" disallows me from changing an infant's diaper in childcare, it forces you to submit yourself to fingerprint checks if you work with children, it forces daycare directors to have at least two staff (females too) on staff at all times, and it doesn't allow me to single-handedly coach my daughter and ten other 6- and 7-year-old girls twice a week on the soccer pitch. In New Zealand that same reorganization, restriction, and intensification assisted the Combined Early Childhood Union of Aotearoa (CECUA) in recommending the following center-based abuse-prevention policies:

1. Increased visibility—it protects both children and staff;
2. Adults must never be alone with a child or children;
3. Caregiving routines, such as toileting, bathing etc., should always be done by the center staff (staff who must never be alone or out-of-sight);
4. Good record keeping and communication with parents is essential. (1993)

The normalization of these types of surveillance and control policies (Duncan, 1997) allows us to continue regulating and producing popular notions of children and childhood as given; a predetermined, innocent, natural, protected, and carefree state, as if there is nothing more to be added to our theoretical deliberations about children. Foucault's work is vital here as he was engaged in rejecting the bureaucratic rationalization of the world that produces the "overwhelming sameness of it all" (Boyne, 1991, p. 139). As a somewhat active, yet critical member of the field of early childhood education, I think the field of early childhood education inspires the least amount of intellectual critique of all the social sciences, and is a reproductive field mostly interested in this "sameness" that Foucault critiqued. Maybe it is because of the ways we've defined children and childhood (e.g., carefree, given, innocent, natural, and to protect), or the way we've politicized our actions by exploiting children ("after all, children can't vote"), or the economy of the profession (i.e., low status, low pay, low reward structure). Nonetheless, as a field we have little power, and what little we do well is disciplined via the ability to "characterize, classify, specialize,…distribute along a scale, around a norm, hierarchize individuals in relation to one another" (Foucault, 1977, p. 231).

An example of this "classification, distribution along a scale, around a norm" is my recent study of sexuality in the field of early childhood education. Ken Plummer noted that, "Anyone who writes about sex these days stands at the intersection of a vast literature speaking about sex from every conceivable persuasion" (1995, p. x). Yet, the scant literature and research in the field of early childhood education is quite distant from the "intersection" Plummer notes. Critical issues of sexuality continue to present themselves in one form or another to our field (Dollimore, 1991; Gagnon & Parker, 1995; Grosz & Probyn, 1994; Irvine, 1995; Millet, 1984), yet other oppositional movements intent on "renaturalizing and reinstating 'ideal' or 'necessary' forms of relations" with children and families (Johnson, 1996) gain more notice and, instead, are placed at the forefront.

The body of research on children and sexuality closely matches the inscripted *body* (Grosz, 1995) of the young child—a pure, innocent, fragile, and immature *body* indeed (Shamgar-Handelman, 1994). Even while we pretend sexuality is not an important issue, that it doesn't exist for children and for the field of early childhood education, our ignorance protects us and keeps us theoretically safe (Stratton, 1996). We remain ignorant and silent at a time when we know children of all ages understand sexual life (Johnson, 1996; Lees, 1993; Zita, 1998). Our fearfulness and suspicion keep us at a safe distance from sexuality (Irvine, 1995), even at a time when sexuality has shifted from the margins to the center in many disciplines highly familiar and interrelated to our own work (Adkins & Merchant, 1996). We model our early childhood practices as we model our sexuality interactions with children by assuming, "We have a need for children to be ignorant. In the face of evidence that they know a lot about sex and birth and even about AIDS and death, we continue to insist that they don't know, can't know, shouldn't know" (Tobin, 1997, p. 136).

To me the previous examples provide clear testimony that our field has to open up to new possibilities (Sikes & Piper, 2010) and "pose different [the right] questions" (Frankenberg, 1992). Like the research on sexuality, another related example is moving beyond simple recognition of the normative, material body to grander visions of a "theory of the body, because human agency involves more than mere knowledge ability, consciousness and intention" (Turner, 1992, p. 91). Intellectual spaces like the opportunity to write this chapter and intellectual people like my co-authors in this collection give me hope. We too can choose to resist, to work against, by broadly (Ussher, 1997) "examining the boundaries of children's bodies and how these are experienced, constructed and shifted by the interpretations and translations of adults, children, nature, and technology" (James, Jenks, & Prout, 1998, p. 168). James, Jenks, and Prout note that "If the body is therefore to be apprehended as both biological and social— but unfinished…we would expect childhood to be one of the most intensive periods in which work on the body is accomplished" (p. 164). Similarly, Bryan Turner's work illustrates,

> The body is a product of knowledge which cannot exist independent of the practices which constantly produce it in time and space…if we are interested in the social representation, for example of the reproductive organs, then it makes sense to think of "the body" as a representation of power. If we are interested in how a missing limb has an impact on body image, then the psychological research of Paul Schilder may be more relevant than the approach of Foucault. (1992, p. 61)

Closing

Early childhood educators, parents, teachers, and administrators must interrogate our complicit beliefs in these ongoing, narrow constructions of children and childhood. For instance, one perspective would be to think of the different types of new conditions in our practice(s) that we can acknowledge, that make it possible to rethink touch (Felman, 1997), as we seek "rupture [as] the only apparent means of escape" (Shaafsma, 1997, p. 256). These new conditions, or new narratives, could mark an "emotional moving forward." In this active stance, we become more "defiant…[we] complain [we] yell" (Abbott, 1989, p. 39) about what we've witnessed and in regard to how we plan to move forward. In similar fashion, Lewis (1997) argues:

> We need ways to visualize the body and its foibles, its awkwardnesses, idiosyncrasies, fumblings and tentative possibilities. We need to address the silences around the real body—not that the "real body" can be fully narrated, but there are certain absences and gaps in everyday discourse about the real body which now carry enormous consequences. (p. 241)

These once untold political stories of transgression, desire, and of the unknown might then help to redefine or (re)position what it means to be a teacher of young children; what it means to be a child protective services case-worker who makes a critical decision to remove children from their home and place them in foster care; what it feels like to be the only male staff in a child care center; what a high school sexual-education curriculum should read like in the age of AIDS; and how college instructors teach early childhood caregivers and teachers about child sexuality.

References

Abbott, S. (1989). *View askew: Postmodern investigations.* San Francisco: Androgyne Books.

Adkins, L., & Merchant, V. (1996). Introduction. In L. Adkins & V. Merchant (Eds.), *Sexualizing the social: Power and the organization of sexuality* (pp. 1–11). New York: St. Martin's Press.

Adler, J. (1994, January 10). Kids growing up scared. *Newsweek*, 43–50.

Baker, B. (1998). "Childhood" in the emergence and spread of U. S. public schools. In T. S. Popkewitz, & M. Brennan (Eds.), *Foucault's challenge: Discourse, knowledge, and power in education* (pp. 117–143). New York: Teachers College Press.

Boyne, R. (1991). The art of the body in the discourse of postmodernity. In M. Featherstone, M. Hepworth, & B. S. Turner (Eds.), *In the body: Social process and cultural theory* (pp. 281–293). London: Sage.

Combined Early Childhood Union of Aotearoa (CECUA). (1993). *Preventing the sexual abuse of children within early childhood services. A practical resource kit.* ISBN13: 9780908828579.

Contratto, S. (1986). Child abuse and the politics of care. *Journal of Education, 168,* 70–79.

Details. (1999, August). Turn her on without touching her. *Details,* 114–117.

Dollimore, J. (1991). *Sexual dissidence: Augustine to Wilde, Freud to Foucault.* Oxford: Clarendon.

Douglas, T. (1995). *Scapegoats: Transferring blame.* New York: Routledge.

Duncan, J. (1997). *New Zealand kindergarten teachers and sexual abuse protection policies.* Unpublished manuscript.

Economist. (1993, February 27). State of the nation: Moral panic. *The Economist, 326,* 62.

Felman, S. (1997). Psychoanalysis and education: Teaching terminable and interminable. In S. Todd (Ed.), *Learning desire: Perspectives on pedagogy, culture, and the unsaid* (pp. 17–43). New York: Routledge.

Ferudi, F. (1994). A plague of moral panics. *Living Marxism, 73,* 20–23.

Foucault, M. (1977). *Discipline and punish: The birth of the prison.* London: Allen Lane.

Frankenberg, R. (1992). Foreword. In S. Scott, G. Williams, S. Platt, & H. Thomas (Eds.), *Private risks and public dangers* (pp. xv–xix). Hong Kong: Avebury.

Fryer, G. E. (1993). *Child abuse and the social environment.* San Francisco: Westview.

Gagnon, J. H., & Parker, R. G. (1995). Introduction: Conceiving sexuality. In R. Parker & J. Gagnon (Eds.), *Conceiving sexuality: Approaches to sex research in a postmodern world* (pp. 3–18). London: Routledge.

Green, B. (1998). Born-again teaching? Governmentality, "grammar," and public schooling. In T. Popkewitz & M. Brennan (Eds.), *Foucault's challenge: Discourse, knowledge, and power in education* (pp. 173–204). New York: Teachers College Press.

Grosz, E. (1995). *Space, time and perversion: Essays on the politics of bodies.* London: Routledge.

Grosz, E., & Probyn, E. (1994). Introduction. In E. Grosz & E. Probyn (Eds.), *Sexy bodies: The strange carnalities of feminism* (pp. ix–xv). London: Routledge.

Holliday, J., & Hassard, R. (2001). *Contested bodies.* New York: Routledge.

Howitt, D. (1993). *Child abuse errors: When good intentions go wrong.* New Brunswick: Rutgers University Press.

Irvine, J. M. (1995). *Sexuality education across cultures: Working with differences.* San Francisco: Jossey-Bass.

James, A., Jenks, C., & Prout, A. (1998). *Theorizing childhood.* New York: Teachers College Press.

Jóhannesson, I. A. (1998). Genealogy and progressive politics: Reflections on the notion of usefulness. In T. Popkewitz & M. Brennan (Eds.), *Foucault's challenge: Discourse, knowledge, and power in education* (pp. 297–315). New York: Teachers College Press.

Johnson, R. (1996). Sexual dissonances: Or the "impossibility" of sexual education. *Curriculum Studies, 4,* 163–189.

Johnson, R. (1997). Contested borders, contingent lives: An introduction. In D. L. Steinberg, D. Epstein, & R. Johnson (Eds.), *Border patrols: Policing the boundaries of heterosexuality* (pp. 1–32). London: Cassell.

Johnson, R. T. (2000). *Hands off!: The disappearance of touch in the care of children.* New York: Peter Lang.

Johnson, R. T. (2011a, May). *Hands off young people! The practice, policy, and politics of touch.* Symposium presented at the Congress of Qualitative Inquiry, Urbana, IL, USA.

Johnson, R. T. (2011b, October). Body representations in early childhood education: Interrogating teacher education *through collective story constellations.* Paper presented at the conference on Reconceptualizing Early Childhood Education: Research, theory and practice, London, U.K.

Johnson, R. T. (2012, March). Ways of being (seeing) with children in sporting and pedagogical contexts. Paper presented at the Annual International Globalization, Diversity and Education Conference. Vancouver, WA.

Johnson, R. T. (2013). Contesting contained bodily coaching experiences. *Sport, Education and Society.* DOI: 10.1080/13573322.2012.761964.

Jones, R. L., Bailey, J., & Santos, S. (2013). Coaching, caring and the politics of touch: A visual exploration. *Sport, Education and Society.* DOI:10.1080/13573322.2013.769945.

Kitzinger, J. (1997). Who are you kidding? Children, power and the struggle against sexual abuse. In A. James & A. Prout (Eds.), *Constructing and reconstructing childhood: Contemporary issues in the sociological study of childhood* (pp. 157–183). Washington, DC: Falmer.

Lees, S. (1993). *Sugar and spice: Sexuality and adolescent girls.* London: Penguin.

Lewis, J. (1997). "So how did your condom use go last night, daddy?" Sex talk and daily life. In L. Segal (Ed.), *New sexual agendas* (pp. 238–252). New York: New York University Press.

Millet, K. (1984). Beyond politics? Children and sexuality. In C. Vance (Ed.), *Pleasure and danger: Exploring female sexuality* (pp. 217–224). Melbourne: Routledge.

National Public Radio. (1994, January 4). Day Care center goes to extremes to protect reputation. *Morning Edition.* Washington, DC: NPR.

O'Loughlin, M. (1995). Daring the imagination: Unlocking voices of dissent and possibility in teaching. *Theory Into Practice, 34*(2), 107–116.

Phillipson, M., & Fisher, C. (1999). Seeing becoming drawing: The interplay of eyes, hands and surfaces in the drawing of Pierre Bonnard. In I. Heywood & B. Sandywell (Eds.), *Interpreting visual culture: Explorations in the hermeneutics of the visual* (pp. 125–144). New York: Routledge.

Piper, H. (2010, May 26). *Touch, risk, allegation: Safeguarding whom?* Department of Social Work and Social Policy, University of Nottingham.

Piper, H., & Stronach, I. (2008). *Don't touch! The educational story of a panic.* London: Routledge.

Plummer, K. (1995). *Telling sexual stories: Power, change and social worlds.* New York: Routledge.

Rose, N. (1990). *Governing the soul: The shaping of the private self.* New York: Routledge.

Shaafsma, D. (1997). Performing the self: Constructing written and curricular fictions. In T. Popkewitz & M. Brennan (Eds.), *Foucault's challenge: Discourse, knowledge, and power in education* (pp. 255–277). New York: Teachers College Press.

Shamgar-Handelman, L. (1994). To whom does childhood belong? In J. Qvortrup, M. Bardy, G. Sgritta, & H. Wintersberger (Eds.), *Childhood matters: Social theory, practice and politics* (pp. 249–256). Hong Kong: Avebury.

Sikes, P., & Piper, H. (2010). *Researching sex and lies in the classroom: Allegations of sexual misconduct in schools.* London: Routledge.

Stephens, S. (1993). Children at risk: Constructing social problems and policies. *Childhood, 1,* 246–251.

Stratton, J. (1996). *The desirable body: Cultural fetishism and the erotics of consumption.* New York: Manchester University Press.

Suaalii, T. (1999, October). Collective responsibility, neoliberal conditions, and sexual risk: Theorizing Samoan events of *"toso teine."* Paper presented at the Annual Pacific Islands Studies Conference, Honolulu, HI.

Terzian, P. (1997, November 5). Childcare dilemma: The trouble with the Woodward case. *Honolulu Advertiser.*

The Conservative Foundation. (1985). *Risk assessment and risk control.* Washington, DC: The Conservative Foundation.

Tobin, J. (1997). Playing doctor in two cultures: The United States and Ireland. In J. Tobin (Ed.), *Making a place for pleasure in early childhood education* (pp. 119–158). New Haven: Yale University Press.

Turner, B. S. (1992). *Regulating bodies: Essays in medical sociology.* New York: Routledge.

Ussher, J. (1997). Towards a material-discursive analysis of madness, sexuality and reproduction. In J. Ussher (Ed.), *Body talk: The material and discursive regulation of sexuality, madness and reproduction* (pp. 1–9). New York: Routledge.

Wagener, J. R. (1998). The construction of the body through sex education discourse practices. In T. Popkewitz & M. Brennan (Eds.), *Foucault's challenge: Discourse, knowledge, and power in education* (pp. 144–169). New York: Teachers College Press.

Zita, J. N. (1998). *Body talk: Philosophical reflections on sex and gender.* New York: Columbia University Press.

SEVEN

Social Justice, Risk, and Imaginaries

Susan Grieshaber and Felicity McArdle

Even though it is 20 years since the first Reconceptualizing Early Childhood Education Conference was held and much work has been undertaken in regard to using alternative theoretical and philosophical perspectives, the current state of the field suggests little headway has been made in reconceptualizing early childhood education and early childhood teacher education programs. Our focus in this chapter is the (missing) dimension of social justice perspectives. We understand social justice to mean a more equitable distribution of societal resources and explain this in greater depth in the section "Social Justice." We consider some of the limitations for the field in dealing with issues of equity, access, and social justice and the reasons for this. A preference for normalization and standardization of thought and practice in terms of what is and can be known is almost always accompanied by governance and regulation that is both technical and instrumental. Possibilities for alternatives are increasingly obscured by the battery of measures, standards, norms, and tests. Our argument relates to how "equity is couched in a new technical vocabulary of risk management, market choice and quality assurance" (Luke, 2013, p. 144). To develop this argument, we look particularly at the concept of risk and draw on both early childhood education and early childhood teacher education. We consider how resistance and "risky practices" can be matters of social justice, and in conclusion, we propose some imaginaries that manage risk through including it as an integral factor in learning, not through continuous (and fruitless) efforts to eliminate risk. We begin by discussing the influence of developmental and human capital perspectives and how these perspectives, in their attempts to "manage" risk, leave little room for social justice and equity.

Social Justice

Early childhood education and early childhood teacher education programs in many western contexts remain dominated by child developmental theories and accompanying prescriptions for practice. A developmental perspective implies educator expertise in child development and prescribes particular ways in which practice is implemented. Developmentally appropriate practice might encompass child-centered approaches, constructivism, and play. The presumption here is that such approaches meet all children's needs. Obviously, one of the purposes of schooling is to foster/nurture/encourage/oversee children's development.

Schooling serves other purposes as well, some overtly, and others are perhaps more nuanced. In their examination of workforce issues, Little and Bartlett (2010) nominate developmentalism as one of the five aspects that constitute the purposes of schooling—the other four being humanist, democratic equality, social justice, and human capital. While combinations of these perspectives are possible, it is the human capital approach that dominates current debates, both about the qualifications needed to teach and the outcomes of teaching (Little & Bartlett, 2010). This logic places the labor market as significantly influencing the types of knowledge and skills that are valued. And this influence is not confined to the workforce. Early childhood settings and classrooms, as well as early childhood teacher education programs, are vulnerable to and also highly influenced by human capital perspectives. Likewise, educational policies are, according to Rizvi and Lingard (2010), "driven more by the values of the market and system efficiency than by cultural and community values such as justice and democracy" (p. 116).

Our concern is that because of the dominance of developmental perspectives and human capital theory, early childhood education and early childhood teacher education pay little attention to those other perspectives—humanist, democratic equality, and social justice. Even though early childhood education in the United States has been a medium for social reform since the mid-1960s through Head Start, the original programs were based on notions of deficit rather than social justice and equity. And the pervasive influence of the normative view in child development means that it still carries enormous authority, with developmental norms used as standards against which children are measured and compared. The problem with developmental norms has always been that they were created from a select group of children and generalized to the child population as a whole (Weber, 1984). Anyone who didn't compare favorably was cause for concern and potential intervention. For some, this equates with goals of democracy, and success for all. It is not unusual for publicly funded early childhood education to be unapologetically aimed at achieving social, political, and economic ends. Nevertheless, there is a difference between funding based on ideas of remedying deficits and those based on social justice and equity.

In education policy, equality is often confused with equity. This is most noticeable with discussions about access to educational opportunities and assumptions that "access alone is enough to produce educational justice" (Rizvi & Lingard, 2010, p. 157). By itself, access cannot produce educational justice or equitable outcomes. Social justice is a contested term, but we understand it to go well beyond access. For instance, a socially just society would involve redistributing societal resources more fairly so that the structure of society and dint of birth are not the sole determinants of who gets what. The achievement of social justice and equity also includes issues of identities, difference, culture, and representation. By necessity, this involves "respect, recognition, rights, opportunities and power" (Rizvi & Lingard, 2010, p. 160).

Developmental psychology is an important area of study, but as Bruce Fuller (2007) remarks in his book *Standardized Childhood*, it has concealed understandings of "social ideals and institutional practices" (p. xxii) that sculpt the institutional settings we create for young children. And, we argue, these institutional settings enact particular versions of respect, recognition, rights, opportunities, and power for the children who inhabit them.

Standards

If developmental psychology is constructed as a universal framework for all children, then the currently popular technologies of standards goes hand in hand with this. A "common-sense" approach to ensuring success for all is to settle/agree on a "standard" (of excellence, performance, achievement, behavior) and to then set about ensuring that every child/student/preservice teacher/practicing teacher can produce evidence that they meet this standard. It is argued that setting these standards works to raise expectations in so-called disadvantaged populations that otherwise might be "exempted"/sidelined from a "standard" education (see, for example, Sarra, 2011).

Standards, interpreted in this way, work like norms. Kagan (2012) sees standards as a universal solution to aligning "early childhood pedagogy and early learning systems" (p. 65). Universal adoption is already occurring: Ghana, Fiji, Romania, and Mongolia are mentioned in Kagan's work as successful examples of a UNICEF-backed "integrated approach to standards" (p. 65). But this integrated approach seems to be about standardizing everything. In the processes of governance and regulation of standards, thought and practices have also become standardized—standards for improving instruction; standards for guiding what parents and the public should know and expect of early childhood education; standards for curricula development; standardized checklists for children's progress; standards for state and/or national monitoring; standards to improve teacher preparation; and standards for teacher education program evaluation (Kagan, 2012). Popular products such as painting by numbers reduce something so complex as the art of painting to a series of simple steps. Likewise the complexity of teaching is reduced to standardized and technical prescriptions—all that is needed is to simply work to standards (numbers/colors) in order to achieve better outcomes. And this is argued as an equity issue. The claim here is that the introduction and regulation of standards ensures "all students—not just the privileged—will have access to challenging content. In doing so, standards level the playing field and promote equity" (Kagan, 2012, p. 58). The fundamental difference between equity and equality comes back again to access. Equality of access to challenging content (whether in school, early childhood education, or teacher education) does not ensure equity, and cannot alone guarantee equitable outcomes. Presuming that universal access is possible, at most this simply enables equal access to challenging content.

The approach to curriculum standards as described by Kagan (2012) seems to illustrate what Luke, Woods, and Weir (2013) would call high-definition curriculum—that is, "extremely elaborated, detailed and enforced technical specifications" (p. 7). Their argument goes on to caution against such an approach, since "over-prescription in the technical form of the curriculum has the effect of constraining teacher professionalism and eventually deskilling teachers, and that as a consequence less equitable educational outcomes ensue" (p. 7). Here, the effect of standardizing teaching is to produce less equitable educational outcomes, even while the stated intent is the opposite.

Similarly, standardizing childhood leads to less equitable outcomes. As Fuller (2007) sees it, differences in child rearing valued by ethnic communities are being pushed aside in the quest to build a universal system that standardizes childhood. He talks of the "contested ideals of development and cultural diversity" (p. xx) and how cultural differences of families are often not considered in the "fusion of school accountability programs with the new push to standardize childhood" (p. xx). In one example, he refers to the drive by kindergarten teachers in public preschools to focus on "narrower academic skills" (p. xx) so that children are prepared for school. In some cases, this has been shown to result in young children knowing more before they commence formal schooling and, in fact, "un-learning" and becoming less competent as a result of their encounters with formal schooling.

On the question of cultural differences, it is claimed that, in relation to the standardized approach to early childhood education advocated by Kagan (2012), the standards are developed "consensually" (p. 65). According to this understanding, standards are as "comprehensive and culturally sensitive as possible" (p. 66), since they are grounded in "the mores of those who create them, so that they reflect the goals, values and desires that adults hold for their children" (p. 66). Our question is whose voices were heard and whose ideas, values, goals, and desires are reflected in the standards?

The experience in Canada with First Nations peoples and the Early Development Index (EDI) was not without controversy and revealed that lengthy, respectful, and ongoing consultation was required in attempts to develop a culturally sensitive index. We ask whether a culturally sensitive index is indeed possible given the many points of mismatch between ideals of child development, equity, and respectful ways of acknowledging cultural diversity in early childhood settings. Amongst other things, the development of the EDI involved negotiations with Elders and concerns about Indigenous languages, identity development, cultural values, and designing research protocols for the ownership and usage of any resulting data (Aboriginal Advisory Group for Best Start in Toronto—Guiding Principles). And finally we ask, what other social ideals and institutional practices are concealed in the creation of measures such as the EDI that might only be revealed after they have been in use? And what are the risks for the families and communities concerned?

Risk

Weather is now a "risk event." We used to experience the weather as an almost random occurrence, although with some element of prediction from the Weather Bureau, based on accumulated records and data, that was subjected to analysis and prediction. In his response to an earlier Education Commission Report, Slattery (1995) used the weather system to illustrate postmodern concepts of time, and chaos theory, and the idea that weather was predictable to a degree, and also unpredictable. However, due to climate change, it seems that this "randomness" and unpredictability of the weather is no longer acceptable. The demand for warnings and preparedness for storms, droughts, and flooding rains has seen the weather produced as a much more modernist concept, and the risks (economic and social) that come with these catastrophes are to be managed and controlled. Risk talk has produced weather as "risk events": risk is news, and it is bad.

The *Oxford English Dictionary* defines risk as both a noun and a verb. As a noun, risk is explained as a "situation involving exposure to danger." As a verb (with an object), risk is to "expose (someone or something valued) to danger, harm, or loss." Risk is therefore defined as the potential for undesired results, and the negative logic that now accompanies this understanding is so dominant that it is almost impossible to think of risk as a positive. The growing aversion to risk in contemporary western societies has been documented by Gill (2007), and in the developmental psychology literature risk-taking behavior is associated with "some probability of undesirable results" (Boyer, 2006, p. 291). However, the news is not all bad as risk can have positive and negative outcomes (Madge & Barker, 2007). The work of risk managers is to try to minimize the possibility that something might go wrong. Nevertheless, talk of risk, associated dangers, and its elimination create expectations of a risk-free state. Risk talk produces a certain kind of knowledge, and the negative logic that accompanies current risk talk means a shift from managing "goods" to managing "bads" (McWilliam & Taylor, 2012). The risk industry, with its systems, operating manuals, audits, and codes of ethics all provide references for those who know risk, can identify risk, and seek to solve the problem of risk. Governments and infrastructure desire risk elimination, or, at the very least, minimization. As accountability mechanisms, audits, operating manuals, and lists of professional standards are supposed to ensure safety and guard against damage, risk is equated with damage and danger, and risk-as-danger must be prevented or minimized. While there are those who have expertise in risk management, all professionals are expected to have knowledge about risk as part of their professional expertise.

Risk-as-Danger

As risk has come to be equated with danger, so too have children come to be understood and spoken of as subjects in need of protection against risk. Indeed, it might be said that children are now almost constructed as risk events. A good example is children's risky play in early childhood settings in contemporary western societies such as the U.S., the U.K., and Australia. When seen from the perspective of risk-as-danger, understandings of children's risky play in these countries is very different from Scandinavian countries such as Norway (see Sandseter, 2009). Consistent with our previous understandings about risk, Sandseter describes risky play as "thrilling and exciting forms of play that involve a risk of physical injury" (p. 93). Safety standards and legislation are now features of settings where children play; and for many early childhood educators, risk assessment is a part of daily working life. Attention to establishing standards has been accompanied by growing concerns about the over-protective nature of contemporary western societies and the regulation of children and childhood (e.g., Stephenson, 2003; Little, 2006). The argument follows the line that children cannot be protected from risks at all times during play and that learning to manage the challenge of risks is an important part of children's development (Adams, 2001).

In Australia, practitioners have acknowledged the value of children's risky play but they are limited by factors such as regulatory requirements and a litigious environment (Little, Sandseter, & Wyver, 2012). Little and colleagues lament the increasing restriction on and control over outdoor play in Australian early childhood settings, remarking that the lack of "sufficiently challenging activities…often resulted in children seeking challenge and at times [engaging in] inappropriate risk-taking in other areas of the physical environment" (p. 308). Other Australian studies have produced similar concerns, with Fenech, Sumsion, and Goodfellow (2006) and Brown and Sumsion (2007) finding that factors associated with standards and accountability compromised the way in which teachers offered children opportunities for challenging play. An overemphasis on safety created an environment of surveillance for both teachers and children, thus restricting what was offered, and therefore the type of play in which children could engage.

Climbing trees is one of the more "risky" types of activities that have come to be understood as a risk management exercise in Australian early childhood settings. It is not that tree climbing is actively discouraged, although this may occur in some places because of the way in which the regulations are interpreted. Rather, it is likely that tree climbing is not actively encouraged because of the risk involved. It has become difficult, if not impossible, to think of children climbing trees without considering the risk involved, and the imminent danger inherent in the activity, of managing something "bad." While precise information about risks in childhood is not possible, Madge and Barker (2007) have used data that is available from the U.K. to compile estimates of the risks children face. The risk of playground injuries for children is far less than the likelihood of their being injured at home, or being involved in a car accident. Nevertheless, the monitoring of risky play has become part of the work of early childhood educators in Australia and the teachers' work is shaped by the risk-as-danger discourse. Managing perceived risk has produced policies and processes aimed at risk minimization, and preferably risk neutralization.

Risk-as-Creativity

Risk has not always been equated with danger. When answers are unknown, there is always the potential for undesired results. But this risk has not always been thought of as bad. For instance, when early explorers set out to sail beyond the horizon, risk was as much about excitement, anticipation, and daring as it was about danger. When the impressionists, like Monet, exhibited in France, their paintings were at first rejected by the conventional art community in Paris. If artists and scientists had stayed with what was known, taken a poll to determine consensus, stuck with standards and manuals, and limited themselves to already established measures, or what could be measured—then no new knowledge would have been created. Good scientists and philosophers cultivate doubt and skepticism. For new knowledge to be generated, risk is involved.

According to Leadbeater (2000), it is knowledge, not ignorance, that stops us from taking risks. He refers to the notion of "useful ignorance," and the discomfort that comes with unfamiliar ideas. If we learn to welcome error (Claxton, 2004) as instructive, then we are more likely to experiment, try out new ideas and new combinations of ideas, invent new solutions, and develop creativity. The risk that comes with not knowing can be the spark for curiosity and inquiry, and eventually the pleasure in acquiring new knowledge or creating new ideas.

This is not to say that skepticism should be left to develop into cynicism; rather, radical doubt can serve to spark the search for new ideas. The important thing is to know what to do when you don't know what to do (Claxton, 2004). Not knowing what to do is not necessarily a crisis. It is the work of teachers to prepare children for a future that we do not know. If creativity is one of the new basics (see Luke & Primary Principals' Association, 2002; McArdle & Grieshaber, 2012), then children need to learn and develop creativity, teachers need to teach creativity, and children need creative teachers. The risk involved in teaching for what cannot be known applies in teacher education as well as in early-years settings and classrooms.

Risk and Professional Standards for Teachers

If children's risky play in early childhood settings in Australia has been compromised because of an overemphasis on being accountable for implementing standards, what might this mean about risk in other areas of teaching and for teacher education? This leads us to contemplate how professional standards for teachers address the question of risk. To this end, we explore aspects of the Professional Standards for Queensland Teachers (Queensland College of Teachers, 2006) and the (Australian) National Professional Standards for Teachers (Australian Institute for Teaching and School Leadership, 2011). The Australian National Professional Standards for Teachers have subsumed previous state standards, such as the Professional Standards for Queensland Teachers (Queensland College of Teachers, 2006), but we explore this latter document because of the way in which it included risk.

In the ten Professional Standards for Queensland Teachers (Queensland College of Teachers, 2006), the word "risk" appears four times in 20 pages, in Standards 3 and 7.

Standard 3: Title: Design And Implement Intellectually Challenging Learning Experiences

PRACTICE:

> *Engage students in learning activities that involve higher-order thinking skills, imagination, creativity, intellectual **risk** taking and problem solving.* (Standard 3, p. 9; emphasis added)

KNOWLEDGE:

> *Teaching and learning strategies for promoting higher-order thinking skills, imagination, creativity, intellectual **risk** taking, critical analysis, reflection and problem solving.* (Standard 3, p. 9; emphasis added)

VALUES:

> *Promoting and modeling creativity, imagination and intellectual **risk** taking.* (Standard 3, p. 9; emphasis added)

Standard 7: Title: Create And Maintain Safe And Supportive Learning Environments

PRACTICE:

> *Undertake explicit teaching of skills to assist students to assume responsibility for themselves and behave responsibly towards others, participate in decision making, work collaboratively and independently, and feel **safe to risk** full participation in learning.* (Standard 7, p. 13; emphasis added). (Queensland College of Teachers, 2006)

In designing and implementing intellectually challenging learning experiences (Standard 3), teachers are required to demonstrate that they engage students in practical activities that involved intellectual risk taking. Teachers are also required to demonstrate that they have knowledge of strategies that promote intellectual risk taking. And they are directed to demonstrate an attitude or belief that would indicate that they value the promotion and modeling of intellectual risk taking.

In Standard 7, which focuses on the learning environment, teachers are expected to demonstrate their capacity to create and maintain spaces where students feel safe to risk full participation in learning. In Standard 3, the risk is intellectual. In Standard 7, where the learning environment might be physical, the word "risk" is coupled with "safe." Nevertheless, in both standards that mention risk, it is constructed as something positive and advantageous to creating meaningful learning environments and teaching strategies, and engaging students in learning. In the more recent Australian National Professional Standards for Teachers (Australian Institute for Teaching and School Leadership, 2011), which have subsumed the state versions of Professional Standards for Teachers, the word "risk" makes no appearance in the 24 pages of this document. This is significant in two ways. First, there is no encouragement for teachers to engage students in intellectual risk taking in the positive ways that it was encouraged in the standards identified by the state of Queensland (2006). Second, the National Professional Standards for Teachers (Australian Institute for Teaching and School Leadership, 2011) claim that use of the standards "will improve educational outcomes for students" (p. 2). The National Professional Standards look like accountability measures that work to audit and circumscribe what teachers are supposed to do (improve outcomes for students). The positive risks encouraged in the Queensland standards have been eliminated in preference for (risk-free?) standardized knowledge, practices, and values that will supposedly deliver improved outcomes for students. In this current culture of audits and accountability, teacher knowledge and professional expectations are standardized. According to Mulcahy (in Brenneis, Shore, & Wright, 2003), this sort of thing does not result in high standards of knowledge or performance, but rather, a "high standard of standardness" (p. 7). In high standards of standardness, there is no place for risk taking or creativity.

Risk and Teacher Education

The backgrounds of children attending early childhood education continue to diversify, yet the composition of the teaching service in the U.S. remains "racially, ethnically, culturally, and linguistically homogeneous" (Little & Bartlett, 2010, p. 288). The story is the same in Australia, with the majority of qualified teachers identifying as white, Anglo, monolingual, and female (McKenzie, Rowley, Weldon, & Murphy, 2011; Reid, 2005). Less than 1% of teachers and leaders identified as being of Aboriginal and Torres Strait Islander origin, which is lower than in the Australian population as a whole (McKenzie et al., 2011). One ongoing issue facing many western countries with a similar teacher demographic is how to "tackle the problems of enduring inequity" (Little & Bartlett, 2010, p. 288).

As we see it, the problem for early childhood teacher education is how to make meaningful connections with those communities and families whose origins are different from the homogeneous teacher demographic. While there is increasing recognition of local ways of knowing, being, and doing and the value of linguistic and cultural diversity, there is scant evidence of change in approaches to teacher education. Matters of cultural diversity must begin, in every country, with knowledge of the original peoples of the land. In Australian teacher education institutions, for instance, little space is made in the curriculum for acknowledging, much less understanding, the complexities of Indigenous knowledge systems (Moreton-Robinson, Singh, Kolopenuk, & Robinson, 2012). And the few attempts that there are to embed Indigenous knowledges in teacher education must first deal with the resistance of preservice students to any interrogation of their position (of privilege) in Australian society in relation to Aboriginal and Torres Strait Islander peoples and cultures (Phillips, 2011).

With Australia's unique version of multiculturalism, it would seem logical that early child-hood settings with populations of children from many different countries of origin might be well-served by teachers with a range of beliefs, ethnicities, and cultures. However, the teaching qualifications of migrants are not always recognized in their new countries and many find themselves working in early childhood education, where their qualifications are not required. Here, in order to be considered "professional," in settings where child-development perspectives dominate, these migrant educators often have to leave their experiential, tacit, and intuitive knowledge systems at the front door (Jipson, 1991) rather than bring these understandings to the contexts in which they work.

If developmental approaches are the only framework, another problem is how teacher educators prepare quality teachers when it is not possible to determine the kinds of work in which children will eventually be employed, or even the kinds of life worlds they will experience. "Readiness" for what? The paradox of being well-prepared to teach is not lost on those teacher educators who espouse a pedagogy that is responsive to site-specific individuals and groups who are diverse and part of particular cultural, social, and other contexts. For these educators, there is no single standardized formula for teaching. However, conducting a teacher education class that resists certainty and encourages experimentation and skepticism has its own risks.

Conclusion

In another 20 years, one certainty is that the project of reconceptualizing early childhood will still be necessary. The only thing stopping this would be if educators were no longer thinkers. Rather than present a grim *Planet of the Apes* view of the future, we prefer to take a creatively optimistic position and imagine a future where early childhood teachers carry status in society because of their significant contributions to the community. They are a diverse workforce, with flexible and varied ways of working with young children. Early childhood settings are places of science, arts, adventures in learning and creativity, influencing the communities and schools around them. Early childhood teachers are admired and respected for their values, attitudes, and expertise. Early childhood teacher educators are leaders of pedagogy and research, and have been instrumental in reengaging students and the reenchantment of teaching and learning. And, in another 20 years (hopefully fewer), it will be the task of the reconceptualizers to not only imagine, but enact, a world that is more fair, just, and equitable.

References

Adams, J. (2001). *Risk*. London: Routledge.

Australian Institute for Teaching and School Leadership (AITSL). (2011). *National professional standards for teachers*. Canberra, ACT: MCEEDYA.

Boyer, T. W. (2006). The development of risk taking: A multi-perspective review. *Developmental Review, 26*, 291–345.

Brenneis, D., Shore, C., & Wright, S. (2003, November 21). Audit culture and the politics of accountability: The price of bureaucratic peace. Paper presented at the Presidential Panel of AAA, Chicago.

Brown, K., & Sumsion, J. (2007). Voices from the other side of the fence: Early childhood teachers' experiences with mandatory regulatory requirements. *Contemporary Issues in Early Childhood, 8*(1), 30–49.

Claxton, G. (2004). Learning is learnable (and we ought to teach it). In Sir J. Cassell (Ed.), *Ten years on: The National Commission for Education report*. U.K., Retrieved February 12, 2014 from http://www.guyclaxton.com/document/new/learning/slearnable.pdf

Fenech, M., Sumsion, J., & Goodfellow, J. (2006). The regulatory environment in long day care: A 'double-edged sword' for early childhood professional practice. *Australian Journal of Early Childhood, 31*(3), 49–58.

Fuller, B. (2007). *Standardized childhood: The political and cultural struggle over early education*. Stanford CA: Stanford University Press.

Gill, T. (2007). *No fear: Growing up in a risk averse society*. London: Calouste Gulbenkian Foundation.

Jipson, J. (1991). Developmentally appropriate practice: Culture, curriculum, connections. *Early Education and Development, 2*(2), 120–136.

Kagan, S. L. (2012). Early learning and development standards: An elixir for early childhood systems reform. In S. L. Kagan & K. Kauerz (Eds.), *Early childhood systems: Transforming early learning* (pp. 55–70). New York: Teachers College Press.

Leadbeater, C. (2000). *Living on thin air: The new economy*. New York: Viking.

Little, H. (2006). Children's risk-taking behaviour: Implications for early childhood policy and practice. *International Journal of Early Years Education, 14*(2), 141–154.

Little, H., Sandseter, E. B. H., & Wyver, S. (2012). Early childhood teachers' beliefs about children's risky play in Australia and Norway. *Contemporary Issues in Early Childhood, 13*(4), 300–316.

Little, J. W., & Bartlett, L. (2010). The teacher workforce and problems of educational equity. *Review of Research in Education, 34*(1), 285–328.

Luke, A. (2013). Generalizing across borders: Policy and the limits of educational science. In A. Luke, A. Woods, & K. Weir (Eds.), *Curriculum, syllabus design and equity: A primer and model* (pp. 144–161). New York: Routledge.

Luke, A., & Primary Principals' Association. (2002). *The new basics: Productive pedagogies* [Video recording]. Hindmarsh, South Australia: SAPPA.

Luke, A., Woods, A., & Weir, K. (2013). Curriculum design, equity and the technical form of the curriculum. In A. Luke, A. Woods, & K. Weir (Eds.), *Curriculum, syllabus design and equity: A primer and model* (pp. 6–39). New York: Routledge.

Madge, N., & Barker, J. (2007). *Risk and childhood*. London: Royal Society for the Encouragement of the Arts, Manufactures & Commerce.

McArdle, F., & Grieshaber, S. (2012). The creativity dis-ease: Or where in the world is creativity? In O. Saracho (Ed.), *Contemporary perspectives on creativity in early childhood education* (pp. 135–157). Charlotte, NC: Information Age Publishing.

McKenzie, P., Rowley, G., Weldon, P., & Murphy, M. (2011). *Staff in Australia's schools 2012: Main report on the survey*. Camberwell, Victoria, Australia: Australian Council for Educational Research.

McWilliam, E., & Taylor, P. (2012, March). Personally significant learning: Why our kids need a powerful disposition to be self-managing learners when they finish their schooling, why they are unlikely to have it, and what we can do about it. Paper for The Innovate ZIS Think Tank 'Learning 2030: Schools Out?' Conference, Zurich, Switzerland.

Moreton-Robinson, A., Singh, D., Kolopenuk, J., & Robinson, A. (2012, February). Learning the lessons? Preservice teacher preparation for teaching Aboriginal and Torres Strait Islander students. Brisbane, Australia: QUT Indigenous Studies Research Network.

Phillips, J. (2011). *Resisting contradictions: Non-Indigenous pre-service teacher responses to critical Indigenous studies* (Unpublished PhD thesis). Queensland University of Technology, Brisbane, Australia.

Queensland College of Teachers. (2006). *Professional standards for Queensland teachers*. Toowong, Queensland, Australia: Queensland College of Teachers.

Reid, C. (2005). Global teachers with global cases. *Australian Journal of Education, 49*(3), 251–263.

Rizvi, F., & Lingard, B. (2010). *Globalizing education policy*. New York: Routledge.

Sandseter, E. B. H. (2009). Children's expressions of exhilaration and fear in risky play. *Contemporary Issues in Early Childhood, 10*(2), 92–106.

Sarra, C. (2011). *Strong and smart. Towards a pedagogy for emancipation: Education for First Peoples*. New York: Routledge.

Slattery, P. (1995). A postmodern vision of time and learning: A response to the National Education Commission Report *Prisoners of Time*. *Harvard Educational Review, 65*(4), 612–633.

Stephenson, A. (2003). Physical risk-taking: Dangerous or endangered? *Early Years, 23*(1), 35–43.

Weber, E. (1984). *Ideas influencing early childhood education: A theoretical analysis*. New York: Teachers College Press.

EIGHT

What About Learning?

Liane Mozère

Two articles I have recently read strongly influence this chapter: "Why Have We Met to Talk About Deleuze, and Why Write Just Now On and Around His *Œuvre*?" by René Lemieux (Giroux, Lemieux, & Cheniér, 2009); and the other is by Ronald Bogue, "Search, Swim and See" (in Semetsky, 2008). Reading these led me to try and understand what it had meant for me and for our little group of radical libertarian students in 1960, involved as we were in politics, to have encountered Félix Guattari in 1965 and, for me at least, to have worked along with him until his death in 1992. What also had it meant to have met Gilles Deleuze in 1969 in Félix's house? It was clear these two crossing points had to do with what Bogue has argued about learning, and more precisely, how one learns to swim. I'll try to develop three main points. First, I will try to express what and how I learned from this closeness. Second, I will argue about what it means for learning, if one is instructed via swimming—this being particularly close to what always troubles us in early childhood. I will do so by commenting on a major political event closely linked to what Guattari called "Ecosophy" (1992); that is, the European elections in 2009 and their pathetic outcome today—strikingly meaningful in relation to Deleuzo–Guattarian tools. Third, I will try to question what and how collective assemblages of enunciation—that is, daycare or preschool settings—are able to link and connect universes; this means to try and actualize new potentialities and to develop what P. L. Chéniér describes as "perpetual work-creating impossibilities" (in Giroux, Lemieux, & Cheniér, 2009, p. 109).

These three entrances to my playground of thought and practice are supported by a major hypothesis based on an unusual perspective: desire is unconscious, and the unconscious is political. This raises the question of how life situations, social and political contexts as well as singular experiences, can escape the dominant status quo (what Deleuze and Guattari call the majoritarian) and develop a minoritarian universe containing possibilities that have previously been unthinkable.

These three examples are only a way of indicating some detours and back routes that it could be useful for us to risk taking in order to engage in acts of resistance through micropolitical *bricolage*. In his article about Guattari, François Fourquet, a member of this group,[1] writes that he was a "speaker" when we first met him. He phrased things in an unexpected but nevertheless immediately familiar way: "Unconscious desire is political," "Subjectivity must be treated as seriously as so called 'political' slogans." To what he called "subjected groups," he opposed "subject groups." A subjected group's first objective was the goal it had given itself officially, and that goal was generally personified by its (natural) leader. The important thing for a subjected group was to survive whatever tragic splits might occur to it: Bolshevik revolution, Trotskyite secession, etc. For Guattari, a subject group was not opposed per se to a subjected group, instead it spread out in quite another universe; it wasn't founded, it was an ad hoc group, set up under given local circumstances, open and permeable to all sorts of unpredictable outside influences. It did not survive in relation to an ideal of eternity, but functioned as a pragmatic, contingent, and immanent tool. It could come to an end at any moment, but might as easily hybridize into other "assemblages of collective enunciation" (*agencements collectifs d'énonciation*); it might divert, spread into a rhizome, or pop up later in another guise.[2] We can say, therefore, that a subject group creates the possibility for all sorts of new and unthinkable possibilities.

So Guattari "talked," and we were not so much fascinated (although of course we were) as deeply, intensely, affected. It had nothing to do with learning; he drew new maps, created an atmosphere, perhaps through an incidental remark about a film—"*Hiroshima, mon amour d'Alain Resnais, quelle merde!*" (when we had all been so enthusiastic!) or a soothing, caring behavior (when we were all tough, revolutionary militants!), playing the piano (were poetry and music revolutionary?). We felt like explorers of new continents, of new oceans. Were we not also capable of seizing the opportunity to grasp these new tools for thinking and living? This became more obvious when we started to work as voluntary helpers in the clinic of La Borde.[3] We were, then, not in a learning process per se, but had to improvise and invent. After all, how can one introduce oneself to a catatonic schizophrenic you are supposed to bathe or to walk in the park? Of course the individual members of staff, as well as the meetings, were there to support us in some of our often ridiculous attempts to overcome our failings. We felt that Félix's words were useless; but were they really as useless as all that? Anyway, we did not feel that they were of any help *hic et nunc*. Making a long story short, we perceived the same sort of discrepancy (*déaccordement*) when Félix met Gilles Deleuze in 1969. Many of us were living in a building next to Félix's house, and Gilles and Félix were working all day long. We would often share meals, picnics, rowing on ponds, listening to music, even indulging in fancy dress on some summer evenings. A lot of laughter and jokes, and no "theoretical" discussions, since we all knew how Gilles hated them. But words floated around as if we were living in an aquarium, and paths were discovered as if we were in a jungle. Last but not least, for me, there was never the feeling that I was "learning" something, but rather I felt as though something was coming toward me. For instance, when Gilles would say, in his very peculiar way, "*Bien oui …*" it bore treasures. And the day when we met Félix, we sensed something different; he would always start a reply by first saying, "Yes, why not?"

So, having known Deleuze and Guattari in daily-life situations inculcated a humorous attitude (never take yourself seriously!), and this readied us for illuminations and intensities of experience, but did not help when it came to reading their work. Even today, I am sure there are many parts of it that I do not understand appropriately, or at all, but then again, it is up to me to seize the tools and make use of them as best I can. Working with the patients at La Borde was a profound shock, but in a way it was only "*nachträglichkeit*" in Freud's sense, and knowing these two men through reading became an absolute necessity: not as a *doxa*, of course, but as a way of experimentally thinking how best to assemble heterogeneous, unmatched, and until then, unthinkable events. It did not help me to become any faster at grasping their meaning—I would even say it made me slower—and reading was always a discontinuous or interrupted movement, in a way comparable to the moments I had shared with them. Some conceptualizations were immediately meaningful and useful, others I just could not approach or tame. When reading was taken up again, it was because there was a specific and urgent need. As Gilles Deleuze often said, he had nothing useless in his cupboards; I could therefore speculate that if it was not a teaching, or a learning pattern, then it was obviously about another way of being in politics, and that is, in life.

Now I address the second issue, which is how I was affected by, or more accurately experienced an epiphany. But first, back to Ronald Bogue and learning how to swim. He bases his argument on parts of Deleuze's *Difference and Repetition*. Deleuze wonders, how does one learn?

> The movement of the swimmer does not resemble that of the wave, in particular, the movements of the swimming instructor which we reproduce on the sand bear no relation to the movements of the wave. ... We learn nothing from those who say: 'Do as I do'. Our only teachers are those who tell us to 'do with me.' (Deleuze, 1968/1994, p. 23)

Deleuze is saying, therefore, that one learns when somebody says "learn with me," and he also says that learning goes through the unconscious; it happens (occurs) *in* the unconscious, thus establishing a deep (profound) complicity between nature and spirit.[4] To learn is politics (*c'est une politique*; p. 215). "One can never know beforehand what somebody will learn—what kind of love makes a good Latinist, what kind of encounters turn you into a philosopher" (Deleuze, 1994, p. 165). I would like to make my point here by referring to a French philosopher, Annie Leclerc, who wrote a beautiful book, *Éloge de la nage*, 2002, (*In Praise of Swimming*). "For a long time I thought I knew how to swim ... [and then] a nasty disease made me decide to go swimming—and there I discovered that I didn't know what swimming was about. Not yet" (Leclerc, p. 12).[5] Swimming, she discovers, enables her to tend toward something that "still needs to be known" (p. 8). "To swim searches to swim" (p. 9). In other words, it is as though the water opens itself to the swimming body, the water per se; which means the swimmer must reverse all his/her previous experiences. And this, Annie Leclerc discovers, means to let go (knowledge), to abandon, to escape (p. 19). How is it possible that water deterritorializes our well-known territories? "If one slides into the water without disturbing it, it approves, it loves it, it winds around your body, it carries your body and smiles" Leclerc (2002). Leclerc always feels approval and experiments with the increasing power of her actions, and this matches well with the way Deleuze and Guattari so often approved at once and said yes. But Leclerc (2002) also experiences the way she is instantly in the middle of things when she starts to use the crawl. "Swimming the crawl has no beginning and no end; you just enter it in the middle of a stroke." It becomes what Deleuze and Guattari call an event. Nevertheless, swimming is also breathing—singular, corporal movements: One has to assemble all these singularities. Will the gesture and the breathing be in phase? Will I have enough breath? What if a wasp bites me, how will my body be affected? Swimming in the Dead Sea, for instance, requires special experimentation. Leclerc posits swimming as an event and says that after swimming she cannot set her feet upon the ground *as if nothing has happened.* Why is this analysis relevant to what Deleuze writes about learning? Actually, Leclerc (re)discovered swimming when she had breast cancer, and swimming was a political act insofar as a new map of experience was drawn, new potentialities were unveiled that until then had been unknown or unrecognized. Leclerc came to see things in their "mortal" evidence. Remember, Deleuze reminds us, learning has to do with mortality (1990, p. 65). Why does Leclerc "obstinately" continue? Isn't it all rather tiresome? Every morning, why start swimming again? Who is demanding such a boring discipline? Is it water, life, or rather being tired of life? Leclerc's swimming always ends with the back crawl, and it is for her a way of facing death. "This is the way you would like the end to come." Deleuze, in *Difference and Repetition*, suggests that there is neither a method for discovering the treasures of experience, nor a method of learning.

> "That is why it is so difficult to say how someone learns: there is an innate or acquired practical familiarity with signs, which means that there is something amorous—but also something fatal— about all education. We learn nothing from those who say: 'Do as I do'. Our only teachers are those who tell us to 'do with me', and are able to emit signs to be developed in homogeneity rather than propose gestures for us to reproduce.… To learn is indeed to constitute this space of an encounter with signs, in which the distinctive points renew themselves in each other, and repetition takes shape while disguising itself. Apprenticeship always gives rise to images of death, on the edges of the space it creates and with the help of the heterogeneity it engenders" (Deleuze, 1994, p. 23).

Our two grandsons, Raphaël (7), and Pierre (4), have very different relations to learning. Before compulsory school age, Raphaël was in a public kindergarten where all the efforts of the pedagogues tended to develop children's own resources, dreams, inventions, and "creations," as some Swedish children called it. (Irène Jonas and I mapped it in a book in which pedagogues told us about the incredible *scenarii* children had enabled them to share; see Mozère & Jonas, 2011.) This education was not school-oriented but clung to what was, at that specific moment, at stake; what was unexpected, nothing to do with a curriculum, or a "program," as the French schooling system loves to develop. When Raphaël entered elementary school he was, paradoxically, handicapped because the other kids had been together in an *école maternelle* (3- to 6-year-olds) and many were already reading and writing. His sense of self-agency in relation to the school's techniques did not mesh; he was told "do as I do" and he resisted. He did not have enough power of action (*conatus*) to seize upon a singular encounter to learn, and he says now, "I hate reading." But on the other hand, he also says, "I want to learn." Having not been led into conformity, he now tries instead to flee rather than follow productive lines of flight. Of course this worries him at times and it is closely linked to the competitive system he is now caught up in. Pierre, on the other hand, was in an *école maternelle* since the age of 3. He is "adapted," tries to read, learns his ABCs, and writes his name. A totally different pattern, but in his case this adaption doesn't mean his potentialities are frozen. He seizes locations where the institution is "leaking" in order to empower his own forces of life. Raphaël will, of course, also snatch the opportunity provided by Pierre's trajectory to link with his own potentialities, in a way, "cutting" through the closures and apparent impenetrabilities of the institution. Nothing is ever given: It must be *created*. And this means that all potentialities remain open for him. Learning is, as one comes to see, a singularity that delineates paths on a plane of immanence. As seen earlier, death is at stake here, but also, centrally, life. That is why the two boys, each with their own singularity—Raphaël, like Bartleby "I prefer not"; and Pierre "Will I catch up with Raphaël?"—will find their specific and contextualized lines of flight. As we can see, learning has to do with an *occursus*, has something to do with the Outside.[6] It is risky, but one distinctly feels, senses, that life is what is at stake. Now a further step: Learning also needs something else. When Guattari wrote *Three Ecologies*, he stressed an important point: To enable a micropolitics (*une micropolitique*) to develop, values other than those of the stock market must be taken into account, that is, social, aesthetic values, and of course, desire itself (Guattari, 1992; Guattari, Ganesko, Pindar, & Sutton, 1989/2008). European elections took place in 2009 and the campaign was dull. Daniel Cohn-Bendit, a European MP who was close to Guattari during the events of May 1968, attempted to assemble an uncertain and bizarre *bricolage* that brought together heterogeneous people who until then had been moving in quite different intellectual, cultural, and political circles: a Norwegian judge in financial affairs in France, a leader of an alternative peasant movement that actually destroyed crops in GMO fields, etc. As Obama did in the United States a year before, they networked in small villages and in cities, focusing on how local, pragmatic issues could only gain political weight by using the European context, or better still, a global scenario. And yet it was a micropolitical endeavor, and Europe Écologie, credited with only 5–6% of the popular vote, had an incredible score, almost as high as the Socialist Party (16%). Everybody was baffled; and Cohn-Bendit, in the first official meeting of Europe Écologie, taught us a great lesson about "learning." He said, "I not only had the guts but a profound desire to make it work." It wasn't only a conscious decision on his part, but also an act of the unconscious, and these unconscious forces (force = *conatus* = heightened capacity to initiate) linked and connected singularities that suddenly had found a space to become part of an assemblage of collective enunciation, totally detached from the "normal" political patterns. Signs were perceived, echoed, magnified, flowed, and "leaking" (Borgnon, see Liselott Borgnon Olsson, this volume) singularities could be turned to one's advantage. In politics also it is necessary to escape existing knowledge: Any politician would have forecast a total flop. But no, this turned out not to be the case; and a French writer (unknown source) recently wrote about Obama's election in 2008 which also was a singular encounter with unconscious desires: "His only faith is to be an unrepentant optimist. He is a true 'man of the people.'"

Can we then propose, as Deleuze and Guattari express it, that "Desire calls forth desire, desire only addresses desire?" There is, as feminists have stated, no division between the private and the political. "Private affairs merge with immediate, social and political issues. Because we are never *alone*, we are always with others, even if this is not recognised" (Deleuze, 1990). In Europe Écologie, social space was opened up to allow experimentation, to create possibilities, to resist the given present; the grouping it mapped ran through unconscious singularities. And in such places a learning process could develop: local groups were discussing, turning political intelligence into a social process, rhizomatially diverting in unpredictable directions, connecting multiple universes. There was—and is—no formal program, but assemblages of differences of practical invention; there were the differences that were then, and are now, making a difference. Nobody is sure it will work since there is no model that can guarantee its success. It is a bet, a risky bet, but one feels that it is both vital and necessary. It is ultimately a question of sensitivity, of perceptions, of affects. It stands ahead of us and becomes a commitment. This is an important point to stress: What is possible does not preexist. You do not *know* what, when, or how you are going to be able to learn. Europe Écologie was a process of learning in the sense that it experimented with impossibilities of thought and practice, a collective dreaming of new subjectivities, heterogeneous universes.[7] Guattari describes how the kitchen in *La Borde* was articulated in relation to different spheres in the clinic: the menu workshop, the daily journal of activities, other workshops (pastry, greenhouse, garden, bar, sports) as well as the meetings between the cook and the psychiatrists (Guattari, 1992, p. 100 French edition). How to make a class room, a hospital ward, a workshop in jail, loci of creation. In other words, how ought we teach? Of course teaching is not a dead end, it only drives us back to the question: What's happening when I teach? What do I, or don't I, let happen while I "teach"? In a sense, it is the same thing as the swimming "event." Deleuze does not want to teach how to swim (by the way, did he know how to swim, and in which environment, and at what age, and so on?)—I am suggesting instead that he is only stressing what is to become the core of his work with Guattari: What is most needed is to experiment. But to experiment means not to be alone, but to be with others. The map becomes both more complex and revealing. Learning means a space, and it means others. I will now end by turning back to daycare studied through empirical research.

Forty years ago, when I started research in daycare, there were only hygienic, medicine-oriented principles at stake. Physical contact was always suspected as a source of microbial infection, and only at the end of the sixties did psychologists start to emphasize the importance of such contacts; they introduced Piagetian, and sometimes Freudian, standards. I have to re-mind you, I think, that in all of those power/knowledge *dispositifs* (practices), the only relation referred to was that of the dual interaction of child and adult. This dualistic pattern was inappropriately applied to situations and loci that were, in fact, far more sophisticated, as you all now know. Daycare means relations of a group of adults and a group of children, but also more microanalytical-level activities: groupings that are mobile, transient, unforeseeable, and never merely "aping" dominant institutional "ideals." So in previous years I needed to roam about continually in order to discover, to unveil these undergrounds—in other words, what lay hidden behind the screens. In *A Thousand Plateaus*, Deleuze and Guattari (1987) write that parents open or close doors to the outside. The same could be said of the pedagogues in daycare: Do they think about, and take charge of, a child as an ideal, rational individual—what I once described as a "standardized" child (*l'enfant moyen-ne*), or are they themselves open to other ways of being? Eileen Honan and Mary Sellers (2008) describe how children escape the commitments of the Piagetian–Freudian–Lacanian model, and how they learn to become clandestine. And here I would like to emphasize that what is discussed earlier has led me to understand how experimentation can occur; in other words, how a process of learning can take place. Liselott Olsson shows, for instance, how Stella Nonna, in learning to walk, is actually experimenting with her body as a surfer would on the waves. This is not simply an interpretation. It has to do with how Stella Nonna's "walking" *affected* Olsson (Olsson, 2009). Desire addresses desire. In the same manner, in daycare settings where Irène Jonas and I led various meetings, these action-research pedagogues told us of the magical discoveries that children had entrapped them in. It was close to what Reggio Emilia pedagogues call, misleadingly, "documentation" (videos, observations). Adults offer the children material, settings, and ideas that they neglect, make use of, transform through "common intelligence"; thus adults may snatch at the children's desiring machines that can connect with their own concerns and discover possibilities to explore and within which they too can flourish.

This means that not only should adults "observe" children, but also accept the risk of being "caught" by the children and their desires, risk sometimes being misled, being wrong, and even sometimes smothering and extinguishing lines of flight. The children as "stowaways" make daycare more liveable and less subjected to dominant standards and patterns. Thus we were able to map the modus operandi the pedagogues made use of to cocreate contexts of space and time within which singularities and their potential could be revealed. But this milieu was not simply constructed from abstract dimensions; there was a density of experience within this context: Movements of desire affect its nature, and it affected desire, lines of flight were actualized, but also weakened—some to the point of becoming ruined endeavors. Such an understanding of mapping can help us acknowledge the pedagogue's competencies as well as construct new planes of immanence where they, the children, and the outside are caught and led to creation—one may journey to the sea in two hours without stirring! When such events occur, one always finds fluidity, leaking, and learning opening out onto new universes of understanding. When Raphaël, then aged 5, got his rubber arm-rings, he discovered, amazingly, that he could not only walk but float and move at the same time; he experimented with a new body. It was not through knowledge but through experimentation; and he shrieked with pleasure as well as fear, splashing all around himself. Is it possible, then, to "teach" young children? Learning is a political act, it means meeting a sign, being with others, and it means what Bakhtin calls autopoiesis, that is, a self-creating process—but perhaps this is a very poor wording. Whatever the case, subjectivity is being created. Can a true learning process be defined as the creation of a subjectivity that escapes the dominant standards? How can one make a classroom or a daycare setting live as a piece of art (Guattari, 1995, p. 83)? Early childhood, Guattari posits, as well as insanity, passion, and art, share aspects of a sort of polysemic, animist, and transindividual subjectivity. A new approach for RECE? A challenge, certainly.

References

Collectif de Chercheurs du Cerfi (Centre de Recherche, d'Étude et de Formation Institutionnelles, CERFI). (1976). *Histoires de La Borde: Dix Ans de Psychothérapie Institutionnelle à la Clinique de Cour-Cheverny*. Fontenay-sour-Bois: Revue du CERFI.

Deleuze, G. (1968/1994). *Difference and repetition*, trans. P. Patton. London: Athlone.

Deleuze, G. (1990). *Pourparlers*, Paris: PUF.

Deleuze, G., & Guattari, F. (1987). *A thousand plateaus: Capitalism and schizophrenia*, trans. B. Massumi. Minneapolis: University of Minnesota Press.

Fourquet, F. *L'accumulation du pouvoir, ou, le desir d'Etat: synthese des recherches du Cerfi de 1970 a 1981 (Recherches, 46, 1982)*.

Giroux, D., Lemieux, R., & Cheniér, P. L. (2009). *Contr' Hommage pour Gilles Deleuze*. Québec: Pressses de l'Université de Laval.

Guattari, F. (1992). *Les trois ècologies*. Paris: Galilée Presse.

Guattari, F. (1995). *Chaosmosis: An ethico-aesthetic paradigm*. Bloomington: Indiana University Press.

Guattari, F., Ganesko, G., Pindar, I., & Sutton, P. (1989/2008). *The three ecologies*. London: Continuum.

Honan & Selbers, M. (2008). *Emerging methodologies: putting rhizomes to work*. In I. Semetsky (Ed.) Nomadic education: Variations on a theme by Deleuze and Guattari. Rotterdam: Sense Publishers, 111–128.

Leclerc, A. (2002). *Éloge de la nage*. Arles: Actes Sud.

Mozère, L. (1992). *Le printemps des creches: Histoire et analyse d'un mouvement* (Collection "Logiques sociales"). Paris: L'Harmattan Presse.

Mozère, L., & Jonas, I. (2011). *On "Garde" des vaches mais pas des enfants: Paroles d'Auxiliares de puériculture en crèche (One herds cows but not children)*. Toulouse, France: Érès.

Olsson, L. M. (2009). *Movement and experimentation in young children's learning: Deleuze and Guattari in early childhood education*. New York: Routledge.

Semetsky, I. (Ed.). (2008). *Nomadic education: Variations on a theme by Deleuze and Guattari*. Rotterdam: Sense.

Notes

1. With its members, Guattari created the Centre de Recherche, d'Étude et de Formation Institutionnelles (CERFI) in 1966. CERFI was a freelance research group and life experiment. These militants, previouly engaged in the radical Students' Union (Union nationale des étudiants de France), had already established relations with the Algerian students' union during the colonial war and with the heterodox Communist Students' Union (Union des étudiants communistes) during the early '60s. They experienced the deep gap between the idealism of their goals (freedom, equality) and the realities of militant, everyday life. If some women were elected as presidents (of the General Assembly of Students, for example) or sat on a board of directors (the Bureau of UNEF, for example), the usual sexist behaviour would quickly reappear: While girls would be typing flyers, men would, in general, be speaking in meetings, and when these ended late, it was the girls who would cook the noodles. The source of Fourquet's quotations are unknown, but believed to be part of Fourquet, Francois, *L'accumulation du pouvoir, ou, le desir d'Etat: synthese des recherches du Cerfi de 1970 a 1981* (*Recherches, 46,* 1982; alternatively they are in Collectif de Chercheurs du Cerfi, 1976 which Mozere cites here and elsewhere.)
2. Field work in early childhood has shown that when desire has been at stake once in a subject-group that is later subjected to institutional goals and demands, when an event connects to the previous subjective map of desire, there is an immediate spark (Mozère, 1992).
3. La Borde was created in 1953 by Jean Oury who had worked in the psychiatric hospital in Saint Alban (Lozère) where François Tosquelles, a Spanish Republican, had adopted the principle that before healing a patient, one had to heal the asylum. This approach was supposed to fight all hierarchies (status, privileges, etc.), which meant that all tasks were to be shared by patients, laypersons, and clinical experts, and there would be a constant turnover in jobs as well as collective discussions involving patients and their carers. The unconscious is, indeed, political. Collectif de Chercheurs du Cerfi, 1976.
4. Deleuze, 1968/1994, p. 192: "In short, representation and knowledge are modelled entirely upon propositions of consciousness … By contrast, the Idea, and 'learning' express that extra-propositional or sub-representative problematic instance: the presentation of the unconscious, not the representation of consciousness."
5. My translation.
6. My student Lionel Querbes, who defended his dissertation on "Desire to learn" in December 2012, shows clearly how dropouts manage to make sense through experiences when the curriculum is exposed to "real life," for instance, by modelling a sculpture for the school.
7. Readers may have noticed how Europe Écologie quickly turned into a group subjected to party standards with all their scandals and renunciations. Today it is a dead apparatus—as is usual with such things. But Deleuze says in his ABCs, for the letter R like revolution, once the revolution is fulfilled it is dead. The only thing that is revolutionary is the revolutionary *process.*

Section II

New Imaginaries Related to Authors' Scholarly Work and Praxis

NINE

Ki te Whai ao, ki te ao Marama: Early Childhood Understandings in Pursuit of Social, Cultural, and Ecological Justice

Cheryl Rau and Jenny Ritchie

To critique the academy is to unlock unseen places, delve beneath the layers, generate spaces of openness and create new possibilities. Reconceptualizing early childhood education exposes inequities and diminished rights. In the early childhood community in Aotearoa/New Zealand, colonial impositions have dislocated Indigenous *tamariki* and *whānau* Māori (Māori children and families), forcing them from their traditional positionality to the margins. In our work we have sought to privilege a pathway of Māori occupation at the center, where merging paradigms of anticolonial tensions, heartfelt voices, multiple literacies, and politicized commitment are powerful. In this chapter we will offer a retrospective revisioning in service of the *kaupapa* (philosophy) of rights and possibilities that can be accessed through a commitment to praxis, activism informed by reflection, and a politicized commitment to social, cultural, and ecological justice.

Māori, as *tangata whenua* (the Indigenous peoples of the land) in Aotearoa/New Zealand trace our *whakapapa* (origins) back to Rangiātea, our ancestral homeland. Generations of *iwi* (tribes), *hapū* (sub-tribes), and *whānau* (families) have resisted imperial impositions, while ancient ways of knowing, doing, and being sustain the *mauri* (life force) of Māori across time and generations. Article 15 of the United Nations Declaration on the Rights of Indigenous Peoples has guaranteed *whakapapa* rights to *tamariki* (children) and their families in Aotearoa/New Zealand: "Indigenous peoples have the right to the dignity and diversity of their cultures, traditions, histories and aspirations which shall be appropriately reflected in education and public information" (United Nations, 2008, p. 7).

Te Ao Māori (the Māori worldview) also prioritizes the cultural concept of *mana* (prestige), interconnected respectfulness for oneself, humanity, and ecology, grounded within *whakapapa*. Linda Smith (1999) advises that:

From indigenous perspectives ethical codes of conduct serve partly the same purpose as the protocols which govern our relationships with each other and with the environment. The term "respect" is consistently used by indigenous peoples to underscore the significance of our relationships and humanity. Through respect the place of everyone and everything in the universe is kept in balance and harmony. Respect is a reciprocal, shared, constantly interchanging principle which is expressed through all aspects of social conduct. (p. 120)

Māori epistemology prioritizes respect as integral to *whānau* (family), *hapū* (sub-tribe), and *iwi* (tribal) relationships and connectedness to the lands, rivers, and seas. For *tamariki* (children) and *whānau* (families), the mantle of *mana* resonates through past, present, and evolving relationships. In this chapter we elucidate ways in which our involvement within the Reconceptualizing Early Childhood Education movement has allowed us to further our theorizing and discussion of these priorities within our work.

The first RECE Conference that Jenny attended was in Honolulu, Hawai'i, in January 1998. She attended with three Māori colleagues—Rita Walker, Amiria O'Malley, and Kura Paul, as well as Margaret Nicholls, all from the University of Waikato. On the first evening, we were invited as a group of conference delegates to take turns introducing ourselves to the collective. This was a familiar process to us, one that is termed in *te ao* Māori (the Māori world) *whakawhanaungatanga*—establishing connections and relationships. One of the plenary presentations at this conference included some young Indigenous Hawai'ian scholars. This privileging of these voices was a strong statement by the program committee. We had found a conference whose *kaupapa* (philosophy, focus) spoke to us.

Māori-Led Partnerships: A Model of Implementation Grounded in Te Tiriti o Waitangi

In 2003 at the 8th New Zealand Early Childhood Convention held in Palmerston North, New Zealand, we presented a paper on "Māori-led partnership" (Rau & Ritchie, 2003) as a model of potentiality for the Aotearoa early childhood sector in upholding the pledges guaranteed within Te Tiriti o Waitangi/The Treaty of Waitangi, the 1840 agreement that allowed for British settlement of Aotearoa New Zealand. Our paper called for educationalists to respect and endorse *tino rangatiratanga* (self-determination), as specified in Te Tiriti, in the quest for achieving Māori aspirations and Māori well-being. This section draws from the paper, highlighting workshop foci that are directly related to advocacy, Māori rights, Te Tiriti o Waitangi, and the early childhood curriculum *Te Whāriki: He Whāriki Mātauranga mō ngā Mokopuna o Aotearoa* (New Zealand Ministry of Education, 1996).

Within majoritarian forms of democracy, it is vital that there be commitment to shared goals prioritizing rights, ethical respect, and generating spaces for Māori voices to be heard (Ritchie, 1992) if there is to be social, cultural, and ecological justice. Recognition that Māori could not "achieve justice or resolve their grievance without Pākehā (citizens of European ancestry) support," as stated by Ranginui Walker (1990, p. 234; author translation) positions Pākehā and Tauiwi (citizens whose origins are neither Māori nor Pākehā) as critical allies within Tiriti-based partnerships:

This role of advocacy in support of Māori aspirations can be considered to be a central tenet of Tiriti-based partnership. What is essential here is that Pākehā do not assume that they can speak for Māori, unless they have a clear mandate to do so. This means that in order to ascertain just what exactly are the aspirations held by Māori, Pākehā/Tauiwi educators need to consider it a professional responsibility to use their initiative to establish responsive and reciprocal relationships (New Zealand Ministry of Education, 1996, p. 14) in which whānau Māori [Māori families] are empowered (New Zealand Ministry of Education, 1996, p. 40) to take the lead in determining priorities for their children's early childhood education programme and identifying processes that will ensure that these aspirations are enacted ... Through tiriti-based partnerships, Māori aspirations for spiritual and practical mechanisms that enhance Māori wellbeing, similar to the whānau models operating within kōhanga reo and kura kaupapa, may also be established in mainstream early childhood settings. (Rau & Ritchie, 2003, p. 9)

A counter-colonial initiative, Ngāhihi, a Māori early childhood professional learning organization established in 1995 by Māori early childhood lecturers from the University of Waikato, privileged Māori-led partnerships located in a *kaupapa* Māori paradigm. One of the directors of Ngāhihi, Rahera Barrett-Douglas, a Maniapoto elder, has provided ongoing guidance to our research projects. In providing professional learning opportunities for early childhood services, Ngāhihi upheld a commitment to the Te Whāriki objective that "In early childhood settings, all children should be given the opportunity to develop knowledge and an understanding of the cultural heritages of both partners to Te Tiriti o Waitangi" (New Zealand Ministry of Education, 1996, p. 9).

The philosophical foundations of Ngāhihi were positioned within a *kaupapa* (philosophy) of *tino rangatiratanga* (self-determination) and *whanaungatanga* (relationships):

> Kaupapa Māori is about validating and legitimising being and acting Māori and this is inclusive of the revitalisation of te reo me ona tikanga (Māori language and culture). Ngāhihi also advocates that tangata whenua [Indigenous people] be recognised as valid service providers to the early childhood sector. Kaupapa Māori is seen to promote excellence within both Māori and Pākehā cultures, prioritising tikanga whakaako (Māori pedagogy) as a preferred way of sharing knowledge. (Rau & Ritchie, 2003, p. 9)

The *kaupapa* (philosophy, focus) of Ngāhihi is consistent with Māori-led partnership within both educational provision and research, maintaining an inclusive approach that prioritizes a collective philosophy prominent in both *kaupapa* Māori (Māori education philosophy) and early childhood ideology (Ritchie, 2001). Ngāhihi continues to advocate for *kaupapa* Māori across the early childhood sector and within the wider community. Democratic process is about generating spaces of openness for Indigenous leadership, for Te Tiriti–based partnerships, for the enactment of social, cultural, and ecological justice praxis across the early childhood sector.

Reconceptualizing Early Childhood Education, Madison 2005

Anchored in a Te Tiriti–based partnership, we again presented together at the 13th Reconceptualizing Early Childhood Education Conference at the University of Wisconsin, Madison (Rau, 2005; Ritchie, 2005) via video link from the University of Waikato. Cheryl presented a paper titled "Indigenous Metaphors of the Heart: Transformative Praxis in Early Childhood Education in Aotearoa. Privileging Māori Women Educators' Voices." It highlighted *"Ko te taonga te reo,* the language is the treasure," as integral to Māori who as a metaphoric people regard the language as a gift handed down across the generations from the elders to the *mokopuna* (grandchildren). Metaphors reflect philosophy and theories, sculpting our thinking, impacting on our ways of knowing doing and being.

A dilemma in Aotearoa is that in early childhood services that are not Māori immersion, Māori are constantly challenged by what it means for them, as *whānau* (families) and educators, to legitimate Indigenous knowledge systems within the early childhood community where Māori children and families, as partners within Te Tiriti o Waitangi, have the right to see themselves reflected within these services. This presentation honored the narratives of Māori women educators as co-constructors in articulating practical and theoretical stratagem for progressing Indigenous education in Aotearoa. The reclamation of *"He taonga te reo"* (the language is precious) applies a decolonizing, demystifying, Indigenous enactment approach in an early childhood landscape where ongoing renegotiation of Indigenous curriculum, praxis, and spaces is occurring.

For Cheryl, this initial RECE academic encounter necessitated critique underpinned in critical theory, postcolonial premises, and Indigenous thinking. Personally it was challenging to present a paper without a *kanohi ki tekanohi* (face-to-face) presence, the virtual distancing making it difficult to feel the *mauri* (life force) and *wairuatanga* of those present. What made a difference was Jenny's relationship with RECE members and the sense of connectedness it created. A question Cheryl raised at the time was, "Postmodernist, postcolonial, are we ready for anti-colonial theorising? We have anti-racism, anti-sexism, anti-bias curriculum, but are we ready for anti-colonial?" This terminology, and the issues it raises, remain an ongoing source of tension (Rau, 2007).

To conclude this section, the relevance of metaphors within Māori theory and methodology must be reiterated. They provide the links to *whakapapa* (origins), *whenua* (land), historical events, heroines, heroes, and places, and nurture our identity and ethical practices as collective people. Narratives and metaphors when considered in this light can be viewed as providing critical inroads to community narrative construction. *Whakatauki* (proverbs, metaphors) are integral to our Te Tiriti based presentations and publications. At the completion of our presentation, the RECE convenors asked us if RECE could come to Aotearoa in 2006. Our response was positive that it could indeed be held in Aotearoa.

"Decolonizing/Anti-Colonial Early Childhood Research and Practice," Rotorua, 2006

Visioning the 14th RECE Conference in Aotearoa 2006 was prioritized as we moved into active mode. Diti Hill (University of Auckland) and Lesley Rameka (University of Waikato) joined us as part of the conference committee; this *rōpu* (group) representative of Indigenous and Pākehā partnership. Diti was the only committee member who was not located in the Waikato region and drove the three- to four-hour journey many times over the year of committee planning meetings. The committee also had a collaborative working knowledge of RECE protocols and practices. Lourdes Diaz Soto was the program chair for the 2006 conference and Jenny Ritchie the key communicator from Aotearoa.

Pedagogy of Place
A critical conversation was where the conference would be held. The committee debated over the location that would best reflect and make visible the *Tiriti o Waitangi* relationship paradigm

of Aotearoa, where *iwi* (tribal) histories, *tikanga* (customs and values), and *kawa* (protocols), achievements, economic initiatives, and cultural strengths are validated. Dr. Wally Penetito articulates that for Indigenous peoples, place-based pedagogy is integral:

> A sense of place is a fundamental human need. The relationship between themselves and their environments is one of cohabitors. A pedagogy capable of embodying ways of knowing and being requires a sense of consciousness, a union of mind and spirit, the mauri [life force] and wairua [spirit]. (Penetito, 2009, p. 20)

The easiest choice for hosting the conference would have been in the Waikato at the University of Waikato with accommodation, lecture rooms, and IT availability. Rigorous discussion highlighted that this university was representative of universities across the globe, that it wouldn't necessarily depict Aotearoa as a nation reflective of its commitment to its Indigenous peoples. It was decided that Rotorua be the designated conference site, its rural nature, density of Māori population, Indigenous cultural setting, and performing-arts strength providing a lens into Aotearoa as a "bicultural" nation. Fortunately a long-term relationship between Jenny Ritchie and Sandy Morrison, a University of Waikato colleague of Te Arawa descent, made it possible to develop an important relationship with Te Arawa elder Ken Kennedy, who supported RECE 2006 being held in Rotorua.

It was equally as important to find a conference site that resonated *te Ao* Māori (Māori world) and a considerable amount of time was spent scanning possible sites until a choice was made that the Millenium Hotel would be the host location for RECE 2006 as it prioritized *te ao* Māori visual and performing arts.

Tikanga a Iwi (Tribal Protocols)
The process of *pōwhiri* (welcoming, greeting ceremony) is integral to guests arriving onto the *whenua* (land) of another *iwi* (tribe). Ken Kennedy (*kaumatua*/elder) opened up Tangatarua Marae (meeting house) at the Waiariki Institute of Technology in Rotorua to welcome RECE attendants. The conference committee viewed this as critical to engaging with *mana whenua* (people who hold the authority within that specific locality/tribal area) and to ensure that processes were adhered to, the conference organizers and delegates were also supported by Tainui *kaumātua*, the late Fred Kana and his wife, Pare Kana, both of them University of Waikato colleagues, who took us on to Tangatarua Marae. The initial *karanga* (call) belongs to *ngā wahine* (women). The *karanga* signals that you are being invited onto the *marae* (meeting place). The traditional *hongi* (pressing of noses) symbolizes the sharing of the breath of life, the *kaikōrero* (speakers) and accompanying *waiata* (songs) acknowledge the past, present, and future. The conference committee viewed this experience as creating space for new learning and possibilities.

Kai Māori (Māori food) or traditional foods were part of the *hākari* (feast), the Māori cultural performance including Sandy Morrison's *mokopuna* (grandchildren) whose contribution is considered a *whakakīnaki* (embellishment) to the meal. Explanations about the carvings represented the history of Te Arawa and Tangatarua Marae.

Conference Proceedings
The relevance of starting each day with *karakia* (spiritual blessings) led by *kaumātua* was to ensure that focussed energies and thoughts were in place throughout the day, and a closing *karakia* also concluded each day. A significant event at the beginning of the conference was the

tribute to the Māori Queen, Te Arikinui Dame Te Atairangikaahu, who had recently passed away, which included the viewing of a special video carried out with the permission of Tainui *iwi*. Waikato has special significance to the conference committee and it was appropriate that we acknowledged the significant leadership of Te Arikinui Dame Te Atairangikaahu.

Center visits were organized, with support of local early childhood educators, which included Te Kōhanga Reo, immersion and early childhood services. Background music between presentations was deliberately created, highlighting the work of the late Hirini Melbourne as well as Hinewehi Mohi.

Indigenous Visibility at RECE 2006

In the initial call for abstracts, Māori responsiveness had been minimal. The conference host committee then became proactive in reaching out to Indigenous participants and services to submit applications. This resulted in further applications, which then had to undergo the review process. Generating spaces for Indigenous articulation and visibility requires prioritization. RECE has been a forum through which to address injustice, inequity, and exclusion of *tamariki* (children) and *whānau* (families) in early childhood education and that values the importance of *wero* (challenge) and of self-challenge that underpins the *kaupapa* (philosophy) of RECE. There are many inspirational contributors within the RECE movement and we feel privileged to have worked closely with them. It is our *moemoea* (dream) that RECE will continue to build the presence of Indigenous peoples, across nations, across time forward into the future.

Towards Reassuming Our Co-Evolutionary Relationship With the More-Than-Human World, Through Reciprocal, Responsive Countercolonial, Postcognivitist, Posthumanist Dialogue

RECE has been a forum in which we have been able to theorize more broadly, deeply, and playfully, and to transgress some of the boundaries that might constrain our writing for other purposes. This section of the chapter focuses on some of the past, current, and future directions of theorizing that has been inspired by our involvement with the RECE movement over the past 15 years. In her paper presented to the 2006 Reconceptualizing Early Childhood Education Conference in Rotorua, Jenny referred to the work of Emmanuel Levinas, for whom "the relationship with the Other represents a sacred journeying of embodied respect, involving a thinking otherwise, an inversion which requires relinquishment of the satisfaction of maintaining control. This remains a relationship to the other as other, and not a reduction of the other to the same. It is transcendence'" (Levinas, 1987, p. 115 as cited in Ritchie, 2007, p. 38).

Grappling with the tension involved in relinquishing the will to know (and thus exert control over) the Other was extended in Jenny's paper presented to the 2011 Reconceptualizing Early Childhood Education Conference in London, in which she offered the following provocation, arising from the devastation wrought on the North Island, New Zealand, coastline of the Bay of Plenty and Coromandel as the result of the then-recent grounding of the container ship *Rena*:

> The imperative of the voiceless other is so evident in the oil-encrusted bodies of the albatross, little blue penguins, diving petrels, and fish in the images from the *Rena* disaster. Levinas wrote of ethical vigilance in responsibility for the other (1987, p. 112). The deaths perpetrated on so many beings, the pain of this responsibility weighs heavily on our shoulders. (Ritchie, 2011, p. 4)

Jenny continued this line of thought in a provocation presented at the 2012 Reconceptualizing Early Childhood Conference:

> As our planet increasingly sends us major distress signals, the strength and severity of which, in the form of storms, droughts, and earthquakes, overwhelmingly impacts those who live in already economically marginalised countries as well as in marginalised circumstances within the Western world; as the machinations of neoliberal hypercapitalism drill and blast deeper in to the earth's skin in search of inevitably finite supplies of fossil fuels whose impact on the atmosphere that we breathe, and the rivers and oceans, the waters that are our life blood, becomes increasing toxic; to continue to ignore these signals is to live blinkered by denial, we dismiss the ethical imperative to care for our planet at our peril. It is clear that, as Gaile Cannella (2011, p. 367) has written, "The time has come for radical, previously 'unthought' conceptualizations and actions." (Ritchie & Rau, 2012, p. 1)

The focus for our presentations at RECE conferences has been to offer postcognitivist, non-Western, Indigenous, countercolonial, and, more recently, posthumanist critiques of early childhood practices. Theorizing a nonhierarchical, nonhegemonic relinquishing/transcendence of the self/other binary shifts us into "a relationship with a mystery" (Levinas, 1987, p. 75). Jacques Derrida deplored the "violent hierarchies" (as cited in Shatz, 2012) implied in constructed binaries of self/other; people/nature; animate/inanimate.

Extending this theorizing beyond the presumptive confines of the bestowal/privileging of enlightenment-derived "human rights" frameworks shifts us into a reconsideration of our relationality with the more-than-human world. Theorists such as David Abram (1996, 2010), Valerie Plumwood (1999, 2002, 2006), Donna Haraway (1997, 2000, 2008), and Rosi Braidotti (2006, 2009) have challenged us to consider ways in which our work can move beyond the confines of humanism, in recognition that dominant neoliberal, market-driven technicist paradigms "distort our sensitivity to and knowledge of nature, blocking humility, wonder and openness in approaching the more-than-human, and producing narrow types of understanding and classification that reduce nature to raw materials for human projects" (Plumwood, 1999, pp. 196–197). For Abram, the shift to a cognitivist-centered literacy has disabled other literacies, those that continue to enable many Indigenous people to hear, read, and respond to the subtle messages of the natural world.

Understanding Indigenous/traditional philosophies may enable us to transcend the Western binary of human/nature; offering a deeper sense of intrinsic belonging within the world founded in embodied, sentient recognition of our spiritual interconnectedness with more-than-human entities. Māori know themselves to be descendants of Papatūanuku the Earth Mother and Ranginui the Sky Father, as are our *whanaunga* (relations), the trees, birds, insects, and other creatures. Mountains (*maunga*) are revered as ancestors, as are, metaphorically, *wharenui*, meeting houses created from the trees of the forest guardian, Tāne-Mahuta. The land (*whenua*), which nurtures all life, has the same name as the placenta (*whenua*), which brings new humans into being. Everything has a mauri (essence, life force energy) both animate and inanimate—a binary that is not salient in *te ao* Māori (the Māori world). All entities are connected through *wairuatanga*, the spiritual interconnectivity energy. *Hau* means wind but also refers to the tracings that people leave as they interact within their environment such as footprints or warmth on the surface of a seat.

The obligation of *manaakitanga* means that one's *mana* (integrity, prestige) is enhanced through one's contribution to the collective, through redistribution of accrued resources within and beyond one's community; there is a fundamental obligation to ensure that those who are in need are cared for, so that the elderly, for example, receive the first of the distribution of fish or crops. Appreciation is always demonstrated to the abundance that has been provided by the *Atua*, the spiritual guardians of these resources such as Tangaroa, the *Atua* of the seas and Tāne-Mahuta, the *Atua* of the forests, trees and birds. *Tohungatanga* is the intergenerational transmission of collective ancestral wisdom, which includes the knowledges pertaining to *kaitiakitanga*, stewardship of the land, seas, and rivers. *Tapu* and *noa* are aspects of a reciprocal spiritual system that needed to be maintained in balance in order for both humans and the more-than-human world to flourish, and *rāhui* (prohibitions) are employed to secure compliance with these protections.

Buddhist teacher Thich Nhat Hahn considers that being *is* interbeing (Hanh, 2008). He warns us that:

> The harmony and equilibrium within the individual, society and nature are being destroyed. Individuals are sick, society is sick and nature is sick. We must reestablish harmony and equilibrium, but how? Where can we begin the work of healing—in the individual, the society, or the environment? We must work in all three domains. (p. 37)

bell hooks, whose writing has been inspirational to our work, continues to invite transgression of boundaries in search of the making of "beloved community" (hooks, 2009, p. 185). In a conversation with fellow Kentuckian author Wendell Berry, she acknowledges his work as one of the first (Western white male) writers to "insist that we cannot have health in mind, body, and spirit if we don't have health in relationship to the land" (hooks, 2009, p. 186) and to link the violence of white supremacy and racism to the exploitation of the land. Both bell hooks (2003) and Vandana Shiva (2012) highlight the sinister, hegemonic nature of "dominator culture." hooks writes that:

> Dominator culture has tried to keep us all afraid, to make us choose safety instead of risk, sameness instead of diversity. Moving through fear, finding out what connects us, revelling in our differences; this is the process that brings us closer, that gives us a world of shared values, of meaningful community. (hooks, 2003, p. 197)

While for us, the Reconceptualizing Early Childhood Education group has served as a meaningful community, and one that has respectfully engaged with Indigenous perspectives, the question remains as to how we, as individuals, scholars, and community members can urgently respond to the crisis of this "age of ecocide" (The Dark Mountain Project, 2009). How can our praxis serve us in the quest to reassume our role as custodians in co-evolutionary relation with our planet? How can we bring ourselves to unknow the dominator paradigm within which we have found comfort, support, status, and identity? How can we cease the objectification and casual everyday exploitation of nature and reattune ourselves to ways of sensing, being, and knowing sourced in embodied interbeing? In what ways can we urgently respond to a planet in pain, drastically rescoping our activities in order to join with the earth, "as the world itself comes to vibrate with its possibilities for being otherwise"? (Gross, 2010, p. 153).

The reconceptualizing early childhood group has been for us a *whānau*, our annual conferences feeling to us like family reunions. As with other "families," there have been many discussions, differences, challenges, provocations over the years, yet the underlying respect for each Other's perspectives means that the dialogue is always enriched through the opportunities to listen and to be heard that our conferences provide. We look forward to ongoing reconceptualizing early childhood dialogues, bringing an ever increasing range of Others' (including more-than-human) imaginaries into our conversations and theorizing.

References

Abram, D. (1996). *The spell of the sensuous: Perception and language in a more-than-human world.* New York: Vintage Books.

Abram, D. (2010). *Becoming animal: An earthly cosmology.* New York: Vintage.

Braidotti, R. (2006). Posthuman, all too human: Towards a new process ontology. *Theory, Culture & Society, 23*(7–8), 197–208.

Braidotti, R. (2009). Animals, anomalies and inorganic others. *Theories and Methodologies, 124*(2), 526–532.

Gross, E. (2010). Feminism, materialism, and freedom. In D. Coole & S. Frost (Eds.), *New materialisms: Ontology, agency, and politics* (pp. 139–157). London: Duke University Press.

Hanh, T. N. (2008). *The world we have: A Buddhist approach to peace and ecology.* Berkeley, CA: Parallax.

Haraway, D. J. (1997). *Modest_Witness@Second_Millennium.FemaleMan©_Meets_OncoMouse™: Feminism and technoscience.* New York: Routledge.

Haraway, D. J. (2000). *How like a leaf: An interview with Thyrza Nichols Goodeve.* New York: Routledge.

Haraway, D. J. (2008). *When species meet.* Minneapolis: University of Minnesota Press.

hooks, b. (2003). *Teaching community. A pedagogy of hope.* New York: Routledge.

hooks, b. (2009). *Belonging. A culture of place.* New York: Rutledge.

Levinas, E. (1987). *Time and the Other*, trans., R. A. Cohen. Pittsburgh, PA: Duquesne University Press.

New Zealand Ministry of Education. (1996). *Te whāriki. He whāriki mātauranga mō ngā mokopuna o Aotearoa: Early childhood curriculum.* Wellington: Learning Media. Retrieved from http://www.educate.ece.govt.nz/~/media/Educate/Files/Reference%20Downloads/whariki.pdf

Penetito, W. (2009). Place-based education: Catering for curriculum, culture and community. *New Zealand Annual Review of Education, 18*, 2008, 5–29.

Plumwood, V. (1999). Ecological ethics from rights to recognition. In N. Low (Ed.), *Global ethics and environment* (pp. 188–212). New York: Routledge.

Plumwood, V. (2002). *Environmental culture: The ecological crisis of reason.* New York: Routledge.

Plumwood, V. (2006). The concept of a cultural landscape: Nature, culture and agency in the land. *Ethics and the Environment, 11*(2), 115–150.

Rau, C. (2005, October). Indigenous metaphors of the heart: Transformative praxis in early childhood education in Aotearoa. Privileging Māori women educators' voices. Paper presented in panel: Counterstories and Reconstructed Metaphors: Indigenous/Pacific Perspectives on Language, Discourse and Power in the Pacific; 13th Reconceptualizing Early Childhood Conference, Madison, WI.

Rau, C. (2007). Shifting paradigms: Māori women at the interface of Te Tiriti (Treaty) based early childhood education in Aotearoa. *Childrenz Issues, 11*(1), 33–36.

Rau, C., & Ritchie, J. (2003). Māori-led partnership. A model for Tiriti implementation. Paper presented at the 8th Early Childhood Convention, Palmerston North, New Zealand.

Ritchie, J. (1992). *Becoming bicultural.* Wellington: Huia Publishers & Daphne Brasell Associates Press.

Ritchie, J. (2001). Reflections on collectivism in early childhood care and education in Aotearoa/New Zealand. In S. Grieshaber & G. Cannella (Eds.), *Embracing identities in early childhood education: Diversity and possibilities* (pp. 133–147). New York: Teachers College Press.

Ritchie, J. (2005, October). Mixing our metaphors. Paper presented as part of panel: Counterstories and Reconstructed Metaphors: Indigenous/Pacific Perspectives on Language, Discourse and Power in the Pacific;13th Reconceptualizing Early Childhood Conference, Madison, WI.

Ritchie, J. (2007). Thinking otherwise: 'Bicultural' hybridities in early childhood education in Aotearoa/New Zealand. *Childrenz Issues, 11*(1), 37–41.

Ritchie, J. (2011, October). Fostering relationality as a pedagogy of hope. Plenary presentation presented at the 19th Reconceptualizing Early Childhood Education Conference, Politics of Care: Sharing Knowledges, Love and Solidarity, University of East London.

Ritchie, J., & Rau, C. (2012, November). 'Aroha ki te tangata': Reconceptualizing early childhood care and education: Critical questions, new imaginaries and social activism. Paper presented at the 20th International Reconceptualizing Early Childhood Education Conference, Penn State University.

Shatz, A. (2012). Not in the mood. A review of *Derrida: A biography* by Benoît Peeters. *London Review of Books, 34*(22), 11–14. Retrieved from http://www.lrb.co.uk/v34/n22/adam-shatz/not-in-the-mood

Shiva, V. (2012). *Monocultures of the mind. Perspectives on biodiversity and biotechnology.* Penang: Third World Network.

Smith, L. T. (1999). *Decolonizing methodologies: Research and Indigenous peoples.* London & Dunedin: Zed Books Ltd. & University of Otago Press.

The Dark Mountain Project. (2009). *Uncivilisation. The dark mountain manifesto.* Lancashire: Bracketpress. Retrieved from http://dark-mountain.net/about/manifesto/

United Nations. (2008, March). Declaration on the rights of Indigenous peoples. Retrieved from http://www.un.org/esa/socdev/unpfii/documents/DRIPS_en.pdf

Walker, R. (1990). *Ka whawhai tonu matou. Struggle without end.* Auckland: Penguin.

SECTION III

Diverse Imaginaries

Situated and Entangled Childhoods: Imagining and Materializing Children's Common World Relations

Affrica Taylor

Legacies and Responses

In the 21st century, the legacies of age-old romantic traditions that couple innocent children and pure nature (Rousseau, 1762/2003) and last-century normative theorizings about individual child development (Bredekamp, 1986) still hold traction in early childhood education. Indeed, it seems that in the increasingly competitive neoliberal educational environment, the primacy of individual child development has been intensified by standardized benchmarking practices and increased pressures for individual achievement. At the same time, growing sections of the community are reacting to this competitive environment by making nostalgic reference to the "good old days" when children were able to play outside "in nature." They are expressing concern about the loss of childhood innocence and the disengagement of 21st-century digi-kids from the natural world (Louv, 2008; Childhood and Nature Network, n.d.). It is in the face of this conundrum of competitive and future-oriented as well as retrospective and protectionist early childhood education imaginaries, which seem so paradoxically at odds, that reconceptualists continue to challenge outdated normative assumptions about individual child development, as well as challenging the notion of the naturally innocent child that needs reuniting with nature.

From Shirley Kessler's and Beth Blue Swadener's (1992) original appeals for a reconceptualization of developmentally appropriate practice, and Gaile Cannella's (1997) ground-breaking deconstructions of natural childhood innocence, through to Kerry Robinson's (2013) recent queering of childhood innocence, reconceptualist scholars have warned of the potentially unjust consequences of holding on to universalist, overly sentimental, nostalgic, and naïve understandings of natural and innocent childhoods. Pointing to the disguised political ploys of such naturalist assumptions, many have adopted Foucault-inspired poststructural perspectives that insist that far from being innocent and natural, childhood is a discursive construction, and thus always implicated in power relations (for instance, Bloch, Holmlund, Moqvist, & Popkewitz, 2003; Cannella, 2000; Cannella & Viruru, 2004; Dahlberg & Moss, 2005; Greishaber & Cannella, 2001; MacNaughton, 2004; Soto & Swadener, 2005). This kind of poststructuralist counter-naturalist argument is exemplified by Kenneth Hultqvist and Gunilla Dahlberg's (2001), declaration that: "There is no natural or evolutionary child, only the historically produced discourses and power relations that constitute the child as an object and subject of knowledge, practice, and political intervention" (p. 9). This statement certainly seems to be borne out by the present conundrum.

Like others in this book, my work contributes to reconceptualizing childhood by troubling the assumed-to-be-natural and thus universalist concept of the innocent child, whose appropriately supported growth and development propels him or her toward becoming an autonomous individual and even, as some would have it, toward being a nature-loving individual activist (see, for instance, Chawla, 2009). The reconceptualizing perspectives I offer build upon the political insights of these poststructural interventions, but take their exclusively discursive framings as a point of departure. Along with other feminist reframings of the human–nonhuman relations (Alaimo & Hekman, 2008; Barad, 2007; Hird, 2009), my work seeks to reclaim something of the liveliness, materiality, and more-than-human agency of the world in which we live. Along with others such as Alan Prout (2005) and Hillevi Lenz Taguchi (2010), I am concerned that if we only ever think about childhood as discursive effect, or in other words, as the product of human meaning making, we risk losing sight of the impact of the nonhuman world upon children's lives and of unwittingly rehearsing the conceit that all the real action is always about us. This is why my current work situates children within the real worlds in which they actually live, and refocuses upon their entangled relations within this world—including their discursive and material relations. Rather than apprehending childhood as a pathway to independence and autonomous agency, I see children's lives as inherently *inter*dependent, and agency as the outcome of intra-actions between entities (both living and inert), not as something that exclusively resides within the (human) individual (see also Pacini-Ketchabaw, 2012).

My approach to childhood is therefore collectivist (rather than individualist), and positioned within a more-than-human (rather than exclusively humanist) framework. It stresses that children are always already enmeshed within the "common worlds" (Latour, 2004) that they inherit and inhabit along with a whole host of human and nonhuman others. As a geographer, children's *emplacement* within these common worlds is particularly important to me, as are the ways in which we think about children's entangled relations with the nonhuman, "natural" world.

In the face of unprecedented global environmental challenges, and the increasingly complex, mixed-up and unequal 21st-century world that we bequeath to children, I believe that it is time to reclaim "nature" from the romantics and realists who uphold it as a pure and sanctified space and therefore a perfect match for innocent children, and from those poststructuralists who would reduce nature (like childhood) to nothing more than a set of human representations. Spurred on by the naming of the Anthropocene,[1] and the increasing recognition of the catastrophic impact of human activities upon the world, I am currently working to refigure both childhood and nature in more political, collectivist, material, and reconstructive terms. My recent efforts to reconfigure childhood as a messy set of embodied, situated, entangled, and noninnocent human and nonhuman relations within lived common worlds is an attempt to tackle the sobering realities of the world that we bequeath to children, and to consider some of the ethically and politically responsive possibilities it opens up for early years learning (Taylor, 2013).

Situated and Entangled Childhoods

It is nearly three decades since the feminist science scholar Donna Haraway (1988) asserted that all those who produce knowledge are "situated" somewhere, and that knowledge is never innocent as it is implicated in relations of power. Her declaration of "situated knowledges" has since become an established maxim for poststructural feminists who recognize the partialities, contingencies, and political implications of knowledge production, and seek to situate or locate their thinking within their particular historical, cultural, social, political, and geographical contexts (for educational examples, see St. Pierre, 2000; Lather, 1991; Pacini-Ketchabaw & Prochner, 2013). As Haraway (1988, p. 587) warns, if we do not situate ourselves, ground our knowledge and recognize our "partial connections," we risk the conceit of rehearsing the "god trick" of making omnipotent and universalist claims that we can know and define the reality of all people, from all times and in all places.

Such were the conceits of the earlier child development theorists, who assumed that all children follow (or should follow) the "natural" and "normal" patterns of growth and development that they had observed and recorded. These theorists—all eminent, white, middle-class European men—appeared oblivious to the fact that the standards they established as the truths and norms of childhood were based upon their own historical contingencies, privileged experiences, limited observations, and partial perspectives. Without the conceptual tools to locate themselves within the politics of knowledge production, they were not able to appreciate how their own universal theories of child development were framed by the Euro-centric and colonialist discourses of scientific progress and development (see Cannella & Viruru, 2004).

I mention this, as the project of denaturalizing and denormalizing (or queering) centric perspectives is central to the reconceptualizations of childhood and of nature that I offer in this chapter. My envisionings of childhoods as made and lived through entangled sets of noninnocent human and more-than-human relations are indebted to the maxim of situated knowledges. When I first registered the significance of this insight—that all knowledge is situated and implicated in relations of power—it helped me make sense of the gut-felt suspicions and aversions that I have carried since my own childhood. These are my suspicions about the moral imperatives that accompany just about all claims to define what is "natural" and "normal," and my aversions to the kinds of totalizing knowledges that remain oblivious to their own centrisms and to ways in which they perpetuate radically uneven geometries of power (Massey, 1993).

Years later, when I moved to the Central Australian desert to teach in an Aboriginal school, the notion of situated knowledges helped me to appreciate why I struggled so hard to understand what was going on in this part of the postcolonial Indigenous Australian world, and why the norms and benchmarks of western child development and learning theories were completely inadequate to the task of teaching Arrernte children. It is not surprising then, that the reconceptualizing theories I am drawn to, and the envisionings of entangled childhood that I offer up as an alternative to orthodox western childhood norms and universalisms, are bound up in the trajectories of my own lived experiences and relations. My re-envisionings of childhood have emerged from the praxis of my own partial and situated knowledges.

A productive notion of entangled human and more-than-human relations is also central to my thinking and writing about childhood. By making children's relations my main concern, I am deliberately shifting the focus away from the western preoccupation with the (paradoxically universal) individual child and towards the entangled networks of relations that constitute children's worlds. This means that I am also challenging the pedagogical wisdom of child-centered learning that flows from the preoccupation with the individual child. My shift away from the individual child as the subject of child development theory (actually it was more like a jolt) began when I was working at an Aboriginal community school in Central Australia in the late 1980s (Taylor, 2013, pp. 95–102), but has been reinforced and extended by my engagement with the relational theories and politics of feminist scholars such as Donna Haraway (1985, 1991, 2004, 2008) and Doreen Massey (1993, 2005). Their elaborations upon the productive or generative nature of all relations have helped me to go much further than simply affirming the formative significance of children's relationships. Rather than approaching children's relationships as bonds established between already constituted individuals (or individuals and things), this productive understanding of relations stresses their mutually constitutive and transformative effects. In other words, it is not just a matter of autonomous, individual children forming relationships; it is the relations with others (not all of them human) that continually make and remake children (see Taylor & Giugni, 2012, p. 112).

Increasingly, my re-envisionings of children's heterogeneous relations (gender relations, relations across cultural difference, relations with other animals, relations with place, and relations with technologies) have led me to question the overarching western humanist axiom that the individual child is and/or should be in the process of becoming a self-determining, autonomous, and agentic adult (Taylor, 2008; Taylor & Richardson, 2005). My work actively challenges both the desirability and the possibility of children's (eventual) autonomy or stand-alone agency. Instead, it emphasizes *connectivities*. It foregrounds the ways in which children are enmeshed within complex networks of relations, and seeks to consider the ethical, political, and pedagogical implications of these entangled relations.

By way of acknowledging the extraordinary diversity and radical inequities of children's lives, I also advocate for situating children's entangled relations. This means approaching children's relations as both the products of a specific time and place and contributing to the making of these times and places. It means appreciating that the continuities and differences that characterize children's relations are not only shaped by their culture and history, but also by the grounds on which their everyday relations take place. And finally, it means tracing the entanglements beyond these grounds, to follow some of the key connecting threads that interweave children's immediate grounded relations with other places and discursive spaces.

Common Worlding Childhoods

At a time when the interest in nature kindergartens, forest schools, and the provision of natural play spaces is booming, I am calling for a careful reconsideration of what we mean by "nature" and flowing on from that, a rethinking of the limits and possibilities of the relationship between nature and childhood. In *Reconfiguring the Natures of Childhood*, I am spurred on by Haraway's (1997) provocation: "what counts as nature, by whom and at what cost?" (p. 104) to explore the question "what does a romantic notion of nature *do* when coupled with childhood?" I argue that when nature is sentimentally valorized and conflated with childhood, it does the work of purifying childhood by locating it in a utopian imaginary and rendering it as essentially innocent (Taylor, 2013).

Moreover, I share Haraway's concern that "the *world* is precisely what gets lost" in the process of representing nature (2004, p. 90, my italics). My concern is that through being inundated with utopian representations of "pure nature" coupled with "innocent children," we can easily lose touch with the composition of real children's much messier, everyday common worlds—including those components that are regularly assigned to the category of "nature." Romantic representations of innocent children abound in literature, popular culture, and advertising, and they are very seductive. For instance, Anne Geddes' popular photographic images of cute babies ensconced in highly aestheticized flowers, nuts, fruit, and other forms of perfect nature, epitomize the kind of romantic and sentimental coupling of pure nature and innocent childhood that has had such enduring popular appeal (see Taylor, 2011). Ironically, it is because such highly contrived cultural representations of childhood *appear* to be so natural and innocent, that they effectively disguise the noninnocent politics of their own representational practices and simultaneously disavow the ways in which real childhoods are implicated within the complexities of down-to-earth and noninnocent common world relations.

To appreciate the enduring seductive appeal and effects of such representations, it is helpful to understand the ways in which they have been constructed and perpetuated. In the first section of *Reconfiguring the Natures of Childhood*, I trace the trajectory of the romantic nature and innocent child coupling, from Jean-Jacque Rousseau's reification of the Nature's Child figure in *Emile* (1762), through some renowned 19th-century Romantic cultural representations in art and literature, and into 20th-century children's literature and legendary Disney nature films. I also consider the various means through which Rousseau's promotion of capital-N "Nature" as the young child's best teacher, has maintained a central influence in early childhood education—from Fröebel's original kindergarten design in the early to mid-18th century, through to the 21st-century nature kindergarten movement that we are currently witnessing.

In today's digital electronic age, in which children spend increasingly large proportions of their time plugged in to electronic devices, it is very hard *not* to be seduced by the romantic alterity of Nature's Child and by the growing chorus that entreats us to "return children to nature" (Children and Nature Network, 2013; Louv, 2008). Although I am very interested in locating childhood firmly within the common worlds that real children cohabit with a whole host of others, including nonhuman "earth others" (Plumwood, 2002), I am equally wary of nostalgic calls to return children to an idealized nature that is assumed to exist in an uncontaminated separate domain and bears very little resemblance to these already mixed-up "natureculture" worlds in which we actually live (Haraway, 2008). As Haraway puts it: "Where we need to move is not 'back' to nature but elsewhere" (Haraway, 2004, p. 90). This shift requires us "to find another relationship to nature besides reification, possession, appropriation and nostalgia" (Haraway, 2004, p. 158). It also requires us to resist the urge to separate nature off from society. The main problem with associating childhood innocence with an idealized and separated-off notion of pure nature—particularly when this nature is used as an antidote to the corrupting influences of adult society, culture, and technology—is that in so doing, we run the risk of denying children's on-the-ground, entangled, messy, and implicated real-world relations.

For all these reasons, my common worlding project sets out to reclaim nature and childhood from the Romantics. This is not about discarding the significance of child–nature relationships, but refocussing upon the ways in which these already entangled relations are produced and materialized on the common grounds of children's actual worlds. In the second section of *Reconfiguring the Natures of Childhood* (2013), I address the question "how might we do childhood otherwise?" by assembling and enacting some different kinds of common world child–nature relations. These include children's significant relations with animals, and with the places in which children and animals co-inhabit. Again, my focus is resolutely upon the productive or generative nature of children's entangled common world relations (Taylor, 2013).

By refusing the nature/culture divide and reconfiguring nature within a series of hybrid naturecultures figurations, such as the "feminist cyborg" (1985, 1991), "oncomouse" (1997), and her "companion species" figure (2008), Haraway has made longstanding contributions to queering what counts as nature. In the second part of my book, I adopt the notion of "queer kin" that Haraway attributes to all her hybrid figures, as a way of acknowledging the unlike and unlikely partnerships and heterogeneous array of significant others (animals, technologies, places) that comprise the naturecultures of children's common worlds. Queer kin is a term that challenges us to consider that it is not only exclusively human relations that count in children's worlds, and not only biological relations that make us who we are (Taylor, 2013; see also Taylor & Giugni, 2012, pp. 112–113).

Yipirinya children, Yipirinya School mural, Alice Springs. Author's photograph.

To help situate and ground children's heterogeneous common world relations in their immediate environs, I draw upon Doreen Massey's (1993, 2005) influential reconceptualizations of place. Massey is one of a number of human geographers who encourages us to rethink place as much more than the inert and static locus of mobile and diverse human relations. Offering an alternative lively and productive sense of place, she invites us to think of place across the temporalities of human and geological instability and change. As she points out, both the human and the more-than-human elements of place are constantly "on the move" (Massey, 2005, p. 158), albeit in nonsynchronous time. Thinking about place in this dynamic way allows us to appreciate it as a heterogeneous time-space event in which geological, human, and more-than-human trajectories constellate or are thrown together (Massey, 2005, pp. 138–142). As well as evoking the time-space convergences of human and nonhuman activities, Massey's notion of place as a heterogeneous event is also highly political. She reminds us that: "politics is the (ever-contested) question of our being-together" (Massey, 2005, p. 142) and asks us to stretch our understandings of who and what belongs in the "throwntogetherness" of place. Massey's lively and productive notion of place as a never-settled event of throwntogetherness is central to my conceptualization of children's common worlds, in which all kinds of unlikely queer kin relations are forged.

Haraway's unlikely queer kin and Massey's lively and productive understandings of the heterogeneous throwntogetherness of place infuse my writings about Indigenous and non-Indigenous Australian children's entangled common world relations. I find these ways of thinking to be quite congruent with Indigenous relational onto-epistemologies that stress the all-important interconnections among children, older people, plants, animals, skies, water, and geological formations (Martin, 2007). They certainly resonate with the Arrernte worldviews that I encountered as a teacher at Yipirinya Aboriginal School in Mparntwe country in Central Australia. All children born in this country are "ayepe-arenye"—which literally means children with "caterpillar-belongings." This hybrid (queer kin) identity is ascribed to these children, because according to the Mparntwe "Dreaming" stories, the "culture-country" that they inherit was originally created by ancestral "ayepe" caterpillar beings (Rubuntja & Green, 2002, p. 161).

Now thrown together with all sorts of heterogeneous newcomers in a culture-country scarred by the impact of colonization, the imperative for these "mixed up together" (Rubuntja & Green, 2002, p. 49) Yipirinya children to learn how to take care of country is even more pressing, and stands alongside their need to be schooled in western ways. Arrernte elders insist that such "two-way" (Indigenous and western) learning is vital to the survival of contemporary Yipirinya children and of their culture-country kin (Yipirinya School Council, n.d.). Bound together by complex sets of reciprocal (queer kin) relations and responsibilities, Arrernte people recognize that the children, culture (Indigenous and non-Indigenous), and country (including all of its nonhuman inhabitants) are inseparable and their futures are irrevocably enmeshed.

It is not only Indigenous Australian children who need to learn how to inherit and co-inhabit in increasingly complex and mixed-up worlds, how to recognize their interrelatedness with their human and nonhuman kin, and how to assume responsibility to care for country. In the face of globally intensifying and entwined social and ecological concerns, such as climate change and diminishing biodiversity, we all stand to gain by forging a new kind of relationship to nature that neither separates it off from society, nor seeks to exploit or dominate it, nor essentializes, reifies, and romanticizes it, nor renders it static and inert. My queer and yet down-to-earth reconfigurations of nature—in part inspired by the quite pragmatic Indigenous relational onto-epistemologies that I first encountered in Central Australia, but also the product of many subsequent scholarly conversations—have given me a way to reconceptualize children's relations with nature without recourse to naturalist claims, nostalgic projections, or normative prescriptions, and without losing touch with the material world in which real children actually live. Unlike Rousseau's romantic Nature's Child treatise, this is not about returning a fictional child figure to some generic notion of essentially good Nature in order to preserve "his" innocence and protect "him" from society's evils, but of situating diverse childhoods and natures in articulating "natureculture" (Haraway, 2008) imbroglios of real-world relations, each with their own contingencies, specificities, layerings, intersections, and geometries of power. It is about supporting children to engage with these noninnocent, often challenging and characteristically heterogeneous real-world relations in respectful and responsible ways.

Ethical, Political, and Pedagogical Implications

My continuing project is to keep pursuing the ethical and political implications of children's entangled relations and to translate these into new kinds of common world pedagogies. As I have stressed elsewhere, "… twenty-first-century children need relational and collective dispositions, not individualistic ones, to equip them to live well within the kind of world that they have inherited…. Such dispositions and capacities will never be fostered through the application of a child-centered and hyper-individualistic developmental framework, nature-loving or not" (Taylor, 2013, p. 117).

Now is the time to reassess the potential risks and consequences of continuing to operate within unreflexively human-centric and overtly individualistic pedagogical frameworks. In place of the ubiquitous child-centered pedagogies that we tend to ascribe with intrinsic moral value and thereafter take as given, I believe that young children would be much better served by relational pedagogies that would support them to learn *with* others in their immediate common worlds (Giugni, in Taylor, Blaise, & Giugni, 2013). These pedagogies would be firmly grounded in a relational ethic that would encourage them to take collective responsibility for these worlds. Rather than celebrating and promoting their autonomy, these common world pedagogies would consistently emphasize children's connectivity to all others in their immediate worlds, including their queer kin (nonhuman) relations. Learning, with children, how to inherit and co-inhabit our interconnected common worlds, and how to ensure an inclusive ethos of more-than-human belongings within these worlds, is perhaps one small step we can take as educators toward making these heterogeneous, messy, and co-implicated real worlds "more liveable" (Haraway, 1994, p. 40) and thus sustainable for future generations.

References

Alaimo, S., & Hekman, S. (Eds.). (2008). *Material feminisms*. Bloomington: Indiana University Press.
Barad, K. (2007). *Meeting the universe halfway: Quantum physics and the entanglement of matter and meaning*. Durham, NC: Duke University Press.
Bloch, M., Holmlund, K., Moqvist, I., & Popkewitz, T. (Eds.). (2003). *Restructuring the governing patterns of the child, education, and the welfare state*. New York: Palgrave Macmillan.
Bredekamp, S. (Ed.). (1986). *Developmentally appropriate practice*. Washington, DC: NAEYC.
Cannella, G. S. (1997). *Deconstructing early childhood education: Social justice and revolution*. New York: Peter Lang.

Cannella, G. S. (2000). Critical and feminist reconstructions of early childhood education: Continuing the conversations. *Contemporary Issues in Early Childhood*, *1*(2), 215–221.

Cannella, G. S., & Viruru, R. (2004). *Childhood and postcolonization: Power, education and contemporary practice.* New York: RoutledgeFalmer.

Chawla, L. (2009). Growing up green: Becoming an agent of care for the natural world. *Journal of Developmental Processes*, *4*(1), 6–23.

Childhood and Nature Network. (2013). Childhood and Nature Network website, www.childrenandnature.org

Dahlberg, G., & Moss, P. (2005). *Ethics and politics in early childhood education.* London: RoutledgeFalmer.

Grieshaber, S., & Cannella, G. S. (Eds.). (2001). *Embracing identities in early childhood education: Diversity and possibilities.* New York: Teachers College Press.

Haraway, D. (1985). Manifesto for cyborgs: Science, technology and socialist feminism in the 1980s. *Socialist Review*, *80*, 65–108.

Haraway, D. (1988). Situated knowledges: The science question in feminism and the privilege of partial perspective. *Feminist Studies*, *14*(3), 575–599.

Haraway, D. (1991). *Simians, cyborgs and women: The reinvention of nature.* New York: Routledge.

Haraway, D. (1994). A game of cat's cradle: Science studies, feminist theory, cultural studies. *Configurations*, *2*(1), 59–71.

Haraway, D. (1997). *Modest_Witness@Second_Millenium.FemaleMan©_Meets_OncoMouse™.* New York: Routledge.

Haraway, D. (2004). *The Haraway reader.* New York: Routledge.

Haraway, D. (2008). *When species meet.* Minneapolis: University of Minnesota Press.

Hird, M. J. (2009). Feminist engagements with matter. *Feminist Studies*, *35*(2), 329–346.

Hultqvist, K., & Dahlberg, G. (Eds.). (2001). *Governing the child in the new millennium.* New York: Routledge.

Kessler, S., & Swadener, B. B. (1992). *Reconceptualizing the early childhood curriculum: Beginning the dialogue.* New York: Teachers College Press.

Lather, P. (1991). *Getting smart: Feminist research pedagogy with/in the postmodern.* New York: Routledge.

Latour, B. (2004). *The politics of nature: How to bring the sciences into democracy*, trans. C. Porter. Cambridge, MA: Harvard University Press.

Louv, R. (2008). *Last child in the woods: Saving our children from nature-deficit disorder* (2nd ed.). Chapel Hill, NC: Algonquin Books.

MacNaughton, G. (2004). *Doing Foucault in early childhood studies: Applying poststructural ideas.* New York: Routledge.

Martin, K. (2007). Ma(r)king tracks and reconceptualising Aboriginal early childhood education: An Aboriginal Australian perspective. *Childrenz Issues*, *11*(1), 15–20.

Massey, D. (1993). Power-geometry and a progressive sense of place. In J. Bird, B. Curtis, T. Putnam, G. Robertson, & T. Tickner (Eds.), *Mapping the futures: Local cultures, global change* (pp. 60–70). London: Routledge.

Massey, D. (2005). *For space.* London: Sage.

Pacini-Ketchabaw, V. (2012). Acting with the clock: Clocking practices in early childhood. *Contemporary Issues in Early Childhood*, *13*(2), 154–160.

Pacini-Ketchabaw, V., & Prochner, L. (Eds.). (2013). *Re-Situating Canadian early childhood education.* New York: Peter Lang.

Plumwood, V. (2002). *Environmental culture: The ecological crisis of reason.* New York: Routledge.

Prout, A. (2005). *The future of childhood: Towards the interdisciplinary study of children.* London: RoutledgeFalmer.

Robinson, K. H. (2013). *Innocence, knowledge and the construction of childhood: The contradictory nature of sexuality and censorship in children's contemporary lives.* London: Routledge.

Rousseau, J.-J. (1762/2003). *Emile: Or treatise on education*, trans. W. H. Payne. New York: Prometheus Books.

Rubuntja, W., & Green, J. (2002). *The town grew up dancing: The life and art of Wenten Rubuntja.* Alice Springs, Australia: Jukurrpa Books, IAD Press.

Soto, L. D., & Swadener, B. B. (2005). *Power and voice in research with children.* New York: Peter Lang.

St. Pierre, E. A. (2000). Poststructural feminism in education: An overview. *Qualitative Studies in Education*, *15*(5), 477–515.

Taguchi, H. L. (2010). *Going beyond the theory/practice divide in early childhood education: Introducing a intra-active pedagogy.* London: Routledge.

Taylor, A. (2008). Taking account of childhood excess: Bringing the elsewhere home. In B. Davies (Ed.), *Conversations with Judith Butler.* New York: Routledge.

Taylor, A. (2011). Reconceptualising the "nature" of childhood. *Childhood: A Journal of Global Childhood Research*, *18*(4), 420–433.

Taylor, A. (2013). *Reconfiguring the natures of childhood.* New York: Routledge.

Taylor, A., Blaise, M., & Giugni, M. (2013). Haraway's "bag lady story-telling": Relocating childhood and learning within a 'post-human landscape.' *Discourse: Studies in the Cultural Politics of Education, 34*(1), 48–62.

Taylor, A., & Giugni, M. (2012). Common worlds: Reconceptualising inclusion in early childhood communities. *Contemporary Issues in Early Childhood, 13*(2),108–120.

Taylor, A., & Richardson, C. (2005). Queering home corner. *Contemporary Issues in Early Childhood, 6*(2), 163–174.

Yipirinya School Council. (n.d.). Teaching two ways. Yipirinya School Council website, Retrieved from http://www.yipirinya.com.au/index.phtml

Note

1. "The Anthropocene" is the proposed name for the new geological epoch that we are now entering. The name indicates that it is human activity that is responsible for fundamentally altering the composition of the earth's surface and biosphere. Events such as human-induced climate change and rapid species extinctions characterize this new epoch.

ELEVEN

Posthumanist Imaginaries for Decolonizing Early Childhood Praxis

Veronica Pacini-Ketchabaw and Fikile Nxumalo

In this chapter, we provide an account of the potential of posthumanist perspectives for "decolonizing" early childhood education practices. Working at the intersection of postcolonial, Indigenous and posthumanist literatures, we outline renewed imaginaries for troubling multiculturalisms and colonialisms in early childhood education. The chapter engages with the following question: How can we conceive a politics for troubling colonialisms in which human individuals are not necessarily the central players, but players among nonhuman others? We explore human and nonhuman entanglements to generate decolonizing early childhood practices.

We employ the term "more-than-human" to refer broadly to all that exceeds the human, including non-human matter, relations, meanings, and understandings. Here both the human and non-human are active co-constitutive participants, and the human is "no less a subject of ongoing cofabrication than any other socio-material assemblage" (Whatmore, 2006, p. 603). We use the term decolonizing with caution. Tuck and Yang (2012) warn that "the metaphorization of decolonization makes possible a set of evasions, or 'settler moves towards innocence,' that problematically attempt to reconcile settler guilt and complicity, and rescue settler futurity" (p. 2). We hope that this chapter joins other approaches to anticolonial practice and creates openings for different and unexpected affectivities, connections, relations, and pedagogical responses—reorientations that might unsettle the relegation of Indigenous peoples and relationalities to "the immaterial and spectral past" (Cameron, 2008, p. 388).

Living and working in what is now Canada requires us to acknowledge the ongoing colonial project that constitutes the country. Settler colonial conditions are ongoing and include material and discursive territorializations, oppressions, and appropriations that shape everyday relations, often in taken-for-granted ways by the dominant society (Barker, 2009). Geographer Emilie Cameron (2011) points out that Canadian geographies "are shaped by histories of imperialism and colonialism, by the racializations elaborated in Canadian settler societies, by historical and contemporary flows of capital and resources, by state and missionary activities" and by Indigenous peoples' "political movements" (p. 170). Colonialist and imperialist legacies form part of our everyday practices as the colonial past inhabits all local presents in what is now Canada.

In addition, although there might be an "official recognition of Canada as a diverse society" because of its adoption of a multiculturalism policy in the early 1970s, "the normative vision of Canada as a white man's country is still pervasive" (Baldwin, Cameron, & Kobayashi, 2011, p. 4). As Baldwin and colleagues note, "despite liberal assurances to the contrary, Canada is a polity whose juridical-political structure, history, spatial arrangements, and social relations are thoroughly racialized and marked by racist ideologies" (p. 8). Even within current claims of a race-neutral and multicultural society, historical racisms and colonialisms remain and, in some cases, are reinforced and revitalized in new ways (Jiwani, 2006; Razack, Smith, & Thobani, 2010). For instance, the commodification of Indigenous lands into global neoliberal economies has often undermined or ignored preexisting Indigenous economies and complex trading networks underpinned by ethical relationalities with the land and all it provided (Cameron, 2011). Extractive mining practices in the Canadian Arctic, which refigure the land as an economic resource and privilege the free market as the "answer" to social and economic challenges, continue to increase even as concerns are raised about environmental destruction and threats to several animal species on Indigenous lands. The racial exclusions and hierarchies of colonialism continue and reemerge in different ways, cloaked as "commodity pricing, multinational capital investment, and federal and territorial bureaucracies" (Cameron, 2011, p. 186) and many other seemingly benign or "progressive" neoliberal formations.

For the past ten years, individually and collectively, we have been experimenting with what it might mean to engage in "confronting, challenging, and undoing the dominative and assimilative force[s] of colonialism as a historical and contemporary process" (De Lissevoy, 2010, p. 280). This chapter tells some of these journeys. We engage with our journeys by employing selected aspects from our collaborative research projects with early childhood educators within the context of what is now the province of British Columbia (Pacini-Ketchabaw, 2010; Pacini-Ketchabaw, Nxumalo, Kocher, Elliot, & Sanchez, submitted; Pacini-Ketchabaw, Benner, & Pence, 2012). We have been using "critically engaged communities" to rethink and re-generate practices in early childhood. At the heart of these collaborations is political work that involves disrupting colonialisms and racisms and attempting anticolonial practices.

Discursive Analyses of Racisms

Much of our initial work has focused on discursive analyses of how racial hierarchies and categories from colonial pasts persist in today's social, political, and material landscapes within the context of early childhood education (e.g., Pacini-Ketchabaw, 2007a, 2007b; Pacini-Ketchabaw, White, & Armstrong de Almeida, 2006). Our emphasis has been on human relations—how humans come together, what happens when differently positioned humans come together, how differences among humans function in always already differential power dynamics, and so on.

In drawing from postcolonial perspectives to critically reflect on early childhood practices, we attempted to move away from judging children as "problem children" and their actions as good or bad. Some questions we employed to critically reflect on our practices as political included: How do colonial histories matter to the children's and educators' positionings and understandings? How are stereotypical colonial discourses enacted in classrooms? How might educators and researchers view children's dialogues and actions as reenactments of powerful colonial discourses that construct racialized hierarchies and position certain groups as inferior to those at the helm of the (neo)colonial order (Jiwani, 2006)? How have racial and economic hierarchies from colonial pasts carried through to frame the social, political, and material landscapes in which children live? What do these hierarchies do to these children's subjectivities? How do they charge certain encounters and the violence therein? What processes of subjectification are made possible (and plausible) through stereotypical discourse in classroom encounters (Bhabha, 1994)?

In asking these questions, we began to engage with the multiple processes and effects of coloniality, including children's and educators' subjectification in relation to "power and resistance, domination and dependence" (Bhabha, 1994, p. 95). We began to make visible the regimes of truth through which colonial power operates in classrooms, and in so doing, "transgress, disrupt and displace them" (p. 96). In making visible these inequitable colonial discourses and their effects on children and families, we saw possibilities to disrupt and reconceptualize colonial legacies.

Drawing Inspiration From Posthumanist Perspectives

Although these discursive analyses of human relations remain important, there are other directions that we believe are worth exploring. These directions involve what Cameron (2011) refers to as re-storying, and draw inspiration from posthumanist perspectives. Cameron explains that posthumanist perspectives shift the approach of analyzing specific narratives from practice as just narratives of "colonialism, whiteness, and racism, which tends to demand in advance the casting of particular people and practices into binaries of colonizer/colonized, white/[Indigenous], power/resistance, and so on" (p. 172). She suggests that we instead narrate stories by attending to the-more-than-human (plants, animals, things). These stories "are not counter-stories, subaltern stories, or even necessarily more true or just stories" (p. 172). The stories are just *different*, and "as such, they order the people and places…in different ways, calling into being not only a different understanding of the past but also animating different futures" (p. 172).

While our discursive analyses might still be valuable to the disruption of racisms and colonization in early childhood education, we agree with Cameron that these analyses still run the risk of "losing sight of the historical and geographical specificity of particular stories and the broader social practices and relations with which they are imbricated, casting them instead as iterations of broader discourses" (p. 172). If all we do is "locate the meaning of the particular in the general," Cameron warns, we might "shore up an understanding of power and the political as sweeping, pervasive, and hegemonic, and thereby [overlook] the very real political possibilities of the local and the specific" (p. 173). Cameron proposes a re-storying that "helps "to open a space to think differently," that aims "to make legible a different set of relations than those demanded by hegemonic…stories, and in so doing to foster different kinds of life" (p. 187).

The goal is "to refigure stories rather than simply critique them" (p. 188). While re-storying may not by itself dismantle structural and systemic colonial and racial formations nor "the 'educated ignorance' enabled by hegemonic narratives" (Cameron, 2012, p. 190), we see important potentials in refiguring stories. Stories that attend to more-than-human relations potentially expand possibilities for what is seen to count as knowledge and actively participate in alternate knowledges-in-the-making (Haraway, 1988, 1997). Refiguring stories does not assume that all the "things," places, people in these stories are in equitable relations: "position in a network matters" (Cameron, 2011, p. 188). Refiguring stories has the potential to highlight political connections that might otherwise remain elusive in a singular human-centered narrative of events and encounters in early childhood settings.

In the rest of the chapter we provide three stories from our own work in which we might begin to generate new imaginaries for decolonizing practices. These stories engage children and early childhood educators but also engage more-than-human aspects of the world in which we live, in the colonial times we live in, and, more importantly, in the challenges we face here and now in a colonial space. We draw inspiration from posthumanist literatures to rethink and re-generate our work on decolonization. These instances are not provided as examples of best practices but rather as struggles of engagement with settler colonialisms. Drawing on posthumanist literature means that we do not run away from the problems that colonialist challenges bring; neither do we provide solutions to these struggles. Yet, we challenge settler colonialism to find ways to create new worlds and embrace what Haraway refers to as re-generation (Haraway, 1992, 1997, 2012).

We speak of re-generation as a way of displacing "development, fulfillment and containment" (Haraway, 1997, p. 12)—interrupting an all too easy move toward interpreting our work with educators through progressive linear trajectories of change. Re-generation, through its gestures to growth as consisting of complicated, entangled, and continually emergent past-present-futures, creates movement away from linearity. Re-generation embraces mutuality, mess, multiplicity, and contradiction. We draw on re-generation as "ways of seeing" that produce mutative interferences to ordered narratives of our research. Haraway (1992) refers to these ways of seeing as "differential artifactualism" (p. 299); where research is relational, embraces difference, and acts in disruptive ways. An important part of these disruptions has been to resist limiting our work to humanist relationships—to put differential artifactualism to work to inhabit *naturecultures* (Haraway, 2008) through located stories of place. Importantly, re-generation provides an entry with which to engage with the more-than-human relationalities that have inhabited our collaborative work with educators.

Stories of Anticolonial Pedagogy

We begin with stories of challenging representative pedagogies, such as what is often referred to as "multicultural education," from Fikile's doctoral research (Nxumalo, 2013a, 2013b). Fikile is currently engaging with educators in the intricacies and messiness of postcolonial spaces in the everyday lives of children and early childhood educators. Fikile's work surpasses the need to outline a pedagogy that transcends the messiness that postcolonial spaces engender. Instead, following Donna Haraway (2010), she stays *with* the trouble and becomes implicated in these messy spaces that are always already racialized and colonized.

In her research, Fikile pays attention to how each pedagogical encounter brings new challenges that always require new responses rather than pre-given solutions. She faces colonialism as a dynamic and complex space that always acts in new ways. Her work underscores how the entrenched forces of racist colonial legacies collide with other political, neoliberal, material, affective, attitudinal, systemic, discursive, and contextual forces in everyday relational encounters and have an impact on human and non-human bodies' capacity to act (Grosz, 2005). She is interested in the possibilities for pedagogical experimentation in ways that might increase others' capacities to act through new connections to things, spaces, and bodies. She is also interested in how openings to the more-than-human, to material-discursive relationalities might not only undo practice-as-usual but also create conditions "under which new ways of thinking and acting can understand themselves, question themselves, and elaborate themselves" (Grosz, 2010, p. 96).

Fikile's work explores relationality as a productive resource for disrupting the static humanistic categories upon which racisms and neocolonialisms rest (Anderson, 2007); for opening up conceptions of subjectivities beyond predefined boundaries and categories of difference. She sees more-than-human relationality, conceptualized from multiple perspectives and world views, not only as interrupting hierarchical dichotomies of difference, but as offering potential for attending to the complexities of encounters with colonialisms and racialization in ways that create affirmative and creative possibilities rather than already known solutions.

Highlighting the risks, fluidities, contingencies, partialities, and potential contradictions that emerge in each pedagogical encounter, Fikile's work engages with what Haraway (1991) refers to as located-responsible-accountable-implicated knowledge-making. This kind of knowledge-making moves away from colonizing "ways of seeing" that assume a detached and neutral observer. Below she stories a pedagogical encounter and then poses questions that gesture toward anticolonial possibilities:

> A large block of brown clay and a small glass bowl of water have been set out on a drop-cloth on a table. Several child-bodies gather around the table and begin to mix water with clay... girl-child-arms and clay-water emerge in mutual engagement:
>
> "I need a little more butter so it can melt."
> [rubbing brown clay-water into her arms] "The butter is going up my sleeve"
> "Look what I've got on my whole arm!"
> "I'm rubbing it on my whole arm"
> "Daba dab dab dab dab dab dab"
> "Now I have brown skin instead of skin"
> "Now you have brown skin?"
> "Lindy, I have brown skin right now"
> Rachel looks over at my adult-researcher-body and smiles as she rubs clay into her hands.
> She looks back down at her arms smiling.
> [Loudly] "I have brown skin!!!" [smiling]
> She looks over at my adult-researcher-body again while smoothing clay into her arms and hands and looks back down; studying her arms with a serious expression.
> [humming and singing, rubbing clay into her arms]:
> "a-a-a-a...eh-eh-eh-eh"
> [in a sing-song voice]: "I ain't going to wash my hands, I ain't going wash my hands before my mom gets herrrre."
> [Gasping]: "How come, how did that happen?"
> [Educator laughing]– "that's what mom would say?"
> "yeah." Later after washing and wiping off the clay;
> [loudly]: "No more brown skin!" (Nxumalo, 2012, pp. 287–288)

In relating this encounter, Fikile focused on the emergent material-discursive relational assemblages that participated in the encounter. She inhabited this encounter by attending to the more-than-human relational becomings it evoked and the dampening affects it created, including the effects of her embodied presence in shaping the encounter; how she "shaped" and was "shaped" by the encounter (Nxumalo, 2012). Her intent was to make visible the inadequacy of dominant multicultural pedagogies for attending and responding to the subtle and unexpected ways in which racialization and colonialisms can emerge in early childhood classrooms. This pedagogical encounter was an invitation to ask how material-discursive encounters might work toward creating movements and openings in early childhood pedagogies to include the affective, the unforeseen and unexpected; ways of seeing that might be otherwise obfuscated in dominant multicultural pedagogies. Fikile writes:

> Perhaps this assemblage of things, affects and human and more-than-human bodies, and all that they "do" this moment can be seen as an "ethical engagement with otherness" that is filled with multiple potentials that escape representation. In my perception this assemblage enacts a transformative and ethical encounter with difference; an intense line of flight created through unpredictable material experimentation. While Rachel seems to make a connection between my brown body and her "brown-skin" clay arms; I did not sense my presence in that moment as an "out-of-place-body", but instead a responsive relationality. In this encounter, brown skin seems to connect to joyful expressions, to shared smiles, to the specific material and discursive dynamics in the room at that moment—to produce an embodiment of brown skin as desirable—at least temporarily. (Nxumalo, 2012, p. 291)

Refiguring this encounter through posthuman postcolonial perspectives, Fikile further asks: How does racialization become connected to colonialisms through the human and more-than-human (clay) in this encounter? How do the pedagogical materials in the classroom act and become connected with the emergence of racialization? What frictional place relations are made visible in "touching" (Haraway, 2008) clay? What histories and stories of clay are children and educators "touching" through this encounter—stories that connect to land/place? What connections can be made to the situated stories of the place where this encounter took place? What interruptions to colonial worldings are made possible through clay and stories? What alternate stories of the clay as an active participant in this encounter might be told (Nxumalo, 2012)?

The subtleties, complexities, and multiplicities of racialization, as well as its entanglements with neocolonialisms, as illustrated by this clay-child-adult encounter, suggest to us that we need to bring creative theoretical and pedagogical approaches to early childhood; approaches that "assemble" in addition to deconstructing; approaches that engage with politically and ethically related questions and that work with the tensions that decolonization brings.

Stories of Entanglements

Our second story comes from Veronica's recent work. Like Fikile, she is interested in encounters among humans and nonhumans in colonial states. Veronica asks, how might we conceive a politics for troubling colonialisms in which human individuals are not necessarily the central players, but are players among nonhuman others? Below she shares a moment at a childcare center that implicates researchers/educators/children/animals in the mess of colonial times and spaces.

> The child care centre where I work is located next to a forest that is home to many indigenous species, including mule deer. The children and educators at the centre love this forest and we often take nature walks through it. The sounds, smells, and sights we encounter on these

walks spark many conversations throughout the day. To our delight, the deer who live in these woods visit our centre regularly, approaching the chain link fence that separates them from the children. The fence is a child care licensing requirement, ostensibly to restrain the children for their own safety; in reality, it restricts the deer more than it does the children, because the children, with adult supervision, can pass through a gate to the other side.

Mature deer visit the centre in the fall and winter; in the spring we greet the new fawns with excitement. We adults remind the children not to startle the deer; when a deer approaches the fence, we ask those children who are in a different room to come quickly to the window; together, we watch as the deer walk the length of the fence; we pay attention to their every movement. We are all deeply interested in the deer.

I am curious, too, about the deer's interest in coming close to the fence to look at us, to look at the children. I wonder who is watching whom and what the risks are of the intersecting gaze. What is this relationship about? What happens when two species with different but entangled histories come together? What kinds of relations are being shaped, right at that moment, between indigenous and settler species? As the deer and the children look at each other, histories are enacted, lives are changed, and new possibilities are generated for responding to each other. The responsibilities we have toward the deer we look in the eyes are real and actual; they shape us as beings and require a response. We cannot innocently ignore the ways in which the deer's lives—and our own—are shaped by our intra-actions. We are in the middle of who the deer are and the deer are in the midst of who we become. For example, in the moment of the gaze, the politics of wild animals might change. Food economies might shift as we encounter the deer face to face. And, as these systems are altered, we and the deer are changed forever. Does this coshaping offer possibilities for learning how to live and to become together in less violent, more "equitable" ways? What can we learn from these encounters about life in a postcolonial state? How has this encounter shaped, and been shaped by, colonial imaginaries? How might this encounter undo us as well as our practices with young children? (Pacini-Ketchabaw, 2012, pp. 303–304)

Here Veronica's interest lies in the complexities and tensions that emerge in the colonized and colonialist spaces where deer and human children "meet." The province of British Columbia, which is home to mule deer, employs narratives of unspoiled wilderness in ways that work to serve the ongoing colonial project (Braun, 2002) while urban and industrial encroachment into deer's habitats continue. The spaces in which humans and non-humans come together in colonial British Columbia are thus contentious, and their relationships are embroiled in complex and evolving dynamics informed by notions of safety and conservation, influenced by socio-politico-economic forces, and shaped through affective investments (Ahmed, 2004) in fear, love, and protection. Early childhood spaces in British Columbia provide rich opportunities to explore these entanglements both as sites that occupy "deer country" and as places that utilize stories, media, and materials featuring infantilized, human-like representations of deer such as Bambi.

Re-storying everyday situated encounters through the more-than-human has potential to disrupt images of innocence in children's relations with nature (Taylor, 2013) and instead make visible entangled multispecies naturecultures and settler colonial histories. Such stories bring attention to the inherent tensions and contestations of particular colonial places and unsettle "dualistic constructions and hierarchical relations with the natural world" (Instone, 1998, p. 457). These stories might animate different understandings, orderings, and relationalities. As Stewart (2012) notes, this is an attention toward "everyday worldings that matter in many ways beyond their status as representations or objects of moralizing" (p. 519).

Our interest is also in how such stories might open up possibilities for encountering "nature" in ways that unsettle colonial imaginaries of an uninscribed timeless landscape, and unsettle the erasures and repression of Indigenous relationalities with the land and its nonhuman inhabitants (Cameron, 2012). What alternative imaginaries and materialities and practices might be made possible? What might it mean for anticolonial early childhood pedagogies to take seriously Haraway's (2008) contention that "species interdependence is the name of the worlding game on earth, and that game must be one of response and respect" (p. 19)? How might multispecies stories make visible "how differences get made, what gets excluded, and how these exclusions matter" (Barad, 2007, p. 30)?

Stories of Diffraction

The third story begins with a moment of practice from a research project that we are working on together. Here we are challenging ourselves to regenerate relating in our practices by bringing what Haraway (1997) refers to as diffractive practices.

> Educators have been concerned about children's prolific use of paper in the centre and have been thinking about how to engage in an inquiry with children on the ethics of caring for paper. One day during my visit to the centre, we discuss possibilities for extending the inquiry beyond the "fact-based" approach educators have been engaging with (trees-pulp-paper making). An educator mentions to me that perhaps a First Nations person could come to the centre to talk about taking care of trees/land. (Pacini-Katchabaw & Nxumalo, field/discussion notes, n.d.)

By attending to the possible worldings enacted through this encounter, rather than its interpretation and representation, we engage with a diffractive approach. We are reminded of what Haraway (1992) explains: "Artifactualism is askew of productionism; the rays from my optical device diffract rather than reflect. These diffracting rays compose interference patterns, not reflecting images" (p. 299). Moving away from explaining and representing this story as "a problem" with the educator that was then smoothly resolved through imparting of "knowledge," we have found that thinking with research practices as relational practices that bring into view particular worlds (Haraway, 1991) has generated more possibilities and brought our discussions to complex layers beyond the individual participants in the encounter.

In this conception, then, relationality is not about imparting expert knowledge but instead to take seriously what ways of "relating" to social and material worlds are enacted through these stories and through our discussions of this encounter with educators—this is not to say that we have overcome or transformed the troubles that this encounter brings, but that we have attended to the multiple relationalities that it has brought into view, including the complex more-than-human relations that emerge and are already embedded in the work that we do, attending to relationalities, "gaps and awkward encounters" (Choy et al., 2009, p. 382) simultaneously.

As Bellacasa (2012) notes, this is a non-innocent engagement with practices that is relational, yet these connections are not without frictions and tensions (Tsing, 2005). For instance, when the educator speaks to us of bringing a First Nations individual into the childcare center, worlds that are affectively resonant with the colonial past-present histories in which our work is situated are instantly enacted, worldings (Taylor, 2013) in which we as researchers are also implicated and embedded. That is to say, the relations we inhabit in this work are not limited to relations between us (educators and researchers), but also to the settler-colonial past-presents including the "colonial histories and neocolonial rhetorics that continue to infuse 'commonsense' categories and identities like 'nature'" (Willems-Braun, 1997, p. 3). How do we account for these colonial relations when engaged in research with educators? What is our responsibility? How do we respond?

As exemplified in the story related by Veronica, we are attempting to attend to relationalities in our research with educators that go beyond human-centric relations. We want to locate our work within the *places* we inhabit as part of human and more-than-human colonial "contact zones" filled with multiplicities, intensive power relations, and unresolved belongings (Taylor & Giugni, 2012). While we have not necessarily resolved these tensions, they have provided a site from which to begin to cause disruptions, such as in unsettling and resituating the static, representation and familiarity underlying so-called natural places (Taylor, 2013; Taylor & Giugni, 2012) as a site for children's experiences in early childhood settings within the specific context of what is now British Columbia. As van Doreen and Rose (2012) note, our approach has been relating to places as inherently vibrant and storied, enacting different questions and histories:

> Places are understood and embedded in broader histories and systems of meaning. But stories and meanings are not just layered over a pre-existing landscape. Instead, stories emerge from and impact upon the way in which places come to be—the material and the discursive are all mixed up in the making of places, as with worlds more generally. If we accept this notion of place, however, an important question remains before us, namely, who stories these places? Whose stories come to matter in the emergence of a place? In particular, we are concerned to ask: What might it mean to take storied-places seriously as multispecies achievements? (pp. 2–3)

We see potential in regenerating conceptualizations of relationality in early childhood practices that attend to relations with place/land and colonial pastpresents. Relations with place/land are always already present, as is exemplified in the story above. Attending to these relations allows us to begin to trouble colonial anthropocentrism that privilege not only humans over other humans, but that are predicated on human mastery over nature and other more-than-human worlds (Tsing, 2012).

Engaging with these messy stories entangles us in relations with place as a site of asymmetric power relations, as a relational place of conflict and friction; where place is not "as static or bounded but...mobile and in process...open to conditionality and emergence" (J. Anderson, 2012, p. 571). We continue to grapple with how encounters with place in our research practices might make visible how "place is far from a static, stable, or fixed entity no longer reliable, consistent, or necessarily coherent; it is wholly provisional and unstable" (J. Anderson, 2012, p. 574), a relational "gathering" of things, bodies, and histories that require close attention to its enactments and sociomaterial multiplicities. In storying troubling encounters with and conceptions of place we have begun to explore with educators possibilities for attending to situated entanglements with and connections to the "sticky materialities" and histories of place, where humans are not necessarily the only actants and where their relationalities are not necessarily determined by human encounters (Tsing, 2005). As Tsing (2005) explains, "our encounters are infused with other social histories—with humans in more or less important roles, depending. And there is nothing about social relations, per se, that requires human forms of consciousness

or anatomy." We see regenerating relationality in practices through more-than-human relations as creating openings to "speak beyond the boundaries of conquest and domination"
(hooks, 1995, p. 297).

Conclusion

Inhabiting posthumanist perspectives in our research is a move toward unsettling colonialisms and toward re-storying practices that "resituate the human within the environment, and
resituate nonhumans within cultural and ethical domains" (Rose et al., 2012, p. 3). We also
see ethical potentialities in posthumanist research practices as creating interferences and disruptions to the exteriorities claimed by colonizing research practices that "teach that knowers
are manipulators who have no reciprocal responsibilities to the things they manipulate" (Battiste & Henderson, 2000, p. 88). In our research with educators, by attending to materialized
practices and their interrelated histories and discourses, we attempt to create openings toward
re-storying colonialisms as material-discursive assemblages of histories, place, practices, bodies, things, materials, economies, discourses, affects, and memories amongst other constituents
and processes.

Importantly, regenerating and re-storying our research is not an attempt to completely
map or represent all the constituent parts of colonial histories, but rather is an intentional
politicized "noticing" of events and encounters (Tsing, 2012). A located and close "noticing the seams" (Tsing, 2012, p. 152) of colonialisms is an important place to begin,
where contradictions and troubles abound. "This is no place to search for utopia" (p.
152) but perhaps can be a productive site to seek out new potentialities, new ethical and
affirmative possibilities for "living well with others" (Haraway, 2008)—including more
than human others (Tsing, 2012)—and for engaging in decolonizing that goes beyond
metaphorization.

References

Ahmed, S. (2004). *The cultural politics of emotion*. New York: Routledge.

Anderson, J. (2012). Relational places: The surfed wave as assemblage and convergence. *Environment & Planning D: Society & Space, 30*, 570–587.

Anderson, K. (2007). *Race and the crisis of humanism*. London: Routledge.

Baldwin, A., Cameron, L., & Kobayashi, A. (Eds.). (2011). *Rethinking the great white north: Race, nature and the historical geographies of whiteness in Canada*. Vancouver: UBC Press.

Barad, K. (2007). *Meeting the universe halfway: Quantum physics and the entanglement of matter and meaning*. Durham, NC: Duke University Press.

Barker, A. J. (2009). The contemporary reality of Canadian imperialism: Settler colonialism and the hybrid colonial state. *The American Indian Quarterly, 33*(3), 325–351.

Battiste, M., & Henderson, J. Y. (2000). *Protecting Indigenous knowledge and heritage: A global challenge*. Saskatoon, SK: Purish.

Bellacasa, M. P. (2012). "Nothing comes without its world": Thinking with care. *The Sociological Review, 60*(2), 197–216.

Bhabha, H. K. (1994). *The location of culture*. London: Routledge.

Braun, B. (2002). Colonialism's afterlife: Vision and visuality on the Northwest coast. *Cultural Geographies, 9*, 202–247.

Cameron, E. (2008). Indigenous spectrality and the politics of postcolonial ghost stories. *Cultural Geographies, 15*(3), 383–393.

Cameron, E. (2011). Copper stories: Imaginative geographies and material orderings of the Central Canadian Arctic. In A. Baldwin, L. Cameron, & A. Kobayashi (Eds.), *Rethinking the great white north: Race, nature and the historical geographies of whiteness in Canada* (pp. 169–190). Vancouver: UBC Press.

Cameron, E. (2012). New geographies of story and storytelling. *Progress in Human Geography, 36*(5), 572–591.

Choy, T., Lieba F., Hathaway, M. J., Inoue, M., Satsuka, S., & Tsing, A. (2009). A new form of collaboration in cultural anthropology: Matsutake worlds. *American Ethnologist, 36*(2), 380–403.

De Lissevoy, N. (2010). Decolonial pedagogy and the ethics of the global. *Discourse: Studies in the Cultural Politics of Education, 31*(3), 279–293.

Grosz, E. (2005). *Time travels: Feminism, nature, power.* Durham, NC: Duke University Press.

Grosz, E. (2010). The practice of feminist theory. *Differences: A Journal of Feminist Cultural Studies, 21*(1), 94–108.

Haraway, D. (1988). Situated knowledges: The science question in feminism and the privilege of partial perspective. *Feminist Studies, 14*(3), 575–599.

Haraway, D. (1991). *Simians, cyborgs, and women: The reinvention of nature.* New York: Routledge.

Haraway, D. (1992). The promises of monsters: A regenerative politics for inappropriate/d others. In L. Grossberg, C. Nelson, & P. A. Treichler (Eds.), *Cultural studies* (pp. 295–337). New York: Routledge.

Haraway, D. (1997). *Modest_witness@second_millennium. FemaleMan©_meets_OncoMouse TM: Feminism and technoscience.* London: Routledge.

Haraway, D. (2008). *When species meet.* Minneapolis: University of Minnesota Press.

Haraway, D. (2010). When species meet: Staying with the trouble. *Environment and Planning D: Society and Space, 28*(1), 53–55.

Haraway, D. (2012). Awash in urine: DES and Premarin® in multispecies response-ability. *WSQ: Women's Studies Quarterly, 40*(1 & 2), 301–316.

hooks, B. (1995). "This is the oppressor's language / yet I need it to talk to you": Language, a place of struggle. In A. Dingwaney & C. Maier (Eds.), *Between languages and cultures: Translation and cross-cultural texts* (pp. 295–301). Pittsburgh: University of Pittsburgh Press.

Instone, L. (1998). The coyote's at the door: Revisioning human-environment relations in the Australian context. *Cultural Geographies, 5*(4), 452–467.

Jiwani, J. (2006). *Discourses of denial: Mediations of race, gender and violence.* Vancouver, BC: University of British Columbia Press.

Nxumalo, F. (2012). Unsettling representational practices: Inhabiting relational becomings in early childhood education. *Child & Youth Services Journal, 33*(3–4), 281–302.

Nxumalo, F. (2013a). Forest stories: Restorying encounters with 'natural' places in early childhood education. Unpublished working paper.

Nxumalo, F. (2013b). Anticolonial research practices in early childhood education: Experimenting with testifying-witnessing and refiguring presences as knowledges-in-the-making. Unpublished working paper.

Pacini-Ketchabaw, V. (2007a). Child care and multiculturalism: A site of governance marked by flexibility and openness. *Contemporary Issues in Early Childhood, 8*(3), 222–232.

Pacini-Ketchabaw, V. (2007b). Racialized migrant women's narratives on child care: An anti-racist, transnational feminist analysis. *International Journal of Equity and Innovation in Early Childhood Education, 5*(1), 69–88.

Pacini-Ketchabaw, V. (Ed.). (2010). *Flows, rhythms and intensities of early childhood education curriculum.* New York: Peter Lang.

Pacini-Ketchabaw, V. (2012). Postcolonial entanglements: Unruling stories. *Child & Youth Services, 33*, 303–316.

Pacini-Ketchabaw, V., Benner, A., & Pence, A. (2012). *The community early learning and child care facilitator project: Evaluation.* Victoria, BC: Unit of Early Years Research and Development.

Pacini-Ketchabaw, V., Nxumalo, F., Kocher, L., Elliot, E., & Sanchez, A. (submitted). *Journeys in Curriculum: Complexifying Early Childhood Education Practices.*

Pacini-Ketchabaw, V., White, J., & Armstrong de Almeida, A. E. (2006). Racialization in early childhood: A critical analysis of discourses in policies. *International Journal of Educational Policy, Research, & Practice: Reconceptualizing Childhood Studies, 7*, 95–113.

Razack, S., Smith, M., & Thobani, S. (Eds.). (2010). *States of race: Critical race feminism for the 21st century.* Toronto, ON: Between the Lines.

Rose, D. B., van Dooren, T., Chrulew, M., Cooke, S., Kearnes, M., & O'Gorman, E. (2012). Thinking through the environment, unsettling the humanities. *Environmental Humanities 1*, 1–5.

Stewart, K. (2012). Precarity's forms. *Cultural Anthropology, 27*(3), 518–525.

Taylor, A. (2013). *Contesting childhood beyond nature.* London: Taylor & Francis.

Taylor, A., & Giugni, M. (2012). Common worlds: Reconceptualising inclusion in early childhood communities. *Contemporary Issues in Early Childhood, 13*(2), 108–119.

Tsing, A. (2005). *Friction: An ethnography of global connection.* Princeton: Princeton University Press.

Tsing, A. (2012). Unruly Edges: Mushrooms as companion species. *Environmental Humanities, 1,* 141–154.

Tuck, E., & Yang, K. W. (2012). Decolonization is not a metaphor. *Decolonization: Indigeneity, Education, & Society, 1*(1), 1–40.

van Doreen, T., & Rose, D. B. (2012). Storied-places in a multispecies city. *Humanimalia: A Journal of Human/ Animal Interface Studies, 3*(2). Retrieved from http://www.depauw.edu/humanimalia/issue%206/rose-van%20 dooren.html

Whatmore, S. (2006). Materialist returns: Practicing cultural geography in and for a more-than-human world. *Cultural Geographies, 13*(4), 600–609.

Willems-Braun, B. (1997). Buried epistemologies: The politics of nature in (post)colonial British Columbia. *Annals of the Association of American Geographers, 8*(1), 3–31.

TWELVE

Radical Theories of Presence in Early Childhood Imaginaries

Chelsea Bailey

These results appear to us to be both exciting and highly provocative. A theoretical picture of the transition to turbulence is just beginning to emerge. … Chaos now presages the future as none will gainsay. But to accept the future, one must renounce much of the past. (Gleick, 1987, p. 39)

Here

There is a standard telling of the historical origins of thinking in early childhood education that begins with Plato and Aristotle and traces itself through a lineage of what could be thought of as an investigative philosophical stance. However accurate this philosophical lineage is, I would propose that we are on the waning edge of an epoch whose ascent began with so-called enlightenment philosophies and reached its apex, at least for our current generation, in the post-Darwinian linear objectivism of the 1950s and '60s.

This point of view, embodied in the theories of the great developmentalists—Piaget, Erikson, Kohler, Freud, etc.—has dominated and continues to dominate what we believe about learning and how we look at, understand, and create relationships with children and their experience. Within this frame, learning and accomplishment are the primary referents around which all physical and ephemeral structures are built.

With the rise of critical, poststructuralist, postmodern, queer, and post-colonial critiques of certainty and power, these well-established narratives of fixity have taken repeated blows. But outside the rarified world of academic discourse, early childhood theory and practice remains stuck somewhere between 1950 and 1989, with a few rare exceptions. However, no narrative, especially one that has outlived its truth-value, can survive beyond its own usefulness. And as the world becomes increasingly undone by what postmodern theory describes but did not start, the disconnection between what was, what is, and what will be becomes more evident and urgent. Past beliefs and narratives that have created and structured the very nature of something called "early childhood education" just won't make sense anymore. They will cease to function, even as we continue to rely on them, even as an object of critique.

The heart of this chapter considers what happens after these narratives have ceased to function and entertains possibilities for how the next chapter of what we currently call "childhood" will be written. Layering systems theory and complexity over theories of radical relational engagement, I look specifically at the potential of nonlinear, unexpected, and tender exchanges as uniquely 21st-century organizing principles for what we currently call "learning." Certainty has been perhaps the greatest privilege of the west, and we are, by and large, unprepared for a future that doesn't look and feel like the past. In this chapter, I draw on stories from my recent work in China to examine how the unfamiliar exposes the uncertain and how this uncertainty can lead us quite suddenly to a breakdown out of which the potential for tenderness arises. Rather than being a simple cross-cultural tale of difference and its failures and misunderstandings in the present, I use the lessons offered by these stories of lateral discontinuity to map a route to tenderness. By engaging in these imaginaries of the present, I make an urgent case for tenderness and suggest one possible course for navigating what I hope will be the best version of what could possibly come next.

I am not offering a radical new set of theories. I am assuming that my readers have a high level of knowledge, commitment, and critical engagement in the field. I am offering, with the humility and perspective of someone who functions largely outside the academy, a set of organizing principles for participating in a future that will exact profoundly different demands on our knowledge, insight, and the quality of our relationships. I hope these can help give rise to a remastered vision of who we are and what we do that is commiserate with the complexity and uncertainty of our own emerging futures.

There

In May 2011, I was invited by a colleague at the University of Pennsylvania to join her in a project to design and open preschools in Hong Kong and China. Having worked on similar projects in the U.S., I was excited for the opportunity to learn about what schooling meant in these locales and contribute in whatever ways I could. We soon began the slow and careful process of forming relationships with the complex network of entrepreneurial funders and their partners, universities here and in China, principals and their schools, local teachers and those we were bringing with us, and each other. These nascent relationships were stretched across the macro-cultures of east and west; the micro-cultures of China, Hong Kong, and the U.S., and the mini-micro-cultures manifest in the interests of seven individual different stakeholders, many of whom were based in Asia.

My job was to co-conceptualize and implement a curriculum design that would create some kind of novel blend of Eastern and Western approaches (co-delivered by Chinese and Western early childhood teachers) and would make sense in a rapidly changing Chinese context. In preparation for this work, I sought out any writings I could find on Chinese early childhood education and East–West educational collaborations there while reaching out to everyone I knew who had done any work in Asia. I was first surprised to find that written documentation of work there was difficult to come by. With one well-known exception, there was just not a lot being written about schooling, early childhood or otherwise, in Asia. And finding anything from an Asian point of view proved even more challenging. Second, I was surprised that the people I spoke to were, for the most part, discouraging about doing educational work in China. The discouragement took two forms. The first was simply people's stories of negative and failed experiences. These stories ranged from frustration over differences in style, particularly around the mechanics of doing business, to the difficulty of gaining access to the more personal side of schools, to the daily challenges of living in China, to the near impossibility of locating high-quality materials for classrooms, all the way to stories of abject failure. The message was: "it can't be done." The other kind of discouragement came in the form of a cautionary tale. China is becoming a huge new educational market, and for those who recognize this, mostly Asian entrepreneurs at this point, there is the opportunity to make a lot of money. The concern, of course, is that in an effort to make money, issues of quality and respect of existing practices and practitioners can be compromised. Because we are working at the behest of business-minded educators in Hong Kong, I was warned against being party to these kinds of exploitative educational ventures.

I was sobered but not discouraged, and what I found in actually doing the work was both the truth of these stories and the limits of that truth. Now, having done real work with real people and having had the chance to live and work in China the better part of the past six months, I certainly don't claim to be an expert on early childhood education in China or East–West collaborations. But I can say that it is in fact the case that all the warnings, stories of failure, and dangers that people told me about are true. I experienced them in real time. And yet, it is also the case that our work has manifested something powerful, profound, and enduring that functions outside and beyond the seeming impossibility of these very real limitations. However valid and real the limitations expressed previously are, ultimately they will not be the determining factor in the success of our efforts. But through these stories, we can come to understand the internal mechanisms of what success can mean in the context of the impossible.

This disjuncture allows us to consider whether the truth of impossibility and the possibility of success have anything to do with one another. It is within this fracture between "by what all accounts should be" and "what in fact is" that the ontological detective must begin their search to understand the relationship between success and the impossible. I feel a personal sense of urgency to do so because I believe it is in fact this disjuncture that will mark the difference between the operating instructions of the world of the past and what the future will require. What lies between is a quieter, more powerful set of operating principles. These principles have always functioned but have historically been silenced by the bombastic, bossy, drunk uncle of Western rationalism that have told us what, when, and where to look and act. It's this myopic vision that is now failing us, and in its failure, we have the chance to see and act beyond these ontological boundaries.

Against the backdrop of what I would loosely call "what I learned in China," or more accurately, "how China created the conditions for me to see clearly what I had suspected all along," I present to you here a set of three organizing principles that I believe can act as a guide for participating in a future that promises to be both completely foreign and utterly impossible.[1]

Principle One: Systems Are Self-Organizing—Learn to Dance With Them

Always start by "attending to the crack." (Scharmer & Kaufer, 2013, Loc 373 of 5044)

Here

Donella Meadows (2008), one of the first thinkers to apply the largely mathematical work of systems theory to the everyday world human experience, offers this definition of a system: "a set of elements or parts that is coherently organized and interconnected in a pattern or structure that produces a characteristic set of behaviors, often classified as its 'function' or 'purpose.'" (Meadows, 2008, p. 188). It is easy to make the case that our lives are filled with systems. They are all around us and within us. Systems structure knowledge as well as thought, experience, and the physical world itself. Some systems we label, understand, and manipulate. Others are oblique but function all the same and do so without our understanding, manipulations, or even our awareness. Gravity is an oblique system, so is love. They can be described, but they were not created. On the other hand, ideology, philosophy, sewage systems, political systems, the Google search engine, biology, table manners, were all invented. But regardless of origin or even hurtful or helpfulness, all systems are subject to the same logic and the same rules of sustainability.

Meadows and her colleagues (Meadows, 2008; McKibben, 2007) have presented in detail the logic of systems and what allow systems to endure or decline. And because naturally occurring systems are entangled with fabricated ones, it is possible for naturally self-sustaining systems to decline and fail if too much pressure is brought to bear by contrived systems. Consider the relationship between the earth's water cycle and the carbon emissions of the combustion engine as an example. Systems that exhaust other systems are not sustainable and will eventually exhaust themselves as well. What do sustainable systems look like? A sustainable system is a balanced, flexible, and resilient system. It is a system that functions and adapts to internal and external perambulations. In short, it can organize and reorganize itself in dynamic relation to itself and other systems. Meadows (2008) offers this definition of self-organization: "the ability of a system to structure itself, to create new structure, to learn, or diversify" (p. 188). In other words, a system must be self-organizing and do it well in order to be sustainable.

There

The first mistake we made in our work in China was to (passively) assume that the concept of time and the nature of interpersonal communications was the same here as there. This was an easy and honest mistake because most of us have lived our lives not having to think otherwise. My wiser readers might think me ignorant and feel impatient with me for not knowing this, but unless you have lived this facet of subjective experience in real time, you cannot possibly understand, even if you accept it theoretically.

It was, in fact, exactly this dissonance that accounted for many of the experiences of frustration I heard about in my early conversations with people about working in Asia. The parts of the work that we expected to be the most straightforward were difficult, protracted, and completely confusing. When it became clear that our new partners were having a similar experience, the more profound implications of this disconnection began to expose our own invisible and deeply written scripts about the nature of time and human communication, the most basic of knowledges.

What did we do? In brief, we overgeneralized about the nature of certain systems, and this overgeneralization first caused discomforts and then caused difficulties. The specifics of the breakdown don't actually matter here. It is the breakdown that is important and how we chose to use that breakdown to reorient ourselves and our understanding of systems (in this instance, the logic of time or how to communicate). The limits of our systemic logic were revealed to us, and we had a choice to insist on the validity (and generalizability) of our old understandings or adjust. In short, we chose to adjust but not without the discomfort of having a core concept of one's life rewritten. And this willingness to be adjusted, for having the DNA of our understanding of time and communication rewritten by a set of vocabularies wholly unfamiliar, is at the heart of the principle of self-organizing systems.

The best way to describe this revision is through a story about how we learned to cross the street in China. During our time working with the kindergarten, we lived about one kilometer from the school. On nice days, we would walk the half an hour to and from school, and in the process we would cross at two major and several minor intersections. We loved the walking but dreaded the intersections. The streets in this city of 21 million people (unknown to most in the West) appeared to us initially as an intense frenzy of bikes, cars, scooters, trucks, motorized carts, buses, pedestrians, and more bikes. But these were not messy, unregulated streets. These were roads with eight clearly marked lanes, designated bike lanes, crosswalks, and sophisticated traffic lights. This only made it worse for us. Despite what looked to us to be these familiar safety systems, the rules around them were terrifyingly unfamiliar. It was clear that there were rules; we just had no idea what they were. Living in New York, I am no stranger to busy street corners; however, I found these corners completely overwhelming. After several weeks of an alternating state of terror (of being hit) and gratitude (for not being hit), I knew I had to get in sync with the streets. The only way to do this was first to let go of everything I knew from the past about crossing streets and second to become a perfect student of every element of the system that is an intersection in this city in China. Once I did these two things, which every smart stranger has ever done in any unfamiliar situation, I was able to find the rhythm and flow and become a functional part of the system, that is, cross the street.

The story of how we adjusted our understanding of time and the nature of communication is exactly the same. It is completely natural that we would rely on our existing knowledge and past experiences to help guide our thoughts and actions in a new place. And as these systems of thought and their accompanying actions failed us, as we sifted through the layers of intention and meaning that goes into trying to express a thought to another, as we stood bleary-eyed not understanding the difference between their "now" and ours, we faced a choice. It is the choice that every "foreigner" has faced when confronted with the fracturing of their irretrievable reality in a faraway place. It is also the choice faced by those who are holding onto systems that have reached the limits of their usefulness. This moment always only holds two options: continue trying to use the outmoded system or give up. The giving up itself offers two options: give up by leaving the context and going somewhere where the system still functions or give up by surrendering the old system for the new that stands before it. The final option is the only one that actually allows for entering into a new place, for participating in a wholly new conversation and context. But this last option also requires the greatest effort, leap, and surrender; therefore, it's the most difficult and where most of us will fail.

Here

All systems, by their nature, are self-organizing because they follow the universal logic of systems and their own defining logic to function. This is true of dysfunctional as well as functional systems. However, in dysfunctional systems, the logic leads to breakdown; in functional systems, the logic is sustaining. The argument that systems theory makes is that if one can understand the logic of how the systems that pervade every aspect of our lives come into being, function, sustain themselves, break down, and cease to be, one can have a profoundly different relationship to and impact on the generation and maintenance of self-sustaining and sustainable systems, those that are ultimately of greatest benefit to all of us.

The relatively simple idea that all systems are self-organizing has profound implications if applied broadly. If one understands that healthy, sustainable systems are ones that learn, grow, and adapt, one learns to follow, engage, and act in concert with the rhythm and flow of its dynamics, to accept and live its logic. Rigidity and over-determinedness are death for a system. If I had continued to follow the rules for crossing the street I brought with me from New York, it would have potentially caused my death. Neither can one enter into a dialogue with a system from a rigid or self-certain point of view. It would not have been possible to force our Chinese colleagues to accept our definition of how time functions. Dialogues require listening to and engaging with the logic of the other, no matter how far away it is from our own point of view. But it is not as simple as giving up your viewpoint for another one. It is not a model based on one idea or system conquering another. Neither is it a passive surrender. It is a model for dynamic encounters in which all parties will be transformed, sometimes by a small measure and sometimes quite large. It is a model where one must enter with the humility of a stranger and attend with the intimacy of a lover if one is to have any kind of success at all. It is my central premise that our current educational system is failing us, and we are already experiencing the breakdown of our ability to participate in the ways we always have. We are fast approaching the moment when we must make the choice between continuing to fight to hold on or to let go and find ourselves anew in the logic flow of the system of learning that is already in emergence, whether we understand it or not.

Donella Meadows reminds us:

> We can't impose our will on a system, we can listen to what the system tells us, and discover how its properties and our values can work together to bring forth something much better than could ever be produced by our will alone. We can't control systems or figure them out. But we can dance with them! (2008, pp. 169–170)

Principle Two: Cultivate Limbic Resonance—Relationships Matter

> Because our minds seek one another through limbic resonance, because our physiologic rhythms answer to the call of limbic regulation—what we do inside relationships matter more than any other aspect of human life. (Lewis, Armini, & Lannon, 2000, p. 192)

Here

Although I was late to come to the book, Thomas Lewis and his co-authors, in *A General Theory of Love* (2000), offer a compelling argument for the critical role of a very specific kind of relationship primarily between parents, particularly mothers, and their children. As an MD psychoanalyst, the first author extends this role to therapists well. This relationship is one grounded in limbic resonance and limbic regulation, and when viewed from the therapeutic context, limbic revision. The limbic system supports basic emotional processes (among other things), and the authors argue that the neurobiology of an infant's present and future emotional life is written as their neurons are formed in response to their mother's emotional and physical engagement. In other words, the neurobiological structure of the brain is directly influenced by a child's experience of love and connection with those whom they are closest.

This is not difficult to accept either from the perspective of common-sense or from what we know of Harlow's cruel research on isolation with rhesus monkeys and later reports on infants who experienced extreme emotional deprivation in orphanage settings. We know that we are social beings and that without love and care our children will not survive, and if they do survive, they are a fraction of who they would have been otherwise. But I think what the book introduces is something more provocative and sophisticated. A foundation for a theory of the neurobiology of learning that would insist upon a level of engagement between those who guide and those who are guided on par with the most resonate and well-regulated mother–child duo is discussed. With the boldness of someone who possesses no real knowledge of the neurobiology of learning, I want to make a special case here, a provocation really, for the possibility of a physical basis for why meaningful, lasting learning can only take place within the context of just such a limically defined relationship.

That the quality of the emotional connection directly impacts the quality of the learning experience is not a particularly new or radical idea. However, if we were to earnestly apply the point of view to educational settings and take seriously the concern about the pervasiveness of poorly regulated limbic brains, then we begin to realize how poorly prepared most of us are to either resonate or regulate, much less revise in a healthy and sustainable way. Lewis, Armini, and Lannon (2000) seem to suggest that most of us are limbic messes, poorly regulated and severely emotionally limited in our capacity for relatedness. Walking around as a human being in this world, I believe this, for the most part, to be true. But I also believe that despite our deficits and our limitations, we are able and do find the flow of another's limbic rhythms, and like the story of self-regulating systems, through this encounter both parties are influenced and changed. With this in mind, I want to initiate a conversation here about what it would mean if it were the case that limbic resonance is in fact the stuff that learning is made from and that without it, learning would be an impossibility.

If we were to explore the premise that learning is an encounter between two sets of complex systems (a "you" and a "me") that must, in order for meaningful sustained learning to take place, engage with one another in such a way that their neurochemistry enters into some sort of alignment, we must immediately consider how it is possible to ensure the best possible conditions, both within and outside the educators themselves, to support these encounters. Of course, this is and has been the work of constructivist educators, who, since Aristotle, have understood the importance of the meaningful encounter as the basis for all learning. However, with the insistence of the critical importance of the well-regulatedness of the initiating adult's limbic system, we must exact a new set of demands on the adults who enter classrooms with young children (as well as those of us who work with the teachers). The idea to grapple with here is that as these dynamic systems engage with one another, minds are written and rewritten in concert with the other, and the health of the one determines the health, well-being, and understanding of the other.

I invite you to consider what a paradigm for learning would look like that took neurobiological resonance as the starting point for all other thought and processes. What does learning and its constituent systems look like then?

There

We arrived in China with *ideas* and *plans*. It's not bad to formulate ideas based on one's training, experience, and expertise and to conceptualize strategies that concretize these ideas; indeed, we were being contracted to do exactly this. We weren't wrong to do so, but we arrived not understanding the relative usefulness of these ideas and plans. We thought of them as our guide and our roadmap as it were. We were sincerely committed to collaborating with our Chinese colleagues; in fact, it was a critical element of our ideas and our plans. In constructing our plan, we did not see any contradiction in "planning to collaborate." And I don't believe many readers would have a problem with the idea of collaboration as an important feature of one's methodology. We designed an intentionally open-format, modular plan for creating curricular encounters (between our ideas and the teachers, children, and administrators) that we felt would leave ample room for negotiating and co-constructing how the curriculum would be lived. Our mistake, however, was that we assumed it would be the exchange of curricular ideas and practices that would form the foundation of our work and act as the primary unit of exchange. And in this we were wrong.

Our ideas and plans were not invalid; they just did not turn out to function the way that we assumed they would based on our past experience. Rather than guiding our work, they acted as ignition points that set into motion reactions, conversations, explanations, negotiations, anxieties, revelations, risks, and intimate engagements. Our ideas and plans became highly charged points of contact that pushed our encounters into a state of dynamic disequilibrium. These strange attractors[2] became an intensely compelling state for all of us, and it is where the real work got done.

I define "real work" here as the space where substantive change can take place. It is not that our plans and ideas were not important or even critical to the process, but rather, that they did not act as the radial point for the transformative change that took place among and between ourselves and our Chinese colleagues. Instead change took place in the realm of relationality beyond the mitigating reach of plans and ideas. The exchange was not of ideas but of the basic elements of human interconnectedness—within the realms of risk, respect, certainty, vulnerability, and love. And this is where we were able to meet each other and where the work got done, under the skin of our everyday selves. It is critically important that this level of work was only possible when well-established professional understandings of curriculum, learning, and the role of the teacher began to break down on both sides. Only when we reached the diminishing edge of our own paradigmatic event horizon did powerful shared connections literally change who we are and how we think about teaching, learning, the world, and ourselves.

If practice (methodology) is reflection of an idea (epistemology), then it is only through relationships experienced in real time that these ideas can come to make sense through the veracity of their usefulness, through the conflation of concept and practice. And if these relationships are not or cannot be defined and regulated by a shared understanding and acceptance of each party's role, then, stripped of our ideas and plans and their attendant identities, we are left standing bare and exposed, no ground or reliable point of reference. From this basis of disequilibrium, we were all equally strangers to the new ideas and no plans had yet to be made. From here, anything was possible, and whatever might be written would be written together.

Our work with our Chinese colleagues was no less powerful or challenging than what I am describing here. Over and over we found ourselves in this cycle of plans and ideas, intense listening and trying to understand, confusion, frustration, befuddlement, letting go, and finally coming to an understanding that arose out of respect and care, and increasingly, out of love.

Here

The intention of this story is to make a case for the primacy of complex, deeply engaged relationships over ideas because ideas are only as flexible and useful as the paradigmatic systems that gave rise to them. I believe that as compassionate as constructivist educational practices might be, they are still vested in a system of thinking that is becoming increasingly outmoded. As systems shift and fail, we can't rely on ideas, even if they are good ones. We must rely on something deeper. Our experience working with our colleagues in China was an object lesson in system failure. It was only because we were able to withstand by degree giving up what we each held to be best practice that we were able to do meaningful work together. And this work included not only building the meaningful connections I describe earlier but also the creation of a courageous classroom practice that reflected the dynamics specific to our particular East–West encounter. I believe these practices reflect an authentic encounter between two outmoded systems and provide a glimpse into the potential what can happen next if we are open and willing to let go of that which we are most certain. And I believe the only reliable navigation tool for this process will be connection.

When we consider what the important factors are in connection, a theory of limbic resonance can be useful in providing us with a complex map for these relational dynamics and their function at the physical as well as psychological levels. It also provides a language for what has been important to educators for a long time as well as a framework for the quality of the relationships necessary for limbic resonance and regulation to be in play. As we move into the uncertain unfolding future, I believe we must be ready to radically engage with whatever encounters of system failure and the unfamiliar that lie before us. And we must do so with our hearts and minds ready to be rewritten in the limbic language of something wholly unexpected and different from what we have known.

Principle Three: Love, Quite Plainly, Love

"I would say this quite plainly, what is truly human is—and don't be afraid of this word—love. And I mean it even with everything that burdens love or, I could say it better, responsibility, is actually love, Pascal said: 'without concupiscence' [without lust] … love exists without worrying about being loved." (Levinas quoted in Marcus, 2008, p. 97)

Here

In a TED talk based on his 2012 book, *Far From the Tree*, Andrew Solomon (2013) offers a powerful corollary between self-organizing systems in the physical world and love to expose the lines that can delineate difference, acceptance, and the limits and possibilities of love. He states: "in the same way we need species diversity to ensure that the planet can go on, so we need this diversity of affection and diversity of family to strengthen the eco-sphere of kindness." Solomon's book is an exploration of how love and acceptance manifest across the horizontal identities of difference between parents and their children. In classrooms, at work, in the gym, on the street, we expect to encounter difference. But when we have a child, we expect, at least in the beginning, a more comfortable mirror of ourselves. It is a subtle unconscious expectation that sneaks up on you over the course of your child's life. I remember, for example, being confused when, seconds after her birth, I gazed upon my daughter's face and saw my mother-in-law staring back. I love my mother-in-law, but my surprise reveals the unspoken (even to myself) expectation that my daughter would reflect my own features back to me. This small example demonstrates the presence of an expectation I didn't know was lurking in my heart. And as she has grown, I have gone through many such experiences of the pleasures and discomforts of sameness and difference. But the latitude of difference has never been so large (so far) that I have had to cross any great divides. It is easy to celebrate her differences along with the ways that we are the same, placing my parenting experience squarely outside the specific scope of Solomon's book. But I also understand how my parenting story could have just as easily been one of those being told if circumstances were even a few degrees different. And that this could be true for any of us.

The concern of Solomon's book and my own anecdote about the unexpectedness of difference are important here because of what they have to tell us about love, the last and most important principle to guide us into the unwritten future of our field. Why love? Solomon speaks of a need for "diversity of affection" to strengthen the "eco-sphere of kindness." These words resonate as critical instructions not just for families but for our culture at large, especially for those of us who have profound influence over the daily lives of children. Given our tendency to love easily what is most familiar and struggle against that which is not, the imperative to love boldly becomes that much more urgent. Why love? Why not simply respect or support? Because true kindness demands nothing less than love, and anything less leaves room for the subtle brutality that arises from the distance and disconnection of not seeing the other as an extension of yourself, as intimately tied to your heart, as your greatest responsibility. If you do not believe me, look at the current classroom conditions most teachers and children are living in today. To be a meaningful participant in the unwritten future of the field, to create meaningful contexts and communities of what we call learning, we can only do through love. But this is not a neatly organized, structured kind of love. It is a deep, messy, rip your heart and stand naked before the other kind of love. I offer that the future will demand nothing less that our whole hearts and perfect passions opened and offered to those whom we have committed our lives.

There

The first time I saw Ms. Liu, I knew she was someone very special. She was dressed in electric-pink spandex pants, off-the-shoulder *Flashdance*-style top, florescent-green glasses with no lenses, globe earrings that touched her shoulders, beaded bracelets to the wrists on both arms, and an afro-style permed ponytail. She also possessed the magic of a powerful master teacher. To watch her teach, even in a language I didn't understand, was mesmerizing. She held the rapt attention of every one of the 35 5-year-olds in her class. It didn't matter whether she was leading a lesson on math calculations or on the importance of dental hygiene. It didn't matter that every lesson was "teacher directed," we all had stars in our eyes as we watched her move around the room as graceful as the dancer she was.

We were incredibly fortunate that Ms. Liu was open and eager to learn whatever we might offer her in the way of Western methods. And it was with much excitement that we (myself and Michele, who would actually co-teach in the classroom) returned one month later to launch the pilot program in her classroom. As soon as we began, I realized right away what a profound gift she was offering to open up her classroom and her mind to our new ideas. Now, coupled with my already existing teacher crush, I was overcome with a debilitating sense of gratitude. I would become so overwhelmed, I would begin to cry and found myself giving her any gift I could find: any jewelry I was wearing, an orange I had picked fresh from a tree in California a few days before my flight, a favorite scarf, my one-of-a-kind knitted coin purse I had bought in a boutique in Shanghai on my last trip, anything I thought she might like. She seemed to feel the same way and brought me gifts regularly as well, but hers were presented with the comportment of proper Chinese gift giving. I was clearly an amateur, a sloppy puppy to her sophisticated lady, but she was charmed as well. We both knew the gift giving was only a courtship for the real relationship we both craved, which was the deep exchange of our most closely held beliefs, hopes, and dreams about teaching and learning.

At the end of the first week, with the assistance of our translator, we had our first real date, that is, we talked about the curriculum we would be introducing. Everything was lovely until I talked about what seemed to me a logistical detail: We were going to break the children up into smaller working groups. Everything, including the romantic soundtrack, came to a screeching halt. She said simply: "That's not possible," with the greatest look of sadness and the smallest hint of betrayal on her still radiant face. As I felt the ground lurch and sway below me, she explained why it wasn't possible, and the entire universe of my professional knowledge, all my ideas and plans, tried to reorganize themselves into the molecular structure that would make what was impossible, possible for her. For her, I would accept that even to split the group in half violated the deepest core of what was most dear to Ms. Liu as a teacher—*guan* [3]—and I would find a way to give her the gift she most wanted, a version of Western curriculum that would make sense in her classroom, something both intelligible and kind.

And so it was with the focus and intention of one who fears the loss of something important that I began to reformulate my/our curriculum for her/their classroom. I would woo her with the curriculum of her dreams, and in order to do that, I had to know what her dreams were. I had to understand the outer edge of her curricular imagination and where she most wished to travel and explore. Therefore, I had to watch and listen with the persistence of one who wishes to please their love. I became a student of her deepest pedagogical desires. She was in turn the embodiment of the children's deepest wishes and desires to know and be in the world, and through her, I came to know them. Day by day, I listened and watched with every one of my senses, especially my heart. I put my plans aside and opened myself up to becoming fully present to her teaching, to her classroom, her children, and her relationships to them, the parents, and the other teachers in the classroom, to put myself in her place. I wasn't going to just meet her halfway, I was going to lose myself in her teaching in order to bring her to me, a classic lover's ploy.

I did learn, and through trial and error, we slowly found together the space where something entirely different could come into being, something neither fully hers nor mine, something intelligible and kind, a space we could all find shelter in. For this to be possible, we had to discover a process for being in the both/and space of neither fully Western nor fully Chinese early childhood curriculum. And we did this quite simply through the trust and love that arises in the risk and struggle between what we know and don't know. The negotiations and translations, both linguistic and cultural, were almost constant, with Michele trapped in the middle to perform a curriculum (often for media audiences) that was neither here nor there, the shadow of an idea, negotiated in the fine line between what we and they recognized as learning. All any of us could do was trust, especially the teachers and administrators at the school. They didn't really understand or recognize what we were doing, and we were rewriting and reformulating our entire plan as we went along, and still they chose to trust us. We showed up every day with ideas and plans and listened to their concerns and tried our best to be responsive to their requests, and every day the trust and respect was tested but more than not, it grew. Through the mistakes and apologies and gifts and challenges, we continued to deepen our respect and care and concern for each other. We struggled, but we never turned away, and this was the critical difference. I would argue that this is the reality of what love is, never turning away.

After a certain point, we knew we were lost to our passions for the project and for each other. When I left the first time, I had to promise over and over again that I would return in a month's time. And during this time, Ms. Liu and I communicated almost every day, sending pictures back and forth, sharing concerns and ideas. Michele developed bronchitis over her birthday (while I was in the U.S.), and the teachers and administrative staff cared for her as sweetly and carefully as they would a member of their own family. We knew then that we had become part of each other, that we were deeply bonded and that something miraculous had happened, because to actually open one's heart to another is nothing less than a miracle and should rightly be viewed as such. And when it was finally time for us to leave at the end of our brief eternity of four months, there were gifts and tears and passionate, desperate embraces with our previously reserved Chinese colleagues who had become our sisters, mothers, daughters, lovers, and teachers, and we all knew we would never be the same. We had all been broken open by the same set of desires, longings, and passions. We began to only be able to imagine a future that would be written together.

Ms. Liu and I still write to each other several times a week. We are anxiously waiting to hear whether the program has been approved to continue in the fall. Michele and I promised to return, so no matter the outcome of funding or official approvals, she and I know we have to go back. A promise of the heart cannot be broken, and we know this. This is not, however, a story about curriculum and what we did in China. There's no shortage of stories written about the miraculous insights gained in faraway places. Instead, it is quite simply a story about love. To read this as a tale of connection and disconnection across culture is to make a profound mistake. Love, care, respect, and tenderness were not byproducts of a successful project; they were the cause. And it is these trajectories that will determine and guide what comes next. I believe that only now, in this state of resonance and love, can a new curriculum begin to be imagined. Now we are ready to begin our work.

Here/Now

If we are to survive the project of early childhood education, which we ourselves help to create and maintain, then we must engage in a new reality defined by the urgency of connectedness. We must show up and fully open ourselves to the possibilities and failings of love. We must take seriously what it means to fall in love with our work and with those with whom we work, and we must give ourselves over fully to its experience and implications with our adult and child collaborators. Love must become the *force majeure* of our work. Emmanuel Levinas (1997; Hand, 2009) made what I feel is one of the most radical philosophical and ethical proposals of our time. He proposed that love is not an equal exchange. It is not the coming together of two who encounter one another with equal responsibilities toward the other. Indeed, he argues that the only truly ethical stance is to view the service and care of the other as one's highest responsibility. No matter what they present or ask of you, no matter your own perceived wishes or needs, the onus falls on you to love and care for the other. Love without limits, without boundaries, without expectations is the most sustainable system of all because it always gives more than it takes. It implores us to be passionate toward the other (*loving fully*), present to the other (*witnessing fully*), and infinitely responsible for the other (*responding fully*).

I can imagine no greater imperative for a new vision of what we currently call early childhood education.

The intention of this chapter is to propose three organizing principles that can guide us through the failing trajectories of our waning educational paradigm. In doing so, I am making an urgent plea for seizing the opportunity for tenderness and what unfolds from the love that arises. I have provided examples of how this happens between adults in faraway places to highlight not only what can come of uncertainty but why it is that our own falling apart will be the greatest guide for moving courageously into the best version of what can come next.

References

Gleick, J. (1987). *Chaos: Making a new science*. New York: Penguin.

Hand, S. (Ed.). (2009). *The Levinas reader*. Malden, MA: Blackwell.

Levinas, E. (1997). *Entre-Nous: On thinking of the other*. New York: Columbia University Press.

Lewis, T., Armini, F., & Lannon, R. (2000). *A general theory of love*. New York: Vintage Books.

Marcus, P. (2008). *Being for the other: Emmanuel Levinas, ethical living and psychoanalysis*. Milwaukee, WI: Marquette University Press.

McKibben, B. (2007). *Deep economy: The wealth of communities and the durable future*. New York: St. Martin's Griffin.

Meadows, D. (2008). *Thinking in systems: A primer* (D. Wright). Ed. White River Junction, VT: Chelsea Green.

Scharmer, O., & Kaufer, K. (2013). *Leading from the emerging future: From eco-system to eco-system economics*. San Francisco: Berret-Kohler.

Solomon, A. (2012). *Far from the tree: Parents, children and the search for identity*. New York: Scribner.

Solomon, A. (2013, June 3). Andrew Solomon: Love no matter what [Video]. Retrieved from http://www.ted.com/talks/andrew_solomon_love_no_matter_what

Notes

1. All the stories I tell in this essay are stories of my experience and mine alone. At times, I use "we" to acknowledge that I did not do this work alone. I have had wonderful partners throughout this journey, and I know that their experiences have led them to meaningful insights. I include them in the "we," but I do not intend or assume to speak for them.

2. A dynamic kind-of-equilibrium is called a "strange attractor." (www.abarim-publications.com/ChaosTheoryIntroduction. html#.UfDTFmRDp9Q).

3. *Guan* is simultaneously translated as care and control and forms the foundation for all educational and even governmental relationships. It is a very complex and subtle concept that guides many aspects of Chinese society. In an early childhood context, one form it takes is that the teacher always guides and controls the children. I was told that children under the age of 6 are, in fact, not capable of self-control, and any group of children not under the strict direction of a teacher would hurt themselves, others, or the materials.

THIRTEEN

Black and Chicana Feminisms: Journeys Toward Spirituality and Reconnection

Michelle Salazar Pèrez and Cinthya M. Saavedra

Inspired by hooks and Mesa-Bains' (2006) *Homegrown*, this chapter is dedicated to a conversational dialogue between Cinthya Saavedra and me (Michelle Salazar Pèrez) about our work enacting Black and Chicana feminisms. We have chosen this format for sharing with each other and our audience in order to provide what is often undocumented insight into the theoretical and methodological influences in our research over the years and thoughts about future possibilities for childhood/s inquiry that foregrounds marginalized feminist perspectives.

We begin with a conversation about our connections with Black and Chicana feminisms and why we are drawn to them. Then, we discuss our past work that stems from our theoretical positioning. Finally, we explore new imaginaries for childhoods research as it relates to marginalized feminist epistemologies and notions of collective/spiritual imaginaries.

Our Relationship With Black and Chicana Feminisms, Our Theoretical Homes

Michelle

As I reflect upon my connections to Black feminisms, I am reminded of some of the graduate master's work I did prior to being exposed to Patricia Hill Collins (2000/2008) in my doctoral studies. I was the coordinator of an urban-education student teaching program while completing my master's degree in Educational Psychology at Texas A&M University. Although I had been exposed to critical thought (Foucault, 1979; Freire, 1970, 1998) in some of my undergraduate and master's-level courses by professors like Gaile Cannella (1997), Radhika Viruru (2005), and Ellen

Demas (Demas & Saavedra, 2004), in my research for a Houston-based student teaching program, I was memorizing codes for the use of a classroom observational instrument, obtaining inter-rater reliability, and even teaching these post-positivist "data collection" methods to other researchers. I couldn't help but feel the imposition this instrument had on the Black, Brown, and white teachers I worked with and the students they served who were labeled as "at risk." With my positioning as a Chicana, I knew in my gut that while our research was seen as rigorous, it was in actuality harming the very communities I had hoped to advocate with/for. As I began to question my role as an educator, academic, and activist, I wondered what research might look and feel like that recognized power as central to the inequities I was witnessing daily and ways in which lived experiences of communities of color (and those from other marginalized positionalities) might be viewed as "at promise" (Swadener & Lubeck, 1995).

Instead of continuing my doctoral studies to learn further about deficit forms of research with young children from marginalized communities, I decided to immerse myself in a PhD program that would expose me almost entirely to critical thought. At that point, my advisor gave me the book *Black Feminist Thought: Knowledge, Consciousness, and the Politics of Empowerment* (Collins, 2000/2008). In my initial reading of Collins, I recall writing pages upon pages of notes, highlighting text, and making comments in a way that I had never done before. I felt as if at last, I had read a text that made sense to me. Although I can remember having a powerful connection to Freire's (1970) *Pedagogy of the Oppressed* in my undergraduate studies, it was Collins' ability to connect her lived experiences to the collective experiences of women of color and to larger social and institutional structures of domination that drew me to her. I could finally understand why and how my everyday feelings of oppression and empowerment were connected to a complex, web-like "system" of power. This led me to learn more about intersectionality (Crenshaw, 1991; Dill, McLaughlin, & Nieves, 2007) and (re) positioning marginalized epistemologies as central to thought, knowledge, and activism (Collins, 2005, 2006; hooks, 2000a, 2000b; James & Busia, 2003; Lorde, 1984).

Cinthya

In many ways, Michelle, I have very similar reasons as you for my connections to Chicana feminisms. For me, it started my junior year in college when I took a Mexican American writers course. I read the works of Gloria Anzaldúa (1987), Cherríe Moraga (1983), and Ana Castillo (1994), to name a few. Looking back, I'm thankful to Dr. Jesus Rosales for centering Chicana feminism in his course. This was the first time in my life that I felt deeply connected to literature. I felt intimately tied to the women we read that semester and my world finally made sense. The complexity of straddling multiple worlds and languages and my ambivalent feelings toward gender roles were ideas that were foregrounded in the pieces we read for class. New to me were the structural and systemic inequalities that minorities faced. This made me want to pursue a master's degree and PhD in education so I could be a better teacher and researcher for bilingual, immigrant, and transnational students despite the structural challenges they face.

It was during my doctoral studies that I also began to feel drawn to postmodern, poststructural, and postcolonial theories of education. These perspectives gave me a different way to examine inequalities and society. I think I was particularly attracted to ideas associated with postcolonialism (Bhabha, 1996; Loomba, 1998; Spivak, 1988), epistemological/ontological considerations (Kincheloe, 2006), and the questioning of grand narratives (Foucault, 1969). I resonated with the many ideas that the world was/is made of and different ways of being that were/are hidden, sometimes violently by Western man's search for a universal truth through Western disciplines and discourses. Though I felt really drawn to the latter, it was the former epistemology, Chicana feminisms, that offered not only methodological and theoretical tools of research that were relevant to my life but also offered fortitude, solidarity, and more importantly, healing, a healing that I believe can be used for the Self and with communities.

In particular, Chicana feminisms have generated unthought spaces for reinvention, navigation, and negotiation of systems of oppression (Delgado Bernal, 1998). I have really appreciated the reworking of theory (Anzaldúa, 1990; Saldivar-Hull, 2000; Trujillo, 1998), Chicana/Latina pedagogies (Delgado Bernal, Elenes, Godinez, & Villenas, 2006), and methodologies (Delgado Bernal, 1998; Villenas, 1996). For many Chicana feminists, theory comes from the flesh (Anzaldúa, 1987; Moraga, 1983), a much different conception of theory from a positivist understanding of the world. Critical and transformative pedagogies are found in everyday exchanges between mothers and daughters and conversations at the kitchen table (Trinidad Galvan, 2001), not just in formal schooling. Upon reading the work, I was able to immediately say "yes, I get it." My life experiences are reflected in the scholarship, despite the fact that I come from Nicaragua. In essence, their work transcends borders, nationalities, and identities, which is my strongest attraction to Chicana feminist theories.

Foregrounding Black and Chicana Feminisms While Enacting Bricoleur Approaches to Childhoods Research

Michelle
I can relate to the interweaving of many forms of critical thought, such as postmodernism, postcolonialism, and poststructuralism, and the blending of methodological approaches that can be utilized as a result; the scholar/researcher can be referred to as a bricoleur (Kincheloe, 2006, 2008). I've been particularly drawn to Clarke's (2005) *Situational Analysis: Grounded Theory After the Postmodern Turn*. One of my PhD committee members at Arizona State University, Mary Margaret Fonow (2003), introduced me to Clarke's (2005) ideas, and as I read and began to work with situational analysis, I could see how Black feminisms fit well with it. Black feminist thought (Collins, 2000/2008) would be the theoretical perspective that framed my dissertation work in New Orleans, and situational analysis a complementary methodological tool to uncover some of the invisible forms of oppression existing in the re-establishment of public education after the failure of the levees post-Katrina.

My time working on my dissertation was a powerful experience for me. I had read and engaged in learning about perspectives that questioned research in itself as exploitative (Smith, 1999), even some forms of critical qualitative inquiry, and so exposure to these ideas drove my desire to resist reifying harmful research practices in my own work, especially amongst communities of color in New Orleans that were being increasingly gentrified by colonial/imperialist circumstances. When I arrived in New Orleans in 2007, I spent a year immersing myself in the culture of the city and began to learn the story of the communities. After witnessing the injustices occurring in the context of what Naomi Klein (2007) termed "disaster capitalism," my research began to focus on examining the privatization of the public school system in New Orleans (Pérez, 2009; Cannella & Pérez, 2009; Pérez & Cannella, 2010, 2011, in press).

Situational analysis (Clarke, 2005) felt like the perfect complement to my Black feminist theoretical framework. It served as a medium to grab hold of what were extremely fleeting circumstances (Cannella & Pérez, 2009); in fact, I even used it to design my study (Pérez & Cannella, 2011). I wanted my research questions to be based on initial "readings" of the discourses surrounding charter schools and public education, so it was important for me to not only gather information about the school system, but engage in the culture of the city and community-driven forms of activism. This occurred mostly through my involvement in a grassroots organization concerning public housing—the members of which introduced me to a network of activists attempting to resist the dismantling of public services across all sectors (such as healthcare, transportation, and education to name a few). I am forever thankful and indebted to the communities that took me in and shared their lives with me and who also taught me about a different form of activism than what I had learned about through my higher education training—they taught me how to *collectively* engage in community rallies and protests while using my body and my "voice" to resist oppression.

I could really see the ties between my closeness to Black feminist epistemologies and the activism in which I participated, even the forms of oppression(s) present within social movements (hooks, 2000a; Morris, 2010; Roth, 2003) as well as what Collins (2000/2008) refers to as both/and identities functioning within/amongst interpersonal power/oppression. In relation to my childhood education research, methodologically, Black feminist thought helped me to frame the structural circumstances creating inequities in children's access to public education. From dismantling public transportation for children trying to get to and from schools, to denying special education services to young children and families, communities were denied services. Further, the dominant rhetoric embedded in media and education policy discourses espoused by appointed education leaders with business backgrounds misled communities and influenced the larger national dialogue to support a privatized system for public education. Black feminisms helped to flesh out and uncover the structural, disciplinary, hegemonic, and interpersonal power (Collins, 2000/2008) fueling the corporatization of the public school system in New Orleans; mapping with situational analysis helped me to decide which stories to tell (Clarke, 2005) within the messy and often overwhelming and ever-changing charter school landscape.

Cinthya
Your thoughts on Black feminisms remind me of how Chicana feminisms, and in particular, borderland-mestizaje feminism (Saavedra & Nymark, 2008), are connected to my very being. As I reflect on my past work, I can see how central it was not only as a lens but as a way of life. I think that is what is missing in much scholarship, that intimate relationship with theory. Even when I use European and American theorists in my work, it is because I deeply relate to them—it feels epistemologically right for me. Just as important have been my critical self-reflections (Pillow, 2003; Villenas, 1996) in all of my research endeavors.

My dissertation was a multiple epistemological examination of the history of the feminization of teaching. What was interesting is that I, too, used Kincheloe's bricolage methodology, which allowed me to see the discourse of the history of the feminization of teaching from multiple lenses. But the central questions started with reflections on my cuerpo/my body that stem from Chicana feminist work and the idea of theory in the flesh (Anzaldúa, 1987; Moraga, 1983). My understanding of Chicana feminism prompted me to ask questions about my inability to perform liberatory pedagogies with third-grade bilingual students. This (re)search led me to examine how teaching has strong ties to its history and how the body of the teacher is socially constructed. Moreover, my work with immigrant, Latina, mostly Mexican women (Saavedra, 2011), has necessitated that I not only use theories that are relevant to their lives but also that help offer new ways to work with and for our communities. My research in North Carolina taught me that being "Latina" did not necessarily mean that I had immediate access, understandings, and solutions for this community. What helped me though were the theories that help researchers to be reflexive such as Chicana feminisms (Villenas, 1996), poststructuralism (Pillow, 2003), and discussions regarding decolonization (Smith, 1999).

But what about research with dominant (privileged) or mainstream communities? What I have learned is that research in itself is colonizing (Saavedra, 2011; Smith, 1999). My work with mostly White, middle-class, pre-K teachers in North Carolina also helped me to reflect about the ways that research imposes a need to find Truth and to change participants (Saavedra, Chakravarthi, & Lower, 2009). Research rarely allows us to reconsider what it is that we are doing and how the very act of research ought to also change research and the researcher (Fernandes, 2003).

I remember thinking at the beginning of the project how *these* teachers were hesitant to change their perspectives about working with immigrant children. Yet through dialogue and critical reflections, my colleagues and I began to see how complex the work of early childhood teachers is, and researchers need to examine how the multiple discourses found in the early childhood classroom create complexities that are hard to tease out and solve. The teachers in the end did show new understanding, but so did we. Both of these research projects deepened and further complicated my role as researcher. For example, it made me question bifurcated categories such as privileged and nonprivileged. The pre-K teachers may occupy some privileged spaces as White women, yet at the same time, in the early childhood classroom, this label is more complicated and cannot be easily thrown on them if we are really looking at our participants with critical lenses.

New Imaginaries for Childhoods Research: Collective/Spiritual Possibilities

Michelle
When I think about (re)envisioning early childhood research, I turn to ideas surrounding more collective approaches to the world. In many ways, while important to highlight the unique struggles and strengths of marginalized communities through the use of theory conceptualized *by* our communities, I wonder what might be possible if we intertwine our ideas more often, to move toward a diversality (Kincheloe, 2008) of critical thought and methodology enacted through our childhoods research and activism. With this braiding, what commonalities/ tensions would we find and what possibilities might be uncovered? For instance, you and I have found ways to blend marginalized epistemologies, finding points of affinity between our Black and Chicana feminist *testimonios* (Saavedra & Pérez, 2012), and have even attempted to forge a third space (Bhabha, 1994; Pérez, 1999) by weaving Black and Chicana feminist

perspectives with Deleuze and Guattari's (1977, 1987) notions of assemblage (Pérez, Cannella, & Saavedra, in press; Pérez & Saavedra, 2012). This braiding of multiple critical lenses, I believe, has great potential to bring us closer together as childhood activist scholars.

Cinthya

Yes, in addition to moving more toward collective forms of research across marginalized/dominant critical epistemologies, I believe that we also have to constantly remind ourselves of the reciprocal relationship between the researcher and researched. Kincheloe (2006) and Fernandes (2003) discuss how we can no longer afford to be the detached observer, or the interpreter. For example, we always look and desire the change in our participants or the phenomenon under investigation, while we ignore how that very examination changes the observer/researcher as well and thereby ignore the symbiotic relationship between observer and observed. Kincheloe (2006) discusses how when we (researchers) encounter difference in our investigations, we enter into a symbiotic relationship where our identity is also changed. We are, he states, "no longer merely obtaining information but are entering a space of transformation where previously excluded perspectives operate to change consciousness of both self and world" (p. 186). Yet he cautions that this space of transformation cannot magically appear, it must involve our "complex hermeneutic abilities" in order for connections to surface and for meaning to be interpreted.

What I believe Kincheloe leaves out, but implies, is what Leela Fernandes (2003) asserts: that we must illuminate the witnessing that transpires in our research endeavors and the "usually invisible question of spiritual responsibility" (p. 91). Spiritual responsibility is to witness the suffering of others. She goes on to note that spiritual responsibility is the "deepest unfolding of the soul…a process in which the suffering of others sparks the soul of the witness [researcher/observer], who may either accept the challenge of understanding and responsibility or who may instead curtail the spiritual possibilities by refusing to see or by seeing voyeuristically" (pp. 91–92). I had never thought of research as such an intimate journey with my participants or phenomena but it surely changes how I approach my scholarship.

Michelle

I, too, find myself moving more toward notions of spiritual responsibility, especially as it pertains to activist conceptualizations of childhood studies research. I have been particularly drawn to spiritual notions of connectivity and the ways in which these understandings of our/selves and the universe urge us to blur the lines of oppositional thought and action (Keating, 2008; Fernandes, 2003; Dillard, 2006). What possibilities surface when we (re)consider our borderlands (Anzaldúa, 1987)? For instance, if we think about our/selves as being connected to each other, the earth, and the cosmos, how might this move us away from approaching activism as oppositional engagement? These ideas have more recently become central to my research/teaching/activism as I have been troubled by the thought that my participation in dissent has in some ways reified many of the oppressions I had hoped to disrupt and dismantle. This is not said without acknowledgement and concern for the need to strongly contest social and institutional imperialism/colonialism, patriarchy, ageism, racism, heteronormativity, ableism, and a host of other acts of domination that create painful and violent circumstances for many (Cannella & Pérez, 2012). However, I do question whether some of my approaches to "fighting" for justice and equity have created new forms of domination. I contemplate how these concerns might cause me to complicate/rethink the borders between ourselves and "others," even within oppositional spaces.

Cinthya

I feel similarly—my journey is now to cross/straddle/stand between new borders, of the cosmological type. I have returned to Gloria Anzaldúa (2002) for inspiration and have found an ally in quantum physics, Indigenous world views, and Eastern spiritualism, which have been staring at me all along. What is even more fascinating to me is that these borders are not so neat, defined, and rigid. Instead they are branches of the same tree, unique drops of water in an ocean. I believe that my reading, performing, and use of Chicana feminist and borderlands scholarship have opened me up to embrace and navigate these new borders.

Two years ago I went to Mexico for a two-week critical language school experience. While there, I went to one of a few Miacatlán sites, Xochicalco. On the side of one of the pyramids was etched an Aztec priest sitting in lotus position and doing mudras with his hands. Here is where space/time/cosmological borders were blurred for me. I didn't know where I was anymore—was I in India or somewhere else in Asia, or Mexico? This small moment made me realize that we are all interconnected, and thus, I have turned to Indigenous peoples' way of viewing the world that can reconnect us to the spiritual world (Cajete, 2000; Duran, 2000). For me now this means that my research is not different or separate from my spirituality, my sense of what it means to be human. Perhaps research is about reconnecting with our world and other human beings.

Michelle

Cinthya, you have explained beautifully some of the imaginaries I have thought about most recently (and that we've talked about in our conversations over the years) when engaging in childhood studies research. As we, and we hope others, reconceptualize connections amongst communities (communities thought of in a broad sense—e.g., across our constructed categories of us/them, human/nonhuman, etc.), how can we continue to break open our colonized minds/bodies/spirits? Notions of spirituality, especially thoughts regarding connectivity, are one way we might rethink and (re)member (Dillard, 2012) our relationship with one another and the world.

Concluding Thoughts

Our past and more recent conversations about Black and Chicana feminist epistemologies have prompted us to (re)consider more collective forms of action across borderlands and also to no longer deny the spiritual realm as part of our ways of being, which include how we conceptualize childhoods research. Although we acknowledge that these ideas are not in any way "new," we have found that they are rarely legitimized or even discussed within academic contexts, and therefore, much work must be done if we are to generate spaces for more collective/spiritual considerations, not only within our critical early childhood organization/s, but also across disciplines and other borderlands. By continuing our work with Black and Chicana feminist thought, attempting to forge more collective approaches to activist scholarship, and engaging more intimately with spirituality, we hope to provide further points of entry for childhood/s imaginaries.

References

Anzaldúa, G. (1987). *Borderlands/La frontera*. San Francisco: Aunt Lute Books.

Anzaldúa, G. (1990). Haciendo caras, una entrada. In G. Anzaldúa (Ed.), *Making face, making soul: Haciendo caras*. (pp. xv–xxviii). San Francisco: Aunt Lute Books.

Anzaldúa, G. (2002). Now let us shift…the path of *conocimiento*…inner work, public acts. In G. Anzaldúa & A. Keating (Eds.), *This bridge we call home: Radical visions for transformation* (pp. 540–578). New York: Routledge.

Bhabha, H. (1994). *The location of culture*. London: Routledge.

Bhabha, H. (1996). The other question. In P. Mongia (Ed.), *Contemporary postcolonial theory: A reader* (pp. 71–89). London: Arnold.

Cajete, G. (2000). *Native science: Natural laws of interdependence*. Santa Fe, NM: Clear Light.

Cannella, G. (1997). *Deconstructing early childhood education: Social justice & revolution*. New York: Peter Lang.

Cannella, G. S., & Pérez, M. S. (2009). Power shifting at the speed of light: Critical qualitative research post-disaster. In N. K. Denzin & M. D. Giardina (Eds.), *Qualitative inquiry and social justice: Toward a politics of hope* (pp. 165–186). Walnut Creek, CA: Left Coast Press.

Cannella, G. S., & Pérez, M. S. (2012). Emboldened patriarchy in higher education: Feminist readings of capitalism, violence, and power. *Cultural Studies <=> Critical Methodologies, 12*(4), 279–286.

Castillo, A. (1994). *Massacre of the dreamers: Essays on Xicanisma*. Albuquerque: University of New Mexico Press.

Clarke, A. E. (2005). *Situational analysis: Grounded theory after the postmodern turn*. Thousand Oaks, CA: Sage.

Collins, P. H. (2000/2008). *Black feminist thought: Knowledge, consciousness, and the politics of empowerment* (2nd/3rd ed.). New York: Routledge.

Collins, P. H. (2005). *Black sexual politics: African Americans, gender, and the new racism*. New York: Routledge.

Collins, P. H. (2006). *From Black power to hip hop: Racism, nationalism, and feminism*. Philadelphia, PA: Temple University Press.

Crenshaw, K. W. (1991). Mapping the margins: Intersectionality, identity politics, and violence against women of color. *Stanford Law Review, 43*, 1241.

Deleuze, G., & Guattari, F. (1977). *Anti-Oedipus: Capitalism and schizophrenia*, trans. R. Hurley, M. Seem, & H. R. Lane. New York: Penguin Books.

Deleuze, G., & Guattari, F. (1987). *A thousand plateaus: Capitalism and schizophrenia*, trans. B. Massumi. Minneapolis: University of Minnesota Press.

Delgado Bernal, D. (1998). Using a Chicana feminist epistemology in educational research. *Harvard Educational Review, 68*(4), 555–582.

Delgado Bernal, D., Elenes, C. A., Godinez, F. E., & Villenas, S. (Eds.). (2006). *Chicana/Latina education in everyday life: Feminista perspectives on pedagogy and epistemology*. Albany: SUNY Press.

Demas, E., & Saavedra, C. M. (2004). Reconceptualizing language advocacy: Weaving a postmodern *mestizaje* image of language. In K. Mutua & B. Swadener (Eds.), *Decolonizing research in cross-cultural contexts: Critical personal narratives* (pp. 215–234). New York: SUNY Press.

Dill, B. T., McLaughlin, A. E., & Nieves, A. D. (2007). Future directions of feminist research: Intersectionality. In S. N. Hesse-Biber (Ed.), *Handbook of feminist research: Theory and praxis* (pp. 629–638). Thousand Oaks, CA: Sage.

Dillard, C. B. (2006). *On spiritual strivings: Transforming an African American woman's academic life*. Albany: SUNY Press.

Dillard, C. B. (2012). *Learning to (re)member the things that we've learned to forget: Endarkened feminisms, spirituality, and the sacred nature of research and teaching*. New York: Peter Lang.

Duran, E. F. (2000). *Buddha in redface*. Lincoln, NE: Writers Club Press.

Fernandes, L. (2003). *Transforming feminist practice: Non-violence, social justice and the possibilities of spiritualized feminisms*. San Francisco: Aunt Lute Books.

Fonow, M. M. (2003). *Union women: Forging feminism in the United Steelworkers of America*. St. Paul: University of Minnesota Press.

Foucault, M. (1969). *The archaeology of knowledge*, trans. A. M. Sheridan Smith. London: Routledge.

Foucault, M. (1979). *Discipline and punish: The birth of the prison*. New York: Vintage.

Freire, P. (1970). *Pedagogy of the oppressed* (2nd ed.). New York: Continuum.

Freire, P. (1998). *Teachers as cultural workers: Letters to those who dare to teach*. Boulder, CO: Westview Press.

hooks, b. (2000a). *Feminism is for everybody: Passionate politics*. Cambridge, MA: South End Press.

hooks, b. (2000b). *Feminist theory: From margin to center* (2nd ed.). Cambridge MA: South End Press.

hooks, b., & Mesa-Bains, A. (2006). *Homegrown: Engaged cultural criticism*. Cambridge, MA: South End Press.

James, S. M., & Busia, P. A. (Eds.). (2003). *Theorizing Black feminisms: The visionary pragmatism of Black women.* New York: Routledge.

Keating, A. (2008). "I'm a citizen of the universe": Gloria Anzaldúa's spiritual activism as catalyst for social change. *Feminist Studies, 34*(1/2), 53–69.

Kincheloe, J. L. (2006). Critical ontology and indigenous ways of being: Forging a postcolonial curriculum. In Y. Kany (Ed.), *Curriculum as cultural practice: Postcolonial imaginations* (pp. 181–202). Toronto: University of Toronto Press.

Kincheloe, J. L. (2008). Critical pedagogy and the knowledge wars of the twenty-first century. *International Journal of Critical Pedagogy, 1*(1), 1–22.

Klein, N. (2007). *The shock doctrine: The rise of disaster capitalism.* New York: Metropolitan Books.

Loomba, A. (1998). *Colonialism/postcolonialism.* London: Routledge.

Lorde, A. (1984). *Sister outsider: Essays and speeches by Audre Lorde.* Berkeley, CA: Crossing Press.

Moraga, C. (1983). *Loving in the war years: Lo que nunca paso por sus labios.* Boston, MA: South End Press.

Morris, C. D. (2010). Why misogynists make great informants: How gender violence on the left enables state violence in radical movements. *INCITE.* Retrieved from http://inciteblog.wordpress.com/2010/07/15/why-misogynists-make-great-informants-how-gender-violence-on-the-left-enables-state-violence-in-radical-movements/

Pérez, E. (1999). *The decolonial imaginary: Writing Chicanas into history.* Bloomington: Indiana University Press.

Pérez, M. S. (2009). *Discourses of power surrounding young children, charter schools, and public education in New Orleans post-Katrina.* Unpublished doctoral dissertation, Arizona State University.

Pérez, M. S., & Cannella, G. S. (2010). Disaster capitalism as neoliberal instrument for the construction of early childhood education/care policy: Charter schools in post-Katrina New Orleans. In G. S. Cannella & L. D. Soto (Eds.), *Childhoods: A handbook. Critical histories and contemporary issues* (pp. 145–156). New York: Peter Lang.

Pérez, M. S., & Cannella, G. S. (2011). Using situational analysis for critical qualitative research purposes. In N. K. Denzin & M. D. Giardina (Eds.), *Qualitative inquiry and global crises* (pp. 97–117). Walnut Creek, CA: Left Coast Press.

Pérez, M. S., & Cannella, G. S. (In press.). Situational analysis as an avenue for critical qualitative research: Mapping post-Katrina New Orleans. *Qualitative Inquiry.*

Pérez, M. S., Cannella, G. S., & Saavedra, C. M. (In press). Combining qualitative research perspectives and methods for critical social purposes: The neoliberal U.S. childhood public policy behemoth. *International Review of Qualitative Inquiry.*

Pérez, M. S., & Saavedra, C. M. (2012). Working within third space(s): Entrenzando Deleuzian, postcolonial, and marginalized feminist perspectives. Paper presented at Mujeres Activas en Letras y Cambio Social (MALCS) Women Active in Letters and Social Change, University of California, Santa Barbara.

Pillow, W. S. (2003). Confession, catharsis, or cure? Rethinking the uses of reflexivity as methodological power in qualitative research. *Qualitative Studies in Education, 16*(2), 75–96.

Roth, B. (2003). *Separate roads to feminism: Black, Chicana, and White feminist movements in America's second wave.* Cambridge, U.K.: Cambridge University Press.

Saavedra, C. M. (2011). De-academizing early childhood research: Wanderings of a Chicana/Latina feminist researcher. *Journal of Latinos and Education, 10*(4), 286–298.

Saavedra, C. M., Chakravarthi, S., & Lower, J. K. (2009). Weaving transnational feminist methodologies: (Re) examining early childhood linguistic diversity teacher training and research. *Journal of Early Childhood Research, 7*(3), 324–340.

Saavedra, C. M., & Nymark, E. D. (2008). Borderland-mestizaje feminism: The new tribalism. In N. K. Denzin, Y. S. Lincoln, & L. Tuhiwai-Smith (Eds.), *Handbook of critical and indigenous methodologies* (pp. 255–276). Thousand Oaks, CA: Sage.

Saavedra, C. M., & Pérez, M. S. (2012). Chicana and Black feminisms: Testimonios of theory, identity, and multiculturalism. *Equity and Excellence in Education, 45*(3), 430–443.

Saldívar-Hull, S. (2000). *Feminism on the border: Chicana gender, politics, and literature.* Berkeley: University of California Press.

Smith, L. (1999). *Decolonizing methodologies: Research and Indigenous peoples.* London: Zed Books.

Spivak, G. C. (1988). Can the subaltern speak? In C. Nelson & L. Grossberg (Eds.), *Marxism and the interpretation of culture* (pp. 271–313). Urbana: University of Illinois Press.

Swadener, B. B., & Lubeck, S. (Eds.). (1995). *Children and families "at promise": Deconstructing the discourse of risk.* Albany: State University of New York Press.

Trinidad Galvan, R. (2001). Portraits of *mujeres desjuiciada*: Womanist pedagogies of the everyday, the mundane and the ordinary. *Qualitative Studies in Education, 14*(5), 603–621.

Trujillo, C. (1998). *Living Chicana theory*. Berkeley, CA: Third Woman Press.

Villenas, S. (1996). The colonizer/colonized Chicana ethnographer: Identity, marginalization and co-optation in the field. *Harvard Educational Review, 66*(4), 711–731.

Viruru, R. (2005). The impact of postcolonial theory on early childhood education. *Journal of Education, 35*, 7–29.

FOURTEEN

The Use of Poststructuralist Storytelling in Early Childhood Education Research

Alejandro Azocar

To make a case about the usefulness of storytelling in early childhood educational research, I start this discussion with an understanding of the word "story" as an account of life episodes manifested in multiple ways; for example as a written piece that describes someone's experiences, as an oral recount, a poem, a song, a short story, a novel, or even as a television show. There is one undeniable fact about human stories: They are told every day, everywhere, and by everybody. Telling stories is a basic human characteristic that reflects our social nature. Stories are told in all forms and shapes; for example in reality shows on television, on blogs, in magazines, in "tell-all" memoirs, on the internet, or even on Facebook and Twitter. For a variety of reasons, we feel the need to tell what happens to others and what happens to us in such a way that our particularities are honored and our feelings get recognized. Through the narration of observable events, we transmit the significance of our daily experiences to those who wish to listen to our words, or those who want to read our words.

A common denominator among all types of stories seems to be their ability to transport the readers' imagination to distant spatial and temporal dimensions. In fact, written and oral narratives produce powerful effects on people's minds. Our words are able to trigger the imagination of the listener or reader, who is able to elaborate a mental picture of the narrated events. Moreover, stories should convey a sense of significance that is intimately felt by the narrator. This significance is contained in messages, many times political ones, which are embedded in the words, phrases, and paragraphs of the story.

I find an interesting parallel between literary excerpts such as vignettes, short stories, and novels, and research in early childhood education. How can we join these two vastly different contexts, namely literature and educational research? How can we transgress traditional forms of research writing in academia? Is this possible in the first place? We still hear a strong push for evidence-based educational research, which for some scholars is the only way to faithfully achieve progress and the betterment of children's education. Like the author of short stories or novels, the educational researcher also aims to convey messages to improve children's education in the words that make up the final research text. However, personal perspectives have usually been disguised in social sciences research under the principle of objectivity and detachment. In the postmodernist era, the writing of stories in educational research has allowed scholars to rethink the concept of investigative legitimacy, which now accepts the situatedness of the writer/researcher as a fundamental characteristic in need of acknowledgement from very early on in the report of research documents. Objective, factual, and empirical values do have a legitimate place in educational research but they reside in approaches that are different from postmodernist perspectives. As Clough (2002) clearly states:

> If we think of the writing of stories in educational research as the creation of a building, the writer becomes an architect. The question, therefore, is not technical; it is not "*how* do I *construct* this building" but rather "what is the building *for*?" So, in setting out to write a story, the primary work is in the interaction of ideas; in the act of thinking, tuning in, and decision making and focusing on the primary intent of the work. And of course, writing a story—like constructing a building—is not carried out outside of a need, a community, a context. These are actually the primary ingredients. (Clough, 2002, p. 8)

I posit an important question: Can an early childhood educational researcher be a storyteller? Can both roles be fused into one? What could the result be: educational research or literary excerpts? I argue that a hybridization of early childhood educational research is possible and, in fact, should be encouraged in present-day postmodernist times where the complex life of the immigrant child, the bilingual child, or the disabled child, to name a few, needs to be told to a larger audience. We need to question the push for normality that surrounds the child's experience, especially the child who happens to be "different" from the mainstream. Orderly progress, which is desired and cherished by modernism, is questioned by postmodernism (Crotty, 2007). The questioning of the "normal" is exactly what present-day storytelling can achieve in the academic realm of early childhood education.

I believe that the benefit of using storytelling is mutual for the child whose experiences are being narrated and for the researcher. Indeed, it is good for the human spirit. Of paramount importance for early childhood education researchers who are committed to social justice is the expression of the messages that lie beneath the final "research report," for instance in short stories, poems, or vignettes. These alternative forms of presenting research projects honor the freedom of the human spirit, and I see it as a liberatory format that offers an alternative to the rigid canons of academic writing. Inspired by Richardson (1994) and Richardson and St. Pierre (2005), I see alternative forms of writing as freer from the traditional canons of academic writing, but still subjected to certain regulations:

> Although we are freer to present our texts in a variety of forms to diverse audiences, we have different constraints arising from self-consciousness about claims to authorship, authority, truth, validity, and reliability. Self-reflexivity unmasks complex political/ideological agendas hidden in our writing. (Richardson, 1994, p. 523)

The Fabrication of Early Childhood Education Ethnographies

A common method of doing research on children is ethnography, which was my choice as a doctoral student. I did an ethnographic study on a group of student teachers who were part of a world-language teacher education program in a large Midwestern university in the United States. The student teachers' goal was to obtain certification in the teaching of Spanish in K–12 settings. As part of the teacher education program, the student teachers were required to student teach for two consecutive semesters in an elementary school. They were to teach Spanish as a foreign language to kindergarteners, and first, second, and third graders, most of whom spoke English as a first language.

Soon after I started my ethnographic data collection, I learned that the ethnographic experience as a researcher is complex, unpredictable, and fundamentally nonlinear. Ethnographies inevitably become entangled with the baggage of our own life experiences that define who we really are as human beings. In my case, my identity as a researcher was bookmarked by virtue of being a Chilean individual whose native language is Spanish. Having grown up in Chile and been immersed in Latin American culture for many years positioned me as a person who inevitably had an opinion about the teaching of my own native language by a group of young, inexperienced, English-speaking Spanish student teachers. How could I express my own struggles, my dilemmas, and my goal of helping these student teachers in their teaching if I was supposed to keep a distance and only be a "participant observer" in the field? I realized that I could not be distant, and I had to acknowledge my feelings toward Spanish education in the context of the elementary school where student teaching took place. Given this unique situation, I discovered that storytelling was a comfortable methodology to be used in order to deal with these issues.

Pole and Morrison (2003) discuss the idea of handling the complexity that derives from ethnographic projects with responsibility. In my opinion, responsibility implies that the researcher not only should acknowledge the realm of the Other (for example, the child), but also the realm of the Self. The infusion of political agendas, which are highly intertwined with human feelings, can be achieved by the fictionalization of the researcher's ethnographic experience in the crafting of stories. By doing this, the researcher keeps in mind an ethical responsibility with the Other that calls for advocacy and defense. Indeed, the fictionalization of educational data becomes a form of representation and advocacy that honors the condition of the Other and the Self. As Clough (2002) states:

> [stories in educational research] could be true, they derive from real events and feelings and conversations, but they are ultimately fictions: versions of the truth which are woven from an amalgam of raw data. (Clough, 2002, p. 9)

MacLure (2003) claims that research texts are indeed "fabrications," therefore ethnographies, as final research reports, can also be seen as "fabricated texts," which neatly corresponds with the application of storytelling in educational research. She states: "[research texts'] truths and findings are put together—that is, built or woven to achieve particular effects and structures rather than artlessly culled from a pre-existing world Out There" (p. 80). Thus, the particularities of ethnographies can be represented through storytelling. Not only does this involve the description of locations, events, and people, but also includes the portrayal of the researcher's humanity and personal interpretation of the observable social phenomena, as an "understanding of social behavior from inside the discrete location, event or setting" (Pole & Morrison, 2003,

p. 3). These authors suggest that ethnographers should attempt to honor the complexity of human experiences, most of which are difficult to describe in final research reports as they need an interpretation by the researcher beforehand. Therefore, storytelling can open a possibility to recognize, in a more powerful and convincing way, the complexity of children's lives.

A Story About Karen and Julia and the Ideal Child as a Spanish Learner

The following vignette is based on notes that I wrote at the end of a long and tedious day at the school where I did my doctoral research. I wrote a very informal journal entry using only bulleted sentences that highlighted the core of a conversation that I had witnessed between two Spanish student teachers. Inspired by this journal entry, I wrote a short vignette that reconstructed the context of the conversation, which pertained to the vision of the "ideal" Spanish student in the opinion of the student teachers.

> What does being a language learner really mean? Specifically, what does being a "Spanish student" really mean? I want to ask myself this commonsensical question to unravel precisely the commonsense that surrounds foreign language learning in America. Karen and Julia jokingly referred to their first-grade students as "Spanish students" by physically exaggerating the expression "Spanish students" with a movement of both the index and the middle finger upward and downwards to signal quotation marks.
>
> "Are they really Spanish students?" Karen uttered, stressing the word "really" with a loud pitch. "You know, sometimes I feel that we are not doing a good job in teaching these kids Spanish greetings, chunks of conversations and stuff like that because they are NOT getting it! They simply DO NOT GET IT! It's ridiculous! Seriously, I feel that I am teaching to a wall, but not even a wall because those kids become unruly so easily. At least walls wouldn't disrupt me as I am teaching. It's just so frustrating…"
>
> "Exactly," Julia said. "My students can barely say 'Hola' to each other, which makes me feel really bad. I feel bad for these kids because our teaching is truly a waste of time for us and for them."

This vignette, which was inspired by a dialogue that I observed at the school, captures the essence of what I heard, and how I interpreted it. The fictionalization of the situation allowed the portrayal of a clear "snapshot," which in essence constitutes a report of educational data. The vignette allowed me to be critical of the discursive formation of educational subjects, namely the subject called "Spanish teacher" and the subject called "Spanish student." The vignette's purpose is to reveal that teaching Spanish appropriately is conditioned by the production of good utterances by the kindergarteners in communicative situations. Moreover, there is a sense of hopelessness in the vignette. Kindergarteners are considered "unteachable" because they get easily distracted. The ideal Spanish student is not a child, but an older student perhaps, who is conscientious, well-behaved, and a producer of oral utterances. If the Spanish teacher is able to trigger a communicative purpose among children, she is considered a "good" Spanish teacher. Julia's utterance that this "makes me feel really bad" encapsulates tensions, uncertainties, and simultaneously an intense reflexivity among student teachers, which is the result of a process of becoming a subject (a Spanish teacher) in a predetermined and unidirectional way. Moreover, the subjectification of kindergarteners as Spanish students, as "it is supposed to be," is not achieved in this particular classroom because children are unruly and cannot produce utterances. In the end, Karen and Julia find themselves at odds with the discursive forces that determine who they should be and who the children should be in a Spanish language classroom.

The Suppression of the Researcher's Self in Educational Ethnographies

It is challenging for early childhood education researchers to represent the complexity of the child's experience if they honor positivistic principles such as objectivity, empiricism, and detachment. Writing in social science research has traditionally been a reductionist activity due to the researchers' tendency to depurate the human experiences of Others (and also their own) from ambiguities or confusions in order to make them clearly presentable to the readers in final research reports. MacLure (2003) provides examples of how traditional ethnographies have resorted to the use of rhetorical devices such as realism and visualism to achieve faithful written descriptions of social phenomena for the readers. The "taming" of the writing, understood as simplification, not only seems to correspond to the pursuit of written clarity, but also to a governing principle of order and truth grasping, which seems quite similar to the features of the project of modernity (Dahlberg, Moss, & Pence, 2007). As MacLure (2003) further states, "[in academic writing], there is a desire for transparency, for language that lets you see through to the *truth or meaning*" (p. 108, emphasis added).

Postmodernist ethnography, on the contrary, embraces the ambiguities and complexities of human experiences as fundamentally normal and worthy of being expressed in social science research. Moreover, the postmodernist side of the ethnographic continuum welcomes exploratory forms or writing such as storytelling that contradicts traditional presentations of research in writing. Postmodernist ethnography honors the subjective intentions of the researchers to persuade readers that their truths are valid. In postmodernist ethnographies, there is "an emphasis on rigorous or thorough research, where the complexities of the discrete event, location or setting are of greater importance than overarching trends or generalizations" (Pole & Morrison, 2003, p. 3). Thus, complexities are fundamentally manifested in the description of human experiences that are felt within social groups, for example children, and inside the researcher in interaction with the social group that is being researched.

Living Ethnographic Data for the Creation of Stories on Children's Experiences

It was not easy for me to decide on the use of storytelling in my doctoral research project. Besides being labeled as a non-rigorous research report, storytelling mixes writing traditions that stand on opposite sides: one is the depiction of the real, and the other one is the portrayal of fantasy. Nevertheless, it is important to ask ourselves: Is human experience always portrayed using a faithful allegiance to reality? Can reality be also manifested in fabricated literary forms? In educational research, human experience in the social sciences traditionally has been confined within "collected" data obtained from the Other and should be able to be attested in empirically observable forms, for example in audio recordings and transcripts. The human experience of schooling is collected, analyzed, and the results are narrated. Presumably these data collected from the Other must not be contaminated by the researcher's biases, actions, or other external conditions in order to conform to the powerful research tradition that calls for objectivity and scientific empiricism (Clough, 2002). Throughout the 20th and early 21st century, we have continued to be told that the purity of data should not be affected, so the researcher's duty should be to handle data with care and responsibility in order to avoid the infusion of subjective ideas into the data (for example, see debates in Shavelson & Towne, 2002; Hatch, this volume). Conversely, I believe that the human experience of Others always becomes tainted with the researcher's biased ideas when s/he elaborates a written report of findings. Furthermore, when the researcher's own human experience happens to be present in the same data that has been empirically "collected," inevitably we must confront and accept a presumed contamination. The presumed impurity of contaminated data may, in fact, be understood as purity because this pollution faithfully encapsulates our humanity, spirituality, and in particular, our complexities as individuals. This condition constitutes a fundamental asset in present-day qualitative research in early childhood education that opens a space for a new dimension in educational research, one that inevitably calls for an attention to the Self (Denzin & Lincoln, 2005).

Postmodernist Ethnographic Data in Early Childhood Educational Research

Inspired by the political side of postmodernism, which stands in opposition to the principles of modernity (Crotty, 2007; Dahlberg et al., 2007), I believe that early childhood educational data can be understood as a cumulative body of information about particular social phenomena in children that refuses to be confined to traditional investigative boundaries. Data transgress limits, invade other territories, and become unconfined. This alternative vision of educational data encapsulates dynamic, active, ever-changing, and elusive knowledge that crosses temporal and local realms. This implies that a postmodernist notion of data includes unconventional areas of knowledge that cannot be considered as "collected" data but as "lived data" that resides in the mind of the researcher. Therefore, by adopting an inclusive understanding of data, researchers can become storytellers because they can resort to the use of their own memories in the crafting of stories. This opens possibilities of researching the spirituality that exists in educational events by focusing on the perspective of the researcher and creation of something new. When researchers include excerpts from their lived experiences as human beings, they contribute to the formation of a wealth of information that blurs the distinction between human experience and ethnographic educational data.

Representing Findings via Storytelling

Postmodernist educational data revealed that traditional early childhood education principles were used in the school, which was not a big surprise as the Spanish program touched upon early childhood education. The Spanish curriculum was supposed to spring from children's interests rather than the superior interests of educators. According to Cannella (1997), child-centered instruction has its origins in the Enlightenment ideas of 18th century that conceived the child as moving naturally into stages of development toward human rationality. By putting the child at the center of pedagogical practices, it is expected that the child will unfold naturally, evolving into a rational human being. Child-centered instruction, which is the dominant principle in early childhood education, has been examined critically in the last decades. Specifically, there is a critique of child-centeredness based on the argument that the curriculum is not something that comes from the children's interest, as it is normally argued, but from the dominant group's interest (Cannella, 1997). In the particular case of Spanish education for children, the dominant discourse seems to be that languages are best learned if they are connected to children's needs, so language activities should appeal to their interests (Lipton, 1997).

I witnessed a peculiar phenomenon in relation to the application of the child-centered philosophy. While Spanish student teachers kept it as a guiding principle in the elaboration of lesson plans, child-centered instruction became subordinated to a higher principle: oral communication in Spanish among children. Therefore, it was believed that dynamic activities had to appeal to children's interests but they had to be communicative. Many times I witnessed lessons that required children to express their emotions, preferences, and opinions in Spanish. Children were given choices that needed to be verbalized. However, as I observed children doing these in-class activities, I wondered whether children were expressing their sincere interests as they fulfilled the communicative requirement of the lesson. The following story reflects such a case.

Me gusta/No me gusta (I like it/I don't like it)

One morning, I arrived at the school with a weird sensation that I couldn't fully comprehend. I suspected that a Spanish lesson that I was going to observe would not be a good one. I had read the lesson plan, for a first-grade class, that Amanda (Spanish student teacher) had emailed me the night before. She and two other student teachers had collaboratively designed the lesson plan under the thematic unit: "Mi comida favorita" (My favorite food). The objective of the thematic unit was quite simple: to teach first graders the names of food items in Spanish within the context of daily meals. Therefore, foods would be taught under "desayuno" (breakfast), "almuerzo" (lunch), and "cena" (supper) over a period of four teaching days. Besides vocabulary, children would learn how to say their true preferences in relation to food in order to give them the chance to express themselves in Spanish.

I stepped into Amanda's first-grade classroom about five minutes before 10:00 a.m. She was already in the classroom, setting things up by the "Spanish corner" that Mrs. Scott, the classroom teacher, had assigned to her. Children were moving towards the corner and began to sit in a semi-circle, facing Amanda directly. Exactly at 10:00 a.m., the Spanish class started.

"Buenos dias estudiantes," she said.

"Buenos dias, Señorita Smith," children answered, chorally.

Amanda proceeded to give each child a smiley face and a sad face that had been drawn on white paper plates. After every child had gotten the two drawn faces, she started to do her "presentational section" of the lesson plan, precisely as she had been taught in the foreign language methods class on campus. The presentational portion of a lesson plan meant that the student teacher had to introduce the Spanish form (also called "linguistic form") to the students before proceeding to engage them in interactive and communicative activities.

"A mi me gusta la leche al desayuno (I like drinking milk for breakfast)," she said, showing the children an actual plastic bottle of a gallon of milk, which was empty, and showing the smiley face simultaneously. Children observed attentively.

"A mi no me gusta la fruta al desayuno (I don't like eating fruit for breakfast)," she continued, showing the children a sad face with a picture of a bowl of fruit. Simultaneously, she signaled a "no no" sign with her index finger.

"Te gusta el pan al desayuno? (Do you like eating bread for breakfast?)" She unexpectedly asked Terry, one of the students who was sitting next to her, who looked at her puzzled and confused.

"Si, te gusta el pan al desayuno (Yes, you like to eat bread for breakfast)," she answered to herself, nodding her own head, and ignoring Terry's reaction, which was a reaction of total confusion. Then, Amanda stood up and said: "Repitan por favor (Repeat after me please) A mi me gusta el pan! (I like bread!)"

The children said chorally: "A mi me gusta el pan!"

"Pan!" Amanda shouted, pointing at a clipart picture of a loaf of bread. "Pan!" she repeated. The children shouted: "PAN! PAN! PAN!"

After the demonstration of the "Me gusta/no me gusta" sentence structure, she showed children a series of clipart pictures that depicted food items that are normally eaten at breakfast in the United States. For example, she showed a picture of a peanut butter jar, a box of cereal, a bottle of orange juice, a carton of milk, and a loaf of bread. As each picture was displayed, she said the name of the food item in Spanish, and then children repeated the word orally, chorally, loud and clear using perfect Spanish pronunciation.

(Needless to say, the breakfast items were familiar to children by virtue of being "American." Wouldn't it have been nicer to incorporate typical foods that are normally eaten for breakfast in Latin American countries?)

Then, Amanda proceeded to go around the circle and explain to her students, in Spanish, that each person would have their turn to tell the whole class their favorite food item that they really enjoyed eating for breakfast. To do this, each child would engage in a mini-dialogue in which they would have to answer this question (asked by Amanda herself): "Que te gusta comer al desayuno? (What do you like to eat for breakfast?)" In the ideal world of language instruction, children would answer in a complete sentence: "Me gusta la leche al desayuno" (I like milk for breakfast)." Simultaneously, children would have to lift the smiley face above their heads in order for everybody to see it. If they chose an item that they didn't like, they would have to say: "No me gusta la leche al desayuno (I don't like milk for breakfast)." In that case they would have to lift the sad face as they replied, uttering a complete sentence as well. The entire explanation of the activity was done in Spanish, very slowly, using lots of body movements and pointing to the pictures and faces many times. It took five minutes of the lesson to explain everything. This explanation was done in Spanish in order to abide by the rule that dictated that English could not be used during Spanish instruction.

As I quietly took notes, I observed that children began to get distracted. They started to play with the smiley and sad faces. As Amanda went around the circle asking each child "Que te gusta comer al desayuno?" they looked at her confused, and lifted the faces on the paper plate randomly. For Amanda, this became problematic because children were not "producing" the desired language. Rather, they were trying to figure out what to do, or they were simply distracted by the colorful pictures of the food items, or by the smiley and sad faces drawn on paper plates.

Amanda realized that the activity wasn't going as well as the lesson plan had predicted. She opted to get the children's attention by pulling out a puppet from a bag: a small lion that roared when its nose was squeezed. "Silencio por favor (silence please)," she shouted. With the help of the classroom teacher, who spoke to the kids in English, Amanda managed to get back the attention of her students. She asked the question again: "Que te gusta comer al desayuno?" By pointing at the pictures of food items, children had to reply accordingly. The assumption was that if a kid liked milk, for example, s/he would say, "Me gusta la leche al desayuno" and the child would lift up the smiley face, and vice versa. Once again, Amanda started to go around the circle and ask each child the question. They simply lifted the smiley face without uttering any words. Confronted with this situation, she decided to answer the question herself loud and clear for everybody to hear them.

I walked out of the classroom moments before the class was over. Vivid in my mind is the image of every child lifting up the smiley face drawn in a paper plate. Nobody lifted up the sad face. Needless to say, they didn't orally respond to Amanda's question.

When Amanda and I met afterwards to debrief the lesson, her frustration was evident. She cried. She told me that she felt like a failure because the objectives of the lesson hadn't been met. She had not been able to engage her students in oral production of the language. Even though she tried hard to engage her students in mini-dialogues, she couldn't.

"I don't know what to say," she confessed to me. "I was supposed to teach them, but I failed. I feel like a real failure."

"Everything will be OK in the end," I replied.

I wrote this story to represent the complexity of the process of becoming a Spanish teacher within the constraints of appropriate teaching practices in Spanish education. Amanda's unsuccessful lesson reveals more than lack of pedagogical effectiveness with a group of kindergarten or first graders. To me, her frustration was not a sign of failure, but evidence of the formation of a particular type of rationality as a Spanish (student) teacher, one that calls for dynamism, engagement, and of course the production of oral communication among students. Amanda's emerging identity was conditioned to the fulfillment of pedagogical goals such as the use of a total immersion method, which Amanda did, and also the capacity of "extracting" orally produced chunks of language from the children. Shrouded by the desire to appeal to children's interests, the real objective of Amanda's lesson, and many others at the school, was to teach children the language (words and sentences) and then have them speak to the teacher or ideally to one another. Her frustration derived from a predetermined and narrow set of objectives that did not envision alternative ways of understanding Spanish instruction for children.

Reflexivity: The Threshold Toward Storytelling

When using storytelling, the researcher/storyteller needs to reflect upon his experiential data before writing stories. The task of drafting a story starts from the very moment when the ethnographer enters in contact with the subjects. Adopting a postmodernist approach to ethnography forces researchers to engage in an in-depth and comprehensive reflective process, which differs from traditional forms of reflexivity that occur "in the analysis stage"; that is, after data have been collected. In my experience, reflexivity started from the first days of my immersion in the school, and it gradually increased with the passing of time. Being reflective became a natural occurrence, intermingled with the observations of daily experiences of Spanish student teachers, children learning Spanish, the audio recordings of lesson debriefings, and the memories from my personal life. Certainly, I did not need to wait until the "analysis stage" to begin to realize that there were particular phenomena in their teaching experiences that were important in their constitution as elementary-school Spanish teachers. Upon entering the school every morning, I would tell myself: What striking situation will I observe today regarding the teaching of my Spanish, my mother tongue? What surprise will I witness today? How will I react to particular pedagogical events? Will I praise student teachers, or will I criticize them? What sort of connection will I make with some forgotten event in my life as a learner of English as a second language?

Everyday observations in the classrooms made me question pedagogical practices in situ in ways that were in total contradiction with the principles mandated by ACTFL (American Council on the Teaching of Foreign Language). In the midst of this immersion in ACTFL philosophy, standards, and especially the need of emphasizing communication during language instruction, I began to feel highly uncomfortable. For example, I would hear conversations about world-language education methods among student teachers, and I would think to myself: Why do these student teachers understand the Spanish language in such peculiar ways? Daily interactions and observations revealed surprises. They triggered thoughts, which made me question why Spanish education and world-language teacher education in general were seen in such peculiar ways, indeed quite differently from my own beliefs about world-language education in general. I link my personal reflective process with the idea that human experience is fundamentally complex and truly unpredictable. The external observable phenomena triggered an auto-reflection in direct connection with the events that were happening at the elementary school.

Reflexivity is an intimate, internal, and inevitable process. It cannot be detached from the process of doing ethnography. Reflexivity allows the extraction of layers of personal data imprinted in the researcher's recollections, or in their lived experience. Data, then, offer a slice of the internal and the external where the researcher is located at the center of the project (Tochon, 1999). Nevertheless, it is interesting to observe how the researcher becomes "tamed" by academic control. Richardson (2000) argues that there is a sense of academic self-control that prevails in academic writing. Self-censorship in the act of writing social science research becomes so powerful that it eventually suppresses the researcher's Self. Therefore order, logic, and science do affect us: They eventually *erase* the Self from our research projects because the Self is still seen today as inconsistent with scientific forms of writing. Richardson states: "Our sense of Self is diminished [in academia] as we are homogenized through professional socialization, rewards and punishment" (p. 925). The very act of reflecting on observations, daily social interactions, and letting the researcher's inner Self emerge in his or her field notes transgresses the traditional principle of objectivity in educational research.

Poststructuralist Storytelling as Revealing the Construction of Subjectivity

I argue that the crafting of a story derived from early childhood educational research should project a message, which may be critical of a specific condition of the child's experiences, or perhaps this message can be politically motivated. Specifically, we can use storytelling to exemplify the ways in which people become subjects of particular dominant discourses. According to Goodley (2004), "poststructuralist storytelling" is a type of narrative research representation that "aims to excavate the power and knowledge that are used to construct versions of humanity" (p. 101). I believe that the formation of particularly defined versions of humanity is closely linked to the discursive construction of who the child is in multiple locations in today's society. The researcher, therefore, can write stories that portray the process whereby children become subjects through schooling. I used poststructuralist storytelling primarily to show how Spanish preservice teachers became subjects in relation to the Spanish language under the premise that there exists a set of linguistic and pedagogical discourses that shape an understanding of who we are and how we are supposed to act when we speak and teach Spanish. The same principles can be applied for the portrayal of the subjectification of the bilingual child, the ESL child, or the disabled child in American schooling.

Dominant discourses have a limiting effect because they constrain possibilities (MacLure, 2003). Foucault (1980) postulates that discourses work in relation to the effects of power, understood not only in a sovereign manner, or in a "top-down" fashion, but as localized power relations. Understanding local power allows for the examination of dominant representations of knowledge in the duality power/knowledge. Therefore, the formation and reformation of subjectivities among specific groups of children in American schools are the result of discursive ideas that are intimately linked to power/knowledge, which coexist locally and nationally.

The Inception of the Stories

Once experiential data has been "lived" by the ethnographer, it is time to fully use storytelling by writing stories from the field. The way to do it is fundamentally intimate and creative, which combines the realms of educational research and creative writing. I have been inspired by Deleuze's principle of "vitality of thought." Deleuze, as cited in Dahlberg and Bloch (2006), makes the distinction between knowledge and thought. While knowledge constitutes what is already known, thought is fundamentally uncertain, and yet productive. As they state: "[Thought] takes place when the mind is provoked by an encounter with the unknown and the unfamiliar. As such, it calls for an openness to the unpredictable and new, a willingness to experiment and make new connections" (p. 108). Based on this idea, I believe that life experiences, memories, field notes, and audio-recorded data are somewhat unknown to researchers. Nothing can be absolutely known because there is always a veil of unknowingness on whatever is presumably "already known," including our life experiences. We may be rich in knowledge, however our stored knowledge is not easily extractable unless we apply methods or techniques to extract it and put it into words. It is also knowledge that is not the same as thought, but might lead to new openings, new thought, if we understand this as possibility rather than impossibilities.

Based on Deleuze's ideas, I believe that a provocation of the mind can be applied as a research method in the generation of storytelling in early childhood educational research. It forces researchers to confront their stored knowledge in order to generate more knowledge via reflective practices. Consequently, we honor our own self by placing our researcher's persona, as a storyteller, at the center of the research enterprise. Researchers become part of their data and part of the story that they narrate. In doing so, they become their own research subject, and they blur the boundary between objectivity and subjectivity in educational research. The provocation of the mind triggers thoughts that are not only subjective, but transgressive of the cannons of dominant forms of research representation in education. This principle of transgression is associated with an attempt to "work in the ruins" of educational research methods, in alliance with feminist poststructural thoughts (St. Pierre & Pillow, 2000). In fact, "Thought opens up—to change, innovation and invention. Thought is critical and creative—of new concepts, problems and learning. Thought respects singularity" (Dahlberg & Bloch, 2006, p. 112).

Poststructuralist storytelling allows educational researchers to give an account of past research experiences using literary techniques with the purpose of deconstructing the subjectivity formation of people. Past experiences in the research field are fundamentally experiential, lived or felt, and as such, the lived experience helps me see data as "experiential data." While traditional views of data locate the experiences of others in some tangible forms, for example in field notes (as written notes) and/or in audio recording (as audible voices), I believe that the experience of living data, or even "creating" data is worth using as a foundational principle in research. It works from the ruins of deconstructed canons of research that impose empiricism and objectivity.

A Story About the Latino Immigrant Child Who Needs to Learn Appropriate Spanish

During my research at the school, I noticed that a substantial number of students in the classrooms where native speakers of Spanish. While the focus of my research was on Spanish student teachers, I observed the participation of Latino immigrant children during Spanish instruction. Many issues arose from the interaction between Spanish student teachers and children who spoke Spanish as a mother tongue. While I encouraged student teachers to use immigrant children as their "classroom helpers," little was done to use their knowledge of the language during instruction. I perceived among classroom teachers and Spanish student teachers the idea that the Latino immigrant children needed constant help with their English in order to be mainstreamed as quickly as possible. Moreover, I perceived that their Spanish was "not quite good." Most of the time, this linguistic deficiency was attributed to the low socioeconomic status of the immigrant families who sent their children to this particular school. Lack of education "back home" affected immigrant children's linguistic capabilities even in their native language. While this assertion was not explicitly discussed among teachers, Spanish student teachers, and school administrators, I perceived it quite clearly.

The following story is based on my observations of Latino immigrant children during Spanish instruction. It tries to capture the experience of the child who is offered ESL reinforcement and simultaneously attends a mainstream classroom. I have written this story from the point of view of an immigrant child who remembers his linguistic experiences during kindergarten many years after the events took place. He is the narrator of the story.

Betrayal

My mother frequently told me: "Obedece a tu maestra" (Obey your teacher). This command, so ingrained in my mind until today, puzzles me as I look back in time and remember my first year in elementary school.

Yes, I was supposed to obey Mrs. Gilford, a "maestra" (teacher) who was so different from me, who spoke an incomprehensible language, and treated me nicely but distantly. We had just arrived in this country where people looked and acted so differently from my parents, brothers, sisters, and cousins. The center of my universe was by my people, its food, and colors. Our house back home was big, but the one we rented in this new American city was three times as big as the old one. Our backyard was my parents' pride. They kept it clean and orderly to receive guests, most of whom I didn't know, but whose physical appearance and language were like mine. My house, and the parade of people who would come to my house on weekends, made me feel a deep sense of belongingness that I could not feel at school.

My "maestra" did not speak Spanish. She spoke only English to me. Her kind, soft-spoken voice exuded compassion and pity for my condition as an outsider; and yet I interpreted her smile as a genuine welcoming gesture to her world. At that time, I couldn't explain why. Today, I can fully comprehend it.

One day, Mrs. Gilford told me this: "You are learning numbers very fast. Great Job, Manuel. Soon you'll be able to sit in my class without the help of Mrs. Garcia."

Mrs. Garcia was the bilingual resource assistant in charge of tutoring me for about two hours a day. Mrs. Garcia would come to my classroom at exactly 10 a.m. to take me to a small office down the hallway where she would teach me English in Spanish. She would gently knock at the door, open it carefully, and looked at me with a smile. I immediately knew that I was supposed to follow her, and I enjoyed following her to her office because stepping out of Mrs. Gilford's class meant liberation for me.

When Mrs. Gilford praised my progress in English, I felt uncomfortable. She had mentioned the fact that Mrs. Garcia would not be my ESL tutor anymore. When she said "You'll be able to sit in my class without the help of Mrs. Garcia," I felt terrified, because Mrs. Garcia was my guardian angel during those first months at Oliverville Elementary School. Obviously, she spoke Spanish, and precisely the same type of Spanish that my parents' spoke. Later on, I learned that she was from the same region where my parents had grown up. I dreaded the fact that I would be mainstreamed. During the tutoring sessions with Mrs. Garcia, I felt protected, which was the same type of protection that a child feels when a mother embraces him. Her language (my language) created an aura of comfort that would suddenly be interrupted by the bell that signaled the beginning of our recess time.

One morning, during the ESL session with Mrs. Garcia, we were visited by Mrs. Gilford, who was accompanied by a very young lady, impeccably dressed in a floral dress. This young woman was blond, her eyes were blue, and she was carrying a satchel. Upon entering the office, Mrs. Gilford started the dialogue:

"I'm so glad I found you here, Mrs. Garcia. I'd like you to meet Jennie Scott. She will do her student teaching in Spanish with my kids until December."

"Nice to meet you, Jenny," Mrs. Garcia said. "I knew that a group of college students are coming to the school to teach Spanish. It's wonderful!"

"Yes, I am very excited. I love children and I can't wait to start," Jenny said.

Mrs. Gilford added: "And here is Manuel. He speaks Spanish at home, and comes to learn English with Mrs. Garcia every day."

"Hi Manuel, *un placer* (pleasure to meet you)," Jenny told me.

As I was beginning to reply to Jenny's greeting, Mrs. Garcia jumped into the dialogue and said, "Oh, no, no, no, Jenny. You should tell him 'que mas!' That's the way he'll understand what you mean. I am sure that he doesn't understand what '*un placer*' means. That is very formal Spanish."

"Oh, I see," Jenny said. "I've learned all my Spanish using mostly Spanish textbooks published in Spain. I studied two semesters in Spain too. I guess that makes my Spanish pretty formal."

"Oh, I am sure it does," Mrs. Garcia continued. "In fact, I am so glad to hear that the kids will learn good Spanish from you. You know, sometimes I don't even understand the dialects spoken with the kids I work with. I think that our Spanish-speaking children will benefit enormously from your teaching. This Spanish program is good for everybody, isn't it?"

"Of course it is!" Mrs. Gilford added.

Even though I was five years old at that time, I understood exactly what these three women were talking about. I understood my place in the school context, as an immigrant child in need of urgent linguistic intervention not only in ESL, but also in my own native language. My voice was silenced in that office, but this dialogue, so clearly imprinted in my mind, watermarked me in ways that, today, energize me to defend the linguistic rights of the diverse groups of immigrants who come to this country.

Poststructuralist Storytelling: Final Remarks

The principles described so far have explained the possible use of storytelling in early childhood educational research under the assumption that ethnographic experiences, both of the Self and the Other, can be better described through narratives. As Polkinghorne states (1988, as cited in Richardson [1997]), a "narrative is the primary way through which humans organize their experiences into temporally meaningful episodes" (p. 27). In a more general sense, Richardson (1997) states that both our lives and our time are intimately connected, so narratives are bridges that help us make sense of our lives and our time. Narratives become a vehicle in which "temporality becomes interpretable in human terms" (p. 29). Time, which is shaped by past experiences, can be narrated. Without a narration, time continues to be amorphous, even nonexistent in concrete forms, and yet interjected with personal knowledge. The narration of a story implies making a choice to highlight events that give meaning to our past and our knowledge. Simultaneously, it makes time human. Poststructuralist storytelling specifically narrates events that highlight subjectivity construction, leaving aside many other events and experiences that are irrelevant to a social constructionist critique of childhood. This alternative way of representing research is in accordance with present-day times where scientific, objective, and evidence-based principles, although still dominant and used by many, have become only one set of foundations in a horizon of possibilities for new research enterprises.

References

Cannella, G. (1997). *Deconstructing early childhood education: Social justice and revolution.* New York: Peter Lang.
Clough, P. (2002). *Narrative and fictions in educational research.* London: Open University Press.
Crotty, M. (2007). *The foundations of social research: Meaning and perspective in the research process.* Thousand Oaks, CA: Sage.

Dahlberg, G., & Bloch, M. (2006). Is the power to see and visualize always the power of control? In T. Popkewitz, U. Olsson, K. Petersson, & J. Kowalczyk (Eds.), *"The future is not what it appears to be." Pedagogy, genealogy and political epistemology in honor and in memorial to Kenneth Hultqvist* (pp. 105–123). Stockholm: Stockholm Institute of Education Press.

Dahlberg, G., & Moss. P. (2005). *Ethics and politics in early childhood education*. London: Routledge.

Dahlberg, G., Moss, P., & Pence, A. (2007). *Beyond quality in early childhood education and care: Languages of evaluation*. London: Routledge.

Denzin, N., & Lincoln, Y. (2005). *The Sage handbook of qualitative research*. Thousand Oaks, CA : Sage.

Foucault, M. (1980). *Power/knowledge*. Brighton: Harvester Press.

Goodley, D. (2004). Gerry O'Toole. A design for life. In D. Goodley, R. Lawthom, P. Clough, & M. Moore (Eds.), *Researching life stories: Method, theory and analyses in an biographical age* (pp. 3–14). London: Routledge.

Lipton, G. (1997). *Practical handbook to elementary foreign language programs FLES*. Lincolnwood, IL: National Textbook Company.

MacLure, M. (2003). *Discourse in educational and social research*. Buckingham: Open University Press.

Pole, C., & Morrison, M. (2003). *Ethnography for education*. Maidenhead: Open University Press.

Richardson, L. (1994). Writing: A method of inquiry. In N. K. Denzin & Y. S. Lincoln (Eds.), *The Sage handbook of qualitative research* (pp. 516–529). Thousand Oaks, CA: Sage.

Richardson, L. (1997). *Fields of play: Constructing an academic life*. New Brunswick, NJ: Rutgers University Press.

Richardson, L. (2000). Writing: A method of inquiry. In N. K. Denzin & Y. S. Lincoln (Eds.), *The Sage handbook of qualitative research* (pp. 923–948). Thousand Oaks, CA: Sage.

Richardson, L., & St. Pierre, E. A. (2005). Writing: A method of inquiry. In N. K. Denzin & Y. S. Lincoln (Eds.), *The Sage handbook of qualitative research* (3rd ed.). Thousand Oaks, CA: Sage.

Shavelson, R., & Towne, L. (2002). *Features of education and education research. Scientific research in education*. Washington, DC: National Academy Press.

St. Pierre, E. A., & Pillow W. S. (Eds.). (2000). *Working the ruins: Feminist poststructural theory and methods in education*. New York: Routledge.

Tochon, F. (1999). The situated researcher and the narrative reference to lived experience. Special issue, *International Journal of Applied Semiotics, 1*, 103–114.

Fifteen

Revisiting Risk/Re-Thinking Resilience: Fighting to Live Versus Failing to Thrive

Travis Wright

Through my work with young children and their families developing in the context of poverty, trauma, and other high-stress environments, I have observed that what might be a source of strength in one part of a child or family's life may be a source of risk in another. Similarly, across individuals, what might be protective for some may be destructive for others. In considering the implications of this observation in the context of child development and the practice of early childhood education, I have begun to question whether current approaches adequately account for such complex development.

Such reflections are timely as increasingly researchers, policymakers, and practitioners are interested in promoting resilience—focusing on positive development as opposed to minimizing risk. However, relatively little work has questioned what is meant by the term "resilience." The prevailing definition, better-than-expected outcomes in the midst of adversity (Masten, Best, & Garmezy, 1990), provides little operational guidance. Consequently, many use resilience as a synonym for whatever adaptive outcome one may be privileging—academic achievement (Cutuli et al., 2013), positive peer interactions (Bulotsky-Shearer et al., 2012), non-depressed (Schroder & Ollis, 2013), etc. Such models tend to assess resilience as an outcome, rather than as an ongoing process of positively responding to one's changing environment. These outcome-oriented models also fail to consider both the influence of context and the developmental processes underlying such adaptive behavior. This is a critical limitation as resilience is fundamentally context specific and an ongoing developmental process.

Drawing on critical perspectives, here I contemplate the advantages and limitations of current discussions of resilience through presentation of three case examples emerging from my ongoing research efforts, one focused on the demands of respect in the preschool classroom, another exploring the risk and resilience associated with various preschool masculinities, and the third focused on the behaviors of maltreated children in the preschool classroom. In the context of this article, I pay particular attention to how discussions of resilience may be reflecting stereotypical notions of race, class, and gender. As well, given their relative powerlessness in the debate, I am also mindful of the ways in which policy and applied interventions implicitly conceptualize children and childhood, and the implications of particular actions on young children and their development. In doing so, I wish to argue that static notions of risk and resilience factors fail to consider the ways that various influences may facilitate both risk and resilience in children's lives. To conclude, I will discuss the implications of such a perspective for educational practice and developmental theory.

Resilience as a Reframing of "At-Risk"

The present focus on resilience emerged, in part, as a response to the language of "at-risk" that permeated the world of research, practice, and policy for much of the last two decades. This conceptualization has been critiqued for framing children and families as lacking the cultural and moral resources for success and being in need of compensatory assistance from the dominant society (Sleeter, 1995). As such, the at-risk discourse has been argued to be implicitly racist, classist, sexist, and ableist (Lubeck & Garrett, 1990). In response, Swadener and Lubeck (1995) advanced the notion of "children and families at promise" as a way to orient to the possibilities of children and families rather than their deficits.

The language of resilience emerged, in part, as a response to these and similar critiques. However, though its intent may have been to orient toward promise, it is frequently used in concert with notions of risk to further classify and demoralize individuals. For example, the language of risk and resilience, or risk and protective factors (i.e., Eklund, Torppa, & Lyytinen, 2013), suggest that one is either at risk or resilient, with those not conforming to dominant expectations of success being further diminished. Typically, resilience is constructed as a constituent element of identity—one is either resilient or not. Thus, resilience (or the lack of) becomes yet another label bestowed upon the individual by dominant society.

Indeed, the prevailing definition of resilience is better than expected outcomes in the midst of adversity (Masten, Best, & Garmezy, 1990). Such ambiguous framing begs the questions: Whose expectations are being privileged? And, on whom are such expectations being placed? Given social inequity, power, and privilege, it is most certainly the values and priorities of dominant society that are imposed. And it is those sitting at the margins who are imposed upon. Thus, it might be argued that the dominant discourse of resilience, much like the one informing the notion of "at-risk," are implicitly racist, classist, sexist, heterosexist, and ableist. In this way, the language of resilience has oriented us to the importance of "promise," but has done little to deconstruct the privileging of dominant notions of success and classification systems, which reify deficit perspectives. As an antidote to these critiques, it is important to develop conceptions of resilience that are dynamic, allowing multiple perspectives of and from the individual to emerge.

Beyond Static Notions of Resilience: Three Twists on the Story

In leveraging this critique, it is helpful to understand the increasing complexity of integrating various aspects of one's self, social environments, relationships, and other developmental contexts (Fischer, Ayoub, Singh, Noam, Maraganore, & Raya, 1997). Fischer et al. recognize that humans often organize their development around positive and negative splits and that development is "naturally fractionated in a kind of passive dissociation, with skills organized independently in terms of task, context, and emotional state" (p. 752). As such, development becomes a process of organizing and coordinating these different strands in levels of increasing complexity over time to develop an integrated self-understanding. However, given the lack of social support, the impact of poverty, and the challenges inherent in sustaining positive relationships, for example, many individuals living in poverty find this integration difficult, if not threatening.

Fischer et al.'s perspective is also helpful in explaining the adaptive, although potentially negative, outcomes that may develop when one is forced to develop along a nonintegrated developmental pathway. Given that individuals with challenging lives must coordinate and integrate seemingly contradictory understandings of their gender and racial identities, social environments, and relationships, such a framework offers a normative framework for representing the challenges and complexity of developing and sustaining an enduring sense of well-being.

Following, I will present three separate case studies that represent and clarify the contextual nature and the dynamic developmental processes underlying resilience.

Listening to Mom and Watching Out for Himself

Located in the midst of one of the city's most monolithic housing developments, Child Works is a Head Start center serving children and families from the neighborhood. I spent four years working at Child Works, both as a mental health counselor and also as coordinator of a university research project. Virtually all of our students live well below the poverty line and come from all sorts of backgrounds. Yet, they share many of the same fears. Though there are many positive aspects about their neighborhood, all of them are haunted by its violence often resulting in everyone trying to make herself or himself smaller, invisible, as they shuffle quickly through the streets. Even the buildings in this part of the city seem smaller than they actually are, dwarfed by the shadows of skyscrapers from the downtown nearby.

After working at Child Works for more than a year, I was asked to begin counseling James,[1] a 5-year-old boy who had been referred for refusing to follow classroom instructions and for variously hitting his teacher and running away from him. During my initial observations, I noted that James seemed fully engaged when playing with his classmates, and that they seemed to respond very positively to him. However, he did seem never to allow his back to be turned to the teacher. A subtle dance, he was always turning to make sure that he could keep an eye on Mr. Elias. Though slightly more tolerant of Ms. Dawson, the assistant teacher in the classroom, James still seemed very guarded around her. Given this, I felt trepidation about how James might respond to working with me one-on-one in the playroom. Nevertheless, I recognized that it was exactly such relationship building that would characterize James' healing and focus our therapeutic goals.

When it was time to begin our therapy sessions, I asked James' mother to meet with him and me, so that she might introduce us. Unfortunately, though she consented for services, she was unable to change her work schedule and asked that Ms. Dawson serve as her surrogate. On the slated morning, Ms. Dawson introduced me to James inside the classroom and explained to him that I would be his counselor. The three of us spent a few minutes talking about what it meant to have a counselor and invited James to ask any questions he might have. He folded his arms. I explained to him that eventually we would be playing together in my playroom, but that we would get to know each other for a while in his classroom.

For almost two months, I spent a few hours each week playing with James and the other children in his classroom. He was reluctant at first, but became a little less guarded as the other children began to feel more comfortable around me. Soon, I thought that it would be time to begin our transition out of the classroom. I began a countdown for James, telling him at the end of each visit in how many days we would be playing together in the playroom. I assumed that his lack of acknowledgment meant acceptance of this plan.

On the fateful morning, I walked to the door with my "magic key," handed it over to James, and asked if he would like to lead us to the playroom. He simply took the key, threw it across the room, and said, "I ain't going nowhere with you."

Attempting a therapeutic response, I replied, "It can be scary to visit a new place." Followed by, "I am your friend and I will do everything possible to make sure you are safe and ok."

James took a swing at my knees and said, "Leave me the #$&^ alone."

Shocked at how quickly the situation was escalating, I asked James: "Can you tell me why you would like to stay here?"

He said, "I don't know you."

"Thanks for sharing that with me, James," I replied. "But I thought we were getting to know each other. "

James said, "Mommy says I can't talk to no strange people. They want to kill little kids."

"Some people do hurt children. I want to help you feel safe," I replied.

Putting his hands on his hips, James looked at me and said, "I keep me safe."

Needless to say, we did not go to the playroom that day.

For the purposes of this vignette, I will not go further into the details of James' therapeutic treatment, nor the painful history underscoring his insistence on keeping himself safe. Even so, this brief interaction provides some insight into his defiance. Quite literally, James is fighting for his life. Though maladaptive in the classroom environment, his behavior does make sense in the context in which it emerged, a community with a high concentration of sexual offenders living in close proximity to children whose parents may frequently be working long hours. While placing him farther and farther away from academic success (or perhaps just positive relationships with teachers), his efforts to distance himself from adults is protective in addressing some more basic survival and self-identity needs. And, though his behavior may have seemed disobedient or disrespectful to his teacher, watching out for himself and keeping his guard up was mindful and respectful of the admonishments of James' mother. Given this, should we say that James is not resilient? Or, would it be more appropriate to say that community resilience is impacting his academic resilience?

A "Good Boy": The Risk of Early Loss

One month short of 3 years old, Jorge was well on his way to becoming a little boy. He was said to be "the mirror image of his father," with short wavy brown hair, dark-brown eyes, and a light-beige complexion that reflect his Latino heritage. Besides his father's physical appearance, Jorge also shares his nickname, "Macho."

I had known Jorge since he was 16 months old, the first child I met while completing a required counseling internship. While uncommon for children to participate in therapy at such a young age, Jorge's daycare center is the site of a university research project aimed at fostering the positive development of children and families living in poverty. Originally, Jorge was referred to therapy mainly as a preventative measure; his family's socioeconomic status and father's sporadic involvement in his life made Jorge particularly vulnerable to future challenges. However, in recent months, therapy had helped Jorge with the unexpected departure of his father and the Department of Social Services' removal of Swahim, Jorge's 6-year-old half-brother, from the home due to a contentious custody dispute between Jorge's mother and the boy's father. Given the impact of these events on Jorge's mother, she had become overworked and depressed, sometimes struggling to maintain a consistent routine for Jorge and his 5-year-old sister, Shanille.

Despite my initial reservation about knowing what to do with small children, I was assigned to work with Jorge by an insightful clinical director who believed "The little guy could benefit from a male presence in his life." For well over two years, Jorge and I spent close to ten hours a week together, in his classroom, on the playground, and in his weekly therapy sessions. Recognizing our special connection, several teachers at Jorge's daycare center often jokingly referred to him as my "son." Despite my corrections, Jorge even called me "daddy" for the first six months of our time together. I heard Jorge's first sentence, held his hand as he learned to hop on one foot, and supported him through his father and brother's departures from his life. My relationship with Jorge has been the most profound learning experience of my educational career.

Becoming part of Jorge's life challenged me to confront parts of my own. Though our experiences and communities are different in many ways, I did see much of myself in Jorge. I know what it is like to live in a home filled with both good times and worry. I was raised by a hard-working single mother in an under-resourced Southern community; I have also felt unsafe. My own father walking out on us when I was still a boy allowed me to connect with Jorge's experiences of loss, not necessarily understanding them, but certainly being able to empathize.

In thinking about the kind of man I wanted to support Jorge in becoming and my explicit charge from the daycare's clinical director, I was challenged to think about the kind of man I hoped to be. Attempts to reconcile the values of my childhood with those of my current life as a gay graduate student at an Ivy League institution allowed me to recognize that communities and cultures often have conflicting notions of what it means to be a good man—and that failure to conform to these standards may be painful. Yet I also wondered, what is lost in conformity? Given that many men in this society struggle to sustain close relationships, experience intimacy, and express emotions, it seemed that being a good man also comes at a cost. In cultures where men are expected to stand on their own, not cry, and be a tough guy from a very young age—around 3 years old in most Western societies—men simply do not have permission or the skills to feel close and vulnerable. Coming to see my journey as one shared by Jorge, and all men, forced me to question the kind of partner, father, and friend I would work to become. I was also led to consider, as a child psychologist, what kind of boys and men would I support my clients in becoming? Years spent reflecting on these questions (Wright, 2007) now leads me to wonder how was Jorge impacted when his behavior and emotional needs contradicted the norms of his daycare environment?

My relationship with Jorge underscored for me that becoming a boy—becoming a man—is a difficult journey. Separating from care and relationships is a critical but painful achievement necessary to becoming the strong independent man so celebrated by society's dominant culture. My relationship with Jorge straddled the time in his life when the challenges of becoming less dependent on caregivers are most acute. Our connection allowed me to empathize with the pain Jorge experienced in moments of conflict between his needs and the social/cultural demands of the world around him.

More particularly, this experience highlighted for me the risk and resilience of various masculinities. For example, Jorge's uncles enjoyed the fact that he frequently fought with other children, got in trouble at school, and maintained a tough exterior. They said that he was a "good boy." However, in the classroom, this behavior placed him at risk of academic failure, poor peer relationships, and greatly limited his educational prospects. As his therapist, I struggled to determine what type of resilience I should be promoting—what might allow him to be successful in school could have estranged him, or worse, from his family and community. However, not preparing him to be successful in the school environment had equally damning consequences. In other words, resilience at school may have placed him at increased risk in other parts of his life, or vice versa. Similarly, he was not viewed as a resilient child at school, even though his behaviors were very adaptive for the environment in which they developed.

For children like Jorge who experience such early loss, the demands of this socialization process are particularly insidious. In the midst of coming to terms with the fact that many in his early life have walked away from him, Jorge was forced to confront another world that was pushing him away. When he cried, he was told that he should not. When he asked for connection, it was sometimes withheld. He was taught that to be caring is to be a girl—at the same time, learning that to be a girl is a really bad thing to be. Much larger than him, the roots of these responses are held in the values of this little boy's world, culture, social class, and location—all forces that are very difficult to circumvent. As a result, depending on the context and who was assessing him, Jorge was labeled as both resilient and not.

Having worked with Jorge for such a long period of time, in different domains, while also building relationships with other people important to him, allowed me to realize that what happened to Jorge in one part of his life had direct implications for how he responded in another. Recognizing that Jorge was telling me his story through his behavioral and emotional responses helped me to better understand his actions and understandings inside the classroom. Taking a holistic perspective on his life was central to the effectiveness of my work with him. While this is not a new or innovative understanding—most of us know that what goes into children is what comes out of them—it has been my experience that it is often not one that is implemented in our work with children, particularly those who are very young. Many times it seems that people use children's life experiences against them, to justify why it would be challenging to foster their development. However, through my work with Jorge and other small children, I have found that in developing a deep understanding of children's life experiences we might engage them in their behavior more fully, reframing and refocusing understandings to become more positively adaptive.

Reframing Risk as Resilience

Sixteen months old, Goddess had never learned to laugh. It is unclear if she never experienced this emotion, or if she had simply given up on it. With a very dark complexion and distant eyes, Goddess most often arrived at school bundled in her dingy pink coat, covered with the smell of cigarette smoke. Spending most days sitting silently in the corner of her toddler classroom, she did not smile, play, or ask her teachers to hug, console, or sit with her. Though taller than most of her 16- to 20-month-old classmates—five rowdy boys and two equally energetic girls—Goddess sought none of the same attention. She did not run around the room, ask the teacher to "Help me, please," cry, throw, pinch, hit, laugh, dance, sing, or annoy. She simply sat. Oftentimes Goddess' gaze was fixed, staring blankly out the window. Other times, she clearly gazed within, her blank expression signaling that, though physically present, her thoughts had carried her to another place.

I met Goddess when assigned to work in her classroom as part of a clinical internship required for completion of my graduate studies in mental health counseling and human development. Though it is uncommon for children to participate in therapy at such a young age, Goddess' school was recognized as a therapeutic preschool by the state's Department of Social Services, with approximately one-third of the students living in state custody or living under the supervised custody of their families due to substantiated claims of abuse or neglect. Initially assigned to the school by the court system, Goddess was born into the protective custody of the state, her mother giving birth to her while incarcerated on drug charges.

Goddess and I spent close to ten hours a week together, in her classroom, on the playground, and in weekly play therapy sessions. Though initially assigned to her for one academic year, I volunteered as clinical staff for more than four years in order to further my support of Goddess and several other children. I heard Goddess' first laugh, rubbed her back as she struggled through naptime nightmares, and supported her through family struggles.

Goddess provides a poignant example of the consequences of negative experiences in early childhood. Learning about life through the perspective of a mother struggling with depression and addiction, Goddess never expressed the typical emotions of childhood, nor had the manifestation of them ever served to meet her needs. Barely more than a year old, she already questioned the world's ability and desire to respond. Goddess rarely enjoyed the moments of pleasure necessary to develop positive emotions, like laughter. As well, growing up in a world that often failed to respond to her cries, she also never fully developed her tears. Internalizing the world as a place of assault, Goddess had already started her retreat.

Unfortunately, the necessary barriers she created to protect herself also began to isolate her from opportunities to develop new knowledge, skills, and expectations. Looking inward, Goddess failed to learn many of the skills necessary to communicate to the outward world, as well as to generate positive responses from it. Though none of us at the school intentionally overlooked Goddess, her lack of affect did not efficiently draw us to her at first—only confirming her perceptions of her place in the world.

Though Goddess should not be expected to advocate for herself at such a young age, it was to her detriment that she did none of the things of "typical" children to draw adults to her. Across my experiences as an educator, through the pre-K through university levels, I have observed that the children most difficult to like almost always receive the worst treatment from peers and adults. In a highly competitive environment like the classroom, Goddess, and those who have never honed their skills eliciting positive responses, are labeled as behavior problems or are lost in the shuffle.

Perhaps this is the most insidious consequence of maltreatment—if one is poorly "loved," it is difficult for one to know how to be loveable. As well, if one is raised by a depressed or absent caregiver, never seeing a smile, one does not know how to manufacture or recognize laughter. Unfortunately, for many maltreated children who never come to expect much from the world, this attitude is often an important determinant of their future life outcomes.

However, Goddess' silence can also be understood as a resilient act of self-preservation inside the environment to which she was responding. While in the classroom her silence did not serve her well, it was an efficient response to experiences of maltreatment. If a caregiver is absent in her response, crying does not serve to have one's needs met. Similarly, if one is uncertain of one's next meal, learning not to cry is a very efficient way to conserve energy for survival. For those children at risk of physical abuse, it makes much sense to become as invisible as possible.

Though initially my emotional response was to feel sorry for Goddess, I soon came to respect her strength. While no child should have to experience such maltreatment, Goddess did endure. Rather than a sign of brokenness, changing my perspective on Goddess' silence allowed me to recognize in her someone who was fighting to live. Through this reframing, I could begin to imagine her laughter. Rather than trying to "save" or change Goddess, I eventually came to understand my role as being to support her own inherent strengths. As I began to see more clearly these possibilities in Goddess, she and those around her began to see them more clearly as well. In the same way that expectations may be the most damning consequence of risk, perhaps they are also the greatest hopes for resilience.

Resilience Through Risk

Through my work with children like these, James, Jorge, and Goddess, I have observed that as they become more trusting, they frequently become more outwardly focused, less temperamental, and share more positive affect. Soon, they begin to receive more positive attention from teachers and peers, building additional social-emotional skills through interactions with them. Similarly, as their teachers begin to see these children in a different light, I have noticed that they often begin to enjoy them more, feel a greater sense of efficacy, and gain energy from their love and affection. Indeed, it is the mutual transformation that occurs between children with messy lives and the important relationships in their lives that inspire and sustain a support network for them—greatly improving their future prospects.

Moving Forward

Such dynamics have important consequences for children's identity development and attitudes about schooling. As such, it is important to develop pedagogies, dispositions, and classroom environments that honor the complex skills that these children have developed to navigate their messy lives. Rather than locating the injustices of their world internal to these children— viewing them as not resilient—we should recognize the ways that their actions are logical and meaningful in the context of a world that may be turned upside down, or which may be functioning according to a different set of values.

Perhaps rather than demanding compliance and "good behavior" as a precondition to learning, classrooms should be structured to provide greater autonomy to children and thus space for respect and interdependence to emerge. Moving from educational narratives that assume respect to perspectives that respect the diversity, and sometimes difficulty of children's lives, we may create space for more positive and less oppositional images of children to emerge. Perhaps this will allow teachers more flexibility in seeing the adaptive capacities of their students, and support them in being more creative in figuring out how to support students in either building on these adaptations that are serving them well outside the school environment or better developing their capacity to differentiate social contexts and appropriate skill sets.

The necessity and potential consequences for children are great. When children are forced to choose between adaptations (beliefs, skills, and values) that keep them safe and/or connected to those whom they love or are dependent on and things that potentially challenge or move them away from them, they will always choose the former. In other words, in the short term, survival is the issue, even if survival choices jeopardize skill development and future opportunities. Consequently, schools must not compete—rather than devaluing what children bring with them into our classrooms, we should find a way to at least honor and acknowledge individual sources of strength in some part of their lives. Failure to do so induces shame and inferiority at worst, and pushes children farther and farther away from embracing schools as safe and emotionally protective spaces at best. Indeed, a child may not be or have all that we wish for him or her, but what he or she does have is the world to them, and in it is the fertile ground of hope. For as the children discussed in this piece suggest, they will be resilient regardless—change always happens—it is in which context they will be allowed to develop that is fundamentally at stake.

References

Bulotsky-Shearer, R. J., Manz, P. H., Mendez, J. L., McWayne, C. M., Sekino, Y., & Fantuzzo, J. W. (2012). Peer play interactions and readiness to learn: A protective influence for African American preschool children from low-income households. *Child Development Perspectives, 6*(3), 225–231. doi:10.1111/j.1750-8606.2011.00221.x.

Cutuli, J. J., Desjardins, C., Herbers, J. E., Long, J. D., Heistad, D., Chan, C., Hinz, E., & Masten, A. S. (2013). Academic achievement trajectories of homeless and highly mobile students: Resilience in the context of chronic and acute risk. *Child Development, 84*(3), 841–857. doi:10.1111/cdev.12013.

Eklund, K., Torppa, M., & Lyytinen, H. (2013). Predicting reading disability: Early cognitive risk and protective factors. *Dyslexia, 19*(1), 1–10. doi:10.1002/dys.1447.

Fischer, K. W., Ayoub, C., Singh, I., Noam, G., Maraganore, A., & Raya, P. (1997). Psychopathology as adaptive development along distinctive pathways. *Development and Psychopathology, 9*(4), 749–779.

Lubeck, S., & Garrett, P. (1990). The social construction of the 'at-risk' child. *British Journal of Sociology of Education, 11*(3), 327–340.

Masten, A., Best, K., & Garmezy, N. (1990). Resilience and development: Contributions from the study of children who overcome adversity. *Development and Psychopathology, 2*(4), 425–444. doi:10.1017/S0954579400005812

Schroder, K. E. E., & Ollis, C. L. (2013). The coping competence questionnaire: A measure of resilience to helplessness and depression. *Motivation and Emotion, 37*, 286–302.

Sleeter, C. E. (1995). Reflections on my use of multicultural and critical pedagogy when students are white. In C. E. Sleeter & P. L. McLaren (Eds.), *Multicultural education, critical pedagogy, and the politics of difference* (pp. 415–437). Albany, NY: SUNY Press.

Swadener, E. B., & Lubeck, S. (1995). The social construction of children and families "at risk": An introduction. In E. Swadener & S. Lubeck (Eds.), *Children and families "at promise": Deconstructing the discourse of risk* (pp. 1–16). Albany, NY: SUNY Press.

Wright, T. (2007). On Jorge becoming a boy: A counselor's perspective. *Harvard Educational Review, 75*(2), pp. 164–186.

Note

1. Pseudonyms have been used in this article to ensure the confidentiality of participants.

Sixteen

Our Story of Early Childhood Collaboration: Imagining Love and Grace

Denise Proud and Cynthia à Beckett

We present our friendship that spans three decades as an example of the way strong bonds grow through shared understandings born out of working with young children in early childhood settings. Stories that are included in education texts help teachers explain themselves and their teaching practises. Fleet, Patterson, and Robertson (2012) provide current examples of the way individual teacher stories clarify key ideas in the book. The reader becomes connected to key ideas through being able to relate to the writers on a personal basis. Whether there are differences or similarities, there is a relational starting point, a meeting place for things to begin. The reader is thus guided from the personal to the larger arguments. Van Manen (2002) provides another example of this process as each writer in the edited volume shares his/her personal teaching experiences before detailing ideas. This is the way we use our personal experiences. Our stories focus first on our social context, to help the reader appreciate the multiple layers we inhabit. This process exposes our similarities, differences, and our ongoing relationship of decolonizing through our intercultural friendship. In our case we met as early childhood advisors after coming directly from working in kindergartens in different states of Australia. We argue that working with young children is a position of grace. In our research project in 2001, we explored our views about working in kindergartens and then with adults in different settings and how our intercultural friendship acted as a decolonizing factor (à Beckett & Proud, 2001). We also raised the question as to whether we fall from grace when we no longer work with children (à Beckett & Proud, 2004). In this chapter, we revisit these ideas and we also present new projects. We encourage those who work with young children to appreciate the pivotal undercurrents evidenced through the sense of grace that comes with this work. We argue that understandings and imaginaries of our work with young children can support a reconceptualized view of early childhood education and further support social activism.

The positions of grace we experienced while teaching in early childhood settings have been revitalized and reconceptualized through our involvement with the Reconceptualizing Early Childhood Education (RECE) group over the past 12 years. Our involvement with the RECE community has nurtured both our combined work and our individual projects (Proud & à Beckett, 2011; Semann, Proud, & Martin, 2012; à Beckett, 2010). We also draw on the idea of playing in the in-between as a way to clarify our definition of grace. We share our individual stories as a background to our current work. While we currently live in different capital cities of Australia, Denise in Brisbane and Cynthia in Sydney, we remain close—watching, listening, responding, caring.

Denise

I'm an Indigenous Australian born in Wakka-Wakka country of Southern Queensland and I grew up in the Aboriginal community of Cherbourg. Back in 1969 in regional Queensland, not many people knew about early childhood education—to many it was considered at the time as "just babysitting." I was lucky enough to observe the Kindercraft program in the Brisbane City Hall. Not only were there passionate teachers engaging with the children, but Aboriginal and Torres Strait Island women were working with the children during the day and attending lectures as night. These women were role models to me and I was so inspired, as I could see a place for me here and a future in this field within my community. After completing the Kindercraft course, I went on to start the first kindergarten in Cherbourg. You can imagine that resources and support were scarce at the time. I also had to motivate others, including officials from the State Department, to view early childhood education as a worthwhile concept in the community. Since I came under "The Act" (The Aboriginal Protection and Restriction of the Sale of Opium Act 1897–1934), I was bonded to the department for two years. This act gave the government the right to keep records and have enormous control over all key aspects of our lives.

A career in early childhood teaching was a logical choice for me. There are many connections between early education and Indigenous community. For example:

> My community was interactive and early childhood teaching is interactive. I felt primary schools were restrictive with too much order. I preferred the early childhood setting—like our culture—observing, watching, listening, interacting, sensing, feeling, being in the moment with a child or children. (Semann, Proud, & Martin, 2012, p. 247)

Cynthia

I grew up in Victoria, a southern state of Australia, and I lived first in inner urban Melbourne and then rural Victoria. My family had come primarily from England in the 1800s making me the fourth generation on both sides of my family born in Australia. At the age of 7 I decided I was going to be a kindergarten teacher and my family supported me and continue to support these abiding interests. I completed my initial early childhood qualification in Melbourne and then worked in various early childhood settings in Melbourne for 11 years.

Teaching and Meeting

We worked in many early childhood centres: Denise in Queensland, Cynthia in Victoria. Both worked in innovative programs, Denise in mobile kindergartens, Cynthia in a demonstration center in the grounds of Melbourne University and another centre, the first combined pre-school daycare center in Victoria. We were both sensitive to the different teaching styles of early childhood educators and also ensured that our programs were always inclusive. This sensitivity to diversity ensured that differences, for example, in culture and socioeconomic circumstance, did not create any barriers. We both worked in centres with diverse populations from inner urban centres with high migrant populations to remote mining and Indigenous communities. We both found this diversity rich and vital. Denise noticed that there were many similarities between the approaches of the Indigenous and early childhood education communities.

We met at the Crèche and Kindergarten Association (C & K) in Brisbane after coming directly from our work with young children and families. We had respect and a fascination with each other from the very start of our friendship, both admiring each other and wanting to know more about the other person's background and knowledge. We seemed to develop our friendship for one another very quickly. We found mutuality in one another with Cynthia willing and receptive to learning about Denise's community, Aboriginal culture, and heritage, and Denise interested in finding out about Cynthia's family ties and community in Melbourne, Victoria.

Over the years we've written papers together, presented together, and are like sisters. We were both advisors in our fields and we learned so much from each other. Cynthia was advisor to C & K centres throughout Queensland as was Denise in her role as the first Indigenous early childhood liaison officer for C & K. In this role she had to travel the state as an advisor to early childhood teachers concerning Indigenous education. She supported teachers with bringing Indigenous knowledges into an early childhood teaching situation. She also advised on the ways to involve parents and the community. During this work she travelled to remote communities and the Torres Strait Islands.

During our time together as advisors to the field, we shared views and ideas about our different roles. We learnt from and supported one another. We trusted one another and we believe that our previous work with young children in early childhood settings supported us to form such a trusting, caring, respectful relationship. This support was more than a professional, occupational link created through shared understandings of settings and the practices of early childhood teachers. There was something more. There was a predisposition to be open to another, in a way that combined trust, appreciation, and pleasure.

Together and Apart

After working together as advisors with C & K in Queensland for two years, we both left advisory work. Denise moved to Denver, Colorado, in the United States, and Cynthia stayed in Brisbane to commence her first academic teaching appointment in early childhood education. During the time Denise was in Denver, she worked with the United Way and George Washington Carver Center—working with children and families from low-socioeconomic areas—many Hispanic, African American, and American Indian.

The friendship continued to flourish even though we were living in different parts of the world. Denise felt that having the experience of living in the United States helped her grow and gave her strength to apply what she had seen in the States back home in Australia. When Denise returned to Australia, Cynthia invited her to give guest lectures to the students about forming partnerships with Indigenous families. As we were once again working with adults, there was great trust and collaboration. We argue that the strength of these connections came from our separate, initial teaching with children in early childhood settings. The students were very responsive to Denise's lectures and she was encouraged to consider work in the university setting. Denise decided not to do this as she was concerned about issues for Aboriginal youth and became a teacher in the Technical and Further Education system in Queensland. She was then approached to work with 25 Aboriginal men in a maximum-security prison teaching a life-skills class. For the next 20 years, Denise worked in prison settings providing life skills for both Aboriginal people and others who chose to come to her classes.

Another change happened when Cynthia took up an academic appointment at the University of New England in rural New South Wales. This was in 2000 and significant because we became involved with the Reconceptualizing Early Childhood Education critical group (RECE) and applied to do a joint presentation at the conference in 2001. Our work with adults in different settings was a continual topic of interest and so it was logical to research this issue and compare our view of teaching children in kindergartens with teaching adults in university and prison settings. The research process, the writing of the paper, and presentation at the RECE conference in 2001 were highly significant events (à Beckett & Proud, 2001). The conference was held in New York City three weeks after September 11, so this created a number of issues. One of the most powerful aspects of this conference was meeting the participants of the RECE group. We were welcomed in, there was a great deal of interest in our research, and we were encouraged in an enduring way that continues, as evidenced by our presentations done separately (à Beckett, 2004; Proud, 2009) and together (Proud & à Beckett, 2011).

Teaching as a Position of Grace (Re)visited

Over the years, we asked why we found working with young children so compelling and so enduring. In our initial research about teaching in early childhood settings, we agreed that times of connection with young children could become moments of wonder (à Beckett & Proud, 2001, 2004). One way to explain this is as a position of grace. Our current responses to such times of wonder and the related idea of grace now include the concept of playing in the in-between (à Beckett, 2007). These are times when children and adults are not constrained by the usual requirements of social exchange, based on the logic of identity (à Beckett, 2007, 2010). While many collaborative, productive times are explained through the social exchange model, this cannot explain times of grace when relations form. Our shared appreciation of these ideas, in their very early forms, motivated our research conducted more than a decade ago (à Beckett & Proud, 2001, 2004). We were influenced by the arguments of Van Manen (1991, 1997), who focuses on the need to break away from the tireless domination of activism so that a more patient, gentle tone can unfold. The elements of playing in the in-between support ways this can be achieved and also clarify our current definition of grace (à Beckett, 2007). The three elements are being fully present, un-knowing, and mutuality through love. When children and staff are part of grace-filled relational times, these aspects will be present.

Early childhood education is unique in its format—it is different to and less formal than other educational systems. It is more visual, more tactile, and more creative. Research, theories, and ideas such as playing in the in-between reveal a sense of passion, a sense of grace. Revisiting issues of grace reveals major explanations in the area of theology. Our work has been influenced by the analysis of grace provided by Metcalfe and Game (2002). They explain how grace allows us to let go and be ourselves, our true selves. This may have implications for the way we do things and suddenly succeed with grace as explained in their ballet example. They argue that the complication and beauty of how grace happens is the mystery of everyday life.

Grace is a topic of focus in many areas other than theology, including psychology and education. Roffey (2012, 2013) has established a blog site on the topic (www.sueroffey.com) and describes grace in terms of behavior. She explains it as "kindness in all situations and (that you) maintain your own integrity regardless of provocation or slight. Grace is being true to your best self." This differs from ideas of grace being part of the mystery of everyday life. Initially, Denise defined grace in this way:

> It seems to me that we are using the word 'grace' in two different ways—the first is our attitude and approach to life that we largely inherited from our parents and life experiences. The second is 'working with children as a place of grace.' But why is working with children a 'place of grace'? Is it because teaching children is somehow felt to be a privilege, because you as a teacher are in a position of trust and influence? Is there more trust in teaching young children than in teaching adults? (Denise, e-mail 8) (à Beckett & Proud, 2004, p. 153)

Denise wrote this because she had moved away from early childhood education into working in youth detention and adult correctional centres. We wanted to understand more about the possible changes that can happen if we move from teaching children in early childhood settings to then teaching adults.

> When I compare teaching in a university and teaching in an early childhood setting I feel that the chance to engage and be responsive often has many pressures and layers that work against direct response and real feelings about things. It seems that it is difficult to know if a tutorial or lecture has been useful because there have been so many factors that impact on students and staff. (Cynthia, e-mail 5) (à Beckett & Proud, 2004, p. 154)

This was when Cynthia had moved on from early childhood settings into university lecturing.

We revisit this research today to help us understand more about this position of grace in early childhood settings. We explore in more detail the actual qualities of early childhood settings. Denise details how the sense of family and community is key and how learning by doing, observing, and imitating are also key aspects of her family life growing up in an Aboriginal community. Friendliness expressed by touching and ways to establish rapport and respect by listening are key features. We agree that the early childhood community values the importance of family and community involvement and learning by doing. There is also a focus on observing, imitating, touching, and physically exploring real things. Again Denise feels these key qualities were also very important in her own family and wider community. We are also coming to understand this is all part of the position of grace found in working with children in early childhood settings.

Social Activism and Grace

The field of early childhood education has a long history of social activism and justice initiatives. In Australia in the late 1800s, many children were destitute due to the economic depression of the times. Great concern for these children and their families led to the establishment of centres for children. This was the beginning of the kindergarten movement in Australia where kindergarten teaching colleges were established in capital cities in Australia, for example, Melbourne and Sydney in the 1920s. The provision of a three-year tertiary undergraduate qualification was one of the first teaching degrees of this type in Australia. These innovations were built on a history of social activism and remain in the field of early childhood education.

Concern for the well-being of destitute children was the starting point for the kindergarten movement in Australia and the focus on well-being remains. Taking an active role in the well-being of others is a key aspect of social activism and is evident in many community-based early childhood centres in Australia. Inclusive practices that support social activism in early childhood settings are enhanced when people operate in circumstances of grace. Everything becomes easier through grace and inclusion. Communities strengthen. In addition, shared notions of care, explained by Noddings (1984) as relational ethics, also contribute to the positive circumstances that often transpire. All are valued and through this are included.

Noddings (1984) also uses the term "engrossment" to explain the way those in caring circumstances, such as early childhood settings, are fully present and available to others. When this type of availability is evident, it predisposes those involved to an enduring legacy. Even when teachers are no longer working together in an early childhood setting, great connections remain. While such bonds can be explained as an expected part of friendship, we argue that more is taking place. Collaborations eventuate that can also involve aspects of social activism.

Our presentations, writing, and publications over the past 12 years have provided new imaginings for our work in early childhood education and new ways of being. These ways help to explain our different states, imaginings, and ways of knowing. Our intercultural friendship has acted to decolonize differences such as unequal positions of power detailed by Foucault (Foucault, 1991; MacNaughton, 2005). Our meeting in Brisbane as fellow early childhood advisors provided a professional platform that enabled the friendship to develop. We worked together with other advisors to provide technical and professional advice to teachers to support their work in early childhood education settings. While the initial meeting and ongoing work provided an important basis for our relationship, this could not ensure that different positions of power and knowledge would be minimized so that we could form the rich, long-term relationship that developed. There was something more. It seems to us now that this extra factor came from our previous work in early childhood education settings with young children. We did not fully understand this as a key factor until we conducted our research years later (à Beckett & Proud, 2001; à Beckett & Proud, 2004). We argue that work in early childhood education settings predisposed us to trust, engage, and share with one another, and that led to us to become close even though we no longer worked with children. This predisposition acted to counterbalance barriers that might have happened due to any unequal positions of power.

There is a danger that the consideration of working with young children as being a position of grace romanticizes work in early childhood settings. Currently, staff in this field often experience poor conditions and lower pay than other areas of education. This results in high demands logically associated with the early childhood field. While these are major challenges, there are many who remain committed to early childhood education and provide inspiring programs. Our research findings demonstrated the way we understood our work with young children as a position of grace:

> Teaching was viewed as times of connection in which things can be transformed in a moment of wonder. There was agreement that defining moments of wonder could be considered as a

position of grace.... There were shared views that our initial work with children was grace filled.... Denise defined grace as wisdom, strength, poise, empathy and other things...we each agreed...and that it also involved a respect for others. (à Beckett & Proud, 2004, p. 152)

We argue that a more specific understanding of teaching as a position of grace can lead to new imaginings and a reconceptualized view of work in early childhood settings. A deeper appreciation of the impact this work has on teachers through an understanding of grace can explain how those who work in this field can find great support from one another. We present ourselves as an example of the way we have been supported through our previous work with young children in early childhood settings.

The presentation of research findings about teaching as a position of grace, presented at the RECE conference, led to even stronger bonds (à Beckett & Proud, 2001). We engaged with others in these settings who took great interest in our views, research, and our work. We were supported by those in the RECE community to publish together for the first time (à Beckett & Proud, 2004). Over the past 12 years we have presented together and separately, internationally at RECE conferences and nationally at other conferences in Australia (à Beckett, 2003; à Beckett, 2004; à Beckett, 2009; Proud, 2009; à Beckett, Proud, & Proud, 2006; Proud & à Beckett, 2011).

The work we have presented together often focuses on a rethinking of inclusive practices in early childhood education (Proud & à Beckett, 2011). This work relates to social activism and social justice. Once again our ability to combine on these projects has been strengthened by our shared bonds, the legacy of our work with young children. They fuel imaginings for future action and are prominent features of RECE gatherings. We believe that such a history combined with daily positions of grace inherent in early childhood settings create circumstances of compassion and mutuality through love.

Dwelling in Places of Love

Our views on these topics were included in the 2011 Australian video project *World Views, Theories and Philosophies in Children's Services* (Producer Australian Research Alliance for Children and Youth, and Director M. Guigni, (2011). This was a response to the new national framework for early childhood education entitled Australian Government Department of Education, Employment and Workplace Relations for the Council of Australian Governments "Being, Belonging and Becoming: The Early Years Learning Framework" (2009). Our interest in new theories such as playing in the in-between and new Indigenous knowledges is evident in this material. All of this work, the ideas, the separate and shared projects are places of love. Collaborations, circumstances, situations, moments of early childhood education, practice, and research are at the same time about dwelling in places of love.

References

à Beckett, C. (2003). Dreaming, breathing, being. New considerations of how relations form: Implications for early childhood education. Presented at the 11th annual Reconceptualizing Early Childhood Education: Research, theory, and practice. Arizona State University, Tempe, Arizona.

à Beckett, C. (2004). The trouble with identities: An argument for otherness and the in-between rather than the logic of identities, implications for early childhood practice. Presented at the 12th annual Reconceptualizing Early Childhood Education: Research, theory, and practice. Oslo University College, Norway.

à Beckett, C. J. (2007). *Playing in the in-between: Implications for early childhood education of new views of social relations.* Ph D thesis, University of New South Wales, Kensington, NSW, Australia.

à Beckett, C. (2009, June 22–25). Pedagogies of hope explored through playing in the in-between. Presented at the 17th annual International Reconceptualizing Early Childhood Education Conference: Pedagogies of hope. Bethlehem City, Palestine.

à Beckett, C. (2010). Imaginative education explored through the concept of playing in the in-between. In T. Nielsen, R. Fitzgerald, & M. Fettes (Eds.), *Imagination in educational theory and practice: A many-sided vision* (pp. 191–208). Newcastle, U.K.: Cambridge Scholars.

à Beckett, C., & Proud, D. (2001). Fall from grace: Reconceptualizing early childhood education from kindergarten to university and prison. Presented at the 10th annual Reconceptualizing Early Childhood Education Conference: Research, theory, and practice. Bank Street College of Education, New York.

à Beckett, C., & Proud, D. (2004). Fall from grace? Reflecting on early childhood education while decolonizing intercultural friendships from kindergarten to university and prison. In K. Mutua & B. Swadener (Eds.), *Decolonizing research in cross-cultural contexts* (pp. 147–158). Albany: SUNY Press.

à Beckett, C., Proud, D., & Proud, M. (2006, Nov. 30–Dec. 4). Decolonizing through intercultural friendships: Creating community, implications for early childhood practice. Presented at the 14th annual Reconceptualizing Early Childhood Education Conference: Research, theory and practice. Rotorua, New Zealand.

Australian Government Department of Education, Employment and Workplace Relations for the Council of Australian Governments. (2009). *Belonging, being, and becoming: The early years learning framework for Australia.* Commonwealth of Australia. http://www.ku.com.au/resources/other/COAG%20EYLF%20July09.pdf (retrieved October 26, 2013).

Australian Research Alliance for Children and Youth (Producer) & Guigni, M. (Director). (2011). World Views, Theories and Philosophies in Children's Services. video. Australia. http://afterhours.wesrch.com/paper-details/pdf-AF1S07R1OWHCP-worldviews-theories-and-philosophies-in-children-s-services#page1, retrieved 10-26-2013.

Fleet, A., Patterson, C., & Robertson, J. (Eds.). (2012). *Conversations: Behind early childhood pedagogical documentation.* Mt. Victoria, NSW: Pademelon Press.

Foucault, M. (1991). *Discipline and punish: The birth of a prison.* London: Penguin.

MacNaughton, G. (2005). *Doing Foucault in early childhood studies.* New York: Routledge.

Metcalfe, A. W., & Game, A. (2002). *The mystery of everyday life.* Sydney: Federation Press.

Noddings, N. (1984). *Caring: A feminine approach to ethics and moral education.* Berkeley: University of California Press.

Proud, D. (2009, June 22–25). Stories of hope: Indigenous Australians share their stories. Presented at the 17th annual International Reconceptualizing Early Childhood Education Conference: Pedagogies of hope. Bethlehem City, Palestine.

Proud, D., & à Beckett, C. (2011, Oct. 25–29). Rethinking inclusive practices in early childhood: A decade of discoveries through RECE. Presented at the 19th annual Reconceptualising Early Childhood Education Conference. Politics of care: Sharing knowledges, love and solidarity. University of East London.

Roffey, S. (2012). *Positive relationships: Evidence-based practice across the world.* New York: Springer Press.

Roffey, S. (2013). Inclusive and exclusive belonging: The impact on individual and community well-being. *Educational & Child Psychology, 30*(1), 34–47.

Semann, A., Proud, P., & Martin, K. (2012). Only seeing colour? Identity, pedagogy and ways of knowing. In A. Fleet, C. Patterson, & J. Robertson (Eds.), *Conversations: Behind early childhood pedagogical documentation* (pp. 245–257). Mt. Victoria, NSW: Pademelon Press.

Van Manen, M. (1991). *The tact of teaching: The meaning of pedagogical thoughtfulness.* London, Canada: Althouse Press.

Van Manen, M. (1997). *Researching the lived experience: Human science for an action sensitive pedagogy.* London, Canada: Althouse Press.

Van Manen, M. (2002). *Writing in the dark: Phenomenological studies in interpretive inquiry.* London, Canada: Althouse Press.

SEVENTEEN

Bring Back the Asylum: Reimagining Inclusion in the Presence of Others

Gail Boldt and Joseph Michael Valente

How to educate children with disabilities has been debated against the backdrop of larger cultural understandings of inclusion and exclusion. Garland-Thomson (2001) argues that disability can be understood as the marker of differences from bodily or behavioral cultural norms and expectations. Although differences in the traits, experiences, and desires of people who may share a particular marker can be vast, this diverse set of people is typically identified as a group based on the perceived "abnormality." Disability is not the impairment or difference that is marked however, but is rather located in oppressive and exclusionary beliefs and practices of cultures (Reid & Knight, 2006; Stiker, 1999). Historically, abledness in gendered, raced, classed, modified, and otherwise marked bodies has produced powerful justifications for inequalities (Baynton, 2001; Campbell, 2009; Garland-Thomson, 1996, 2001; McRuer & Bérubé, 2006; Snyder & Mitchell, 2006; Stiker, 1999, 2007). The traits of an inclusive society can be evidenced by how "people 'live everyday life as an everyday thing, with and *in the presence of* special, specific human beings who are our disabled equals'" (Masschelein & Verstraete, 2012 citing Stiker 1997, p. 11, emphasis added).

Central to debates about inclusion has been the question of *place* (Masschelein & Verstraete, 2012). Children with disabilities have been and continue to be placed in countless locations and arrangements somewhere along the continuum of segregated to integrated/mainstreamed to partial- and full-inclusion settings. This includes separate "asylums" and special schools and programs within public schools. Internationally, the movement toward inclusion education arose as part of the rights-based movements for broader inclusion of all people with minority status to be able to participate in mainstream society. The 2003 United Nations Educational, Scientific and Cultural Organization (UNESCO, Booth, & Lynch, 2003) position paper outlines how the right to inclusive education is a basic human right covered by long-standing international agreements,[1] sharply critiquing segregated settings in its introductory remarks, and noting that inequities and abuses most often arise "outside the mainstream—special programmes, specialized institutions, and specialist educators" (p. 3). Concerns about exclusions extend then to "second-class" or second-rate educational opportunities that lead children with disabilities to further social, cultural, and economic inequities as well as these children's experiences of social isolation and abuse.

Supporters for inclusion argue that inclusive education respects the unique contributions of each child and supports the civic, social, and educational rights of all children to participate in the normal daily life of the school. However, to imagine *place* as the primary indicator of the best approach or the most enlightened commitments is to deny or erase the complicated differences that are produced through any policy or practice. Inclusion policies and practices can sometimes give rise to and hide forms of systematic exclusion. Most notably, reports by the United States Government Accountability Office (2009), Human Rights Watch, ACLU, and Farmer (2009), and the U.S. Department of Education's Office of Civil Rights (2012) each detail alarming findings about children being subjected to abusive restraints and seclusion that have led to physical and emotional trauma and even deaths. The Office of Civil Rights (U.S. Department of Education, 2012) called special education to task with critiques of long-hidden data revealing that preschool children and special education students from culturally and historically marginalized groups in inclusive settings were being physically and mechanically restrained, subjected to seclusion and isolation, placed in in-school and out-of-school suspensions, expelled, and arrested, at rates far exceeding white and able-bodied peers. Still more, *The Lancet* recently reported that children with disabilities are almost four times more likely to be victims of violence and more than three times more likely to be victims of sexual violence (Jones et al., 2012). Additionally, arguments over place can ignore or dismiss the mundane, day-to-day realities of decisions parents have to make about how and where to educate their children that are embedded within socioeconomic and cultural realities and dependent on financial resources, transportation, work schedules, personality matches and conflicts with school personnel, religious and cultural beliefs, expectations, and pressures, and their own complicated histories with schooling (Valente & Boldt, in review).

In this chapter, we follow the argument of Masschelein and Verstraete (2012) to assert that in order for place to matter, it has to be coupled with commitments about what it could mean to "live in the presence of others" (p. 2). Masschelein and Verstraete frame place or space through French pedagogue Ferdnand Deligny's use of the word "asylum."[2] Asylum is a loaded word, conjuring the "insane asylum" and the inhumane warehousing of children with disabilities. Deligny was an experimental special educator who worked from the 1930s to the 1990s, first with children who were criminal offenders or considered "feebleminded" and later with children diagnosed as schizophrenic and as autistic. Deligny used the word asylum both in the original Greek sense of the word "asulon," which signified a sanctuary or inviolable place of refuge and protection from which one cannot be forcibly removed without sacrilege (*Old English Dictionary*, 1989 [Simpson & Weiner, 1989], cited in Masschelein & Verstraete, 2012), and also as a place wherein Deligny had the ability to live in very particular ways in the presence of children who did not communicate verbally. In other words, as Masschelein and Verstraete argue, place for Deligny was not just a location but could only be understood as it was formed through the presence of all participants living together in shared circumstances.

Additionally, the word asylum was important to Deligny because "the French word 'asile' completely encompasses the French word 'île' meaning island in English" (Deligny & Álvarez, 1976/2007, quoted from Masschelein & Verstraete, 2012, p. 9). For Deligny, an asylum was an island floating in a sea of expert psychological and pedagogical language that threatened to take over all possible meanings of the lives and experiences of children and teachers alike. For the non-speaking children with whom he lived and worked in his later years, the demand that they prove the existence of a recognizable subjectivity and desire through languages understood by others often meant that they were condemned to permanent valuelessness and objectification within society. Masschelein and Verstraete point out that for Deligny, living in the presence of the other means that the other is not viewed in terms of the ways that s/he contributes difference to the establishment of a common good—that is, greater appreciation of human diversity—but "precisely in the extent to which they produce interstices[3] in this communality" (p. 5). In other words, Deligny did not need the children to somehow make clear "their personal wishes, to express their fears and longings and make explicit their immediate and pressing needs in order to promote a new and improved conception of communality" (Stengers, 2005, p. 996, cited in Masschelein & Verstraete, 2012, p. 4). The extent to which a given child may or may not contribute a recognizable self was irrelevant. What concerned Deligny was that:

> The voices, gazes and gestures of individuals are not dumb, they do mean something, and they do express something. However, what is signified cannot be grasped by existing ideologies, ways of behaving or traditional discourses. To put it even stronger, they produce interstices in the linguistic spaces of those disciplines. (Masschelein & Verstraete, 2012, p. 10)

Living in the presence of others then, is welcoming the power of interstices that open between the children as subjects of professional discourses and the children's efforts to live their own lives, between the beliefs and knowledges of the teacher and what it is that the children present, and perhaps most importantly for Deligny, within the teacher him/herself:

> Seeking refuge and looking for asylum thus cannot be put on a par with a foremost Western tradition of diagnosing and putting children in isolated and walled spaces where they are loved and treated according to the newest insights of psychology and other disciplines. On the contrary, time and again Deligny has stressed the fact that rather than being outward, the action radius of the educator should be transformed towards a gaze which focuses on itself. The focus of any educational initiative for Deligny was not the child which had been described as in need of help or special support, but was the educator her/himself. What should be transformed then was not so much the incurable child, but precisely the way of relating and the language used by the educator to approach the situation. (Deligny & Álvarez, 1976/2007, cited in Masschelein & Verstraete, 2012, p. 10)

In what follows, we draw on Deligny's concept of asylum and Stiker's concept of living in the presence of others as expanded upon by Masschelein and Verstraete. Our thinking is framed through our reading of Deleuze and Guattari (1987), and especially the concept of assemblage (defined later). We use these concepts to help us think about our recent research at an inclusive French preschool, L'Ecole Gulliver, that unconditionally admits (subject to space[4]) all children regardless of the nature or severity of their disability or chronic illness.

This work began three years ago when, engaged in a university reading group making our way through Deleuze and Guattari's *A Thousand Plateaus* (1987), Joe noticed a short section describing the work of Deligny. Ever attuned to any references offering an applied approach to disability studies (or likeminded orientations) in education, Joe recruited Gail in an effort to learn all we could about Deligny's written, film, and practitioner work and how it related to Deleuzoguattarian theory. During a seminar on "French Notions of Disability" hosted by the Council on International Educational Exchange in Paris in 2012, Joe mentioned this interest in Deligny's work to a panel that included Henri-Jacques Stiker, Simone Korff-Sausse, and Eric Plaisance, all major writers in French disabilities studies, who suggested he visit APATE, an organization that oversees inclusion preschools, and its director, social-worker-turned-educator Cécile Herrou, who is inspired in part by the work of Deligny and also of Deleuze and Guattari.

Deligny worked closely with Guattari for a number of years at the psychiatric clinic La Borde in central France.[5] La Borde was founded in 1951 by Jean Oury as an asylum (in Deligny's sense of "sanctuary") in which patients and staff collaborated in running the facility and in which all participants searched for ways that their living together could contribute to their ability to creatively work in ways that suited each. This included a sharp rejection of the normalizing and pathologizing languages of professional psychiatry and psychoanalysis. Oury, borrowing from the earlier work of François Tosquelles at Hospital Saint Alban, named this approach "Institutional Psychotherapy." Guattari joined the staff in the mid-1950s and named his work at La Borde "schizoanalysis."[6] Deligny lived and worked there through the 1960s. On the website of APATE (see http://www.apate.fr/ retrieved October 26, 2013), the larger organization that oversees Gulliver and the other two (soon to be three) inclusion preschools that Cécile Herrou directs, the deregulating and depathologizing practice of institutional psychotherapy is specifically cited as closely related to APATE's work.

Gulliver as Interstice

The plan to make an ethnographic film of a typical day came from Tobin's video ethnographic methods (Tobin, Wu, & Davidson, 1989; Tobin, Hsueh, & Karasawa, 2009). These methods gave us specifics to direct our film crew, which was made up of three undergraduate students with limited experience with shooting film who came with us from our university. We worked to calm their anxieties and our own by coaching them to film with particular attention to routines (e.g., arrival/departure, play lessons, class activities, and recess). This was important if we were to create a narrative arc in the film, a sense of beginning, middle, and end. Capturing routines was also important to the teachers and to Ghada, the Gulliver director, and Cécile.[7] Their concern was that viewers should understand that the structures that framed a typical day at Gulliver were very carefully planned. In addition, consistent with Tobin's method, we instructed our film crew to try to track what was happening in the classroom in order to capture moments that raised interesting or provocative issues. They were also instructed in having two cameras trained on a single scene as often as possible, to give us high-quality cross shots for our film-making needs. Finally, they were instructed to help us watch for children who seemed particularly interesting, who might become "focal children" who we could particularly follow the next day.

On the first day of filming, however, it became evident that while these strategies were important, sticking to them too closely meant failing to capture something important about Gulliver. For one thing, the children changed spaces, groups, and teachers[8] constantly. This meant that following focal children almost always required having the two cameras in different spaces. More importantly, somehow capturing the constant movement of teachers, children, materials, and waves and bursts of affective tensions and energies happening among and within spaces and activities began to seem more important than following the arc of a given event. In fact, many of the things the children were doing did not have discernible beginnings, middles, and ends, but seemed, in the language of Deleuze and Guattari (1987), to be all "middles" or what Deleuze and Guattari, borrowing from Bateson (1972), called "plateaus"—something with no peak or climax but many intensities. Our experience of Gulliver, often more felt than articulated, caused us at the close of the first day to talk seriously about what it would mean to shoot a more "Deleuzoguattarian film," a film in which we could highlight middles or capture something that suggested that perhaps the essence of Gulliver was not the stories of individual children or teachers but of flows and movements emerging within carefully organized structures.[9]

In her 2009 book *Movement and Experimentation in Young Children's Learning: Deleuze and Guattari in Early Childhood Education*, Liselott Olsson describes the work of pedagogic documentation as not being about recognition and representation of "what really took place" but as a part of a process that helps to create new relations, new problems, and new potentials (p. 19). This reframes filming from an act of "capturing" to being a participant in an assemblage. In Deleuze and Guattari's (1987) writing, an assemblage, simply defined, is the collection of things that happen to be present in any given context. These include both discursive and non-discursive elements—bodies, passions, material objects, the composition of the space, as well as discourses and practices. These elements have no necessary relation to one another, and they lack organization, yet their happenstance coming together in the assemblage produces any number of possible effects on the elements in the assemblage (Leander & Boldt, 2013; Patton, 2000).

Understanding the assemblage is key to understanding Deleuze and Guattari's radical reconceptualization of social and cultural formations and indeed, of the unfolding of events in time and space. They begin with the assumption of an open system (Marcus & Saka, 2006). Humans are themselves open systems—changing constantly, becoming something new, something singular. The body is both singular in the momentary embodiment of its own assemblage, yet enters into and out of the heterogeneous productivity of other assemblages. Assemblages, including the assemblage of the body, exist in constant movement in an environment that is itself always in motion; therefore the potential for variation is almost infinite. As Leander and Boldt (2013) describe it:

> The body is always indeterminate, in an immediate, unfolding relation to its own potential to vary: this is what Deleuze and Guattari name as "emergence" (Massumi, 2002, pp. 4–5). The human body is the site that experiences and gives (or doesn't give) expression to the energies and potentials of the present that are constantly generated as the always-emerging body interacts with the always-emerging environment. (pp. 29–30)

As humans we move materially through time and space and our bodies perceive and register the nearly infinite patterns, variations, flows, objects, and potentials in our environment. Many of these affect us and elicit response from us at levels that are below conscious awareness; some rise to consciousness, and we give them meaning in the form of discourse that may be in the register of emotion, narrative, physical response, and energy (Leander & Boldt, 2013; Massumi, 2002). Olsson (2009) describes this as everything always existing in a relational field (p. 20). In the relational field of the assemblage, we affect and are affected by flows of emergence felt as energies and momentum, things speeding up and slowing down, unexpected things entering the field or flying off in unexpected directions. Because of this, as Olsson describes, what is happening is not fixed. The humans involved are not fixed. Each person is singular but that singularity enters the assemblage to become something else that far exceeds the singular as it mixes, activates, speeds, and slows elements in the assemblage, again and yet again.

For us as researchers, the feeling of Gulliver cut through the ways we thought about what we would follow in the filming and we begin to see material objects, the rising and falling waves of energy and engagement, and the random pieces entering and exiting the assemblage as all potentially equally important. Although it was deeply disturbing to our sense of what we needed to accomplish through filming relative to our goals for the research and future funding, on the second day we asked the camera crew to attend to how what was happening was affecting them and to follow what they thought they should follow. This meant that the camera crew was in near-constant motion, often in different rooms, trying to follow the affective flows of a particular emergent event. We had to worry less about getting cross shots. While knowing that this would produce a great deal of unusable footage, we gave ourselves over to the faith that regardless of what happened, there were things going on that the camera and the crew were part of and that we would end up with something.

Perhaps seeking to reassure Cécile about our conduct at Gulliver that suddenly felt and perhaps looked more uncertain and chaotic than we were comfortable with, we described to her the ways Gulliver affected us and therefore our research plan. We explained that thinking through our experiences of the first day of filming caused us to try to do something that would be philosophically more responsive and in tune with the community we were studying. Cécile told us that the APATE schools often have strong and surprising effects on visitors and that responsiveness to what is being experienced is at the heart of what they do. She explained that structure is very important at Gulliver. They know where every child is all the time and this is carefully planned. At the same time, also structuring their work is their strong belief in what she called "spontaneity," that something will happen, that the children will initiate or respond, interact or not interact, and that will show the teachers something and the teachers adapt and change in response. She and the teachers also know, she said, that repetition doesn't exist, that what happens in each moment is something new. "What is happening from moment to moment slips through your hands and you can't hold it," she said. "It must be hard for researchers, but for me, it got to the point where I said, 'Okay, I can't manage all that. I know things happen. I can see some of the things but I can't see everything and I can see something in one situation but I miss another really big thing. But it just happens and I sit still with that. The important thing is that it happens.'"[10] In what follows, we will give a single example of something that happened during our first day of filming at Gulliver, an exchange between a boy named Laurence[11] and his teachers.

Playmobil and Parakeets

It is early afternoon and while the younger children nap, a group of 15 4- and 5-year-olds gather in front of the television to watch a video. We first notice Laurence, a slender, blonde boy of 5 with a diagnosis of autism, when he begins to say, "No, no, no, no," and to shake his head repeatedly. He is staring toward the back of the room. The reason for his distress is indiscernible to us when we later watch the film. Laurence looks like he is about to cry, but instead returns to repeating "no." The children and teachers glance at him, but offer no other response. Laurence begins chewing his finger, continuing to stare at the back of the room and occasionally groans, but then becomes swept up in the energy of the other children debating what video to watch. Laurence does not speak, but joins in the excitement, crawling forward into the group of children to watch as the teacher holds out their choices. As the discussion among the children continues, Laurence again focuses on the back of the room. He points at something, begins again to repeat no, and now begins to cry softly. One of the teachers, Bernadette, comes to comfort him. She rubs his back and takes him onto her lap as he fights against his tears. He says nothing and Bernadette rocks him, looking often at his face to see how he is feeling. She says something to him that we can't hear and he nods, continuing to cry.

Now Rosalie, the teacher who has been organizing the video, comes over and asks him what is wrong. The children's conversation stops and all attention turns to Laurence. He tells her that he didn't do it, but neither the teachers nor we know what he is referring to. Rosalie hands the television remote to Bernadette, takes Laurence's hand, and walks him to the back of the classroom to talk with him privately. We cannot hear what she says, but Laurence makes sounds that seem to indicate distress, then looks back over his shoulder as the movie starts. Rosalie takes her cue from this and walks him back to watch the movie. He continues to look and sound distressed, and Rosalie lifts him onto her lap as they both sit facing the television. Laurence becomes absorbed in the movie and Rosalie offers him a seat of his own in front of her, which he takes.

After about 15 minutes of watching the film, Laurence begins to lose interest. He turns around and sees that two additional teachers, Marie and Stephanie, have entered and are sitting at a table in the back of the room. He stares at Marie and Stephanie, bobbing his head and sucking his fingers. They begin to imitate him. He points to his nose and they do the same. Laurence laughs and takes up this impromptu game with Marie and Stephanie in which he leads and they follow. He grabs his head, elbow in the air, and they do the same. He points to his nose again; the teachers do the same. He laughs and both of the teachers laugh, not in imitation but in obvious pleasure about the game and his responses. They all appear engaged now, having fun. In spite of Laurences' loud laughter, the other children pay no attention. They maintain this game for five minutes, then Rosalie, who had earlier left the room, comes back in and seeing their play, approaches Laurence and says, "Go on, go play with them," sending him to the back of the room to be with Marie and Stephanie. Marie pulls Laurence into her arms and kisses him on the cheek. His smile is enormous.

Marie gets up and pulls down a plastic Playmobil Noah's ark play set. As she sets out the animals, Laurence watches, then picks up the zebra and walks it onto the ark. She asks him, "Where should we put the lion?" but Laurence does not respond. Half a minute passes while Laurence continues to play with the zebra and she continues to set out pieces. Now Marie says, more to herself than to Laurence, "Twenty-eight years old and playing with Playmobil." This time, Laurence responds, "Twenty-eight? Twenty-nine years old?" Marie laughs and says something inaudible. She continues the conversation, but unlike the earlier imitation game, this time she takes the lead. Holding out a parrot, she asks, "What is this?" Laurence responds, "What is?" She points to the parakeet and repeats, "What is this?" and Laurence repeats, "What is?" Marie says, "You know what it's called" and Laurence says, "Called." Marie says, "It's called a parakeet. A parakeet." Laurence responds, "Par-a-keet." He pauses, then adds, "Like me." Ten minutes later, as the camera turns away, they are still playing and talking about colors, animal names, and movements.

Later, when we show clips from this event to the teachers, they tell us that Laurence is just beginning to play in an interactive way with others. Having identified Laurence as a focal child by the middle of the first day, our cameras have often followed him and indeed, throughout our two days of filming, we see that Laurence frequently sits and watches. He appears to enjoy the affectionate holds of his teacher, but rarely speaks or engages in a way that would be thought of as interactive play. Laurence has no trouble following the routines of the day and appears to engage willingly in the activities that are provided, but he also appears to do so in a way that looks like he is alone in a crowd. While the other children appear happy to sit and play around him, they rarely attempt to engage Laurence as his teachers frequently do. The teachers tell us that though they had tried to engage Laurence previously in Playmobil play, our film crew happened to catch the first time he played with it.

Breaking the Reflection

What are we to make of this segment of Laurence's day? It is tempting to describe this through a triumphant narrative in which an important developmental moment or perhaps curative step took place. Stephanie and Marie allowed Laurence to take the lead in engaging them, showing obvious pleasure in his actions. Rosalie, noticing his happy engagement, sent him to the back of the room to play. Not knowing what the outcome would be, Marie nevertheless tried to engage him in a form of play that he had previously ignored, and this time, he followed her lead, interacting and speaking more than we saw him do in any other parts of the film. Perhaps, we speculate, one thing caused the other.

There are two difficulties with this narrative. The first is that of making sense of the first half of the event, wherein Laurence is clearly in great distress for reasons no one understood. What we can say is that Laurences' unhappiness set in motion a series of responses that landed him in the back of the room, nearer to Stephanie and Marie. Laurence then watched the movie for 15 minutes, but for reasons of his own, turned around, making gestures that were carried over from earlier and were not directed at his teachers. On a whim, Marie and Stephanie began to imitate Laurence, not knowing whether or how he would respond and this spontaneous movement set in motion a whole string of new events, which eventually wound up in their back-of-the-room play. Things happened. This is not extraordinary. What is perhaps extraordinary is that in an era where scripts and rules and diagnoses dominate, at a time when a sea of expert psychological and pedagogical language threatens to take over all possible meanings of the lives and experiences of children and teachers alike, Laurence, Rosalie, Marie, and Stephanie had the good fortune to find themselves in a place where the fact that "things just happen" matters.

These things that "just happen" are what Biehl and Locke, in their 2010 reflection on implications of Deleuze and Guattari's work for anthropologists, name as "the life in things" that "carries so much potentially transformative vitality" (p. 320). For Biehl and Locke, engaging the life in things has to do with writing that is in addition to and also challenges or perhaps opens up Marxist and Foucauldian theories of power, structures and institutions, and identity formations that have dominated contemporary social theory for the past half-century. They argue that strict application of these analytic sensibilities in naming normalized and normalizing subjectivities and social relations misses the open-endedness of life, the ways that assemblages come into and go out of existence, "the journeys people take through milieus to pursue needs, desires, and curiosities or to simply try to find room to breathe beneath social constraints" (p. 323).

Children with disabilities and their teachers live within a system of enormous social constraint. The second problem with a triumphant narrative is the implicit assumption that what existed in the end is better than what existed in the beginning, that it is better that Laurence spoke and interacted than had he not. Returning to Deligny, do we value what happened here because it was interactive, because it involved speech that was recognizable to the teacher and us, because Laurence seemed to have taken a step toward more social communality?

When we put this question to Cécile, she told us that the children that Deligny worked with were older, and that many of them were abandoned and not even institutions would take them. They lived in the countryside, far removed from the demands and pressures of crowded city life. In that context, Deligny and the children found good ways of living together. She described that for Deligny, who did not feel the need for shared language or connection, there was no problem if the children crawled on the floor or screamed in public. The children at Gulliver live with their parents in a different context, in Paris and in the contemporary era, and this creates different work. Cécile and her teachers know, she told us, that there are many ways to live a happy life, whether or not the children follow the social trajectories that are expected or wanted for children. But it matters to them that, living within the constraints and potentials not only of who the children are, but who their parents are and what society is, they find ways of living together that allow for the children to be happy and have a good life.

We cannot name a series of causal events that led to Laurence's interaction and speech, nor can we know what any of it meant to him. We do not know what Laurence thinks or feels, or whether that exchange was important to him in some internal sense. Neither does Cécile claim to know, just as Deligny refused to speak for the children with whom he worked. Nevertheless, Cécile draws on themes of connectivity and love, by reminding us that Laurence lives among people who, unlike Deligny, have the need to find ways to feel connected to him. These are the people who have a great deal to do with creating the environment of love, care, and nurturance in which the child exists. Ghada described to us that part of the work they need to do is to help the parents to see their children in ways that the parents can tolerate and love, to support parents in thinking that they can parent their child. We do not know if Laurence feels connected but we do know when Laurence affects us or when we see Laurence affecting others. So this Laurence story is not about Laurence, the individual, but about how those in Laurence's world, including us as researchers, are affected in relation to Laurence. This is a movement toward the assemblage, toward assuming that dilemmas of difference reside in and emerge from assemblages, not individuals.

In Andrew Solomon's 2012 book *Far From the Tree*, he describes the struggles that occur for parents and children when they are very different from one another in unexpected ways. He argues that at least initially (and for some parents, permanently), the ability to love and value a child lies in the expectation that the child will share at least some important traits that the parent values. He calls these "vertical identities." These can be traits transmitted through DNA, but are also often cultural traits and values. He describes "horizontal identities" as those identities that are foreign to the parents. Solomon argues that parents from earliest childhood reinforce their children's vertical identities whereas horizontal identities are often opposed or treated as flaws. Parents can often experience horizontal identities as threatening, frightening, and something to be altered at any cost. Solomon includes among others, children with deafness, dwarfism, Down syndrome, autism, schizophrenia, intellectual disabilities, social disabilities, physical differences, and gay and transgendered children as just some of the horizontal identities that challenge parents and cause distress for parents and children alike, perhaps especially as they are moved into what Valente (2011) describes as "the diagnosing ritual" that pathologizes difference.

In Solomon's interviews with more than 300 parents, he finds that many parents come to love their children's horizontal identities because of the person they believe it makes their child and it makes them. We can read the episode with Laurence by saying that he is feeling the pleasure of connection, but by expanding the horizon of the event, including all the things before, during, and after that don't fit with this narrative, our confidence is shaken. An interstice is recognized, and we begin to realize that maybe we are reading onto Laurence the presumption that what is important to us is important to Laurence. Masschelein and Verstraete (2012) describe Deligny as writing about pearl fishers on a raft who "take away the bottom of a cookie box, replace the bottom by a piece of glass...they immerse the box a bit in water and they see, underneath 'something other' than the mirroring reflections of the sun" (Deligny & Álvarez, 1976/2007, pp. 1007–1008, cited in Masschelein & Verstraete, 2012, p. 11).

In demonstrating an ability to engage in play with human and non-human objects—what we might see as demonstrating a set of interpersonal competencies—we feel more connected to Laurence because he is more familiar to us. But we need a way to break through this reflective surface. We have to recognize the limitations and problems with imagining or insisting that others should be recognizable to us. Danforth (2009) warns about the dangers of patronizing celebrations of "discovered competences" that keep those competencies in place as the desired goal. It raises the question of how we imagine that what matters to us might not be what matters to a child. Danforth challenges us by asking how arguments for "the presumption of competence" will allow us to value the lives of children who will never be more familiar to us.

Interstices occur when the intensities of affect—our sense of connection to a child or situation, for example—get broken and we are forced into the messiness of examining and critiquing the norms and desires that structure our own meaning making, our desires for communality, as we witness events. However, it is helpful to remember that in Deleuzoguattarian thought the assemblage is not a place of either–or. Experiences, ideas, contexts, events, and bodies all exist on a plane, coming into and going out of assemblage. The goal of any Deleuzoguattarian analysis is not to create greater truth—a new synthesis that replaces the previous theses and antitheses—but rather to create a new set of relations or possibilities that is thrown back into the asignifying field, to become one assemblage among many (Boldt, Valente, & Garoian, in review). Cécile's perspective likewise reminds us that it is not an either–or, either the lives the children and adults experience together, or the limitations of that. She reminds us that all of the children and teachers are singular in their differences yet stand side by side, and that this difference puts the norm, the limit, or boundary in constant motion, producing engagement and change for everyone. To return to Biehl and Locke (2010), Laurence, his teachers, his peers, and family are journeying together through milieus, following their needs, desires, and curiosities and at Gulliver, often finding breathing room.

Asylum

Our experiences at Gulliver are helping us to think about how as researchers and teachers we work in places—which are really all spaces—where the affective body moves within ever-emerging and changing assemblages. How do researchers and teachers work with the messiness that results from the fact that humans are constantly different than we were before? Although we are early in our work with Gulliver, what stands out to us, for now at least, is their embrace of emergence, an anticipation of constant arrivals, a privileging of curiosity and openness about what each singular relationship with each singular child will bring to the assemblage of Gulliver. They do not get caught up in the normalizing "treatments" of experts, but rather the teachers live in the presence of the children.

When we asked Cécile how new teachers are prepared to work with the children, she told us, "We don't know how to work with the children when they come. When they arrive is when we work with them and the families to begin the process of learning about this child. We engage the child and through engaging with the child we learn over and over how to engage with the child."

While clearly teachers all over the world would say that they don't know what a particular child will need before the child is present, it is common, regardless of the setting—separate, mainstreamed, or inclusive—that in a certain sense, the children arrive without ever really coming into the presence of the teacher. There is too much that stands between the child and the teacher: the teacher's anxiety, the reports and recommendations of experts, the sterile limitations of risk managers, the desperate or confident faith in the ability of diagnoses to tell us who a child is or what s/he will need.

Difference is relational and this is operationalized by living in the presence of others. Gulliver then is an asylum not only for the children but also for their teachers and often, we suspect, for the children's parents. It is a place of refuge from a world overly concerned with labeling and remediating difference, rather than being curious in the presence of the child. For us as researchers and teacher educators, it is likewise an asylum. As we pore over our films and anticipate our next trip to interview the teachers, the interstices that our few days there opened and continue to open have already allowed us to begin to think differently about living in the presence of others.

References

Bateson, G. (1972). *Steps to an ecology of mind*. New York: Ballantine Books.

Baynton, D. (2001). Disability and the justification of inequality in American history. In P. Longmore & L. Umansky (Eds.), *The new disability history: American perspectives* (pp. 33–57). New York: NYU Press.

Biehl, J., & Locke, P. (2010). Deleuze and the anthropology of becoming. *Current Anthropology, 51*(3), 317–351.

Boldt, G., Valente, J. M., & Garoian, C. (In review). *The rhizome of the cochlear child: A Deleuzoguattarian analysis of cochlear implantation*.

Campbell, F. K. (2009). *Contours of ableism: The production of disability and abledness*. New York: Palgrave Macmillan.

Danforth, S. (2009). *The incomplete child*. New York: Peter Lang.

Deleuze, G., & Guattari, F. (1987). *A thousand plateaus: Capitalism and schizophrenia*. Minneapolis: University of Minnesota Press.

Deligny, F., & Álvarez, T. S. (1976/2007). *Oeuvres*. Paris: l'Arachnéen.

Garland-Thomson, R. G. (1996). *Extraordinary bodies: Figuring physical disability in American culture and literature*. New York: Columbia University Press.

Garland-Thomson, R. G. (2001). *Re-shaping, re-thinking, re-defining: Feminist disability studies*. Washington, DC: Center for Women Policy Studies.

Human Rights Watch, American Civil Liberties Union, & Farmer, A. (2009). *Impairing education: Corporal punishment of students with disabilities in US public schools*. New York: Human Rights Watch.

Jones, L., Bellis, M. A., Wood, S., Hughes, K., McCoy, E., Eckley, L., Bates, G., & Officer, A. (2012, September 8). Prevalence and risk of violence against children with disabilities: A systematic review and meta-analysis of observational studies. *The Lancet, 380*(9845), 899–907.

Leander, K., & Boldt, G. (2013). Rereading "A pedagogy of multiliteracies": Bodies, texts, and emergence. *Journal of Literacy Research, 45*(1), 22–46.

Marcus, G., & Saka, E. (2006). Assemblage. *Theory, Culture & Society, 23*, 2–3.

Masschelein, J., & Verstraete, P. (2012). Living in the presence of others: Towards a reconfiguration of space, asylum and inclusion. *International Journal of Inclusive Education, 16*(11), 1189–1202. doi: 10.1080/136003116.2011.557444.

Massumi, B. (2002). *Parables for the virtual: Movement, affect, sensation.* Durham, NC: Duke University Press.

McRuer, R., & Bérubé, M. (2006). *Crip theory: Cultural signs of queerness and disability.* New York: NYU Press.

Olsson, L. (2009.) *Movement and experimentation in young children's learning: Deleuze and Guattari in early childhood education.* New York: Routledge.

Patton, P. (2000). *Deleuze and the political.* New York: Routledge.

Reid, D. K., & Knight, M. G. (2006). Disability justifies exclusion of minority students: A critical history grounded in disability studies. *Educational Researcher, 35*(6), 18–23.

Simpson, J. A., & Weiner, E. S. C. (1989). *Oxford English Dictionary* (2nd ed). Oxford: Clarendon.

Snyder, S. L., & Mitchell, D. T. (2006). *Cultural locations of disability.* Chicago: University of Chicago Press.

Soloman, A. (2012). *Far from the tree: Parents, children and the search for identity.* New York: Scribner.

Stengers, I. (2005). The cosmopolitical proposal. In B. Latour & P. Weibel (Eds.), *Making things public: Atmospheres of democracy* (pp. 994–1003). Karlsruhe: ZKM Center for Art and Media.

Stiker, H.-J. (1999). *A history of disability.* Ann Arbor: University of Michigan Press.

Stiker, H.-J. (2007). The contribution of human sciences to the field of disability in France over recent decades. *Scandinavian Journal of Disability Research, 9,* 146–159.

Tobin, J. J., Hsueh, Y., & Karasawa, M. (2009). *Preschool in three cultures revisited: China, Japan, and the United States.* Chicago, IL: University of Chicago Press.

Tobin, J. J., Wu, D. Y. H., & Davidson, D. H. (1989). *Preschool in three cultures: Japan, China, and the United States.* New Haven, CT: Yale University Press.

UNESCO. (1960, December 14). *Convention against discrimination in education* (adopted by the General Conference, 11th session). Paris: UNESCO.

UNESCO, Booth, T., & Lynch, J. (2003). *Overcoming exclusion through inclusive approaches in education: A challenge and a vision* (conceptual paper). Paris: UNESCO.

United Nations. (1948). *The universal declaration of human rights: United Nations.* United States: U.N. Department of Public Information.

United Nations. (1989). *Convention on the rights of the child.* New York: United Nations Children's Fund.

United Nations. (2006). *Convention on the rights of persons with disabilities and optional protocol.* New York: United Nations.

United States Department of Education. (2012). *Civil rights data collection.* Washington, DC: Office for Civil Rights, U.S. Department of Education.

United States Government Accountability Office. (2009). *Seclusions and restraints: Selected cases of death and abuse at public and private schools and treatment centers. Testimony before the Committee on Education and Labor, House of Representatives. GAO-09-719T.* Washington, DC: U.S. Government Accountability Office.

Valente, J. M. (2011). Cyborgization: Deaf education for young children in the cochlear implantation era. *Qualitative Inquiry, 17*(7), 639–652.

Valente, J. M., & Boldt, G. (In review). *A Deleuzoguattatian intervention: Contemporary deaf childhoods, pediatric cochlear implants, and deaf monolingual education.*

Notes

1. As addressed in Article 26 of the Universal Declaration of Human Rights (U.N., 1948), the *Convention against Discrimination in Education* (UNESCO, 1960), the *Convention on the Rights of the Child* (U.N., 1989), and Article 24 of the U.N. *Convention on the Rights of Persons with Disabilities* (U.N., 2006).

2. Although as we will describe later, our interest in Deligny's work predated and led us to Masschelein and Verstraete's work, Deligny's writing is not translated into English and our lack of French means that we are dependent upon—and acknowledge our indebtedness to—those few academics who have pieces published about Deligny in English, and most especially for this chapter, Jan Masschelein and Pieter Verstraete.

3. Interstice: (a) a space that intervenes between things, especially one between closely spaced things; (b) a gap or break in something generally continuous (*Merriam-Webster Online Dictionary*, www.merriam-webster.com/dictionary/interstice).

4. Government policy stipulates one-third of the children admitted to Gulliver have identified disabilities.

5. Thanks to Liane Mozère for helping us understand the importance of LaBorde in this history.

6. Additionally, Cécile Herrou's husband, the psychiatrist and psychoanalyst Jean-Claude Polack, worked at La Borde with Guattari and continues with the practice of schizoanalysis.

7. Ghada is the director in charge of the day-to-day operations of Gulliver while Cécile is the director of all of the APATE schools.

8.   Throughout this chapter, we refer to the teaching staff at Gulliver as "teachers." This is not quite right in the French education system, since the word "teachers" is reserved for those with a four-year university degree. The staff at APATE, like early childhood professionals throughout France, go through a three-year training that is not based at a university. They refer to themselves as "educators." Using the term "educator" or even "staff" rather than "teacher" throughout this chapter sounded too awkward and unfamiliar in English, however, so we chose to use "teacher."

9.   There is nothing particularly new about rethinking how filming techniques have to change in relation to one's filming environment. Tobin, Hsueh, and Karasawa (2009) write about how the video-ethnographic method works as a "reflexive" tool. What we are trying to point to here is something specific about how our experience of Gulliver caused us to try things that were new to us, not that trying new things is new.

10. Quotes from Cécile are based on what our translator, Adeline Lebeaux, translated during the recorded interviews. We have not yet had them translated into text.

11. Pseudonym.

EIGHTEEN

Affective/Effective Reading and Writing Through Real Virtualities in a Digitized Society

Liselott Mariett Olsson and Ebba Theorell

Within contemporary society, literacy practices and theories stand in front of great challenges. There is a worldwide, expanding, and never-before-seen focus on educational policy in the field of literacy (e.g., Revised Curriculum and mushrooming local policies and programs in Sweden, No Child Left Behind in the United States, the National Literacy Strategy in the United Kingdom) in order to enhance and promote literacy skills in students of all ages (Kennedy, 2010). At the same time, globalization and new technologies completely transform the features of literacy. One such evident transformation concerns the increase in digitized devices and languages. Even the very youngest children are today immersed in a digitized culture from very early age: surfing the web, playing video or computer games, sending emails, participating in instant messenger systems, or text messaging with cell phones (Carrington, 2005; Dahlberg & Olsson, 2009; Kress, 1997, 2003; Lankshear & Knobel, 2003; Lewis & Fabos, 2005; Marsh, 2005; Nixon, 2003). However, within early childhood education, these "new literacies" (Street, 2003) have yet a somewhat ambiguous and scarce place. Early childhood teachers report a pressure and lack of confidence and experience in relation to new technologies (Chen & Chang, 2006), and early childhood classrooms are often ill-equipped with outdated or limited hardware, sustaining "old" rather than "new" literacy activities, and if new technologies are used it's mainly to support and sustain already existing literacy practices (Lankshear & Knobel, 2003; Wohlwend, 2009). The pressure that teachers feel in relation to integrating new technologies into their classroom has also been exposed as due to an inconsistency in government guidelines, programs, and policies, as these call for the insertion of new technologies in early childhood, but define learning goals and assessment criteria in relation to print-based alphabetic literacy skills and knowledge (Burnett, 2010; Lankshear & Knobel, 2003). The steadily increasing demands on standards, accountability, and high-stake goals in policies and programs put teachers in a situation where they are forced to focus instruction of isolated literacy skills rather than engaging in inquiry and experimentation with new technologies (Dahlberg & Moss, 2005; Masny & Cole, 2009; Mozère, 2007; Olsson, 2012; Taubman, 2009; Wohlwend, 2009). There are also voices within the field that express a fear of children engaging in new technologies in an uncritical way, exposing themselves to inappropriate content and relations, as well as being distracted from more beneficial and "natural" activities (Miller, 2005). A recent overview of research in the field from 2003 to 2009 (Burnett, 2010) confirms an earlier overview (Lankshear & Knobel, 2003) and shows that the field is largely under-researched, especially concerning the very youngest children. Out of 36 available studies, none focused on children under age 3 and only 11 out of the 36 studies focused on children under age 5. Furthermore, the theoretical field is extremely homogenous, with the majority of research focused on a psychological-cognitive perspective, while others were framed by a sociocultural theoretical framework. Research and practices in the literacy field need further expansion of theoretical bases as well as exploration of practices that children clearly encounter in literacy and technology experiences. Through such an encounter between children of today and their educational context, it is possible to give children opportunities to navigate, use for their own creative purposes, but also criticize and choose how they want to be part of digitized society. Burnett (2010) also suggests the need for more extensive and explorative research in the field to bring in new and uncommon theoretical perspectives. This chapter will introduce theoretical perspectives joining the scientific and early childhood didactical work with analog and digital literacy in the setting of a larger research project: "The Magic of Language."

The Magic of Language Project

The research project "The Magic of Language" (earlier described in Dahlberg & Olsson, 2009), has been given funding by the Swedish Research Council in order to work with preschool children's relations to, as well as early childhood didactic tools for, language, reading, and writing, departing from the assumption that these questions are strongly affected by the fact that today we live in a globalized and digitized society. Our preliminary work with young children confirms earlier findings and indicates that preschool children are absolutely immersed in and great users of all sorts of digital devices. Most important, the children approach digital devices through a *productive* representational linguistic logic. What seems to interest them is the playful experimentation with and creation of linguistic representations in a digitized setting, where they collectively can produce sense of linguistic signs (Olsson, 2009, 2012, 2013). Children in these contexts create their own settings, stories, and tools, and use digital devices and language for their own purposes. It is what collectively interests them for the moment that will decide how they use the digital. Children also display great desire and taste for beauty and surprises. They spend a lot of time arranging their settings beautifully and they immensely enjoy the appearing and often surprising effects that digital devices promote. We have found theoretical support for this in perspectives claiming that digital devices do appeal to registers of experience that differ from the strictly defined linguistic representational logic and its predefined sense, in that they harbor affect, sensation, intensity, play, appearance, decoration, spectacle, and style (Darley, 2000; Massumi, 2002). Within the setting of the project, we have tentatively experimented with digital devices in preschool classes. These experimentations point toward even very young children being familiar with digital devices—and skilled at using them. Through these devices they deal with linguistic problems, but always through such features as affect, sensation, intensity, play, appearance, decoration, spectacle, style, and the creative production of linguistic representations and their sense. Children seem to do this also when approaching analog reading and writing. Whether working with crayons on paper or with digital devices, children seem to be engaged exactly in these somewhat more subtle registers of experience. When joining this with cultural theorist Brian Massumi's writings (2002) on affect, sensation, and intensity, it becomes evident that all reading and writing—analog reading and writing with its linguistic representational logic included—is harboring affective, sensuous, and intensive registers of experience. Moreover, Massumi describes (2002, 2011) that, despite claims that the "digital revolution" and the latest digital devices blur the borders between the real and the unreal, the existent and the nonexistent, the visible and the invisible, the most common approach toward the digital is to confound it with a *virtual*, that is, possible, but still, fictive world. But children, through their continuous production of linguistic representations and their sense, treat the digital/virtual world as equally real as the real world. What differs in the children's way of treating the digital/virtual is that they find themselves in and act in different ontological settings.

Thinkers such as Brian Massumi (2002, 2011), Gilles Deleuze, and Félix Guattari (1994) give a different conception of the virtual that seems to align itself with the ontological setting of young children. For these thinkers, reality has more dimensions than the actual one we schematically think, feel, see, speak, and hear through given representations, as this is only the *actual* dimension of reality. To this perfectly real and actual reality is added a virtual dimension of reality. Most important, this virtual dimension—in contrast to common approaches to the digital as a virtual, possible, but still fictive world—has its proper reality; it is no less real than the actual dimension. The virtual actualizes itself into the world that we recognize as real, but has no resemblance whatsoever with the actual. Virtual and actual are two dimensions of reality, intimately intertwined but still distinct. Moreover, and again in sharp contrast to the common approaches to the digital, the virtual is not the same thing as the possible; the possible is still opposed to the real as a given. The possible is just yet another version of what we already know and it is only capable of "realizing itself." This is why these thinkers claim that the digital is, in fact, run by analog logic, and that is also why the digital and its devices do not, by themselves, increase potential in learning to read and write:

> *The medium of the digital is possibility, not virtuality,* and not even potential…. Nothing is more destructive for the thinking and imaging of the virtual than equating it with the digital…. Digital technologies in fact have a remarkably weak connection to the virtual, by virtue of the enormous power of their systematization of the possible…. Equating the digital with the virtual confuses the really apparitional with the artificial. It reduces it to simulation. This forgets intensity, brackets potential, and in the same sweeping gesture bypasses the move through sensation, the actual envelopment of the virtual. (Massumi, 2002, pp. 137–138, emphasis in original)

When children relate to language, the digital *and* the analog, through affect, sensation, intensity, play, appearance, decoration, spectacle, style, the production of linguistic representations and their sense, they probably plunge into the most intense actualization of the virtual. These subtle registers of experience constitute, as Massumi says above, "the envelopment of the virtual." They are the *seismographs* of the process of actualization of the virtual, and it seems that these are very important parts promoting increased potential for children's literacy learning processes. All this invites early childhood literacy didactics to carefully arrange "irresistible opportunities" for children to engage in language, the digital and the analog, where these subtle registers of experience and the production of linguistic representations and their sense can be further explored and made use of within the formalized educational system.

The following part of this chapter describes how we have tried to perform this in our didactic and scientific work in a group of children ages 1 to 2, working with these very young children and experimenting with "the line" through the use of both "old" analog and "new" digital technologies.

The Line

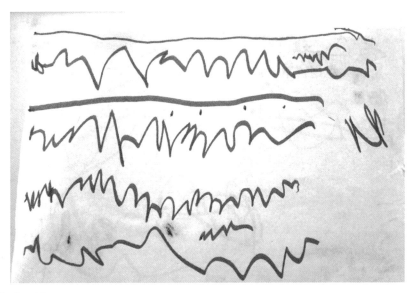

Image 1. Theo's writing.

Theo draws a line and states proudly: "I am writing." He is accompanied by millions of children doing this every day. These "Himalaya lines" are produced over and over again in our early childhood settings. When children, already at a very early age, state that they are writing, they often produce this kind of line. Now, how do we understand this line? We could call it "pre-writing," but if we want to try to appreciate, valuate, and acknowledge children's writing strategies as being equally important as the already established conception of writing, we might need to find other ways of understanding.

Gunter Kress has acknowledged children's attention to the line as part of their first experimentations with giving shape to writing, and he has argued that this reveals their early understanding of writing as a visual and spatial phenomena:

> Children do often show awareness of this factor: not only in the page designs which they produce in their image-based texts—though often these are designs incorporating language and image—but also in the attention they give to the *line*, for instance. Frequently, especially in their earlier writing, they experiment with visual/spatial unit of the *line*, as a means of giving shape to their writing, before the line develops into the grammatical/syntactic unit of the sentence, which then takes over as the relevant unit. (Kress, 1997, p. 121, emphasis in original)

Children in Kress' sense are closer to a more extensive conception of writing, and that, according to him, is also more accurate in contemporary digitized society: "Contemporary technologies of writing are in favour of designers, and expose the linguist's view as having always been too narrow and too abstracted" (p. 120).

When pursuing Massumi's reasoning on the misconception of the virtual and the need to not simply equate it with the digital, we can see that this can be paired with Kress' analysis. Quoting the American pragmatist philosopher Charles S. Peirce (1839–1914) in his *Reasoning and the Logic of Things*, Massumi (2011) also makes us understand the necessity of extending the conception of writing, and moreover, how we can possibly use the concept of the virtual in a didactical setting and in relation to children's writing of and experimentation with the line:

> I draw a chalk line on the board.... What I have really drawn there is an oval line. For this white chalk-mark is not a *line*, it is a plane figure in Euclid's sense—a surface, and the only line that is there is the line which forms the *limit* between the white surface and the black surface.... But the boundary between the black and white is neither black, nor white, nor neither, nor both. It is the pairedness of the two. (Peirce as cited in Massumi, 2011, p. 89)

Massumi recalls Peirce's reasoning and adds: "The separation is across an insubstantial boundary, itself imperceptible. Pure edge. Neither black nor white. Not neither not both. A virtual line" (Massumi, 2011, p. 89). The virtual, as earlier said, is here to be understood as an added dimension of reality, paired with but distinct from the actual dimension that we hold for real. The relation of the virtual to the actual must be understood according to the above-described pairedness of black and white surface. Or as Massumi says: "The virtual line is the activity of the relation between the black and the white" (Massumi, 2011, p. 89). From this definition of the virtual, it is not only when children engage with digital devices that they come in contact with the virtual. When children with crayon and paper draw their very first lines, they activate an actualization of the virtual dimension of reality, and following Massumi, it is only this definition of the virtual—as freed from belonging only to digital devices and, for us, as applied both to analog and digital writing—that can promote potentiality.

In a strictly formalized educational system where you are forced to simply repeat and imitate already defined and designed lines, there is less chance for the more subtle registers of experience and the potential of the virtual to take place. If, within the formalized school system, the first contact with letters and writing that children have consists of being forced to imitate lines in specific orders and designs with preset significations—be it through analog or digital devices—not only motivation but also the more affective, sensuous, and intensive registers of experience accompanying the actualization of the virtual, and thereby potential, are all blocked out and neglected.

Wanting to pay attention to the youngest children's first experimentations with the line, equally wanting to avoid these blockages, and with inspiration from Massumi's definition of the virtual, we formulated the ambition to try to experiment with its potential. As described by Massumi, the virtual dimension of reality is enveloped in more subtle registers of experience such as affect, sensation, and intensity. It is these "parables for the virtual" (Massumi, 2002) that we have tried to put into work in the experimentations together with the children described later. We decided to invite the very youngest children to experimentation with the line with both analog and digital devices.

Crayon Bodies: Affective Learning to Write

The pictures that follow are taken from a longer filmed sequence and it shows a group of 1- to 2-year-olds during one of our first experimentations in class. Deliberately and in order not to be confused by the actual tools, whether analog or digital, we arrange a very simple context for the first experimentation.

Image 2. Large paper and a basket of crayons.

The children were offered a large white paper that covered most of the floor and a basket of crayons. The teachers were very careful to keep themselves in the background, in order to show the children that it was their working area. The children spend a long time discovering the crayons, watching, touching, and smelling before they start to use them on the paper. They also watch each other carefully and await the others' action, as well as joining or borrowing each other's strategy. One girl, for instance, starts putting all the crayons back into the basket. The others carefully observe her and start helping her out with this task. One boy then tentatively takes a crayon out of the basket, looking at the girl, as if to check that it is fine with her. He draws a little line where he is sitting, exclaims "Ah!" and then bends forward to carefully watch the little line he has produced on the paper closer. He slowly continues to bend forward, closer and closer to the line, and then scratches with his fingernail on the line. He then takes a new grip on the crayon and draws a longer line. His whole body follows the movement of the crayon. He stretches out in his full length now, lying on the paper as he continues to draw the line. He continues like this, pulling his body over the whole length of the paper, while every now and then exclaiming sounds, always with different intonation.

Or, rather than saying that the child is pulling his body over the paper, it is as if the crayon is pulling his body over the paper. Or, maybe even better, what we see is not a child with a crayon, but a "crayon body" moving over the paper. The child becomes one with the crayon in his writing. During this time we also notice how the room is filled with joy, excitement, and energy. The children seem to be immensely enjoying this very simple situation and activity.

Image 3. Crayon body.

How is it then possible to appreciate this child as a child learning to write? Within the most common idea of language as an abstract, homogenous system with universal representations (Deleuze & Guattari, 2004), what is going on above is not worth being called writing, but with a different conception of language and learning, it might be possible. Returning to Massumi's definition of the virtual made us pay attention to how "affect" is described as one of the parables for the virtual and how this concept might help us value the process described earlier as learning to write. Affect is originally a concept fetched from the philosopher Baruch de Spinoza (1632–1677) and it has been frequently used by Massumi, Deleuze, Deleuze and Guattari, and also several researchers in early childhood education and literacy education (Cole, 2009; Dahlberg, Manuscript in Progress; Dahlberg & Olsson, 2008; Deleuze, 1988; Deleuze & Guattari, 1994; Dufresne, 2006; Hickey-Moody & Haworth, 2009; Knight, 2009; Masny & Waterhouse, 2011; Masny & Cole, 2009; Massumi, 2002, 2011; Mozère, 2006; Olsson, 2009). According to these references, Spinoza draws up the contours of a universe that consists of bodies (organic as well as nonorganic) that transform and act. Affect indicates a body's (organic or nonorganic) *potential* to transform and act. In Deleuze's writings (1988) on Spinoza, this also concerns a devaluation of consciousness, indicating that "We do not know what a body can do," and showing how "the body surpasses the knowledge we have of it, *and that thought likewise surpasses the consciousness we have of it*" (Deleuze, 1988, p.18; emphasis in original). When our body is being restricted in its capacity to act, we feel "sad passions" and when it is extending its capacities to act, we feel "joyful passions." This is what conscious minds experience, but these emotions are really only "after-effects" only the *effects of affect*.

Children normally love learning to write—in the beginning—because it enables them to increase bodily potential in themselves *as well as in language itself*. It is only when they are being cut off in their actualizations of the virtual, when affects—pertaining to their own bodies as well as to the body of language—are blocked and when everything is reduced in its capacity to act and transform that it becomes boring. For it then becomes non-vital, non-alive, and non-changeable.

If we choose to use these theories, what happens is that the child is learning to write through increasing his body's capacity to act and through joining his own body with the body of the crayon, through becoming one with the crayon, through engaging in writing in an affective way. The joy and energy that fills the room are indicators pointing toward increased potential for all involved bodies (organic and nonorganic). The task for early childhood literacy didactics in relation to such an affective and playful learning to write could be to create a preschool context that promotes and extends affective potential.

Walk the Line — Read the Line: Sensuous Learning to Read

From the previously described reasoning on emotions as an effect of affect, it becomes clear that what we're talking about is not the same thing as any simple idea of "fun learning." And still, emotions are indicators of how potential has possibly been stretched or reduced in any situation. Therefore, when discovering how the children worked with the line through the affective features described earlier, and in order to try to further extend affective potential, we decided to arrange a number of "irresistible opportunities" to further work and experiment with the line. For instance, we repeat the situation with the youngest children, but invite new friends to join in. The second time the children are offered crayon and paper, we observe another child joining his body with the paper and the crayon by literally folding out his body and crawling and drawing one single long line through the whole length of the paper. He is immensely concentrated and when finished he turns around to look at his friends. All of a sudden one child starts walking on the line, several children follow, and they then all start running on the line back and forward. Again, there is a high level of energy in the room and the children laugh and joke with each other, the teachers, and the camera.

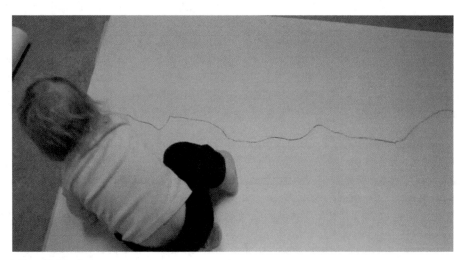

Image 4. Drawing the line.

This time, we're under the impression of having the rare opportunity to understand what we are seeing as we see it; this intense actualization of the line is nothing less than the actualization of the virtual. We are as captured as the children are by seeing this line apparently coming from nowhere rapidly grow before our eyes and invest the paper. When the children start running on the line, we're struck by the fact that they are actually in one sense *reading* the line. Again, the joy, the laughter, and the jokes with the camera tell us that for all involved bodies, this situation promoted and increased capacity to act and transform. The children's way of writing and reading the line and their attention to each other's lines invite us to arrange more opportunities for them to work as a whole group.

Image 5. Walking the line.

On one occasion we therefore decide to gather the whole group together and they get small squared papers and thin black inks. They all sit on the floor, the strategies are flowing in between them; somebody starts drawing lines on the other side of the paper and friends follow, somebody tries to draw lines with the paper in the air and friends follow, somebody starts drawing a line on the body and friends follow. There's a lot of laughter and they seem to have a fabulous time! They are then given adhesive tape and are invited to put their papers on the wall. They all start running around and waving with the papers, sticking them to their heads and bodies; there is so much joy in the room and we all laugh.

Image 6. Small squared papers and black inks.

What strikes us in all of these situations is the pertinent presence of strong sensations and sensing bodies. The joy, the laughter, the sharing, the attention to each other's lines, the relating, the high energy level in the room, the little craziness, the sticking of the paper on to one's own and one's friends' bodies, the striking traces of engaging collective and singular processes. There is, in all these situations, a specific companionship between the children that could be expressed through the second parable for the virtual, that of "sensation." Sensation, as Massumi describes it, is: "the direct registering of potential" (Massumi, 2002, p. 97), and from the examples presented earlier it seems that this is what the children are experiencing.

When thinking about learning to read from a more formalized and strictly linguistic point of view, one is easily led to believe that these sensing and sensuous features have no importance. The focus is more often on purely intellectual capacities associated with meta-linguistic features. But what is learning to read really about? There is always a sensing body that performs the act of reading and also, most important, in order to get something out of reading all your senses must be touched in some way. If not, you are only technically decoding a certain number of signs. Massumi shows how all reading—even when thought of as a purely cerebral adventure—also harbors these sensuous features; reading is here described as seeing through the letters in an engagement of all senses:

> There is no thought that is not accompanied by a physical sensation of effort or agitation (if only a knitting of the brows, a pursing of the lips, or a quickening of heartbeat.... When we read, we do not see the individual letters and words. That is what learning to read is all about: learning to stop seeing the letters so you can see *through* them. Through the letters, we directly experience fleeting visionlike sensations, inklings of sound, faint brushes of movement.... In the experience of reading, conscious thought, sensation, and all the modalities of perception fold into and out of each other. Attention most twisted. (Massumi, 2002, p. 139)

Moreover, and most important, sensation in this sense—as a parable for the virtual—is not something that can be directed or domesticated. One of the most current attempts to deal with young children's learning processes consists in promoting "self-reflection" over one's own learning processes. This has been described by some researchers as part of a neoliberal way of governing, aiming no longer only to discipline students' and children's bodies from the outside, but rather to reach for the child's very innermost desires and *sensations* (Elfström, 2012; Dahlberg & Moss, 2005; Fendler, 2001; Olsson, 2009).

But from the point of view of sensation as a parable for the virtual and from the earlier examples, it turns out that it's never possible to use sensation for rational didactic intervention. It is rather a highly complex and continuously changing feature. Massumi makes a clear distinction between self-reflection and what he calls the "self-referentiality" or "self-complication" of sensation, and that seems to be of utmost importance in order to distinguish between what we try to do here in contrast to neoliberal governing techniques:

> Sensation is never simple. It is always doubled by the feeling of having a feeling. It is self-referential. This is not necessarily the same as "self-reflexive." The doubling of sensation does not assume a subjective splitting and does not of itself constitute a distancing. It is immediate self-complication. It is best to think of it as a resonation or interference pattern. (Massumi, 2002, pp. 13–14)

This would imply that all attempts to domesticate children's sensuous learning processes would fall short, because self-reflection immediately creates a distance between the I that thinks about the Me, and according to the previous quote this is somewhat of a metaphysical impossibility. Thinking and reflection is here rather described in terms of "resonation" in between the "sensory walls" of the body (Massumi, 2002, p. 14). Again, this concerns a devaluation of consciousness, and moreover, for our purposes, it includes the promotion of a learning that is not learning to read *either* by brain *or* body. It concerns an insistence on paying attention to the fact that *both* body and brain, simultaneously, are engaged in reading. This also points toward the fact that these learning processes cannot be rationally domesticated in any way. Following the logic of affect and sensation, the only thing one can do in a didactical setting is to try to create opportunities that will stretch the potential of everyone and everything involved. Learning to read must, from this perspective, be arranged so as to also encourage the use of resonating sensuous registers of experience, but without any ambition to supervise or control the outcome. These more subtle registers of experience can only become vital when allowed to appear as ungoverned and for every situation unique *effects* of increased potential. The proposition is then to see language, reading, and writing as something much more than just a set of techniques for decoding, imitating, and reproducing. Teachers here need to be immensely present in the children's learning processes in order to be able to create learning opportunities that might invite to the use of more subtle registers of experience, but that also carries a strong and clear connection to linguistic problems. In this very case, for instance, during our analysis we also see how one child is extremely occupied by making sounds to his and his friends' signs. Almost every time he produces a new sign he makes a new sound and vice versa. We remember that he has been doing this in almost every situation we have arranged. From our chosen theoretical perspective, this is very important and valued as a work with the linguistic problematic concerning the representation of graphemes and phonemes. This problematic is often seen as governed by a given and predetermined cause–effect relation, that the child needs to imitate and reproduce. It is also this linguistic problematic that is seen as the very base of all writing and reading and considered the most challenging gap that the child needs to bridge in order to be able to read and write: to understand that letters are the representation of sounds (Kress, 1997); although here, the child is *producing* rather than *acquiring* such representations. We tentatively go in search of a problematic to work upon this: to give the child opportunity to further explore and produce sense of the linguistic problematic concerning the *affective* and *sensuous production* of representations of phoneme and grapheme. We decide that we want to invite the child to an irresistible opportunity to continue his experimentation with the producing of graphic and phonetic representations.

The Confetti Room: Intensive Writing of the Heart

The child is this time being invited into a carefully prepared room, where the floor is beautifully covered with crayons and papers in different sizes, colors, and textures. This was thought of as a way to support his ongoing production of different graphemes and phonemes. We wanted to give him access to a great variation in surfaces, colors, and textures to encourage further production. The child walks straight up to a centrally placed blue paper and starts drawing signs.

Image 7. The confetti room.

Image 8. At the blue paper.

He spends a long time with the blue paper before he moves over to explore the other papers.

Image 9. At the transparent paper.

He works with an extreme concentration and to our surprise he doesn't utter a word or sound during the whole process! The only thing one can hear in the room is his rhythmical breathing. He continues working and does not stop until two hours later, when actually falling asleep, still with the crayon in hand. The crayon and the hand are still moving as he closes his eyes and falls asleep.

Image 10. Falling asleep.

When analyzing the process and the signs produced, it becomes clear that they are not without intention and that what took place was the entering into a most intensive and creative process. We are reminded once again that this way of working really is all about careful and tentative experimentation; we can never know beforehand what will happen, or in any way claim that we know exactly what children are after in their learning. This time the child did not continue his experimentation with grapheme and phoneme, even though we thought we had arranged for that to happen. Something else got a grip on him this time. We will probably never know what, but that does not stop us from continuing, tentatively, to arrange for new opportunities to investigate the chosen problematic. Most of all, this situation touches us deeply in its intensity. Despite our long and rich experience of children's sometimes under-evaluated capacities, we are completely taken aback by the fact that such a young child has such a span of concentration and such focus on a task in a given context. There is something in this situation that still gives us goose bumps.

During this period of experimentation together with the children, we continue to be on the lookout for unconventional theories that can help us understand the children's strategies for learning. We go back to all the lines produced by the children and try to find new ways of associating what we see that they are doing.

Image 11. Theo's writing and calligraphic writing.

Our associations stretched from seeing these as an expression of rhythm, as a composition, maybe jazz-like, to the image of an ECG, and the notion of the "writing of the heart." Looking for theoretical tools to reinforce this beautiful association, we fell upon Thomas Lamarre's text "Diagram, Inscription, Sensation" (2002). In this text, Lamarre presents and analyzes a calligraphic tradition, the Heian calligraphy, born in the Japanese archipelago in the 9th century. It seems to us that the way this tradition works and the way Lamarre analyzes it fit very well with our association of "the writing of the heart" and in relation to what we see that the children are doing. It also gives new and interesting connotations to the name of our project, "The Magic of Language":

> Part of the art of the brush then consists of diminishing the dissonance between world and heart, with respect to compositions, motions, operations. At this level, the brush does not

function as a tool of conscious expression but as a kind of seismograph, feeling the oscillations and vibrations of the world and of the heart, and signing these on paper, silk, bamboo splints, etc. If writing is a medium, it is a medium in the occult sense—it delivers signs from other realms through the human body, or rather, through its heart/mind…. The heart is an aperture made sensitive to natural movements; it dilates and contracts with them, and the hand/brush twitches in response…. The heart truly is that which moves through the middle. (Lamarre, 2002, pp. 165–166)

The calligraphic writing is, then, about joining movements in the world and movements of the heart. It concerns diminishing the distance between world and heart. The connection to our association of an ECG and a "writing of the heart" is striking. To write with the heart, the writing of the heart, feels very close to how we see that the child in the confetti room works with the line, as a composition, a rhythm, an ECG registered above all through his rhythmical breathing.

But maybe more than anything, the concept that seems most appropriate in relation to this situation is that of intensity. Intensity is described by Massumi (2002) in relation to image-reception, as something different than the sociolinguistic definition of relations between content and conventional meanings or significations in any intersubjective context, that is, the *qualities* of an image. Intensity, rather than determining the qualities of an image, concerns the image's *effect*, and the strength and duration of that effect. Moreover, and most important, there is no correspondence or conformity between qualities and effects, or between given content and the intensity that an image can produce.

When we deal with children as young as 1 to 3 years old, it is obvious that conventional content and meaning qualities will be changed by the children, but it is equally obvious that intensity—without any conformity or correspondence to sociolinguistic qualifications—will play a greater role in all their learning. Even though Massumi's earlier example concerns image-reception, we believe that it touches as much on children's reception of signs in general. What Massumi offers us is an argumentation and a motivation for a literacy learning that departs as much from intensity as from conventional sociolinguistic definitions of signs:

> Approaches to the image in its relation to language are incomplete if they operate only on the semantic or semiotic level, however that level is defined (linguistically, logically, narratologically, ideologically, or all of these in combination, as a Symbolic). What they lose, precisely, is the expression *event*—in favour of structure. (Massumi, 2002, pp. 26–27)

Massumi continues to claim that much could be gained if the dimension of intensity could be introduced in cultural theory, and we believe that much could be gained if intensity could be introduced into literacy theory and practice. Again, it is not a question of doing away with structure or conventional content-meaning qualifications, but of highlighting that these are always accompanied by other registers of experience, such as intensity, which young children make especially great use of in their literacy learning. Language is, in fact, not committed only to structure:

> Language, though headstrong, is not simply in opposition to intensity…. The relationship between the levels of intensity and qualification is not one of conformity or correspondence but rather of resonation or interference, amplification or dampening. Linguistic expression can resonate with and amplify intensity at the price of making itself functionally redundant. When on the other hand it doubles a sequence of movements in order to add something

to it in the way of meaningful progression…it runs counter to and dampens the intensity. Intensity would seem to be associated with nonlinear processes: resonation and feedback that momentarily suspend the linear progress of the narrative present from past to future. (Massumi, 2002, pp. 25–26)

Language then works on two levels: one narrative and one intensive, and it is because of this that purely linguistic approaches to any system of signs are incomplete. The very youngest children clearly make great use of the intensive level in language and the child's literacy experimentation in the confetti room is a striking example of this.

Through the chosen theoretical perspectives, through our preliminary results and the examples presented earlier, it becomes clear that children's relations to language, reading, and writing are not reduced to only one faculty, the mind, but involve so many other elements of the process of reading and writing. Lamarre talks about reading and writing in a *magical* sense. It is as if the world is writing through us, and our heart is that which finds itself in the center. Massumi has us talking about this as an affective, sensuous, and intensive reading and writing. Massumi and Lamarre's writings gave us the courage to continue experimenting with the line within the setting of working with a magical language that must be described as nothing less than finding itself beyond the strictly linguistic representational logic.

The Line and the iPad:
Learning to Read and Write on That "Seeping Edge of the Virtual"

At this moment in the working process with the line, we decide to experiment with the use of digital devices in accordance with the linguistic problematic worked upon: affective, sensitive, and intensive registers of experience in the production of linguistic representations of graphemes and phonemes. We wanted a tool that appealed to and answered up to the affective, sensuous, and intensive registers of experience displayed by the children and also to the linguistic problematic of the creation of graphic and phonetic representations that we had seen one child engage in at several occasions. After much consideration and analysis, we decide to present this child with an iPad with two software programs, Bloom and Trope. This software functions through inviting the child to draw a line or press a point with his or her finger on the screen, producing a line or a point, and the software then responds with a tone of music. This specific software was chosen, not without hesitation, as an open-ended and flexible tool that corresponded to the child's experimentation. The hesitation resided in our acknowledging of Massumi's distinction of the virtual as not belonging only to digital devices and our ambition to not crush the child's own strategies, as these tools might be too similar to what he was already fully capable of producing only with his hands and his voice. But finally we decided to see it as a gift back to the child possibly encouraging him to further experimentation but on another surface and with a different tool.

The child is delighted with the iPad and he very quickly discovers how it works. When the software changes from Bloom (where you draw lines with your finger) to Trope (where you press with your finger), it takes him only a second to realize how he needs to push with his finger instead of drawing with it.

Image 12. Drawing with finger.

His rhythmical breathing and his immense focus and concentration remind us of when he worked in the confetti room. It becomes clear to us that we are witnessing the entering into yet another creative and intensive process of learning.

Image 13. Pressing with finger.

Discussion: Affective/Effective Learning to Read and Write Through Real Virtualities in Digitized Society

That young children engage in much more creative and complex ways of learning language, reading, and writing is not a problem for children—and here we join Günter Kress (1997); the problem rather lies "in our current firmly established common-sense about literacy and what it is." And as Kress states it is up to *us* to deal with that problem. Indeed, we very much share this political endeavor concerning rethinking "the role and the status, the 'standing' of the child… in the processes of representation and communication" (p. 113).

Our didactical and theoretical findings point toward the importance of using digital devices very purposefully and with the intent to make a clear and defined connection to a linguistic problematic, but also toward the importance of acknowledging and giving children opportunities to live registers of experiences harboring affect, intensity, sensation, play, appearance, decoration, spectacle, and style, as well as the *production* of sense and linguistic representations also in their analog reading and writing. The way children plunge into intense actualizations of the virtual with both analog and digital productions of the line seems very close to how Massumi describes what is important with concepts of the virtual, as enabling triggerings of novelty, emergence, and change:

> Concepts of the virtual in itself are important only to the extent to which they contribute to a pragmatic understanding of emergence, to the extent to which they enable triggerings of change (induce the new). It is the edge of virtual, where it leaks into actual, that counts. For that seeping edge is where potential, actually, is found. (Massumi, 2002, p. 43)

Our temporary conclusion is that, an *affective* learning to read and write might also be an *effective* learning to read and write. Children—if allowed to work from their own premises, may it be with analog or digital devices—seem to continuously find themselves on that very "seeping edge" of the virtual, in potentiality (no wonder they need to sleep a lot!), and, still, always in *real* literacy learning.

References

Burnett, C. (2010). Technology and literacy in early childhood settings: A review of research. *Journal of Early Childhood Literacy, 10*(3), 247–270.

Carrington, V. (2005). New textual landscapes, information, new childhood. In J. Marsh (Ed.), *Popular culture: Media and digital literacies in early childhood.* London: Sage.

Chen, J. Q., & Chang, C. (2006). Using computers in early childhood classrooms: Teachers' attitudes, skills and practices. *Journal of Early Childhood Research, 4*(2), 169–188.

Cole, D. R. (2009). Deleuzian affectivel for teaching literature: A literacy perspective on multiple literacies theory. In D. Masny & D. R. Cole (Eds.), *Multiple literacies theory: A Deleuzian perspective* (pp. 63–78). Rotterdam: Sense.

Dahlberg, G. (Manuscript in Progress). *Immanent pedagogy and ethics.* Unpublished manuscript.

Dahlberg, G., & Moss, P. (2005). *Ethics and politics in early childhood education.* Oxfordshire: RoutledgeFalmer.

Dahlberg, G., & Olsson, L. M. (2008). Micropolitically global. *Hong Kong Journal of Early Childhood, 7*(1), 6–15.

Dahlberg, G. & Olsson, L. M. (2009). *The magic of language: Young children's relations to language, reading and writing.* Research proposal.

Darley, A. (2000). *Visual digital culture: Surface play and spectacle in new media genres.* New York: Routledge.

Deleuze, G. (1988). *Spinoza: Practical philosophy.* San Fransisco: City Light Books.

Deleuze, G., & Guattari, F. (1994). *What is philosophy?* London: Verso.

Deleuze, G., & Guattari, F. (2004). *A thousand plateaus: Capitalism and schizophrenia.* London: Continuum.

Dufresne, T. (2006). Exploring the processes in becoming biliterate: The roles of resistance to learning and affect. *International Journal of Learning, 12*(8), 347–354.

Elfström, I. (2012). *Pedagogisk dokumentation och/eller individuella utvecklingsplaner: Om att synliggöra och bedöma förskolebarns lärande* (Pedagogical documentation and/or individual development plans: Making visible and assessing preschool children's cooperative and individual learning). Doctoral dissertation, Department of Child and Youth Studies, Stockholm University.

Fendler, L. (2001). Educating flexible souls. In K. Hultqvist & G. Dahlberg (Eds.), *Governing the child in the new millennium* (pp. 119–142). London: RoutledgeFalmer.

Hickey-Moody, A., & Haworth, R. (2009). Affective literacies. In D. Masny & D. R. Cole (Eds.), *Multiple literacies theory: A Deleuzian perspective* (pp. 79–92). Rotterdam: Sense.

Kennedy, E. (2010). Improving literacy achievement in a high-poverty school: Empowering classroom teachers through professional development. *Reading Research Quarterly, 45*(4), 384–387.

Knight, L. (2009). Desire and rhizome: Affective literacies in early childhood. In D. Masny & D. R. Cole (Eds.), *Multiple literacies theory: A Deleuzian perspective* (pp. 51–62). Rotterdam: Sense.

Kress, G. (1997). *Before writing: Rethinking the paths to literacy.* London: Routledge.

Kress, G. (2003). *Literacy in the new media age.* London: Routledge.

Lamarre, T. (2002). Diagram, inscription, sensation. In B. Massumi (Ed.), *A shock to thought: Expression after Deleuze and Guattari* (pp. 149–170). London: Routledge.

Lankshear, C., & Knobel, M. (2003). New technologies in early childhood literacy research: A review of research. *Journal of Early Childhood Literacy, 3*(1), 59–82.

Lewis, C., & Fabos, B. (2005). Instant messaging, literacies, and social identities. *Reading Research Quarterly, 40*(4), 470–501.

Marsh, J. (Ed.). (2005). *Popular culture, new media and digital literacy in early childhood.* London: RoutledgeFalmer.

Masny, D., & Cole, D. R. (2009). *Multiple literacies theory.* Rotterdam: Sense.

Masny, D., & Waterhouse, M. (2011). Mapping territories and creating nomadic pathways with multiple literacies theory. *Journal of Curriculum Theorizing, 27*(3), 287–387.

Massumi, B. (2002). *Parables for the virtual: Movement, affect, sensation.* Durham, NC: Duke University Press.

Massumi, B. (2011). *Semblance and event: Activist philosophy and the occurrent arts.* Cambridge: MIT Press.

Miller, E. (2005). Fighting technology for toddlers. *Education Digest: Essential Readings Condensed for Quick Review, 71*(3), 55–58.

Mozère, L. (2006). What's the trouble with identity?: Practices and theories from France. *Contemporary Issues in Early Childhood, 7*(2), 109–118.

Mozère, L. (2007). In early childhood: What's language about? *Educational Philosophy and Theory, 39*(3), 291–299.

Nixon, H. (2003). New research literacies for contemporary research into literacy and new media? *Reading Research Quarterly, 38*(4), 407–413.

Olsson, L. M. (2009). *Movement and experimentation in young children's learning: Deleuze and Guattari in early childhood education.* London: Routledge.

Olsson, L. M. (2012). Eventicizing curriculum: Learning to read and write through becoming a citizen of the world. *Journal of Curriculum Theorizing, 28*(1), 88–107.

Olsson, L. M. (2013). Taking children's questions seriously: The need for a creative thought. *Global Studies of Childhood, 3*(3), 230–253.

Street, B. (2003). What's "new" in new literacy studies? Critical approaches to literacy in theory and practice. *Literacy, Education and Development, 5*(2), 1–10.

Taubman, P. M. (2009). *Teaching by numbers: Deconstructing the discourse of standards and accountability in education.* New York: Routledge.

Wohlwend, K. E. (2009). Early adopters: Playing new literacies and pretending new technologies in print-centric classrooms. *Journal of Early Childhood Literacy, 9*(2), 117–140.

NINETEEN

Learning From the Margins: Early Childhood Imaginaries, "Normal Science," and the Case for a Radical Reconceptualization of Research and Practice[1]

Mathias Urban

Policy discourses that frame "the sum total of the social reaction to the fact of ontogenetic postnatal development" as Siegried Bernfeld (1925, 1973) referred to education, reflect a fundamental dilemma: that education inevitably addresses both the child and the society, leading to often contradictory aims, aspirations, and in consequence, practices. European Union policy references to early childhood education and care, since the early 1990s, have reflected these contractions. The recent EU strategic framework, "Europe 2020: A Strategy for Smart, Sustainable and Inclusive Growth" (European Commission, 2010) provides a bleak analysis of the situation the EU finds itself in at the beginning of the second decade of the 21st century. Without explicitly mentioning it, the description of the economic, social, demographic, and environmental crises facing Europe in a global context resembles the "complex intersolidarity of problems, antagonisms, crises, uncontrolled processes, and the general crisis of the planet" that Edgar Morin identifies in his 1999 manifesto for the new millennium (Morin & Kern, 1999). The need to "resolve" those crises is the underlying narrative in this framework, and a key role is given to early childhood education and care in a set of policy measures to "put Europe back on track" (European Commission, 2010). Starting from what appears to be a paradigm shift in recent EU policies toward young children, the chapter asks what are the imagined and projected (European?) childhoods, who is the child who emerges from this discourse? At the center of the interrogation lies a critical enquiry into a mainstream research-policy-practice complex that, the chapter argues, shows the characteristics of what Thomas Kuhn (1962) refers to as "normal science." Whose questions are seen as relevant in this relationship? Who benefits, who speaks, and who is silenced? Making the case for a radical paradigm shift, the chapter aims at identifying and questioning the narratives that are employed to justify policies and practices focusing on young children and on early childhood education and care in particular. The questioning, the chapter argues, opens a space for possible and necessary counter-discourses, re-narrativisation, democratic experimentation (Moss & Urban, 2010), and "untested feasibility" (Freire, 2007).

Early Childhood Practices Are Political—And So Is Early Childhood Research

Our societies' engagement with the upbringing and education of the youngest children has finally become a highly political issue. At least this is the impression one could get by browsing through the rapidly increasing collection of international policy documents concerned with early childhood education and care. The World Bank, the Organisation for Economic Cooperation and Development (OECD), and UNICEF have been hugely influential in promoting systematic investment in services for children below compulsory school age and in outlining and underpinning early childhood policies in many countries (e.g., OECD, 2001, 2006; UNICEF Innocenti Research Centre, 2008; World Bank, 2003). Childcare and early education have played a role in European Union policies for some time, with the 1992 Council Recommendations on Childcare being an early example of an EU policy document emphasizing the need for coherent policymaking across several areas that are seen as affecting families with young children: childcare services, parental leave, labor regulations, and gender equality (Council of the European Communities, 1992). More recently, the EU policy interest in early childhood has increased significantly. This is manifest in the publication of a number of high-level policy documents linking early childhood and the services set up by member states to support young children and families to the overall framework strategy for the EU for this decade (European Commission, 2010). The 2011 EU communication "Early Childhood Education and Care: Providing All Our Children with the Best Start for the World of Tomorrow" (European Commission, 2011) has a key role among these documents. The renewed interest in early childhood has created a growing demand in research to inform, orient, and legitimate the policies promoted by the European Union.

There is a second approach to the relationship between policy and practice in early childhood. Caring for and educating young children lie at the core of any human society. Childrearing practices in society and the institutions and professions we establish around them are the most fundamental manifestations of the relationship between the private and the public. These relationships are not static, universal, or uncontested. Due to unequal distribution of both private and public resources, they are more favorable for some than for others. There are growing numbers of children and families for whom this most basic relationship has become precarious. Approached from this perspective, early childhood education and care have always been a "res publica," a political issue.

The questions we ask as researchers depend on how we position ourselves in the micro- and macro-politics of early childhood (Dahlberg & Moss, 2005). They are shaped by our own personal and professional backgrounds and histories (and biases) and they shape the image of the child and the possible, desirable, imaginable practices and policies.

In this chapter, I explore the questions we might ask in early childhood research and how they relate to the constructions of both the child and to our understandings of the role of research. The chapter begins with a brief examination of recent European policy documents that have been influential in promoting a particularly important, but, as I argue, narrow view of children and early childhood education in a changing European policy context. I then discuss current research in early childhood in relationship to the policy analysis and argue for a much broader understanding of the challenges we are facing and the implications for doing research in our field. The final two sections make the case for a radical reconceptualization of research as democratic, transformative, and inevitably political practice.

ECEC in a Changing European Policy Context

Since the 1992 Council Recommendations on Childcare (Council of the European Communities, 1992), early childhood education and care have been a recurring topic on European policy agendas. Reasons for the continued interest in services for the youngest European citizens and their families have varied widely over the years and have often been contradictory. The 1992 Recommendations urge EU member states to "take and/or progressively encourage initiatives to enable women and men to reconcile their occupational, family and upbringing responsibilities arising from the care of children" (article 1). This, the recommendations argue, requires coherent policies addressing the provision of childcare services, matching parental leave arrangements, organization and structure of work in order to meet the needs of workers with children, and a general commitment to gender equality: "the sharing of occupational, family and upbringing responsibilities arising from the care of children between women and men" (ibid, article 2). The document then goes on to specify the characteristics of each of the previously mentioned policy areas: childcare services should be affordable and accessible to all children and families and offer reliable care of high quality combined with pedagogical approaches. There is further emphasis on initial and continuous training of staff, close collaboration with local communities, and appropriate public funding for services. "The provision of childcare services needs to be complemented by much greater flexibility in the workplace in general, which take[s] into account the needs of all working parents with responsibility for the care and upbringing of children" (ibid, article 5). Childcare, as a field of employment, is in need of attention, and member states are asked to ensure that "due recognition" is given to childcare workers, their working conditions, and "the social value of their work" (ibid.; Moss, 2012).

Following the Maastricht Treaty (1993), the EU saw the development of an ambitious socioeconomic policy agenda. It culminated in 2000 in a set of policies known as the Lisbon Strategy. The orientation of the EU in the first decade of the new millennium was to become "the most competitive and dynamic knowledge-based economy in the world capable of sustainable economic growth with more and better jobs and greater social cohesion" (European Council, 2000). Hence, childcare was now increasingly seen as an *investment* and a tool to achieve the ambitious policy goals. However, come 2010, it was obvious that Europe was far from being the "most competitive and dynamic knowledge-based economy in the world." Even from the perspective of its architects, the Lisbon Strategy had to be considered a failure. In June 2009, the then-prime minister of Sweden, Fredrik Reinfeldt, stated: "Even if progress has been made it must be said that the Lisbon Agenda, with only a year remaining before it is to be evaluated, has been a failure" (www.euractiv.com/priorities/sweden-admits-lisbon-agenda-fail-news-221962).

The changes in the role given to early childhood are particularly visible in the successor of the Lisbon Strategy and the policy documents that have been developed in its context. *Europe 2020: A Strategy for Smart, Sustainable and Inclusive Growth* (European Commission, 2010) provides the current strategic orientation for the European Union. It builds on a rather bleak analysis of the state of the EU at the beginning of the second decade of the 21st century. Two terms that feature most prominently in the EU 2020 strategy are "crisis" and "transformation":

> Europe faces a moment of transformation. The crisis has wiped out years of economic and social progress and exposed structural weaknesses in Europe's economy. In the meantime, the world is moving fast and long-term challenges—globalisation, pressure on resources, ageing—intensify. The EU must now take charge of its future. (European Commission, 2010, p. 3)

Crisis—What Crisis?

Clearly, what the European Commission has in mind when it redraws the picture of the present and future Union is an economic and financial crisis: the dramatic failure of global capitalism to provide and maintain the sound foundation for social and political progress, and its disastrous capacity to "wipe out" social achievements built on previous economic prosperity. Again, it is not within the remit of this article to speculate why, despite the dysfunctionality of our global economic system, the authors of the strategy hold on firmly to the primacy of the economy over every other aspect of life. Could it be that, despite the ubiquitous talk of transformation and change, the architects of the future European Union are unable to question the dominance of the "neoliberal imaginary" (S. J. Ball, 2012)? A more critical analysis of the situation we find ourselves in, I want to argue, along with Stephen Ball (ibid.) and Aihwa Ong (2007), would focus on the complex relationships between micro- and macro-politics of everyday neoliberalism in our societies. It would question an economic system that perpetuates the economisation of every aspect of social life and its need to constantly create opportunities for profit (what Ong, 2007, p. 4, refers to as neoliberalism with a big "N".) The analysis would extend to addressing the fundamental dependence of such an economic system on individuals who are "willing," "self-governing," and "entrepreneurial"—a Foucauldian mindset of governmentality (Foucault, 1982; Lemke, 2002). Ong (2007, p. 4) to the latter as neoliberalism with a small "n" (cf. S. J. Ball, 2012).

Choosing the frame of analysis is critical, as it orients the questions we ask (*research!*) and the ways forward we suggest in order to deal with the crisis (*policy!*).

Defining the situation in which we find ourselves as an "economic" or "financial" crisis is likely to lead to economic questions and answers. In other words, it contributes to further the neoliberal assumption that everything, including the upbringing of young children, can and should first be understood in economic terms. In this mindset, putting Europe (or other global regions) "back on track" (European Commission, 2010) translates to putting the economy back on track, raising questions about to whose rules this should happen, and based on which philosophies and values.

But continuing to use the EU as our case example—and similar to the much more enthusiastic feel of the Lisbon Strategy ("most competitive and dynamic knowledge-based economy in the world"), early childhood education and care does appear to have its role to play. Influential EU policy documents depict early childhood education and care as a powerful means to achieve economic progress, both individually and collectively. Early childhood education and care (ECEC), it is claimed, can remedy "socioeconomic disadvantage," break the "cycle of poverty" (European Commission, 2010, p. 4), and increase children's "employ-ability when they become adults" (p. 1). The language used in recent policy documents can be so confident about the outcomes of children participating in "high- quality" ECEC because the far-reaching claims are backed up by "scientific" and universalized research findings (e.g., Barnett, 2010).

However, defining both the "crisis" and the "solution" as economic prevents us from taking into account other views. Edgar Morin, in his "Manifesto for the New Millennium" (Morin & Kern, 1999) insists that, on a global scale, we can no longer pretend to identify *one* key problem, the solution to which would miraculously lead to ending the "crisis":

> One is at a loss to single out a number one problem to which all others would be subordinated. There is no single vital problem, but many vital problems, and it is this complex intersolidarity of problems, crises, uncontrolled processes, and the general crisis of the planet that constitutes the number one vital problem. (Morin & Kern, 1999, p. 74)

We are indeed facing global challenges and life-threatening catastrophes including, but not limited to:

- the increasing danger posed by proliferation of nuclear weapons
- the global climate crisis, threatening, among others, to unleash unrest, conflict and mass-migration due to growing shortages of water, food and fuel
- the threat to biodiversity
- the impossibility of unlimited economic growth
- the dysfunctional economic and financial system. (Moss & Urban, 2010, p. 15)

These "challenges" should provoke radical new approaches to education and to early childhood education in particular as we have argued in "Democracy and Experimentation" (Moss & Urban, 2010):

> All of these challenges mean we cannot continue as we are, and they should provoke major democratic debate in all countries. In relation to education, the question of its purpose becomes even more critical and urgent. The dangers we face require spreading and deepening democratic values and practices, collaborative action and a willingness to think and act differently, trying new approaches: "more of the same" is no longer an option. (p. 16)

This view seems to find support from José Manuel Barroso, president of the European Commission. He writes in his preface to the EU2020 strategy document:

> The crisis is a wake-up call, the moment where we recognise that "business as usual" would consign us to a gradual decline, to the second rank of the new global order. This is Europe's moment of truth. It is the time to be bold and ambitious. (European Commission, 2010, preface)

However, the question in early childhood policy and practice is not so much whether we can continue with "business as usual." It is, much more fundamentally, whether "business" is an appropriate concept for the societal engagement with the youngest children at all.

Researching Complexity

The policy arguments for early childhood education and care brought forward in recent EU policy documents seem to be strangely at odds with Barroso's "wake-up call." Instead of opening the debate for radically new questions (and actors), they seem to rely on and ask for ever "more of the same" evidence to legitimate the most effective interventions, for example, to "close the gap" by promoting early literacy and numeracy, especially for children from the most "disadvantaged" communities.

In fields of research other than education, the complex "problematiques" (as the Club of Rome refers to the interwoven crises of the planet [cf. Max-Neef, 2005]) have raised questions of transdisciplinarity and critical epistemology: How can we collaborate to understand the complexity and bring in many different perspectives? How can we come to new understandings of *knowledge* and how (and by whom) it is produced? There are, transdisciplinary thinkers suggest, at least five dimensions shaping the complex realities we address as researchers:

1. **Multidimensional**—complex problems straddle different levels of reality at the same time and therefore imply a thorough understanding of the simultaneity of both the discontinuity *and* coexistence of natural and social systems;

2. **Systemic**—complex problems are interconnected—it is not so much the individual problem areas that are complex, but rather the sets of overlapping relationships between them that define and constitute the bigger, planetary, nexus of problems;

3. **Emergence**—complex problems tend to reveal new or different sides as our perceptions of them change—understanding complex problems therefore implies a multi-referential epistemology with its point of departure in a non-separable subject – object relationship and which involves all our faculties of knowing and understanding—the mind, body and feelings/intuition;

4. **Global – local context**—complex problems do not manifest themselves exclusively at either the macro-, meso- or micro-levels—they are not restricted to a particular "scale" or "level"—neither are they limited to a specific geographical place or region—complex problems are by definition planetary, which means that their presence is observed and experienced both *globally* and *locally*;

5. **Long-term consequences**—complex problems pose severe/adverse implications for the continued existence of the human species if left unattended or unresolved—this implies the urgency of sustainability or finding sustainable solutions to these problems. (Swilling & van Breda, 2005, pp. 3–4)

All this implies that we can no longer study and interpret the world with concepts of certainty (e.g., linearity, local causality, predictability), but need to embrace concepts of uncertainty instead (e.g., non-linearity, global causality, unpredictability). The implications for research methodology and for the questions we ask are far reaching, but rewarding: "Using these new lenses not only changes our *perceptions* of reality, but they allow us to observe a radically different 'reality'" (ibid., p. 5). Beyond "limited situations," writes Paulo Freire, lies "untested feasibility"—and hope (Freire, 2004).

European research in early childhood tends to fall into two distinct categories. On the one hand, there are large-scale, often international studies with a strong element of comparison and/ or evaluation (between countries, programs, groups of children, etc.). They include landmark studies such as the first two *Starting Strong* reports (OECD, 2001, 2006), SEEPRO (Oberhuemer, Schreyer, & Neuman, 2010), EPPE (Sylva, Melhuish, Sammons, Siraj-Blatchford, & Taggart, 2004) or the recent Roma Early Childhood Inclusion (RECI) study (Bennett, 2012), to name only a few. On the other hand, there is an increasing number of small-scale, mainly qualitative (and often unfunded) local research, for example, documenting the experiences in a particular setting, program, or community. Many of these studies are conducted by practitio-ner–researchers who are closely involved with their specific enquiry. There is also a small but growing body of small-scale qualitative research that pushes the boundaries of traditional ECEC research and introduces new theoretical frameworks, for example, using the work of Deleuze and Guattari as basis for analysis and interpretation (e.g., Mozère, 2007; Olsson, 2009). Only a few studies seek to bridge the "global" and the "local," not by adding up distinct local experi-ences into a comparative picture, but by creating spaces for encounter and collaborative enquiry between the macro-, meso-, and micro-aspects of early childhood policy and practice. In our recently completed CORE project (Urban, Vandenbroeck, Van Laere, Lazzari, & Peeters, 2011, 2012) we attempted this by systematically connecting local case studies (and the local research-ers who conducted them) with the overarching European policy environment.

There are obvious problems of perspective and vantage point in both large-scale transna-tional and small-scale local studies in early childhood. Researchers, like cartographers, must find the right scale for their various representations of the world (how these differ fundamen-tally in different knowledge systems is discussed by David Turnbull in his 2003 book *Masons, Tricksters and Cartographers*). The larger the scale, the less detail can be included in the map, the smaller, the less likely it is to see the big picture. Peter Moss, in his contribution to the launch of the first *Starting Strong* report (OECD, 2001) in Stockholm 2001 reminds us of the dilemma in early childhood research:

> Cross-national studies of early childhood can lose sight of the child. Or rather, their focus on structures and technologies runs the risk of producing an image of the child as a universal and passive object, to be shaped by early childhood services—to be developed, to be prepared, to be educated, to be cared for. There may be little sense for the child as a social actor, situated in a particular historical and spatial context, living a childhood in these services, and making her own meanings from the experience. (Moss, 2001)

The problem with the studies that produce the type of data that are most appealing to those committed to "evidence-based" policymaking is not just one of scale, of proximity, or distance. The concept of "comparison" itself is problematic, as it is often connected to the number-one question in evidence-based policymaking: What works? Posed in contexts of policymaking and governance, the underlying question of comparative studies tends to be a question of transfer-ability: How can what works *there* be made to work *here*? Pursuing this rationale inevitably shapes the *what?* and *how?* of research: the questions we ask of the complex, diverse, multifac-eted, and often contradictory worlds of children, families, practitioners, and communities and the approaches we take to explore and understand the "swampy lowland [of] messy, confusing problems" (Schön, 1987, p. 28) that constitutes the reality of early childhood practices. It also carries the risk of restricting the *who?*—the choice of participants in the enquiry into, analy-sis, interpretation, and transformation of the world—to those on the "high ground" (Schön, 1987), the experts and academic researchers.

The focus on "what works" obscures the fundamental *democratic deficit* in educational research, argues Gert Biesta, because it "makes it difficult, if not impossible, to ask questions of what it should work *for* and who should have a say in determining the latter" (Biesta, 2007, p. 5).

As I have discussed elsewhere (Urban & Dalli, 2011), critical researchers such as Robert Stake (Stake, 2003) remind us that "comparison is a grand epistemological strategy, a powerful conceptual mechanism" (p. 148). The problem with this grand and powerful strategy is, he argues, that it necessarily and systematically obscures any knowledge that fails to facilitate comparison. Complexity, the "thick of things," is not only lost; it becomes fundamentally threatening as it undermines the imposing edifices constructed from comparative data. Instead, "comparability" has to be constructed, proactively, by systematically eradicating from the picture anything that is juicy, contradictory, puzzling, alive—in short: meaningful. The result, too often, are pieces of decontextualized information—"evidence nuggets," as recently discussed by a British research initiative (www.whatworksforchildren.org.uk/).

It must be mentioned that, unlike policymakers who see comparative data as a basic commodity, comparative educational researchers have long been aware of the simplification trap. Joe Tobin, visiting and revisiting "preschools in three cultures" (Tobin, Hsueh, & Karasawa, 2009; Tobin, Wu, & Davidson, 1989), removes the comparative *inter-* from his conceptual framework and argues for negotiation as a process of meaning-making. Robin Alexander, in his seminal *Culture and Pedagogy* (2000), urges us to "bite the methodological bullet and progress beyond policy and structure to the classroom" (p. 3). The authors of the first OECD *Starting Strong* reports (OECD, 2001) are also well aware that it is impossible to decontextualize early childhood without losing meaning:

> ECEC policy and the quality of services are deeply influenced by underlying assumptions about childhood and education: what does childhood mean in this society? How should young children be reared and educated? What are the purposes of education and care, of early childhood institutions? What are the functions of early childhood staff? (OECD, 2001, p. 63)

While my depiction of the European early childhood research "landscape" is sketchy at best, it does point to some fundamentally critical issues that require urgent attention if we want to overcome the limitations of a research environment in which the perceived *problems*, the resulting *research questions* and *methodologies*, and the desirable (imaginable?) *solutions* are caught in the same paradigm.

What Counts? Who Counts?
The Case for a Democratic Turn in Research

> For apart from inquiry, apart from the praxis, individuals cannot be truly human. Knowledge emerges only through invention and re-invention, through the restless, impatient continuing, hopeful inquiry human beings pursue in the world, with the world, and with each other. (Freire, 2000b, p. 53)

I argue for a radical democratic turn in early childhood research. I do so not out of naïve sympathies with participation or out of a belief in the importance of giving a voice to children, parents, and practitioners (a deeply undemocratic concept, I would argue, as it implies that the power to grant or withhold the possibility to speak lies with the researcher). A democratic reconceptualization of *how*, with *whom*, and for *what purpose* we conduct research, I argue, is a necessary step toward the needed shift of paradigms to break the cycle where more-of-the-same research predictably leads to more-of-the-same "solutions." Early childhood research (in its established, funded, listened-to variants) has become what Thomas Kuhn called a "normal science" (Kuhn, 1962). It has adopted forms of enquiry that remain safely within the boundaries of the dominant (western natural and positivist social scientific) world view and that serve to "solve" the accepted problems within that paradigm. It is widely accepted and supported by research, for instance, that children from poor and marginalized communities are disadvantaged in the education system and therefore fare considerably worse in life than their privileged peers. Research has identified "the gap," provided the "evidence" for policymakers, and is now offering "solutions" and interventions that "work" to close "the gap." The problem here is that the question implies the solution (e.g., increased participation in early childhood education and care, in order to raise children's literacy and numeracy levels). Once the "problem" is identified as one of lacking educational attainment, or a "lacking" in general in home and community, "more" education—in out-of-home/community settings—is inevitably offered as the solution.

But what if the situation is not as straightforward as it seems through the educational lens? What if the question of educational attainment is tangled up with structural injustice, systemic inequality, oppression, or blatant racism (Murray, 2012; Murray & Urban, 2012)? How is it possible to reframe the question of who does well in education as a question of dominant and widely accepted knowledge versus other knowledges, for example, Indigenous, that are ignored, seen as irrelevant, or openly suppressed? What if, as Paulo Freire (Freire, 2000a, 2000b) argues, the education system itself, its preschools, schools, and universities, played an active role in perpetuating the oppressive situation? How do poor housing, poverty, exclusion come together with educational experience in multifaceted "problematiques," an "intersolidarity of crises" (Morin & Kern, 1999) in the lived experience of "disadvantaged" children and communities? Access to "high-quality" early childhood education has an important role to play, but on its own it certainly does not provide a "solution." Furthermore, the apparent consensus on the importance of "high-quality" services completely ignores that the concept of "quality" itself is highly contested (Dahlberg, Pence, & Moss, 2007).

"Normal" scientists, argues Kuhn, "do not usually ask or debate what makes a particular problem or solution legitimate" (Kuhn, 1962, p. 46). In other words, they do not question the rules of the game where the problems are framed by those who define what counts as problems to be solved. This is the argument John and Jill Schostak make in their 2008 book *Radical Research* (2008). In it, they argue that in order to bring about the kind of paradigmatic change Kuhn talked about in his *The Structure of Scientific Revolutions*, "normal" research will have to be challenged by questions raised "by people face to face with issues in their everyday lives" (Schostak & Schostak, 2008, p. 8).

What does current "normal research" in early childhood look like? An example can be found in a recent program of a high-profile seminar with "internationally renowned scientists" for early childhood PhD students. The event was hosted by a foundation committed to counter the "foreseeable dearth of qualified young academics" in our field, and firmly grounded in the conviction that the "importance of education in early childhood for an individual's personal development is uncontested" (www.boschstiftung.de/content/language2/html/25076.asp). Guest lectures were given on topics such as emotional and behavioral self-regulation and learning skills, quality assessment in early childhood care and education (ECE) using the ECERS (Early Childhood Environment Rating Scale) and the CLASS (Classroom Assessment Scoring System), and promoting literacy and numeracy development (the role of curriculum and teacher in ECE).

I have no intention to belittle the importance of the initiative or to question the motives of funders and participants. My argument is that where in "normal research" in early childhood the importance of the early years of life is largely uncontested, so are the questions, the procedures, and the answers. *What counts*, the researchable topics (e.g., self-regulation and learning skills, quality assessment, curriculum), is clearly defined by those *who count* (internationally renowned "scientists"), rarely by those *who are counted*. The solutions to be suggested by this research are already implied in the questions: programs and interventions to support children's "self-regulation" in order to increase their "leaning skills," to measure "quality" using externally defined criteria, and to support teachers to "deliver" effective curricula. Assumed is a normality of the individual child (behavior, skills), the environment (quality), and the content (curriculum) that remains unquestioned. But if "behavior" and lack of learning skills is a general problem (to pick just one of the issues as an exemplar), how then is it that ADHD diagnosis rates for children from marginalized groups in society (e.g., Roma in Europe and Indigenous children in Canada and Australia) are regularly "significantly higher than expected based on prevalence rates in the general population" (Baydala, Sherman, Rassmussen, Wikman, & Janzen, 2006)? What *other* questions could we ask if we turned the focus of our attention from the child to the relationship between the marginalized and the dominant and their privilege to define what behavior is acceptable in educational settings?

Schostak and Schostak (2008) ask "why so much research contributes so little to democratic questioning of the powerful" (p. 1). They continue to outline a program for research that is "radical" in at least two respects: first, the etymology of "radical" (roots) implies a focus on the essential assumptions, foundations, values, and ethics that frame our perspective on the world. It is concerned with identity, race, class, gender, religion, and politics. The question of the radical, they write, "emerges in conflict, where fundamental approaches to life, to ways of thinking, to ways of seeing the world are in dispute" (p. 6). Research, conceptualized from this "radical" vantage point, insists on asking *why?* questions.

Second, reframing research as "radical" implies a political dimension. Not to accept the social reality as a given, but to ask why things are the way they are implies there are other ways of seeing and doing things. Questioning the taken-for-granted may not in itself "effect the transformation of the world," as Freire (2004) wrote about the practice of education, "but it implies it" (p. 23). The political dimension of "radical" research lies in its suggestion that it is possible to "overthrow...a previously stable or at least dominant order of ways of knowing, thinking believing, acting" (Schostak & Schostak, 2008, p. 1).

Radical, transformative research and radical democracy (Moss & Urban, 2010) go hand in hand because the questions that matter (*what* counts?) are not exclusive, they cannot be defined by the academic researcher alone (*who* counts?). On the contrary, with "faith in the capacity of human beings for intelligent judgment and action if proper conditions are furnished" (Dewey, 1939, p. 227), everyone is capable of asking questions like:

- Why do things have to be like this?
- Why am I considered to be inferior to them?
- Why do they have more than me?
- So, what is actually going on here? Who benefits from these circumstances and who loses?
- Why can't I do just whatever I want?

- How do I stop them from doing whatever they like and in the process hurting me?
- Why can't we all just get on with each other? (Schostak & Schostak, 2008, p. 1).

Research that encourages and enables asking these—and other—questions cannot be designed and "conducted" within the boundaries of traditional disciplines. It implies transdisciplinary approaches (for a detailed discussion, see Fairclough, 2005), a "refocusing of research and action on the political, the cultural [the educational, M.U.] and the social without splitting them up into separate disciplines" (Schostak & Schostak, 2008, p. 8).

Researching ECEC in Europe as Political Practice

> My discourse in favor of dreaming, of utopia, of freedom, of democracy is the discourse of those who refuse to settle and do not allow the taste for being human, which fatalism deteriorates, to die within themselves. (Freire, 2007, p. 26)

Mainstream research in early childhood has not yet embraced the transdisciplinary, transformatory, and radically democratic challenge (and possibility!) arising from the complex and often contradictory realities of children, families, and communities. Despite debates taking place in other fields of social science, humanities and beyond (Fairclough, 2005; Nicolescu, 2002, 2008), early childhood appears to be stuck in a dated paradigm where the subjects and objects of research are constructed from limited perspectives only, and without them taking an active role in that process. Mono-dimensional constructions of children (e.g., in relation to their *learning skills*), families, and communities (e.g., in relation to their ethnicity) contradict a fast-growing body of knowledge and professional experience that confirm children's holistic and multidimensional ways of learning, developing their multifaceted identities, and making sense of the world. Hilary Lenz-Taguchi (2009), exploring this puzzling theory – practice divide, suspects a "desire to control" as a leitmotif:

> the more we seem to know about the complexity of learning, children's diverse strategies and multiple theories [of] knowledge, the more we seek to impose learning strategies and curriculum goals that reduce the complexities and diversities of learning and knowing. The more complex things become the more we seem to desire processes of reduction and thus control, but such reduction strategies might simultaneously shut out the inclusion and justice we want to achieve. (Lenz-Taguchi, 2009, p. 8)

Returning to the EU's research-informed approach to early childhood education and care, we find a conspicuous "construction" of children from a very specific perspective. The importance of "high-quality" early childhood education and care is clearly stated: ECEC can "close the gap in social development and numeracy and literacy skills between children from socially advantaged and disadvantaged backgrounds" (European Commission, 2011, p. 4), and generate future "employability" (p. 1). While the value placed on early childhood education and care is to be welcomed, this perspective seems to be based on two fundamental assumptions:

1. Children (especially from "disadvantaged" communities) are deficient.
2. Children (in general) are potential future contributors to the economy.

Research is an inevitably political *praxis* (Freire) as it requires the researchers to position themselves in relationship to the world they are engaging with. A central question here is whether we choose to maintain and support the status quo, or commit ourselves to questioning the accepted and to enquiries that aim at transformation and more just and equitable experiences for all. Transformative, "radical" research would fundamentally challenge the assumptions made about children, families, and communities. The first questions it would ask would not be about how to treat the deficiency or how to ensure "best practices" for future outcomes. Rather, it would start with questions about *here and now*:

- What are the lived experiences (Van Manen, 1990) of children, families, and communities, for example, in and with the education system?
- What knowledges other than the dominant worldview do marginalized and oppressed children, families, and communities employ to make sense of the world?
- What are their *capabilities* (Nussbaum, 2000); what contributions could they make *now* if "proper conditions were furnished" (Dewey, 1939)?

In early childhood education and care, such questions extend beyond the immediate classroom, program, or early childhood setting to the relationship between children and adults, between the private and the public, and the governance of the institutions and systems we establish around this relationship. They challenge the position of the researcher-as-expert, as they require a radically different understanding of the nature of the body of knowledge underpinning our policies and practices and of those who contribute to it (Murray & Urban, 2012). Elsewhere, I have argued that the "epistemological hierarchy," the top-down structure of knowledge-production-and-application in our field can be replaced by much more reciprocal and inclusive ways of understanding, orienting, and theorising early childhood practices as a "critical ecology" (Miller, Dalli, & Urban, 2011; Urban, 2007, 2008). Recent European research has taken this approach as a vantage point and has shown how a "competent system" in early childhood depends on the systematic and reciprocal relationship between individuals, institutions, research, professional preparation, and governance (Urban et al., 2011, 2012). However, to fully engage with the diversity of children's, families', and communities' lived experiences in Europe, and especially experiences of dominance, marginalization, exclusion (Herczog, 2012; Murray, 2012), I suggest that more radical steps are necessary to reconceptualize research, policy, and practice in early childhood. But how, for instance, could we reframe the relationship between the "advantaged" and "disadvantaged" communities (e.g., Roma, Traveller, Immigrants) in a more equal and respectful way and move beyond the deficit model of early childhood intervention?

Could we learn, for instance, from experiences outside Europe in the "majority world"? (from ECD interventions in Africa that "are more successful when built on local knowledge" [A. Pence & Schafer, 2006, p. 2]). Referring to cross-cultural psychologists Judith Evans and Robert Myers, Pence and Schafer point to the value of Indigenous knowledge and child-rearing practices not only from an ethical and philosophical perspective. They are "intrinsically sound and valuable," and important to "understand, support, and improve child-rearing; respond to diversity; respect cultural values; and provide continuity during times of rapid change" (Evans & Myers, 1994, pp. 2–3 cited in A. Pence & Schafer, 2006, p. 2).

Alan Pence and colleagues have applied the recognition that there are multiple *ways of knowing* that can mutually enrich each other to develop an early childhood curriculum jointly with First Nations communities in Canada, a process they refer to as "generative curriculum" (J. Ball & Pence, 2000). Their experiences with the effectiveness of including Indigenous knowledge in ECD curricula have informed successful professional development and capacity building initiatives in Canada and, in particular, the Early Childhood Development Virtual University (ECDVU) in Africa (A. R. Pence & Marfo, 2004).

In Europe, as elsewhere, policy interest in early childhood education and care is to be welcomed. However, in Europe, as is the case in many other regions of the world, the dominant research paradigm carries the risk of perpetuating rather than countering exclusion and marginalization. In order to challenge this, we need to learn from and engage with experiences from the margins.

References

Alexander, R. J. (2000). *Culture and pedagogy: International comparisons in primary education.* Oxford: Blackwell.

Ball, J., & Pence, A. R. (2000). Involving communities in constructions of culturally appropriate ECE curriculum. *Australian Journal of Early Childhood Education, 25*(1), 21–25.

Ball, S. J. (2012). *Global Education Inc.: New policy networks and the neo-liberal imaginary.* London: Routledge.

Barnett, S. W. (2010). Benefits and costs of quality pre-school education: Evidence-based policy to improve returns. Paper presented at the 7th OECD ECEC network meeting.

Baydala, L., Sherman, J., Rassmussen, C., Wikman, E., & Janzen, H. (2006). ADHD characteristics in Canadian Aboriginal children. *Journal of Attention Disorders, 9*(4), 642–647.

Bennett, J. (2012). *Roma early childhood inclusion: The RECI overview report, a joint initiative of the Open Society Foundations, the Roma Education Fund and UNICEF.* Budapest: OSF/REF/UNICEF.

Bernfeld, S. (1925). *Sisyphos oder die grenzen der erziehung.* Leipzig: Internationaler Psychoanalytischer Verlag.

Bernfeld, S. (1973). *Sisyphus or the limits of education.* Berkeley: University of California Press.

Biesta, G. (2007). Why "what works" won't work: Evidence-based practice and the democratic deficit in educational research. *Educational Theory, 57*(1), 1–22.

Council of the European Communities. (1992). Council recommendation of March 31, 1992 on child care. Brussels: Council of the European Communities.

Dahlberg, G., & Moss, P. (2005). *Ethics and politics in early childhood education.* Oxfordshire: RoutledgeFalmer.

Dahlberg, G., Moss, P., & Pence, A. (2007). *Beyond quality in early childhood education and care: Languages of evaluation.* London: Routledge.

Dewey, J. (1939). Creative democracy: The task before us. In J. A. Boyston (Ed.), *John Dewey: The later works, 1925–1953* (Vol. 14, pp. 224–230). Carbondale, IL: Southern Illinois University Press.

European Commission. (2010). *Europe 2020: A strategy for smart, sustainable and inclusive growth.* Brussels: European Commission.

European Commission. (2011). *Early childhood education and care: Providing all our children with the best start for the world of tomorrow.* Brussels: European Commission, Directorate General for Education and Culture.

European Council. (2000). *Presidency conclusions.* Brussels: European Council.

Evans, J. L., & Myers, R. G. (1994). Childrearing practices: Creating programmes where traditions and modern practices meet. *Coordinators' Notebook, 15*: Consultative Group in Early Childhood Care and Development.

Fairclough, N. (2005). Critical discourse analysis in trans-disciplinary research on social change: Transition, re-scaling, poverty and social inclusion. *Lodz Papers in Pragmatics, 1,* 37–58.

Foucault, M. (1982). The subject and the power. In H. L. Dreyfus & P. Rabinow (Eds.), *Michel Foucault: Beyond structuralism and hermeneutics* (pp. 208–226). Brighton: Harvester.

Freire, P. (2000a). *Cultural action for freedom.* Harvard Educational Review: Monograph Series.

Freire, P. (2000b). *Pedagogy of the oppressed* (30th anniversary ed.). New York: Continuum.

Freire, P. (2004). *Pedagogy of hope: Reliving pedagogy of the oppressed.* London: Continuum.

Freire, P. (2007). *Daring to dream: Toward a pedagogy of the unfinished.* Boulder, CO: Paradigm.

Herczog, M. (2012). Rights of the child and early childhood education and care in Europe. *European Journal of Education, 47*(4), 542–555.

Kuhn, T. S. (1962). *The structure of scientific revolutions.* Chicago, IL: University of Chicago Press.

Lemke, T. (2002, September). Foucault, governmentality, and critique. *Rethinking Marxism: A Journal of Economics, Culture & Society, 14*(3), 49–64.

Lenz-Taguchi, H. (2009). *Going beyond the theory/practice divide in early childhood education: Introducing an intra-active pedagogy.* London: Routledge.

Max-Neef, M. (2005). Foundations of transdisciplinarity. *Ecological Economics, 53,* 5–16.

Miller, L., Dalli, C., & Urban, M. (Eds.). (2011). *Early childhood grows up: Towards a critical ecology of the profession.* Dordrecht: Springer.

Morin, E., & Kern, A. B. (1999). *Homeland earth: A manifesto for the new millenium.* Cresskill, NJ: Hampton Press.

Moss, P. (2001). Beyond early childhood education and care. Paper presented at the Starting Strong OECD Conference, Stockholm.

Moss, P. (2012). Caring and learning together: Exploring the relationship between parental leave and early childhood education and care. *European Journal of Education, 47*(4), 482–493.

Moss, P., & Urban, M. (2010). *Democracy and experimentation: Two fundamental values for education.* Guetersloh: Bertelsmann Stiftung.

Mozère, L. (2007). In early childhood: What's language about? *Educational Philosophy and Theory, 39*(3), 291–299.

Murray, C. (2012). A Minority within a minority? Social justice for traveller and Roma children in ECEC. *European Journal of Education, 47*(4), 569–583.

Murray, C., & Urban, M. (2012). *Diversity and equality in early childhood. An Irish perspective.* Dublin: Gill & Macmillan.

Nicolescu, B. (2002). *Manifesto of transdisciplinarity.* Albany: SUNY Press.

Nicolescu, B. (2008). *Transdisciplinarity: Theory and practice.* Cresskill, NJ: Hampton Press.

Nussbaum, M. C. (2000). *Women and human development: The capabilities approach.* Cambridge: Cambridge University Press.

Oberhuemer, P., Schreyer, I., & Neuman, M. J. (2010). *Professionals in early childhood education and care systems. European profiles and perspectives.* Opladen & Farmington Hills: Barbara Budrich.

OECD (Organisation for Economic Co-operation and Development). (2001). *Starting strong: Early childhood education and care.* Paris: OECD.

OECD (Organisation for Economic Co-operation and Development). (2006). *Starting strong II: Early childhood education and care.* Paris: OECD.

Olsson, L. M. (2009). *Movement and experimentation in young children's learning: Deleuze and Guattari in early childhood education.* London: Routledge.

Ong, A. (2007). Neoliberalism as a mobile technology. *Transactions of the Institute of British Geographers, 32*(1), 3–8.

Pence, A., & Schafer, J. (2006). Indigenous knowledge and early childhood development in Africa: The early childhood development virtual university. *Journal for Education in International Development, 2*(3), 1–16.

Pence, A. R., & Marfo, K. (2004). Capacity-building for early childhood education in Africa. Special issue, *International Journal of Educational Policy, Research and Practice, 5*(3), 6–12.

Schön, D. A. (1987). *Educating the reflective practitioner.* San Francisco, CA: Jossey-Bass.

Schostak, J. F., & Schostak, J. (2008). *Radical research: Designing, developing and writing research to make a difference.* London: Routledge.

Stake, R. E. (2003). Case Studies. In N. K. Denzin & Y. S. Lincoln (Eds.), *Strategies of qualitative inquiry* (pp. 134–164). London: Sage.

Swilling, M., & van Breda, J. (2005). Post-graduate programme in transdiciplinarity and sustainability studies. Towards introducing transdisciplinarity at MPhil and DPhil levels. Paper delivered at the 2nd World Congress on Transdisciplinarity. Brazil.

Sylva, K., Melhuish, E., Sammons, P., Siraj-Blatchford, I., & Taggart, B. (2004). *The effective provision of preschool education (EPPE) project: Final report.* Nothingham, U.K.: Department for Education.

Tobin, J. J., Hsueh, Y., & Karasawa, M. (2009). *Preschool in three cultures revisited: China, Japan, and the United States.* Chicago, IL: University of Chicago Press.

Tobin, J. J., Wu, D. Y. H., & Davidson, D. H. (1989). *Preschool in three cultures: Japan, China, and the United States.* New Haven, CT: Yale University Press.

Turnbull, D. (2003). *Masons, tricksters and cartographers:Comparative studies in the sociology of scientific and indigenous knowledge.* London: Routledge.

UNICEF Innocenti Research Centre. (2008). *Report card 8. The child care transition. A league table of early childhood education and care in economically advanced countries.* Florence: UNICEF Innocenti Research Centre.

Urban, M. (2007, August 29–September 1). Towards a critical ecology of the profession. Systemic approaches to policies, practices and understandings of professionalism and professionalisation in early childhood. Paper presented at the European Early Childhood Education Research Association Annual Conference, Prague, Czech Republic.

Urban, M. (2008). Dealing with uncertainty: Challenges and possibilities for the early childhood profession. *European Early Childhood Education Research Journal, 16*(2), 135–152.

Urban, M., & Dalli, C. (2011). A profession speaking—and thinking—for itself. In L. Miller, C. Dalli, & M. Urban (Eds.), *Early childhood grows up: Towards a critical ecology of the profession* (pp. 157–175). Dordrecht: Springer.

Urban, M., Vandenbroeck, M., Van Laere, K., Lazzari, A., & Peeters, J. (2011). *Competence requirements in early childhood education and care. Final report.* London and Brussels: European Commission, Directorate General for Education and Culture.

Urban, M., Vandenbroeck, M., Van Laere, K., Lazzari, A., & Peeters, J. (2012). Towards competent systems in early childhood education and care: Implications for policy and practice. *European Journal of Education, 47*(4), 508–526.

Van Manen, M. (1990). *Researching lived experience: human science for an action-sensitive pedagogy.* Albany, NY: SUNY Press.

World Bank. (2003). *Lifelong learning in the global knowledge economy: Challenges for developing countries.* Washington, DC: World Bank.

Note

1. This chapter was adapted from an original paper titled "Researching Early Childhood Policy and Practice: A Critical Ecology" published in the *European Journal of Education, 47*(4).

SECTION IV

Social Action and Activism(s)

TWENTY

Critical Qualitative Research and Rethinking Academic Activism in Childhood Studies

Gaile S. Cannella

Most critical reconceptualist scholarship (from a range of fields, including scholarship in early childhood education/care/studies over the past 20 years) has not resulted in the elimination of patriarchy or intersecting forms of oppression. Systemic and institutional oppressions and perspectives that continue to support injustices, as performed upon particular individuals, groups, non-humans, knowledges/ways of being, and the environment, have intensified (Cannella & Lincoln, 2009, 2012; Ellsworth, 1989). Further, reasons for the lack of transformative impact of critical scholarship have been examined. A continued oppressive condition can be understood as embedded within backlashes against diversity (e.g., moves to discredit feminisms), reinscriptions of oppressive forms of knowledge/action (e.g., evidence-based discourse practices, movements toward exclusionary quality ratings), and the corporatization of knowledge (e.g., transformation of higher education toward profit-oriented managerial and entrepreneurial functions, curriculum profiteering). These example performances represent just a few of the technologies that have been employed to disqualify, muzzle, and make invisible critical scholarship and the public actions that can accompany that work (Cannella & Lincoln, 2012; Cannella & Miller, 2008; Lincoln & Cannella, 2004).

During the 1980s, 1990s, and early part of the 21st century, scholars from around the globe and in a range of fields attributed much of these anti-critical reinscriptions and lack of critical transformations to the increasing dominance, and globalization, of western neoliberalism—most commonly associated with capitalism that privileges free markets, profiteering, and managerial orientations (Andrews, 2006; Saltman, 2007). Poststructural, feminist, and postcolonial critiques abound. Some even refer to the condition of the most recent version of patriarchy as capitalist patriarchy. Academic theoretical work has generated perspectives that point to the transformative, rhizomatic, becoming characteristics of capitalism (Deleuze & Guattari, 1977, 1987). Scholars from a range of fields have attempted to use critical perspectives and performances for local and global actions toward social justice; yet again, the context in which we find ourselves continues to be predominantly capitalist, oppressive, disparaging, and even uses reinscribed, unthought conceptualizations and infusions of capital to perpetuate new forms of power.

The purpose of this chapter is to provide an exploratory outline for the use of critical social science, especially critical qualitative research, as an instrument for the construction of critical academic activism in early childhood studies (and other fields). I recognize that many scholars have worked as activists locally and globally for their entire careers; as critical academic forms of activism are generated, this work provides a range of possibilities for thought/action and should at all points be acknowledged. Further, the outline is not original, but rather uses ideas generated from a range of locations. I simply hope that this initial sketch will serve as either a framework for those who feel that they need a form of solid grounding for beginning critical activist scholarship, or as a position from which to construct critical lines of flight for those who would continue (and increase the transformative power of) their own critical work. I know that as a researcher who is concerned about a more just world (socially and otherwise), I continue to struggle with both positions and with how to work as a scholar in a way that is both humble and transformative. First, to acknowledge that we are never single authors (Foucault, 1977) and that our lives and work are embedded within the histories and knowledges that surround us, I provide a brief overview of critical qualitative research perspectives to this point. Second, using these multiple learnings/knowledges, I then create an outline for critical qualitative research that would embed and be embedded within, produce, and be produced by, critical academic activism. The illustrative example uses Foucault's (2003, 2008) discussions of neoliberalism as a historical and theoretical foundation, then uses his work on *The History of Sexuality* (1985, 1986) to generate possibilities for challenges to, and constructions of, academic activist subjectivities.

The reader is encouraged to use all or parts of these poststructural perspectives in her/his own constructions of research, and/or to construct a similar outline with diverse histories and ways of understanding the world as the foundation and informed knowledge base for critical qualitative research (e.g., using Black feminist thought, Chicana feminisms, histories/knowledges of Indigenous peoples, new feminist materialisms, feminist communitarian ethics, even thinking with theory, just to name a few). The work may be hybrid and emergent, but should most certainly be informed, related to issues of justice, and facilitate a condition in which the critical researcher is both intimately and ethically involved academically and performatively.

Critical Qualitative Social Science Research

To clarify without constructing a universalist definition, critical research recognizes and acknowledges power relations, analyzes the taken-for-granted to understand unjust and oppressive conditions, may attempt to illuminate hidden structures of power and/or intersecting oppressions, and is concerned with discourse practices (from language, to artifacts, to performances) that shape and limit perspectives, opportunities, inclusions, and exclusions (Cannella & Lincoln, 2009, 2012). As Popkewitz discussed more than 20 years ago, critical social science "considers the conditions of social regulation, unequal distribution, and power" (1990, p. 48). From Marxist concerns over the division of labor in capitalism, to Frankfurt School critical theory or Freirean critical pedagogy, to poststructuralism's analyses of discourse practices, to those views that often reject the label "critical" but are intimately concerned about issues of patriarchy, power, regulation, and equity like feminisms, postcolonial and subaltern, or queer theories—a massive amount of scholarly work and diverse peoples have played major roles in constructing the broad field. Additionally, because of the universalizing assumptions that are commonly associated with post-positivist and quantitative research, qualitative perspectives and methodologies of inquiry are most often associated with possibilities for critical social science.

Critical qualitative inquiry also acknowledges the role of history(ies) in contemporary social/environmental arrangements that are inequitable, is concerned with the ways that subjects of oppression come to accept that condition, is always and already aware that the practice of research is implicated in the reproduction of systems of inequitable power relations, and ultimately imagines and performs social and environmental transformation toward a more just world (Cannella & Lincoln, 2012; DeMeulenaere & Cann, 2013; Kincheloe, McLaren, & Steinberg, 2012; Steinberg & Cannella, 2012).

The early childhood studies group most involved with critical social science has been the reconceptualizing scholars who have met to share their work for the past 20 years. Early critical work tended to challenge dominant understandings and labelings of perceptions of child, development, and psychology (for examples, see Bloch, 1987; Kessler, 1991; Silin, 1987; Swadener & Lubeck, 1995). Summaries of the work, as well as the range of reconceptualist researchers, can be found in Cannella and Bailey (1999) and Grieshaber and Cannella (2001). This inquiry has been influenced by scholars from a range of locations including Walkerdine (1984), Spivak (1988), and Burman (1994, and recently 2008). Most recent work acknowledges multiplicities, diverse contexts, thinking with diverse theories, and definitely reinforces concern for justice and academic action. See Swadener, Lundy, Blancet-Cohen, and Habashi (2013), Cannella and Soto (2010), Perez and Cannella (2011), O'Loughlin and Johnson (2010), Burman (2008), Bloch, Kennedy, Lightfoot, and Weyenberg (2006), and Swadener (2000) for examples.

Challenges to dominant forms of research overall have recognized the Eurocentric, colonializing, patriarchal error (Jaimes, 1992)—the assumption that researchers have the right to and can represent the "other," and that interpretations can to some extent be accurate. Critical scholarship from this range of perspectives has been "labeled" feminist, postcolonial, and even decolonial (Viruru & Cannella, 2006) and would propose that the researcher be transformed. Further, the work has been called anti-colonial by Rau (2005) and requiring "an orientation that is radically activist and does not support a false separation between academic research and transformative actions in the contemporary world" (Cannella & Manuelito, 2008, p. 49). Voices, theories, and perspectives that have been traditionally marginalized are now considered the locations from which to generate research questions, methods, interpretations, and actions. As an example, Cannella and Manuelito (2008), using a Diné (Navajo) Changing Woman feminine organic archetype mixed consciousness (Jaimes Guerrero, 1997), related to Collins' (2008) notion of body as life force and (Chicana) mestiza mixed consciousness (Trujillo, 1998), propose that the researcher be transformed by constructing a nonviolent revolutionary consciousness (hooks, 2000):

> This anticolonial social science would no longer accept the assumptions that human beings have the ability or "right" to define, know, or judge the minds, cultures, or ways of being of others. Rather, the focus of research in such a social science would be to (a) reveal and actively challenge social systems, discourses, and institutions that are oppressive and that perpetuate injustice…and explore ways of making those systems obviously visible in society; (b) support

knowledges that have been discredited by dominant power orientations in ways that are transformative (rather than simply revealing); and (c) construct activist conceptualizations of research that are critical and multiple in ways that are transparent, reflexive, and collaborative. Some of our research practices can be transformed and/or extended; many must be eliminated. Others will emerge as we struggle together to hear, respect, and support each other and the collective environment that surrounds us all. (Cannella & Manuelito, 2008, p. 56)

Denzin and Giardina (2009) describe the contemporary radical critical position as a "third moment" (p. 21) in which dominant paradigms and normative objectivities can be subverted. Further, common research practices would be anchored in critical traditions that employ "increasingly diverse standpoints" and "the coloring of epistemologies" (p. 21). New critical scholarship and transformation actions can be based on knowledge(s)/theories/"what's happening" to lives/environments on the ground; awareness of locations in which critical social science has successfully addressed critical purposes; placing revolutionary, critical, social, and environmental work at the center; and constructing alliances and direct actions within/between academia and the public (Cannella & Lincoln, 2009, 2012).

Using this challenge to work in the third moment and a range of critical positions, I propose a set of researcher performances/components (potentially an outline) for critical qualitative academic activism. These actions would include the following: (1) explore contemporary conducts, theories, and subjectivities from marginalized locations, specifically to acknowledge and employ (a) informed, yet often unthought, explanations of the dominant, and (b) perspectives from which to transform or think/be outside the dominant (e.g., diverse knowledges, unthought perspectives, thinking with theory); (2) practice forms of ethical humility and critical subjectification in the reimagining of discourse practices (e.g., multilateral humility, becoming ethical, connected academic subjects); and (3) construct critical ways of being and acting.

Constructing Critical Qualitative Research as Academic and Public Activism

The following discussion of possible components of research as academic activism uses Foucault's work as an example of a traditionally marginalized perspective from which to interpret a contemporary condition(s) (in this case, neoliberalism), as well as Foucault's more familiar scholarship to illustrate the ways that researchers can join the struggle to transform their own subjectivities. As previously mentioned, other diverse ways of being/perspectives could also be used (e.g., Black feminist thought, Chicana feminisms, Indigenous knowledges). Diverse locations/perspectives serve as lenses and avenues from which research questions, values, and methods, even researcher subjectivies, can be generated/influenced.

1. Explore Contemporary Conducts/Subjectivities From Diverse Location/Perspective(s)

Activism, Biopolitics, and Neoliberal Shifts in Forms of Governmentality: Considering a New Foucauldian Lens. Although the work of a range of others (like Deleuze and Guattari) has been taken up to deal with our neoliberal context for a variety of reasons (including possibilities generated by the 21st-century description of the capitalist assemblage, as well as counter conducts that could be generated by notions like rhizome and lines of flight), within the past five years, scholars are also more closely examining Foucault's discussions of German, French, and American constructions of neoliberalism (a topic not often associated with Foucault). These lectures, published in the *Birth of Biopolitics* (2008), and *Society Must be Defended* (2003), and the range of scholarship emerging based on the lectures, have much to say regarding our understandings of contemporary governmentality and the forms of truth and subjectivity that produce that governmentality.

Although most of Foucault's work does not address neoliberalism, his lectures in the late 1970s (2008), do reveal his views regarding the differences between liberalism's focus on exchange (as described by Adam Smith) and neoliberalism's focus on competition. Exchange has been considered natural, while competition is understood as something that must be protected (even from the market) through state intervention. Neoliberalism is considered a massive expansion of the field of economics that interprets all human behavior as a cost – benefit calculation. The operative terms of governmentality under this condition have become entrepreneur, interest, investment, and competition rather than the classical notions of rights and laws (e.g., literally protection from the market as discussed by Foucault). Human beings are no longer partners in market exchange, but are now individuals who must invest in themselves. Neoliberal forms of governmentality consume freedom by avoiding the direct marking of bodies, but rather constructing an environment of intensification, a context in which less restriction actually leads to saturation.

A technology of the self is created, a new subject as *homo economicus* or *homo entrepreneur*. Individuals are scattered through privatization and isolation. Saturating all aspects of human functioning, neoliberalism can be thought of as capitalism without capitalism (so infused that it is no longer visible). Further, this form of governmentality silences multiplicity. Discourses are individual and market based rather than multidirectional and participatory. Foucault discusses neoliberalism as the imposition of a self-interested governmentality that ultimately silences conceptions of collective transformation and resistance; alternatives are viewed as impossible. Marketing and management have become the forces (Miller & Rose, 2008) facilitated by the state, but the entrepreneurial individual has become the subject, the driver, the natural competitor.

Entrepreneurialism: Self as Human Capital. This conceptualization of *homo economicus* as competitive creature results in a major shift in thinking and discourse practices and, especially, in human subjectivity. Human nature is conceptualized as constituted by the tendency to compete, a nature that must be fostered and protected (read as: protect the competitive nature, not the individual). This neoliberal *homo economicus* is naturally self-interested; an interpretation that explains all human activity as investment and requiring cost – benefit calculations (ranging from who one marries, to childhood government programs, and/or any other decision, program, or activity). Discourse practices (whether specific language, or even masked behaviors) redefine labor and worker as "human capital." To quote Foucault as he elaborates in the lectures: "In practice, the stake in all neo-liberal analysis is…*homo economicus* as entrepreneur of himself, being for himself his own capital, being for himself his own producer, being for himself the source of [his] earnings" (Foucault, 2008, p. 226). Terminology like "wage" (which is often more related to exchange) shifts to the language of "income," a return on investment, on one's human capital. Rather than "work" being exchanged for wages, the human being is herself/himself the embodiment of the income. Streams of income are "dependent on specific attributes of particular bodies" (Dilts, 2010, p. 5).

Epistemologically, although we are still discussing an economic interpretation of all human activity, the focus becomes the human individual rather than the market. Again, this is a major shift. While many have interpreted this as obviously depressing, some of us would insist that we must consider Foucault's interpretations of neoliberalism. This neoliberalism (especially American neoliberalism), is not an ideology that one can accept or reject, but rather performances, actions, policies, strategies, and circumstances that "create subjects of interest, locked in competition" (Read, 2009, p. 30). (Note: How many of us feel that we must function this way even though we disagree?) The individual, and all other subjects (whether firms, households, or any other contemporary assemblage), are expected to actively yield to, and engage in/with, competition and economic analysis. The entrepreneur is to govern him/herself, to rationally conduct systematic, nonrandom modifications to variables in the environment. All actions are investments. This analysis is always about human capital; other forms of human subjectivity are ignored, erased, or put forward as resolved, acknowledged, and unimportant. Workers, human beings, *homo economicus* are encouraged to see themselves, not in solidarity, but as companies of one. Capital/capitalists and workers are no longer oppositional. For *homo economicus*, entrepreneurial discourses and functionings (skills, development, achievement) are the entire way of life. Workers have become their own capital.

Education has long accepted, and supported, this neoliberal turn that makes children bundles of abilities, attributes, skills, and qualities inseparable from particular bodies either innately or through acquisition (e.g., through development, education, training, or even particular parental behaviors). *Homo economicus* as entrepreneur of self certainly reinforces the notion of children as colonized bodies (as Viruru and I have discussed, 2004), but even more complexly as entrepreneurial bodies—both as *active* economic competitive subjects, and as objects of entrepreneurialism. This neoliberal turn certainly is a form of governmentality that goes beyond ideological choice (Foucault, 2008), beyond simplistic constructions of victims of power, or even the complexities of capitalist assemblage. There is choice—there are all manner of possibilities for entrepreneurial selves—and boundless forms of schizophrenia are surely the result (Deleuze & Guattari, 1977, 1987).

2. Practice Humility in the Reimagining of Discourses: Becoming the Ethical Self

Acknowledgement of, and concerns about, the neoliberal entrepreneurial self as contemporary capital draws further attention to the subjectivity that is constructed through less obvious individual investment notions like the "good researcher," the "academic activist," the "transformative intellectual," or to discourses that construct individual performative states like obligations for citizens to be free and responsible as discussed by Rose (1999). In earlier work, Foucault proposed disciplinary practices like the "political technologies of individuals" (1985, p. 87), self-governing subjectivities (like the good researcher) that no longer require public policing because controlling mentalities have become so internalized. These technologies can be intimately related to the self as entrepreneur, and/or interconnected ways of being that have facilitated the neoliberal shift in governmentality. Locked within an individualistic, capitalist entrepreneurial world, researchers must continually inquire within themselves addressing issues like:

- How do we avoid political technologies of the individual and continue to be research-ers who must often perform as individuals?
- How do we avoid becoming the entrepreneurial activist? Are there counter conducts that can avoid entrepreneurial reinscription (Cannella & Lincoln, 2007; Cannella & Viruru, 2004; Demas, 2003)?
- Can we avoid becoming the "benevolent" (white, or male, or western, or privileged, or educated) "hand" that would save the world (Escobar, 1995, p. 193)?
- How do we reconceptualize research and ourselves at a time in which research will continue to be practiced whether we reject it as power-oriented or not?

Avoiding entrepreneurial inscription does not necessarily mean rejecting all that is individual; the neoliberal condition may even be a circumstance in which new forms of unthought sub-jectivities are crucial. Further, agreeing with Deleuze and Guattari (1987), Foucault (1985) reminds the reader that we must struggle with the fascist power orientations within us. Some scholars have even interpreted Foucault's work on the history of sexuality (1985, 1986) as incor-porating the neoliberal attention to the subject. Hamann (2009) proposes that Foucault's work potentially serves the aim of producing free, active, entrepreneurial individuals who would cultivate themselves, stating "Foucault actually provides a kind of technical support manual for the neoliberal agenda of recoding society and its subjects" (p. 48). However, Foucault does not accept the simplistic assumptions embedded within the neoliberal notion of human capital, that freedom is simply development of and investment in "self" in an environment of choice. Rather, Foucault transforms and disqualifies the neoliberal subjectification of the self as he turns to one's relationship with oneself. This relationship "is not simply 'self-awareness' but self-formation as an 'ethical subject,' a process in which the individual delimits that part of him(her)self that will form the object of his/her moral practices" (Foucault, 1985, p. 28). Further, Foucault used this becoming of the ethical subject in constructing notions like tacti-cal reversal and aesthetics of existence as forms of resistance (Dilts, 2010; Thompson, 2003).

Just as there is no universal moral code, which as a construct would actually be catastrophic (Foucault, 1985), there would be no one universal ethical subject or form of subjectivity. How-ever, the critical ethical subject would at least consider the avoidance of self-absorption, even struggling continuously with the development of multiple forms of humility. Acknowledging that research, writing, and publishing are *not* acts of humility, the struggling ethical self would continue to engage with the complex intersections between informed knowledge construction and the arrogance of educational elitisms. Concerned with the complexities and multiplicities of becoming the ethical self, Foucault proposes a genealogy of the self that includes examina-tion of one's ethical axis, or the components of self as a moral agent. Potential elements of the ethical axis are: *ethical substance*, moral constitution of the researcher self; *mode of subjectifica-tion*, self-establishment related to contemporary dominant rules; *ethical work*, methods chosen or constructed for ethical transformation; and *telos*, disassembly and transformation of self toward practices of research that reject/refuse power over others (Cannella & Lincoln, 2007; Foucault, 1985; Lincoln & Cannella, 2007; Rabinow, 1994).

Ethical Substance. Foucault describes the ethical substance of the self as the will to truth, or "that which enables one to get free from oneself" (Foucault, 1985, p. 9). This substance is different for different individuals. As examples: For some, conceptualizations of social justice may be the ethical substance; for others, Christian concepts of a higher power. For some, belief in science, logic, and progress; for others, belief in the power of diversity. For some, universal forms of spirituality—and, on and on. Questions for the critical researcher can be:

- What part of me is concerned with moral/ethical conduct, and how is that played out in my behavior as an academic researcher activist?
- Does the conceptualization and practice of research contribute to the constitution of a particular ethical substance (Cannella & Lincoln, 2007, p. 324)? Is that substance consistent with critical perspectives?

Mode of Subjectification. In his discussions of rules and obligations (as imposed by ethical substance), Foucault tends to accept the idea that regulation results in subjectification. For example, Kant's focus on the obligation to "know" produced, and was produced by, an ethical mode of subjectification that required reason for self-governance. Analysis of one's mode of subjectification requires that the "self" engage with itself as Other, asking historical and critical questions concerning disposition:

- What rules are subsumed within my ethical substance (e.g., for individual selves as researchers; within particular conceptualizations of research)?
- How are these rules acted on in research activities?
- Are there individuals/groups who are privileged/harmed as particular ethical modes of subjectification are implemented in the conduct of research (Cannella & Lincoln, 2007)? How do my ethical modes influence/impact others?

Ethical Work. For Foucault (1986), self-forming, ethical actions that literally transform the self are considered ethical work. Historical examination of the constitution of oneself that critically involves "the possibility of no longer being, doing, or thinking what we are, do, or think" is necessary (p. 27). Some refer to this as turning the world upside down, challenging all of one's beliefs, or removing the foundation upon which one stands. The ethical work is to learn how to challenge and question self, and then invent new ways of thinking, being, acting, and forming relationships. Example questions include:

- How would the ethical paths not taken in my research be envisioned?
- What new modes of ethical relations do I invent within the practices of my research (Cannella & Lincoln, 2007, p. 325)?

Telos. Telos involves committed and long-term, yet flexible and emergent, actions and movement toward the becoming of an ethical self/researcher. A form of self-bricolage is practiced for the purpose of thinking differently rather than legitimating the known. The critical scholar explores ways of assembling self as an ethical researcher (Foucault, 1994), asking (and taking actions related to) questions like:

- How is my ethical being reflected in the conceptualizations of research that I choose and practice?
- What are the patterns of conduct performed by my ethical self (e.g., questions chosen, inclusions/exclusions, forms of contextual/historical recognition, methodological performances, daily practices) (Cannella & Lincoln, 2007, p. 326)?
- Can we cultivate ourselves as those who can desire and inhabit unthought spaces regarding research (about childhood, diverse views of the world; Lincoln & Cannella, 2007, 2009)?

3. Construct Critical Academic Research as Ways of Being/Acting

Even critical scholars disagree as to whether transformative activism is possible through research and publication (perhaps a critical transformative academic activism in some cases), or if direct community work on the ground—in homes, on the streets, working with legislatures, or engaging directly in schools and other institutions—is necessary for transformative activism (DeMeulenaere & Cann, 2013). Critical researchers must decide this for themselves; the actions may vary dependent on the issue, the type of academic work that is conceptualized, and even individual scholar strengths.

However, most could likely agree that within neoliberal conditions, constructions of ethical counter-colonial alliances/performances are critical actions that should be taken. A range of scholars have provided us with maps that can facilitate this ethical turn including Tuhiwai Smith (1999) and Maori collective ethics; Ritchie and Rau (2010), who propose an ethics of alterity that shifts the researcher focus from "us" or "them" to the collective "we", and Glesne (2007), who proposes that the purpose of research should be solidarity. "If you want to research us, you can go home. If you have come to accompany us, if you think our struggle is also your struggle, we have plenty of things to talk about" (p. 171). Using the work of Spivak, Fanon, Foucault, and Butler, Alessandrini (2009) even calls for an ethics without subjects, an ethics of relationships that acknowledges the aftermath of colonialism. Drawing upon all of this work, and emphasizing the work of Ritchie and Rau (2010), Yvonna Lincoln and I have proposed critical academic actions/activism that would include, at least, the following:

- Expose the diversity of realities;
- Engage directly with webs of oppression;
- Reposition problems and decisions toward social justice; and
- Join in solidarity to create new ways of functioning. (Cannella & Lincoln, 2011)

Minimally, actions require identification and physical engagement with females, people of color, and other groups that have been traditionally disqualified, as well as unthought and marginalized theoretical perspectives and knowledges (Cannella & Manuelito, 2008; hooks, 2000; Kincheloe, 2008). Researcher bodies can no longer be docile, but must perform whatever actions necessary to move scholarly work one (or more) step(s) farther toward justice (either social or environmental, or both). Finally, while taking action, researchers must struggle to avoid technical substitutions and sophisticated reinscriptions, complex inclusions into the dominant (Charkiewicz, 2007). As illustrated by the title of the book *The Revolution Will Not Be Funded: Beyond the Non-Profit Industrial Complex*

(INCITE, 2007), old forms of oppression are often recreated through progressive, contemporary forms of activism. The forming of ethical alliances and actions within diverse forms of solidarity also requires continued flexibility and openness, but also always/already a critical and humble disposition.

Considering the Critical Research Outline

For those who would hope to construct critical research and actions that would attempt to both systemically and incidentally move toward social and environmental justice, I have attempted to outline possibilities. Please note that this is a humble attempt that should always be viewed as emergent and flexible, and certainly not a truth. The components have included: (1) Exploring contemporary conducts and subjectivities from diverse location(s)/perspective(s). The illustrative perspective used here is Foucault's work on neoliberalism and the construction of entrepreneurial subjectivities. A range of other unthought, or traditionally marginalized theories, knowledges, and perspectives (e.g., Black feminist thought; feminist new materialisms; see Perez & Cannella, 2011 for example using Black feminist thought) could be chosen dependent on the needs and alliances constructed by the researcher(s). (2) In the "becoming" of the ethical critical self, practicing humility in the reimagining of discourses and actions. Since Foucault's work can also be used related to the ethical self, notions of ethical substance, mode of subjectification, ethical work, and telos were discussed here as researcher practices. These or other forms of subjectification as related to the perspective chosen by a particular researcher could be used separately or combined. (3) Construct critical academic research as ways of being/acting. As Glesne expresses (2007), perhaps the purpose of research should be solidarity, to learn to struggle and take actions with all who would increase social and environmental justice. There are no sets of actions or outlines that we can follow to ensure transformations; but we can make every effort to join together to be hopefully, honestly, and humbly connected and allied in the struggle.

References

Alessandrini, A. C. (2009). The humanism effect: Fanon, Foucault, and ethics without subjects. *Foucault Studies, 7*, 64–80.

Andrews, J. G. (2006). How we can resist corporatization? *Academe, 92*(3), 16–19.

Bloch, M. N. (1987). Becoming scientific and professional: An historical perspective on the aims and effects of early education. In T. S. Popkewitz (Ed.), *The formation of school subjects* (pp. 25–62). Basingstoke, U.K.: Falmer.

Bloch, M. N., Kennedy, D., Lightfoot, T., & Weyenberg, D. (Eds.). (2006). *The child in the world/the world in the child: Education and the configuration of a universal, modern, and globalized childhood.* New York: Palgrave.

Burman, E. (1994). *Deconstructing developmental psychology.* New York: Routledge.

Burman, E. (2008). *Developments: Child, image, nation.* New York: Routledge.

Cannella, G. S., & Bailey, C. (1999). Postmodern research in early childhood education. In S. Reifel (Ed.), *Advances in early education and day care* (Vol. 10; pp. 3–39). Greenwich, CT: Jai Press.

Cannella, G. S., & Lincoln, Y. S. (2007). Predatory vs. dialogic ethics: Constructing an illusion, or ethical practice as the core of research methods. *Qualitative Inquiry, 13*(3), 315–335.

Cannella G. S., & Lincoln, Y. S. (2009). Deploying qualitative methods for critical social purposes. In N. K. Denzin & M. D. Giardina (Eds.), *Qualitative inquiry and social justice* (pp. 53–72). Walnut Creek, CA: Left Coast Press.

Cannella, G. S., & Lincoln, Y. S. (2011). Ethics, research regulations, and critical social science. In N. K. Denzin & Y. S. Lincoln (Eds.), *The Sage handbook of qualitative research* (4th ed.; pp. 81–90). Thousand Oaks, CA: Sage.

Cannella, G. S., & Lincoln, Y. (2012). Deploying qualitative methods for critical social purposes. In S. R., Steinberg & G. S. Cannella (Eds.), *Critical qualitative research reader* (pp. 104–114). New York: Peter Lang.

Cannella, G. S., & Manuelito, K. (2008). Feminisms from unthought locations: Indigenous worldviews, marginalized feminisms, and revisioning an anticolonial social science. In N. K. Denzin, Y. S. Lincoln, & L. T. Smith (Eds.), *Handbook of critical and indigenous methodologies* (pp. 45–59). Thousand Oaks, CA: Sage.

Cannella, G. S., & Miller, L. L. (2008). Constructing corporatist science: Reconstituting the soul of American higher education. *Cultural Studies <=> Critical Methodologies, 8*(1), 24–38.

Cannella, G. S., & Soto, L. D. (2010). *Childhoods: A handbook*. New York: Peter Lang.

Cannella, G. S., & Viruru, R. (2004). *Childhood and postcolonization: Power, education, and contemporary practice*. New York: RoutledgeFalmer.

Charkiewicz, E. (2007). *Beyond good and evil: Notes on global feminist advocacy*. Women in Action. Retrieved from http://www.isiswomen.org/index.php?option=com_content&view=article&id=517:be

Collins, P. H. (2008). *Black feminist thought: Knowledge, consciousness, and the politics of empowerment* (2nd ed.). New York: Routledge.

Deleuze, G., & Guattari, F. (1977). *Anti-Oedipus: Capitalism and schizophrenia*, trans. R. Hurley, M. Seem, & H. R. Lane. New York: Penguin Group.

Deleuze, G., & Guattari, F. (1987). *A thousand plateaus: Capitalism and schizophrenia*, trans. B. Massumi. Minneapolis: University of Minnesota Press.

Demas, E. (2003). *Critical issues*. Unpublished manuscript, Texas A&M University, College Station.

DeMeulenaere, E. J., & Cann, C. N. (2013, October). Activist educational research. *Qualitative Inquiry, 19*(8). Advanced print online: http://qix.sagepub.com/content/early/2013/07/05/1077800413494343

Denzin, N. K., & Giardina, M. D. (2009). Qualitative inquiry and social justice: Toward a politics of hope. In N. K. Denzin & M. D. Giardina (Eds.), *Qualitative inquiry and social justice* (pp. 11–50). Walnut Creek, CA: Left Coast Press.

Dilts, A. (2010). *From 'entrepreneur of the self' to 'care of the self': Neoliberal governmentality and Foucault's ethics*. Chicago, IL: Western Political Science Association 2010 Annual Meeting.

Ellsworth, E. (1989). Why doesn't this feel empowering? Working with the repressive myths of critical pedagogy. *Harvard Educational Review, 59*(3), 297–324.

Escobar, A. (1995). *Encountering development: The making and unmaking of the third world*. Princeton, NJ: Princeton University Press.

Foucault, M. (1977). What is an author? In D. F. Bouchard (Ed.), *Language, counter-memory, practice: Selected essays and interviews by Michel Foucault*, trans. D. F. Bouchard & S. Simon (pp. 113–138). Ithaca, NY: Cornell University Press.

Foucault, M. (1985). *The history of sexuality, Vol. 2: The use of pleasure*, trans. R. Hurley. New York: Vintage Books.

Foucault, M. (1986). *The history of sexuality, Vol. 3: The care of the self*, trans. R. Hurley. New York: Vintage Books.

Foucault, M. (1994). On the genealogy of ethics: An overview of work in progress. In P. Rabinow (Ed.), *Michel Foucault: Ethics, subjectivity, and truth, 1954–1984* (Vol. 1; pp. 253–280). New York: New York Press.

Foucault, M. (2003). *Society must be defended: Lectures at the College de France, 1975–1976*, trans. D. Macy. New York: Picador.

Foucault, M. (2008). *The birth of biopolitics: Lectures at the College de France, 1978–1979*. Translated by Graham Burchell. New York: Picador.

Glesne, C. (2007). Research as solidarity. In N. K. Denzin & M. D. Giardina (Eds.), *Ethical futures in qualitative research: Decolonizing the politics of knowledge* (pp. 169–178). Walnut Creek, CA: Left Coast Press.

Grieshaber, S., & Cannella, G. S. (Eds.). (2001). *Embracing identities in early childhood education: Diversity and possibilities*. New York: Teachers College Press.

Hamann, T. (2009). Neoliberalism, governmentality, and ethics. *Foucault Studies, 6*, 37–59.

hooks, b. (2000). *Feminism is for everybody: Passionate politics*. Cambridge, MA: South End.

INCITE! Women of Color Against Violence (Eds.). (2009). *The revolution will not be funded: Beyond the non-profit industrial complex*. Cambridge, MA: South End Press.

Jaimes, M. A. (1992). La raza and indigenism: Alternatives to autogenocide in North America. *Global Justice, 3*, 4–19.

Jaimes Guerrero, M. A. (1997). Civil rights versus sovereignty: Native American women in life and land struggles. In M. J. Alexander & C. T. Mohanty (Eds.), *Feminist genealogies, colonial legacies, democratic futures* (pp. 101–121). New York: Routledge.

Kessler, S. (1991). Alternative perspectives on early childhood education. *Early Childhood Research Quarterly, 6*(2), 183–197.

Kincheloe, J. L. (2008). Critical pedagogy and the knowledge wars of the twenty-first century. *International Journal of Critical Pedagogy, 1*(1), 1–22.

Kincheloe, J. L., McLaren, P., & Steinberg, S. R. (2012). Critical pedagogy and qualitative research: Moving to the bricolage. In S. R. Steinberg & G. S. Cannella (Eds.), *Critical qualitative research reader* (pp. 14–32). New York: Peter Lang.

Lincoln, Y. S., & Cannella, G. S. (2004). Qualitative research, power, and the radical right. *Qualitative Inquiry, 10*(2), 175–201.

Lincoln, Y. S., & Cannella, G. S. (2007). Ethics and the broader rethinking/reconceptualization of research as construct. In N. K. Denzin & M. D. Giardina (Eds.), *Ethical futures in qualitative research: Decolonizing the politics of knowledge* (pp. 67–84). Walnut Creek, CA: Left Coast Press.

Lincoln, Y. S., & Cannella, G. S. (2009). Ethics and the broader rethinking/reconceptualization of research as a construct. *Cultural Studies <=> Critical Methodologies, 9*(2), 273–285.

Miller, P., & Rose, N. (2008). *Governing the present: Administering economic, personal and social life.* Cambridge: Polity Press.

O'Loughlin, M., & Johnson, R. T. (Eds.). (2010). *Imagining children otherwise: Theoretical and critical perspectives on childhood subjectivity.* New York: Peter Lang.

Perez, M. S., & Cannella, G. S. (2011). Disaster capitalism as neoliberal instrument for the construction of early childhood education/care policy: Charter schools in post-Katrina New Orleans. *International Critical Childhood Policy Studies, 4*(1), 47–68.

Popkewitz, T. (1990). Whose future? Whose past? Notes on critical theory and methodology. In E. G. Guba (Ed.), *The paradigm dialog,* (pp. 46–66). Newbury Park, CA: Sage.

Rabinow, P. (1994). *Michel Foucault: Ethics, subjectivity, and truth, 1954–1984* (Vol. 1). New York: New York Press.

Rau, C. (2005, October). Indigenous metaphors of the heart: Transformative praxis in early childhood education in Aotearoa, privileging Maori women's educator's voices. Presented at the 13th International Conference on Reconceptualizing Early Childhood Education: Research, theory, and practice, Madison, WI.

Read, J. (2009). A genealogy of homo-economicus: Neoliberalism and the production of subjectivity. *Foucault Studies, 6,* 25–36.

Ritchie, J., & Rau, C. (2010). Kia mau kit e wairuatanga: Counter narratives of early childhood education in Aotearoa. In G. S. Cannella & L. D. Soto (Eds.), *Childhoods: A handbook* (pp. 355–373). New York: Peter Lang.

Rose, N. (1999). *Powers of freedom: Reframing political thought.* Cambridge, U.K.: Cambridge University Press.

Saltman, K. (2007). *Capitalizing on disaster: Breaking and taking public schools.* Boulder, CO: Paradigm.

Silin, J. (1987). The early childhood educator's knowledge base: A reconsideration. In L. G. Katz (Ed.), *Current topics in early childhood education* (pp. 17–31). Norwood, NJ: Ablex.

Smith, L. T. (1999). *Decolonizing methodologies: Research and indigenous peoples.* London: Zed Books.

Spivak, G. (1988). Can the subaltern speak? In C. Nelson & L. Grossberg (Eds.), *Marxism and the interpretation of culture* (pp. 271–313). Urbana: University of Illinois Press.

Steinberg, S. R., & Cannella, G. S. (Eds.). (2012). *Critical qualitative research reader.* New York: Peter Lang.

Swadener, B. B. (2000). *Does the village still raise the child? A collaborative study of changing child-rearing and early education in Kenya.* New York: SUNY Press.

Swadener, B., & Lubeck, S. (Eds.). (1995). *Children and families at promise: Deconstructing the discourse of risk.* Albany, NY: SUNY Press.

Swadener, B. B., Lundy, Blanchet-Cohen, & Habashi, J. (Eds.). (2013). *Children's rights and education: International perspectives.* New York: Peter Lang.

Thompson, K. (2003). Forms of resistance: Foucault on "tactical reversal and self-formation." *Continental Philosophy Review, 36,* 113–138.

Trujillo, C. (Ed.). (1998). *Living Chicana theory.* Berkeley, CA: Third Woman Press.

Viruru, R., & Cannella, G. S. (2006). A postcolonial critique of the ethnographic interview: Research analyzes research. In N. K. Denzin & M. D. Giardina (Eds.), *Qualitative inquiry and the conservative challenge* (pp. 175–192). Walnut Creek, CA: Left Coast Press.

Walkerdine, V. (1984). Developmental psychology and the child-centered pedagogy. In J. Henriques, W. Hollway, C. Urwin, C. Venn, & V. Walkerdine (Eds.), *Changing the subject: Psychology, social regulation and subjectivity* (pp. 153–202). London: Methuen.

TWENTY-ONE

None for You: Children's Capabilities and Rights in Profoundly Unequal Times

Valerie Polakow

As I look back at the past 30 years during which progressive early childhood educators, critical reconceptualists, advocates, and allies have attempted to reframe early childhood policies and practices, several moments stand out. There has been a critical interrogation of the bureaucratization of childhood, of at-risk deficit categories, of developmentally appropriate practice, of voice and agency, of race and gender, of working conditions of child care workers, of deconstructing and decolonizing discourses of care, and, more recently, of neoliberalism and its impacts—all have engendered prolific forms of scholarship. Yet the crisis of child poverty that reemerged during the Reagan years in the 1980s, and the intersectionality of child poverty and the acute deficit of child care have not been urgent priority agendas addressed by activists and critical scholars. More recently, deconstructing neoliberal power regimes, the corporatization of accountability, the emphasis on standardized testing, and the impact of privatization and deregulation on early education and schooling have gained far more traction as is evidenced by the vast array of publications and presentations on these topics.

Clearly theoretical critiques are important as are analyses that unpack the deleterious impacts of neoliberalism's reach; but placed within the context of appalling child poverty that encompasses more than 40% of our children in the United States, we need to question misplaced priorities and the role of scholar-activists. There is a puzzling silence about poverty; yet, arguably, child poverty is *the* crisis of our times and demands redress. It is the neurobiologists and pediatricians, such as Jack Shonkoff at Harvard's Center for the Developing Child, who have raised alarm bells, but these bells are rung from different medical and policy terrains. To what extent has the critical left normalized child poverty through silence and inattention to one of the most fundamental human rights violations in the United States?

This chapter examines how poverty is played out in the micro-worlds of impoverished children in the United States. Child poverty is analyzed both as *the* existential and *the* policy crisis of our times, and as a violation of human capabilities and human rights. For young children, poverty and the politics of care create a tangle of inequalities with far-reaching physical and psycho-social consequences. What does it mean to be a poor child in the second decade of the 21st century in the United States? How do we see children whose lifeworlds are bounded by poverty, inequality, and social and educational exclusion?

Prisms of Poverty

Material Income-Based Poverty and Instrumentalism

When we analyze poverty from a narrow income inequality perspective, the results are alarming. While children account for 24% of the U.S. population, they represent 34% of all poor people with over 16.1 million children (22%) living in poverty and 32.4 million children (45%) in low-income households.[1] The United States uses an artificially low poverty threshold based on an outdated formula developed by Mollie Orshansky in the 1960s during Johnson's war on poverty (Addy, Engelhardt, & Skinner, 2013; Katz, 1989). This poverty threshold has been critiqued as inadequate and various alternative measures have been proposed. Both the Economic Policy Institute (EPI) and the National Center for Children in Poverty (NCCP) use a Family Budget Needs Calculator (Bernstein & Lin, 2008; see also www.nccp.org/tools/frs/budget.php) that calculates minimum daily necessities by region—housing, food, health, child care, transportation, and other costs. Moreover, NCCP also calculates the number of low-income children living in households below 200% of the FPL (see Cauthen & Fass, 2008). This income threshold closely approximates the international calculation of relative poverty (calculation of half of the national median income). If we used the international standard, almost half of children in the U.S. would be classified as living in poverty.

The international *Innocenti Report Card 9* on inequality and child well-being ranked the United States last among all 24 OECD industrialized countries in overall inequality and 23rd in material well-being of children, and in highlighting "bottom-end inequality" argued that "protecting children during their vital, vulnerable years of growth is both the mark of a civilized society and the means of building a better future" (UNICEF, 2010, p. 1). The most recent 2013 *Report Card 11* is even worse, ranking the U.S. 26th of 29 countries in material child well-being, below Slovakia, and trailed only by Lithuania, Latvia, and Romania. Furthermore, in terms of relative child poverty, the U.S. ranks second to last behind Romania, one of the poorest countries in the European Union (UNICEF, 2013).

The severe recession of the last four years with its epidemic of mortgage foreclosures triggered by predatory lending to vulnerable buyers has created a further class of dispossessed families, who, in an age of austerity and severe budget cuts in the states, have lost their homes and their communities. Children have been displaced from their schools and neighborhoods, and loss of a home frequently means loss of the familiar—school, friends, neighborhood, and those social spaces that hold symbolic meaning and identity. Widespread food insecurity has ensued (Child Hunger Facts, n.d.), although food stamps under the SNAP program remain one of the last vestiges of a frayed social safety net. Eviscerating the welfare state has been a very visible thrust of the right-wing political agenda led by the Tea Party and slavishly followed by conservative Republican legislators in Congress and in the state legislatures. Welfare assistance, Medicaid, and social and educational spending have all been cut to trim deficits in state budgets amid a national clamor to erode the role of government. At the time of writing, hundreds of thousands of poor families will be harmed by the refusal of half of the states to expand Medicaid as part of the Affordable Care Act (Pear, 2013). Deregulation, privatization, and the shrinking of public entitlements always hits children the hardest, creating multiple "circuits of dispossession" (Fine, Stoudt, Fox, & Santos, 2010, p. 30).

Such politics of distribution lead to targeted human costs that disproportionately affect children as part of the collateral damage of the war on the poor. While welfare cuts to poor families, particularly single mothers, are heralded in the language of personal responsibility, standing in the shadows behind every poor single mother are young children who experience the developmentally damaging effects of severe poverty that serves as a toxic stressor in early childhood, producing damage to social-emotional, cognitive, and physiological health (National Scientific Council on the Developing Child, 2005).

When investments in young children are discussed as a part of political discourse, it is always in a language of instrumentalism—is it less costly to spend money now or to pay later? Nobel economist James Heckman is a prime exponent of the "invest now, or pay later" cost – benefit discourse and he is widely cited by policymakers and advocates for making a convincing economic argument for why money should be targeted to early childhood (Heckman, 2006, 2008; Heckman & Masterov, 2007) and the Heckman equation, "Invest, Develop, Sustain, Gain" disseminates the evidence on his website (www.heckmanequation.org/ heckman-equation). Frequently model programs like the High/Scope Perry Preschool with its 40-year longitudinal positive outcomes is cited as yielding economic returns of $12.90 per every dollar invested (Schweinhart, 2004). While there is ample evidence to substantiate the claims that good early intervention programs do point to developmentally healthier outcomes when young children in poverty receive high-quality early education (Peisner-Feinberg et al., 1999), none of this is premised on the rights and well-being of the child. It is clear that from a human capital investment perspective, it makes good-sense to invest in the education and early care of children, in order to lay the foundations for future economic productivity, but the inherent rights of the child to be free from poverty and to experience developmentally enriching childcare is not part of the discourse in the United States.

Child Poverty: Capabilities and Rights

In the European social policy debates, child poverty has been shaped by a children's rights framework and human capability theories as well as the growing sociological and social welfare literature on child well-being and social exclusion, which has also filtered through to the international human development arena. Sen's work on human capabilities (1981, 1989, 1999) changed the paradigm for mapping human development across the globe. Advocating for a multidimensional view of poverty, that takes participants' own perspectives and agency into account, Sen has argued that the metric of income poverty is a reductionistic frame. Although increasing resources is vital for economic sustainability in poor households, resources are insufficient to combat the non-material effects of poverty such as stigmatization, social isolation, and exclusion. Hence, while poverty is a deprivation of means, it is agency and choice that are central to developing human capabilities. Sen defines capability as the opportunity for individuals "to do and to be" with the autonomy and freedom to choose and act on behalf of what they value (see Alkire, 2009). In advocating for the global importance of incorporating stakeholder perspectives about their own experiences of poverty into international human development work, Sen points out that poverty results in "capability failure" when human functioning is derailed by poverty, famine, war, violence, and other obstructions to the living of sustainable lives; and it is ultimately agency and capability that comprise human freedom and the capacity to live a life of dignity.

Nussbaum (2000, 2011) in elaborating on Sen's capability approach and anchoring it within a social justice framework, also argues that "the key question to ask when comparing societies and assessing them for their basic decency and justice is, 'what is each person able to do and to be?'"(2011, p. 18). The failure of human capabilities occurs when individuals experience discrimination, exclusion, and marginalization—where capabilities are truncated and individuals cannot exercise choice nor make autonomous decisions. Nussbaum argues that there is a minimum social threshold below which governments cannot permit their citizens to fall. Hence, for individuals to realize their internal capabilities, governments must provide fundamental resources that support families and provide infrastructures that support human development such as education. Internal capabilities can only be realized in interaction with social, political, and economic conditions that create the possibility for the exercise of "combined" capabilities.

The body of work produced by Sen and Nussbaum is significant when we analyze child poverty. Neither theorist explicitly focuses on child poverty, but their work is aligned with a human rights framework and transfers directly to the key principles of the Convention on the Rights of the Child (CRC) in terms of children's voice and participation. Furthermore, the explicit rights accorded to children all speak to the affirmation and facilitation of children's human capabilities: children's economic, social, and cultural rights (Articles 4, 26); the establishment of institutions, facilities, and social programs for the support of children, and the right to child care (Article 18); rights and access to services for all children with special needs (Article 23); access to quality health care (Article 24); the right to a standard of living adequate for the child's development (Article 27); and equality of opportunity in education and the development of the child's fullest potential (Articles 28, 29) (Convention on the Rights of the Child, 1989).

Heather's Story: Disrupted Capabilities and Violated Rights

Many years ago, when conducting ethnographic research in classrooms, I observed a young, tearful, 7-year-old child sitting at a desk in the hallway in an elementary school. Heather was not allowed to participate in classroom activities and had been banished from her classroom for "stealing" free lunch on a Friday from the cafeteria. As I entered the school, several children pointed at Heather telling me that they were not allowed to speak to her because she had been "bad," nor was she allowed to speak to anyone. While more than 20 years have passed since I witnessed this punitive exclusion, I have never forgotten Heather. She was the older child of a teen mother, and together with her younger sister, was living in a trailer with no electricity in a very fragile household facing eviction from the trailer park for unpaid rent. She "stole" the extra lunch on a Friday, telling me later that her little sister liked the lunch cookie and she anticipated that there would be a shortage of food over the weekend.

During the following weeks, Heather's isolation in her second-grade classroom increased. She was consistently excluded from participation by her teacher, Mrs. Mack, and marginalized by her classmates. On a scheduled field trip day, because she did not have $4 for a rock and mineral collection, she was given other busy work to do and was unable to accompany her classmates on the field trip. She was in tears the day her teacher left her alone with an aide, but she also understood how isolated she was, telling me "Mrs. Mack always picks on me and I hate her.... I hate this school and I don't got no friends here"(Polakow, 1993, p. 140).

From a capabilities framework, Heather's basic human functioning was obstructed by poverty, intermittent hunger, and tenuous shelter, and her human capabilities were thwarted as she confronted social, economic, and educational conditions that created searing forms of social exclusion. She was isolated from her classmates, denied the equal opportunity to learn in her classroom, and subjected to stigmatization and humiliation. She was also excluded from field trips and other activities as she could not produce the currency that permitted participation. On all counts Heather suffered extreme forms of discrimination and exclusion. Her rights to an education with respect and dignity were violated. Yet in the face of this, Heather, a little girl who carried a backpack of burdens on her back, demonstrated remarkable agency. Not only did she actively strategize to increase the household food supply, but she also figured out how best to accumulate that as she took left-over food for her hungry family. She was punished by exclusion and social isolation, but actively resisted with her own counter-text of "I hate this school."

When the school operates as a site of shaming and exclusion, other forms of poverty become very apparent—the poverty of exclusion and isolation. Jones and Sumner (2011), who have analyzed child poverty in relation to children's rights, outline a Three-Dimensional Well-Being approach that is part of a rights-based understanding of child poverty in contrast to the more traditional income-based metric. Such 3-D mapping of child well-being encompasses the material, the relational, and the subjective dimensions of a child's lifeworld. While the material relates to income poverty and the basic human correlates of survival—what Maslow (1962) termed basic physiological and safety needs—it is the relational and the subjective that begin to take account of children's meaning-making, their social networks, their participation in their community and school, and how they experience their lifeworlds with agency and voice. If we consider Heather's situation from a 3-D well-being framework, we can see how the relational and subjective dimensions of her world were harshly circumscribed and the overriding experience of shaming caused her to hate her school and feel isolated.

Redmond, in reviewing several international qualitative studies of low-income children's agency and participation, comments on the power of schools to function as agents of inclusion or exclusion, and how children who feel stigmatized and isolated suffer from the "profoundly social costs of children's poverty" where "it is usually not poverty per se that hurts but the social exclusion that accompanies it" (2008, p. 4). Yet, the ways in which children cope with their daily lives of poverty and hardship, and how, when, and why they assume active rather than passive roles in strategically marshaling resources, has been under-researched both in terms of children's rights and human capability frameworks. Neither Sen nor Nussbaum explicitly discuss children in their capability theories, and in the poverty policy literature, children are typically constructed as household members, and passive recipients of support or stigma. Yet in Heather's case, she became an agent of the family, attempting to exert, in Nussbaum's words, "the fundamental functions of a human life" (2000, p. 1) in her construction of necessity and a plan of action.

There are other questions that arise when one considers the emblematic case of a hungry young child. What is the role of the adults in the school environment—the teacher, the social worker, the principal—in attending to Heather's fundamental safety and security, as well as her educational and social-emotional needs? No school personnel mediated Heather's harsh lived realities nor attempted to support her development and learning. Rather she was a condemned and targeted child—a thief—experiencing a public shaming as she sat at her desk in the hallway.

School Exclusion and Silenced Voices

Schools are powerful loci for exclusion and "othering" of poor children, children of color, and children with disabilities. In many schools, children and youth exist in circumscribed rule-governed hierarchical social spaces. Children have very few rights in relation to power and agency, and in the educational at-risk literature, those who are noncompliant are usually constructed as problem kids to be silenced, socialized, and placed under surveillance and subjected to various forms of disciplinary technology. Expressing one's views is often characterized as "talking back" and insubordination. Robbins points out how zero-tolerance disciplinary policies have led to militarized schools with surveillance technologies that severely limit "the future social, political, and economic viability of youth, especially youth of color" (2008, p. 12). Zweifler and De Beers (2002) argue that the school lives of poor school-age children and youth of color are characterized by high drop-out rates, low graduation rates, disproportionate expulsions, and unmet special education needs. The American Civil Liberties Union (ACLU; 2008) reports that violations of due process, racial disproportionality in suspensions and expulsions, and the increasing criminalization of student infractions "reflects the prioritization of incarceration over education" as long-term suspensions and expulsion cast hundreds of thousands of youth into the streets, and in many school districts, there are few viable alternative education programs. The exclusion trajectory from suspension and expulsion to incarceration has created a school-to-prison pipeline that has been documented across the states with disproportionate impacts on impoverished youth and youth of color where "denying access to education can produce life-altering results … [that] are often especially dire" (Georgetown Law Human Rights Institute, 2012, p. 7). Social and educational exclusion by schools has set in motion a youth incarceration industry and is an alarming anomaly that has been met with widespread acceptance and indifference by educators as children's educational rights are eroded.

Stories of Adolescent Exclusion: Obstructed Capabilities and Violated Rights
In interviews with low-income students in Michigan who had been suspended and expelled, the students, who were predominantly African American, spoke about the silencing of their voices, their inability to participate in decisions that affect their lives, and the abuse of power by school authorities. Jenny, a 13-year-old who was expelled for a full academic year as a consequence of being in the wrong place at the wrong time, when friends were smoking marijuana, describes how her voice was silenced and no one listened to her:

> It was really hard 'cause they don't care what we have to say. They think that they already know the situation so they don't care. Like, it's kind of sad that they can't hear from all of us…. I think I was treated unfairly by the school board…and they already had their mind made up that they were going to expel all of us. (Baiyee, Hawkins, & Polakow, 2013, p. 14)

Schools and childcare settings are the fundamental institutions where children and youth spend many years "living" in a community; yet they are also profoundly undemocratic social spaces and an ongoing source of rights violations, where students lack both due process and the right to participate in decisions affecting their lives—from school rules and disciplinary policies, to dress and appearance, as well as the right to communicate freely with their peers. For young children, the right to participate and also to resist is even more circumscribed. It is significant that the highest rate of expulsion in the U.S. is now in pre-K settings where children are expelled for a variety of toddler infractions such as biting, scratching, hitting, and throwing tantrums. This downward trend of zero-tolerance policies has also severely impacted young children's educational futures as more and more expulsions take place before children ever enter public schools. Preschool expulsion is emerging as a new crisis of access in early education where "uncontrollable behavior" and even potty accidents result in snap removals. For single-parent families in particular, an expulsion may induce a downward spiral of events that threatens to destabilize the entire family: Lack of child care leads to loss of a job, which in turn leads to eviction, homelessness, and destitution. Chiquila, a single mother, describes her situation of desperation when her 4-year-old daughter, Anita, was expelled from her childcare center for having "a meltdown."

> And they came to me at Christmas time, and they say, "We no longer want your daughter to return!" I felt like I was helpless.... I had no options and I had to work.... And suddenly they put my child out of school.... And I was devastated. (Polakow, 2007, pp. 94, 99)

Feminized Poverty, Child Poverty, and Child Care

Child poverty and social and educational exclusion exist on a nexus of gendered intersectionality. The feminization of poverty, which is pervasive globally, takes particular forms in the U.S. where the residual welfare state has been eviscerated creating extreme forms of commodification. Esping-Anderson (1990) has argued that societies with strong social citizenship rights and social care infrastructures have successfully created decommodification from the market in order to decrease income vulnerability, so that citizens are not adversely affected by the ravages of the free market. Hobson and Lister (2002) and other feminist social theorists point to the specific struggles and forms of discrimination (the labor market and pay inequity) that poor women encounter that create greater risks of commodification, and they advocate for universal social policies such as child care and family leave that create specific gender-differentiated rights.

Currently, 17.7 million women live in poverty in the U.S. and the gender wage gap (women earn 77% of what men make in comparable occupations), occupational segregation in unstable, low-wage jobs, and the dual responsibilities of being both provider and caregiver for dependent children are all key factors in feminized poverty. Forty percent of women living in poverty are single mothers with dependent children, and they are twice as likely to be poor compared to single fathers. The poorest and youngest children (58%) live in single female-headed households, yet only 27% of poor families with dependent children received any TANF (welfare) cash assistance, and the benefits levels are far below the federal poverty line (less than 30% in 29 of the states; Finch & Schott, 2013; National Women's Law Center, 2012).

The intersectionality of feminized poverty, child poverty, and lack of access to high-quality child care has produced an acute crisis for low-income women; child care is a fundamental, gendered right for mothers, as well as for their young children. Countries that have remediated child poverty have invested in social care infrastructures that support families, specifically women and children, and have created strong, universal child care systems. In countries where universalism is strong and children's well-being is premised on rights, there are generous cash transfers, parental and maternity leave policies, and high investments in child care spending per child. There are dramatic differences in spending on child care when the Scandinavian expenditures are contrasted with those in the United States: Sweden spends $6,409 per child; Norway, $6,425 per child; Denmark $8,126 per child; but the United States spends a mere $794 per child (Economic Policy Institute, 2013). The consequences of such policy deficits hit the ground in spirals of accumulating damage to young lives.

Jasmine's Story:
Obstructed Capabilities and Violated Rights in Two Generations[2]

Jasmine, a young teen mother from Michigan, experienced a traumatic childhood. Much of her childhood was spent in foster care, and she became pregnant in the 11th grade. With no family support and indifferent teachers, Jasmine "dropped out" of school. Living on the streets until moving in with her abusive boyfriend and his aunt, Jasmine weathered her pregnancy and gave birth to Che. Once she turned 18, she was required to report for "Work First" training when her son Che was 12 weeks old (Michigan has one of the harshest mandatory welfare-to-work work requirements under the 1996 PRWORA welfare legislation). Unable to find a satisfactory child care place at a nearby family daycare home, priced out of child care centers, and unable to obtain child care subsidies because she has been sanctioned by the Department of Human Services for not working the required number of hours, Jasmine is desperate. "I didn't know what to do.... I couldn't find someone to watch my baby." When Jasmine finds a full-time housekeeping job at a nearby hotel, she relies on her younger sister, who lives in an adjacent city, to take care of baby Che. But with minimum wage and no access to affordable, stable childcare, Jasmine must make child care arrangements on the fly. Her options include a friend, her sister (who is herself at risk because she has missed so much school in her senior year and may be unable to graduate), Jasmine's abusive boyfriend whom she suspects of leaving Che unattended, and the boyfriend's aunt, who is harsh and who Jasmine feels does not care for Che. Hence, Jasmine faces a multitude of obstacles that reverberate through her family: Che endures multiple child care spells with different (sometimes harsh and indifferent) caregivers. Kristin, Jasmine's sister, has her own education placed under threat for "truancy" as she regularly misses school to care for Che. During the school spring break, Kristin stays over at Jasmine's and cares for him daily. However, when Kristin returns to school, Jasmine scrambles to find childcare, misses several days of work, and is fired. Despite her best attempts to make things work, her desperate struggle to piece together makeshift childcare arrangements continually fall apart. "It's been so hard," she says. "I been looking and looking for child care. If it's not the area, it's the amount of money. If it's not the amount of money, it's the transportation" (Polakow, 2007, pp. 17–18).

For Jasmine, as with so many other millions of low-income mothers, childcare is the tipping point; and without safe, affordable, accessible, and decent quality childcare, family viability is on the line. There are over half a million children (560,000) in Michigan living in poverty; and almost 500,000 young children under 6 have working parents; of those, 40% are living in single-parent households. Yet there are only enough licensed slots to serve 75%

of children who need child care, and income eligibility for state child care assistance is limited to those with an annual income of $23,880 (129% of the FPL). The need for child care is particularly acute for mothers like Jasmine with an infant or toddler. The average annual cost for full-time infant care in Michigan is $10,114, and is considerably higher in the city where Jasmine lives (Child Care Aware, 2012). Furthermore, only 47% of licensed centers and 50% of licensed family child care homes will accept subsidies, due to chronic late and delayed payments from Michigan's Department of Human Services. If Jasmine does succeed in accessing subsidies, they will not pay the full cost of care and she will still have a hefty co-pay of about $100–$400 a month.

As we consider the thwarted dreams of Jasmine, who wants to get her GED and go to a community college to study for an associate degree in child development, we can see how her human capabilities have been obstructed—by poverty and by pernicious welfare policies that thwart her autonomy and possibilities for success. While she demonstrates determination and resilience trying to create a home for herself and her child, her fundamental rights as a child, adolescent, and young adult have been violated by poverty and lack of social protections. Strong social and educational supports would have ensured a better childhood for her, and could have enabled her as a young mother, to secure good child care for her son. Without access to good-quality care and family support, she cannot function successfully as provider and nurturer to her son. For Jasmine's sister, Kristin, who wants to be a teacher, her own life trajectory has been threatened because if she fails to graduate, her own educational goals will be derailed, and her capabilities to become who she wants to be will not be realized. For little Che, who is in a vulnerable period of development, bounced around from one caregiver to another, the strains are visible. He is not an easy baby and screams and cries when held, seemingly experiencing difficulties with bonding and attachment to both his mother and his aunt. The toxic effects of poverty will, in all probability, impact his development at all levels: neurobiological, social, and emotional. Because he has been priced out of good-quality child care, his early years are imperiled and his functioning and capabilities—walking, talking, playing, interacting, constructing meaning—are all likely to be truncated. His rights too are violated by the lack of social protections and public policies that would enable him to develop in a high-quality child care setting.

There is an appalling national deficit of care that hinges on access, quality, and affordability. High-quality child care can be purchased by affluent parents—as much as $18,000 a year for infant care and almost $14,000 a year for full-time preschool (Child Care Aware, 2012). Yet for low-income parents, particularly single parents, good care is simply not available in most states and the waiting list for subsidies is lengthy; only one-seventh of low-income parents actually receive child care subsidies across the nation. Subsidies also do not pay the full cost of care, which is typically pegged at 75% of market rates, leaving parents with high co-pays of several hundred dollars per month (Child Care Aware, 2012; Polakow, 2007).

Furthermore, state licensing and oversight systems are inadequate. Lack of regulation and monitoring, low standards, inadequate staff training, poor facilities, high costs, a low-paid work force, and generally inferior quality of care characterize the majority of child care settings in the United States. Only 10% of centers and 1% of family child care homes are nationally accredited, and 32 states require only a high school diploma or less for "lead teachers." Child care workers are underpaid—the average annual income is $21,320—leaving many single mothers who work full-time in child care settings in poverty. In addition, less than one-third of the

10.9 million children under 5 in need of child care actually attend childcare centers and family childcare homes; the rest (the majority of whom are poor) are in unregulated care by relative and non-relative providers (Child Care Aware, 2012; Helburn & Bergmann, 2002; Polakow, 2007).

Whither Capabilities and Rights?

It is clear that the lives of poor children in the United States are embedded in a tangle of policies and practices that fail all three P's of the CRC: provision, protection, and participation. For Heather, a young stigmatized second grader, for young mother Jasmine and her baby Che, for expelled teens such as Jenny, and for Chiquila's 4-year-old daughter, Anita, there is a glaring policy indifference to their development as young human beings, their capabilities to be and to do, and their social, economic, and educational rights. Their voices were silenced and their participation in decisions that profoundly impact their lives and their futures was denied in institutions that functioned in undemocratic ways, failing to protect and provide the possibilities for healthy human functioning that promotes autonomy and choice. Healthy human functioning creates the possibility for developing the human capabilities to do and to be; yet widespread material poverty creates a poverty of capabilities—leading to exclusion, isolation, and a landscape of social toxicity (Garbarino, 1995). From hunger and housing insecurity to denied access to good schools and high-quality child care, to disrupted capabilities, diminished well-being, and a lack of safety and stability—poor children's lives have been stained by the politics of welfare evisceration, exclusionary policies of "None for you," and a generalized public and academic indifference to the toxic consequences of poverty.

Agency and Resistance

How children and adolescents confront domination and the violation of their rights is important to consider. In her analysis of the meaning of poverty and agency, Lister (2004) emphasizes personal, political, and citizenship agency. The different dimensions of "getting by," "getting (back) at," "getting out," and "getting organized" (p. 130) are part of a taxonomy of actions that depict different forms of agency. This analysis, useful for understanding the agency of adults living in poverty, can also be stretched and applied to children and adolescents, whose agency is rarely analyzed. Heather used different coping strategies to "get by" and yet also exercised resistance, "getting at" when she chose to "steal" free lunch. Jasmine and her sister Kristen were also "getting by" and struggling to marshal strategic resources. Jasmine engaged in several forms of everyday resistance, refusing to attend Work First orientations and claiming to her caseworker that Che was ill when she had no one to take care of him and could not work. Kristen feigned illness to school authorities when she was actually taking care of Che so Jasmine could find a job. In Che's case, his coping and resistance (if a child's unhappy instability can be viewed that way) to multiple caregivers was to express his unhappiness through constant crying and sleeplessness.

As Lister (2004) points out, there are considerable personal resources that are drawn on in the struggle to survive, such as resilience and resourcefulness, and this is demonstrated by children and adolescents in multiple ways and is typically constructed as non-compliant or as a rule infraction. Understanding poverty and its impact on children, as well as understanding children's ways of experiencing and meaning-making, also necessitates understanding childhood as a dominated and undemocratic social space; and when participation is denied, forms of resistance and noncompliance frequently result in harsh and punitive sanctions that lead to exclusion. When poverty and exclusion intersect, as we have seen in these children's stories, their life trajectories are imperiled.

For children's rights to be affirmed and realized in the families and institutions that children inhabit, they clearly need adults to protect and provide for them, and government institutions to legislate *for*, not *against* them, in order to realize the full implications of Article 27 of the CRC that affirms "the right of every child to standard of living adequate for the child's physical, mental, spiritual, moral, and social development" (Convention on the Rights of the Child, 1989). But they also need adults to respect their voices and participation, as social and cultural identities mediate the interpretation and construction of those lifeworlds. For voice and participation to be actualized, the structures that govern children's lives must be stretched, expanded, and revisioned so that children's voices are heard within their local micro-worlds as well as in the broader policy discourse. This becomes a particular challenge for educators in the United States because it means addressing profound inequality amid increasing "private affluence" and "public squalor" (Judt, 2010, p. 12).

Yet, where are the voices of educators and critical scholars? Where are the analyses of the isolation engendered by a failure of resources that impacts the capacity of children to engage in schools and communities, in social and civic participation? Why do educational critics and early childhood reconceptualists direct valuable intellectual resources and time to critiques of neoliberal, corporate education regimes, while largely ignoring the appalling consequences of deepening inequality on the impoverished ground upon which so many thousands of children walk? Cornell West, in a recent address, questions whether we have "become callous to catastrophe" and "well-adjusted to injustice" (West, 2013) as poverty is normalized and asks, "What can I do to wake up my fellow citizens?"

Deep and persistent child poverty is an appalling condition and a crisis that demands redress in the United States. For those of us engaged as allies in the struggle for social and economic justice, there is an urgent need to crack the silences, to use our positions of public visibility and accumulated intellectual capital to name the outrages committed daily against the youngest members of our society. If not now, when?

References

Addy, S., Engelhardt, W., & Skinner, C. (2013, January). *Basic facts about low-income children: Children under 18 years, 2011*. Retrieved from http://www.nccp.org/publications/pub_1074.html

Alkire, S. (2009). Concepts and measures of agency. In K. Basu & R. Kanbur (Eds.), *Arguments for a better world: Essays in honor of Amartya Sen*, (Vol. 1; pp. 455–474). Oxford: Oxford University Press.

American Civil Liberties Union. (2008, June 6). *What is the school to prison pipeline?* Retrieved from http://www.aclu.org/racial-justice/what-school-prison-pipeline

Baiyee, M., Hawkins, C., & Polakow, V. (2013). Children's rights and educational exclusion: The impact of zero tolerance in school. In B. B. Swadener, L. Lundy, J. Habashi, & N. Blanchet-Cohen (Eds.), *Children's lives and education in cross-national contexts: What difference could rights make?* (pp. 39–62). New York: Peter Lang.

Bernstein, J., & Lin, J. (2008, October 29). *What we need to get by*. Retrieved from http://www.epi.org/publication/bp224/

Cauthen, N. K., & Fass, S. (2008). *Measuring income and poverty in the United States*. New York: National Center for Children in Poverty, Columbia University, Mailman School of Public Health.

Child Care Aware of America. (2012). *Parents and the high cost of child care*. Retrieved from http://www.naccrra.org/sites/default/files/default_site_pages/2012/cost_report_2012_final_081012_0.pdf

Child Hunger Facts. (n.d.). Retrieved from http://feedingamerica.org/hunger-in-america/hunger-facts/child-hunger-facts.aspx

Convention on the Rights of the Child (CRC). (1989, November 20). Retrieved from http://www2.ohchr.org/english/law/crc.htm

Economic Policy Institute. (2013). *State of working America preview: A world of difference in child care funding.* Retrieved from http://www.epi.org/publication/state_of_working_america_preview_a_world_of_difference_in_child_care_f/

Esping-Anderson, G. (1990). *The three worlds of welfare capitalism.* Cambridge, U.K.: Polity Press.

Finch, I., & Schott, L. (2013, March 28). *The value of TANF cash benefits continued to erode in 2012.* Retrieved from http://www.cbpp.org/files/3-28-13tanf.pdf

Fine, M., Stoudt, B. G., Fox, M., & Santos, M. (2010). The uneven distribution of social suffering: Documenting the social health consequences of neo-liberal social policy on marginalized youth. *The European Health Psychologist, 12*(3), 30–35. Retrieved from http://www.ehps.net/ehp/issues/2010/v12iss3_September2010/12_3_fine_etal.pdf

Garbarino, J. (1995). *Raising children in a socially toxic environment.* San Francisco, CA: Jossey-Bass.

Georgetown Law Human Rights Institute. (2012). *Kept out: Barriers to meaningful education in the school-to prison pipeline.* Washington, DC: Georgetown University Law Center. Retrieved from http://www.law.georgetown.edu/academics/centers-institutes/human-rights-institute/fact-finding/upload/KeptOut.pdf

Heckman, J. (2006, January 10). Catch 'em young. *Wall Street Journal.* Retrieved from http://jenni.uchicago.edu/papers/WSJ_Heckman_01102006_Catch_Em_Young.pdf

Heckman, J. (2008). Schools, skills, and synapses. *Economic Inquiry, Western Economic Association International, 46*(3), 289–324. Retrieved from http://www.nber.org/papers/w14064

Heckman, J., & Masterov, D. (2007). The productivity argument for investing in young children. *Review of Agricultural Economics, 29*(3), 446–493.

Helburn, S., & Bergmann, B. (2002). *America's child care problem: The way out.* New York: Palgrave Macmillan.

Hobson, B., & Lister, R. (2002). Citizenship. In B. Hobson, J. Lewis, & B. Siim (Eds.), *Contested concepts in gender and social politics* (pp. 23–54). Cheltenham, U.K.: Edward Elgar.

Jones, N. A., & Sumner, A. (2011). *Child poverty, evidence and policy: Mainstreaming children in international development.* Bristol, U.K.: Policy Press.

Judt, T. (2010). *Ill fares the land.* New York: Penguin.

Katz, M. (1989). *The underserving poor: From the war on poverty to the war on welfare.* New York: Pantheon.

Lister, R. (2004). *Poverty.* Cambridge, U.K.: Polity Press.

Maslow, A. H. (1962). *Towards a psychology of being.* Princeton, NJ: D. Van Nostrand.

National Scientific Council on the Developing Child. (2005). *Excessive stress disrupts the architecture of the developing brain: Working paper no. 3.* Retrieved from http://developingchild.harvard.edu/index.php/resources/reports_and_working_papers/working_papers/wp3/

National Women's Law Center. (2012). *Downward slide: State child care assistance policies 2012.* Retrieved from http://www.nwlc.org/sites/default/files/pdfs/NWLC2012_StateChildCareAssistanceReport.pdf

Nussbaum, M. (2000). *Women and human development: The capabilities approach.* Cambridge, U.K.: Cambridge University Press.

Nussbaum, M. (2011). *Creating capabilities: The human development approach.* Cambridge, MA: Harvard University Press.

Pear, R. (2013, May 24). *States' policies on health care exclude some of the poorest.* Retrieved from http://www.nytimes.com/2013/05/25/us/states-policies-on-health-care-exclude-poorest.html?_r=0

Peisner-Feinberg, E. S., Burchinal, M. R., Clifford, R. M., Culkin, M. L., Howes, C., Kagan, S. L., Yazejian, N., Byler, P., Rustici, J., & Zelazo, J. (1999). *The children of the cost, quality, and outcomes study go to school: Technical report.* Chapel Hill: University of North Carolina at Chapel Hill, Frank Porter Graham Child Development Center.

Polakow, V. (1993). *Lives on the edge: Single mothers and their children in the other America.* Chicago, IL: University of Chicago Press.

Polakow, V. (2007). *Who cares for our children? The child care crisis in the other America.* New York: Teachers College Press.

Redmond, G. (2008). *Children's perspectives on economic adversity: A review of the literature.* Innocenti Discussion Paper IDP 2008-01. Florence, Italy: UNICEF Innocenti Research Centre.

Robbins, C. (2008). *Expelling hope: The assault on youth and the militarization of schooling.* New York: SUNY Press.

Schweinhart, L. J. (2004, November). *The High/Scope Perry preschool study through age 40: Summary, conclusions, and frequently asked questions.* Ypsilanti: High/Scope Educational Research Foundation. Retrieved from http://www.highscope.org/file/Research/PerryProject/3_specialsummary%20col%2006%2007.pdf

Sen, A. (1981). *Poverty and famines: An essay on entitlement and deprivation.* Oxford, U.K.: Clarendon Press.

Sen, A. (1989). Development as capability expansion. *Journal of Development Planning, 19*, 41–58.

Sen, A. (1999). *Development as freedom.* New York: Alfred A. Knopf.

UNICEF. (2010). The children left behind: A league table of inequality in child well-being in the world's rich countries. *Innocenti Report Card 9.* Florence, Italy: Innocenti Research Centre. Retrieved from http://www.unicef-irc.org/publications/pdf/rc9_eng.pdf

UNICEF. (2013). Child well-being in rich countries: A comparative overview. *Innocenti Report Card 11.* Florence, Italy: Innocenti Research Centre. Retrieved from http://www.unicef-irc.org/publications/pdf/rc11_eng.pdf

U.S. Department of Health and Human Services. (2013). *2013 poverty guidelines.* Retrieved from http://aspe.hhs.gov/poverty/13poverty.cfm

West, C. (2013, February 16). Unstuck: Reviving the movement for social justice, human dignity, and the environment. Keynote Address, Ann Arbor Michigan.

Zweifler, R., & DeBeers, J. (2002, fall). How zero tolerance impacts our most vulnerable youth. *Michigan Journal of Race and Law, 8*(1), 191–220.

Notes

1. The 2013 Federal Poverty Level (FPL) is $23,550 for a four-person family and $19,530 for a three-person family. Families living between 100% and 200% of the FPL are classified as low-income (Addy, Engelhardt, & Skinner, 2013; U.S. Department of Health and Human Services, 2013).
2. Jasmine's story is based on a narrative drawn from *Who Cares for Our Children?* (Polakow, 2007).

TWENTY-TWO

The Costs of Putting Quality First: Neoliberalism, (Ine)quality, (Un)affordability, and (In)accessibility?

Mark Nagasawa, Lacey Peters, and Beth Blue Swadener

Economic globalization and related neoliberal policies continue to be pervasive forces, impacting wider societies, their systems of care provision, and marginalized communities. Drawing from our life experiences and research, in this chapter we deconstruct the prevailing discourse of quality in the U.S. state of Arizona's "Quality First" childcare rating program and discuss how this effort reflects neoliberal discourses and *common-sense* notions about what constitutes a coherent, quality-focused early childhood system. Our analysis draws upon Antonio Gramsci's (1971) notions of common- and good-sense to illuminate concerns about Arizona's burgeoning system focused on improving the quality of childcare, which currently touches only a fraction of childcare providers, families, and children in the state and in ways that may (re)produce social inequalities rather than ameliorating them as is ostensibly intended.

As longtime participants in an array of state, federal, and nonprofit early childhood programs and systems, we use this case to explore how state and national policies reflect persistent hegemonies of power, privilege, and neoliberal ideology, even as they attempt to be *inclusive* and *democratic*. Previous critiques highlight that neoliberalism is a hybrid discourse with conservative, libertarian, and modern liberal features but whose unifying logic is the free market wherein the public good is served by consumer choices and product quality is assured through competition (e.g., Dahlberg & Moss, 2005; Perkins, Nelms, & Smyth, 2004; Swadener, 2003). Our interpretations of this state's system-building provide a localized perspective on globalized neoliberal ideology in practice.

As authors, to position ourselves more reflexively, Mark became interested in policy issues early in his career as a preschool teacher/social worker, as he (and colleagues) struggled to implement new policy mandates such as licensing their public-school preschool classrooms as individual childcare centers and incorporating learning standards that they had no part in developing. Some of his early reflections included, "Who's making decisions about us? What does this have to do with what kids and their families are struggling with?" These questions eventually led him to experiences in the Arizona Governor's Office, the Arizona Department of Education, and a return to graduate school. Beth met Mark in the Arizona Governor's Office and they began a critical dialogue about systems and power dynamics in early childhood that continues. Beth has done cross-nationally comparative studies of early childhood policy and enactment of programs related to children's participation rights; has worked extensively with community-based early childhood agencies; and has conducted intensive early childhood professional development with Indigenous teachers and (*othered*) Head Start teachers. Lacey was a preschool teacher prior to her doctoral work. Early on she recognized the tensions that can arise between and among various constituents in classroom communities, most notably as they emerged during the period families prepared for the transition to kindergarten. More to this point, she was struck by the gaps and inconsistencies that formed between adults and children as they constructed beliefs about kindergarten. Those observations inscribed a deep value in her scholarship to meaningfully include perspectives commonly underrepresented in education reform discourses. A common thread throughout our work is a desire to put theory into practice, which drew us to Gramsci's ideas of common- and good-sense.

Common- and Good-Sense

In Gramsci's conception, common-sense is unquestioned, fluid, and apparently coherent but often contradictory knowledge shaped by political-economic and historical context (Crehan, 2002, p. 110). Each stratum of a society may have its own common-sense; however, certain common-sense is more privileged and pervasive, which adds nuance to his notions of how coercion and consent interact to form hegemony. However, within common-senses lie atoms of good-sense, practical philosophies of life (Gramsci, 1971; Jones, 2006). While nebulously defined, recognizing the existence of good-sense provides avenues for being grounded and connected to people, organic, rather than engaging in critical projects only at the level of abstraction. This engagement involves opposing and transforming common-sense, by seeking out and dialogically knitting together fragments of good-sense into coherent counternarratives (Crehan, 2002; Jones, 2006).

The common- and good-sense analytic frame aids consideration of the (un)intended consequences of focusing too narrowly upon improving childcare quality. We argue that, while few would disagree about the need to provide more and higher quality options for parents in need of care for their young children (good-sense), this program's unreflective emphasis on prevailing (common-sense) assumptions about quality has resulted, to this point, in de-emphasizing the issues of accessibility and affordability of childcare for the majority of low-income parents in Arizona. This is also a theoretical perspective that promotes joining with other scholar-activists to rethink our understanding of "the neoliberal turn" and its impacts on the field's engagement with policy issues and structures that intimately affect people's lives. In the following sections, we provide a brief overview of early care and education in the U.S.; followed by a section on neoliberalism and the discourse of quality that frames our analysis of Arizona's initiatives to address the interrelated problem of childcare quality, affordability, and accessibility. We conclude with a discussion of *insider-outsider* scholar activism, the pressing need to reinvigorate the concept of praxis within contemporary neoliberal common-sense, and the importance of diverse perspectives for the ongoing work of the Reconceptualizing Early Childhood Education movement.

The State of Early Care and Education in the United States

There is no consensus on what constitutes early care and education (ECE) in the United States (Gomby et al., 1996). Does ECE mean early childhood education or early care and education? Are childcare and preschool the same things? Does healthcare for young children count as care, or does this really refer to childcare? Even with this lack of clarity, ECE has become linked to education reform, with the time before children begin school entering the reform gaze with the issuance of the National Education Goals Panel's (1991) *Education Goals 2000*, which identified children's readiness for school as the number-one goal.

Despite this official pronouncement, federal efforts with regard to ECE have historically taken a narrow focus on existing programs such as Head Start, childcare subsidies, and special education (see Gallagher, Clifford, & Maxwell, 2004). In 2002, the scope broadened following the issuance of George W. Bush's plan for early education, *Good Start, Grow Smart*, which conceptually linked federal and state ECE reform activities to federal and state reforms resulting from the reauthorization of the Elementary and Secondary Education Act as the No Child Left Behind Act of 2001 (P. L. 107–110).

More recently, Barack Obama announced general support for universal preschool and has carried the general thrust of his predecessor's plan forward, most notably with competitive grants through a program called Race to the Top, which provide funding to states to improve coordination among ECE programs, refine learning standards, and focus on teachers' professional development (The White House, 2013). These recent presidential initiatives acknowledge that what is referred to as ECE is multidimensional and made up of different programs with different aims, professional development systems, funding, and regulations (Gallagher et al., 2004). Given the administrative fragmentation, and the resulting policy diffusion, it should come as no surprise that one point of consensus is the need to fix the United States' ECE non-system, with program quality at the center of these reforms (e.g., Barnett, 1993; Gallagher et al., 2004).

Neoliberalism and the Discourse of Quality

In ECE, "quality" is often assumed to be a fixed and objective set of features, both among professional and general publics (*Education Week*, 2002; Helburn & Cost, Quality and Child Outcomes Team, 1995; Wilgoren, 1999). This notion lends itself to neoliberal arguments for choice and free-market logics that lead *naturally* to thinking of ECE as a commodity, that is, "you get what you pay for" (Cochran, 2007, p. 47). However, as ECE-the-intervention has risen in prominence, advocacy has focused on high-quality programs, with both researchers and advocates frequently citing the finding that 70% of childcare centers can be characterized as mediocre in quality and nearly 13% as a threat to children's health and safety (Helburn & Cost, Quality and Child Outcomes Team, 1995). This is an alarming and serious claim, making conceptual clarity important. What is quality? What can be done to improve it? And what are the policy mechanisms needed to support it? While many might argue that the answers to these questions are known and the main issues revolve around political will (Brauner, Gordic, & Zigler, 2004), it is actually a more complex idea than might be thought; a common-sense one built with equal parts scientism (Soto & Swadener, 2002), a limited number of quality rating instruments, and cultural assumptions (Tobin, 2005) that leave little room for questions of whose definition of quality counts (Adams, 2006).

A key task in our project is to clarify the common- and good-sense of quality. Dahlberg, Moss, and Pence (2007) suggest that there are some key, critical questions to ask: (a) Who has been involved in the process of defining quality? Who has not? (b) Might there be multiple perspectives or understandings of the idea? and (c) What is the context in which the idea has been formed?

Ceglowski and Bacigalupa (2002) organize the field's thinking on the concept into four categories. They call the first perspective "structural," which focuses on issues of children's group sizes, adult/child ratios, and staff qualifications/levels of experience. The second perspective, global, is concerned with the general quality of the classroom environment and practices. The third, process, speaks to the nature and types of adult – child interaction. Importantly, their fourth category, perspectives of children, parents, and staff, has been less commonly addressed by the field (for notable exceptions see Barbarin et al., 2006; da Silva & Wise, 2006; Hallam, Fouts, Bargreen, & Caudle, 2009; Tobin, 2005).

While Tobin (2005) has argued that notions of quality should be locally negotiated and focused on dialogues among parents and professionals, children are typically omitted from research on quality (cf. Hallam et al., 2009) and the policy focus has been solidly on the *measurable* features, each of which contribute to one of the most vexing problems in ECE, the interaction of quality, affordability, and accessibility to families, which some have called the child care "trilemma" (Lash & McMullen, 2008). The trilemma's structural dynamic is as follows: In a business—and in the U.S., the majority of ECE settings are private—where personnel is the highest cost (Cochran, 2007), setting more stringent group size and ratio requirements necessitates hiring additional staff members. This in turn may have adverse effects upon the supply and variety of services available to families and the costs they are expected to bear (Barnett, 1993; Helburn & Cost, Quality and Child Outcomes Team, 1995).

The dimension of accessibility is further compounded by limited and constrained options for low-income families, such as shifting and nontraditional work hours, a limited range of providers, and limited knowledge of how to navigate the child care *market* (Chaudry et al., 2011). Resolving this problem has real implications for working parents as well as children's life chances, as there is evidence that lends credence to the idea that participating in ECE programs that have been identified as *higher* quality is related to improved language, cognitive, and communication abilities, effects that have been observed to endure into the second grade (Burchinal, Roberts, Nabors, & Bryant, 1996; Peisner-Feinberg et al., 2001). While we problematize the notion of quality, and will later critique scientistic assumptions undergirding universalized measures of quality and exclusion of othered children, parents, and ECE professionals, there is still an important good-sense consideration that has serious social justice implications—the kinds of resources, emotional support, and care that adults in these programs can provide to children to foster their capabilities (see Polakow in Chapter 21 of this volume).

A Local Case: The State of Arizona

Arizona presents an interesting case of how globalized neoliberal discourses express themselves through policies and programs, despite being less recognized for its ECE policies than other U.S. state programs such as those in North Carolina, Georgia, or Oklahoma. For unlike nations with centralized education planning, the United States' federal model has historically provided for local decision making (Martin, 2012). As in many other U.S. states, advocates for ECE in Arizona have fought for both the existence of early care and education programs, as well as increasing systemization (Nagasawa, 2010). These efforts have reflected the unclear and contested definitions of what constitutes ECE, permeated by a discourse of quality.

Arizona's Response to the Early Care and Education System Problem

In 2006 Arizona voters passed an initiative creating the Early Childhood Development and Health Board, a new state agency whose purpose is to develop a coordinated, accessible, and high-quality early care and education system focused on promoting health, improving ECE programming, and supporting parents (*Proposition 203*, 2006). This scope is notably broader than other states, such as New Jersey, Georgia, Oklahoma, and Illinois, which more commonly focus only on preschool education. This new system is funded by a dedicated tax on tobacco products.

First Things First. The ballot initiative defined a system directed by a state board, which has taken the public name "First Things First," and is made up of regional partnership councils (RPCs) that direct funding to address locally defined needs—with the state board's approval. One of the initiative's central messages was, and continues to be, that this is a locally responsive system as illustrated in the report *Ready for School, Set for Life*:

> We need to move beyond an incremental approach—one pilot project after another, a slew of disconnected programs—to create a comprehensive approach that addresses all elements of the system…. Different communities will focus on different elements, depending on their local priorities. But having a holistic perspective will help everyone stay on track, working on the priorities that matter most. (First Things First, 2011b, p. 4)

However, in keeping with contradictory neoliberal discourse extolling the virtues of choice while forwarding a specific agenda, staying "on track" has seemed to mean encouraging RPCs to "invest" in a "Strategy Toolkit" that provides more than 70 programmatic options, all of which are carried out through a web of state and local grants, contracts and subcontracts (FTF, 2010a, 2011a, 2011b, 2012a).

Addressing the cost, quality, and access problem. The enduring influence of the *Cost, Quality and Child Outcomes Study* and the childcare trilemma (Helburn & Cost, Quality and Child Outcomes Team, 1995), informs First Things First's quality-improvement strategy, which is made up of three "signature" programs: Quality First, Professional Reward$, and Teacher Education and Compensation Helps (T.E.A.C.H.), in addition to childcare scholarships and what is called a "preschool expansion." It is a common-sense strategy, in keeping with the field's conventional wisdom about how to raise program quality. Quality First is the state's Quality Rating and Improvement Rating System (QRIS), joining 38 other states that are systematizing quality through: (1) program standards; (2) monitoring; (3) professional development through coaching; (4) incentivizing improvement; and (5) providing *consumer* information (QRIS National Learning Network, 2013; Child Trends, 2010, p. 1).

Finally, FTF approaches the problems of cost and access through childcare scholarships and a preschool expansion, which sounds like a positive step but when examined closely is more complicated. For in 2010, as a part of deficit reduction measures, the State Legislature did away with funding for the state's Early Childhood Block Grant (ECBG), which supported the state preschool program (Nagasawa, 2010). FTF's continued support for public-school preschools may seem encouraging, but it is important to consider that the total amount for this "expansion" was $5,047,880–$7,644,409 less than the peak funding for state preschool of $12,692,289 (in 2007; Arizona Department of Education, 2009; FTF, 2011a). While FTF's activities may follow the field's common-sense, we ask how the sum of all these parts will lead to the ideal system that FTF and others envision (FTF, 2011b; Gallagher et al., 2004), who is meaningfully involved in these decisions, and what are opportunities to engage in more *good-sense* systems development?

The Costs of Putting Quality First

Well before the start of drafting the ballot initiative that led to First Things First, advocates' discourse reflected an emphasis on *raising the floor of quality* in Arizona childcare. Arizona is routinely rated among the lowest-ranked states for child well-being, with high rates of child poverty and among the lowest investments in education, early care, and child health in the nation. According to the 2013 Annie E. Casey *Kids Count Data Book* (Annie E. Casey Foundation, 2013), Arizona ranked in the bottom five among the 50 U.S. states for overall conditions for children. Thus much of the early public discourse regarding FTF has emphasized the lack of access to quality programs to meet diverse community and family needs, with the implicit neoliberal assumption that raising the numbers of childcare providers deemed to be of higher quality will serve to *raise all boats* through competition over increasingly savvy consumers who have been educated to know good care when they see it. The rhetoric used by FTF follows economic arguments that high-quality ECE programs are an investment in human capital that will lead to innumerable societal gains and strong economic returns in the form of reduced costs for social and educational remediation and a more productive workforce (e.g., Heckman, 2011). In addition, the policies and programs used to structure FTF are established through regulatory or governing mechanisms intended to promote what Kagan and Kauerz (2010) refer to as consistency, continuity, and predictability across early childhood programs and systems. We argue that there is a two-fold, good-sense dimension embedded within the Quality First program: Increasing both programmatic quality and access to these programs is meaningful. However, we caution that the emphasis has been disproportionately on quality over affordability and accessibility; that is, the strategy fails to address the structural problems inherent in a system predicated upon two assumptions: (1) childcare as a commodity and (2) supplies following consumers' demands—assumptions that favor the affluent. Further, we are concerned about the relatively low number of childcare programs participating in the Quality First by the seventh year of FTF's existence. Of the 2,012 childcare centers and 1,415 family childcare homes that are regulated by the state, only 759 of these are enrolled in Quality First, with another 309 programs on a waiting list (FTF, 2012b). This leaves 78% of regulated childcare providers minimally affected or unaffected by the influences of the state's quality-improvement system, not to mention the number of unregulated care settings that would (or could) also benefit from participating in Quality First. While the question must be asked whether nonparticipation in this system is a negative, Polakow (see Chapter 21 this volume) reminds us that the "tangle of inequalities" (p. xx) associated with poverty—including radically different access to childcare based on family income at least mirrors structural inequalities, if not contributing to their reproduction.

Our analysis critiques common-sense notions of quality but without rejecting the good-sense notion that quality can matter, most importantly for children and families whose capacities and rights have been systematically undermined. Polakow (this volume) writes:

> It is clear that the lives of poor children in the United States are embedded in a tangle of policies and practices that fail all three P's of the [United Nations Convention on the Rights of the Child]: provision, protection and participation. (p. xx)

The case in Arizona both punctuates her critique of how these failures are systematized while also suggesting opportunities for action.

Following Dahlberg and Moss' (2008) convincing argument that "the concept of quality assumes the possibility of deriving universal and objective norms, based on expert knowledge" (p. 22), we are concerned that Quality First centers and homes are assessed with a battery of popular environmental rating scales (e.g., the Early Childhood Environmental Rating Scale [ECERS], its applicable counterparts, and the highly commercialized Classroom Assessment Scoring System [CLASS]), along with a Quality First-specific scale that measures staff qualifications, administrative practices, curriculum, and child assessment. While such standardized measures may seem like a common-sense starting point for constructing more uniform definitions of quality, and are in widespread (inter)national use, there is a rising debate about the applicability of these measures with programs serving economically, culturally, and linguistically diverse children and how unquestioned assumptions about quality may do little to address (in)equity (Campaign for Quality Early Education [CQEE], 2013; López, 2011; cf. Vitiello, 2013). Much as early reconceptualist work critiquing "developmentally appropriate practices" (e.g., Cannella, 1997; Jipson, 2001; Kessler, 1991; Lubeck, 1998) raised concerns about the dominant, Euro-American, middle-class bias embedded within notions of *universal* best practices in early childhood, many of the same arguments can be made today regarding the assessments that are actively marketed and part of quality rating systems (CQEE, 2013; López, 2011). Raising further concerns about the discourse used to promote Quality First is that the language reflects "hegemonic globalization" (de Sousa Santos, 2006), perpetuating universalized notions of *effective* and *appropriate*, as well as privileging formally recognized types of caregiving and undervaluing the programs or approaches that fall outside of rubricated systems of quality.

We also consider the question of how centers and family providers find out about and apply to participate in Quality First. The criteria for accessing and applying to the Quality First program are vague. Moreover potential participants are offered only an opaque view of the requirements for participation via the program's website (FTF, 2010b). Additionally, early childhood professionals have expressed to us concerns about the complexity of applying to Quality First. From this perspective, we can surmise that potential participants who could benefit from the Quality First program are excluded at the onset, as those who are unaware of the process or who are unable to take the initial steps required to enroll have no access to these supports. Following market logic, these providers will either survive or fail based on consumers' choices, how the children in their care fare would seem to rest on parents' responsibility to choose well—or not. A good-sense approach to test our assumption might be to look more closely at the programs selected to participate to determine whether patterns exist—who is participating, where are these providers located, etc. There is currently no easily accessible aggregate listing of Quality First programs. When looking at available reports on programs' quality ratings, only about 12% (665/759) of centers in the program had reached between three and five stars, and only 3% (22/759) of the centers were at four- or five-star ratings (with three reaching the highest rating; FTF, 2012b). To their credit, FTF and the agencies contracted to administer Quality First have given priority to centers that begin at lower ratings on the five-star system; that is, such centers have been actively recruited and approached with incentives for participation, such as participation in T.E.A.C.H., Professional Reward$, and childcare scholarships (FTF, 2011c).

This last incentive raises the issue of increasing access through increased affordability. In the narrowest of senses, the scholarship program does this—for families who receive them. However, the way scholarships are awarded, and for how long, is unclear. From a broader perspective, the Quality First strategy does little to support the 32,800 low-income families who have been denied support through the federal/state childcare subsidy program, despite their eligibility (Arizona Child Care Association [ACCA], 2013). Nor does Quality First, according to their website, assist the 7,200 children on the state childcare administration's childcare waiting list for working-poor parents (ACCA, 2013). More to this point, FTF's "preschool expansion," discussed earlier, funds state preschool at 60% of its previous high point. Quality First is not designed to address the other two components of the childcare trilemma—inequities/lack of access and affordability. The common-sense assumption is that heavy investment in Quality First will likely build a more comprehensive system of care and education and parents will make *the right* choices—but is this good-sense? How many families living in poverty, in areas with few formal childcare options, or who prefer kith and kin care are or will be reached by Quality First? And importantly, how many of them have been consulted about their needs, their desires, and their views of what the care their children receive should and could look like?

Concluding Thoughts: On Activism

Bearing in mind Polakow's (this volume) admonition that neither policymaking nor policy studies are abstract endeavors and, in an attempt to advocate for different forms of agency across various early childhood locales, we close by addressing the question of whether it is possible to maintain a critical "reconceptualist" stance while working with(in) these systems? We believe that this is an attainable goal. Having drawn upon Gramsci, what about hegemony, which is often thought of and experienced as totalizing and unassailably agile? Gramsci's ideas are ultimately about seeking understanding to awaken agency. As Marx (1852/1972) famously wrote, people "make their own history, but they do not make it just as they please; they do not make it under circumstances chosen by themselves, but under circumstances directly found, given and transmitted from the past" (p. 437). If one accepts the construct of globalized neoliberal discourse, then it follows that everyone is immersed in neoliberal common-sense. Therefore a key existential question is how to act within these conditions. As no one can be completely separated from this discourse, working from within is a necessary tactic—one among many yet-to-be-imagined others—for the next phases of the Reconceptualizing Early Childhood Education (reconceptualist) movement. The problem of co-option may be ameliorated by the union of reconceptualists who have very different answers to the question of what to do—and with whom to collaborate. Our ongoing inquiries as insider-outsiders are quests to engage in dialogue with other scholars—including those who do not share our views—as well as with parents, children, and ECE providers about the assumption that so-called market-based (but publicly subsidized) approaches can address concerns about basic health and safety, developmental enrichment, and "school readiness" that drive this focus on quality. In service of this aim, we offer some concluding thoughts about activism with(in) related to our scholarly work, direct participation in the system, and facilitation of more diverse participation.

Returning to the questions raised by Dahlberg, Moss, and Pence (2007): (a) Who has been involved in the process of defining quality? Who has not? (b) Might there be multiple perspectives or understandings of the idea? and (c) What is the context in which the idea has been formed? Whereas some studies on quality in ECE bring forward information on the different factors parents and professionals use to evaluate the quality of an early care or education environment (e.g., Barbarin et al., 2006; Peisner-Feinberg et al., 2001), there lacks deep insight on *other* perspectives of quality that may offer good-sense contributions to efforts such as Quality First. Serving as allies of these perspectives is a reconceptualist opportunity: challenging, problematic, contradictory, meaningful, and therefore in keeping with the most vital of the reconceptualist curricular and research traditions.

As discussed, we share serious concerns about ways in which Quality First may be reproducing familiar categories of exclusion and structures of inequality in Arizona. While the history of the reconceptualist movement has productively questioned power-imbued notions of science and empiricism (e.g., Bloch, 1987; Cannella, 1997; Soto & Swadener, 2002), we argue that empirical and empirically informed approaches are necessary tactics for communicating across ideological perspectives and social positionalities to address persistent and growing inequities and social exclusions. Critiques of scientific discourse will simply not be heard by those we seek to influence. There are critical-empirical questions to be pursued about these policies: What has happened, is happening, how and why? What are these policies' underlying rationales? What are the intended and unintended effects? What are the distributional impacts? (Ball, 2005). The results of these kinds of inquiries can shine light on processes that get elided by a singular focus on child outcomes. As insider-outsiders one of our roles is to continually push ourselves and our colleagues to consider the relationship between intents, actions, and effects.

For example, we have completed qualitative interviews with 110 professionals across the state to understand their perspectives on FTF (Arizona University Consortium, 2012) and continue to combine existential and instrumental perspectives in our work that blend stories about experiences with Quality First and other policy initiatives with a range of approaches to data analysis. A next step in our analysis will involve examining where these Quality First childcare providers are located, by *quality* ratings, and in comparison with community demographics. Is this system addressing quality and access—and for whom? What are parents' and children's viewpoints about what is happening and what needs to happen to address their aspirations? Addressing these types of questions is an important activist tactic. Demonstrating *empirical credibility* aids our direct participation in the system that has involved program evaluation, sitting on task forces and boards, providing staff support to those groups, and of course teaching within this system. While there is real risk that these activities may only reinforce the practices that concern us, these demonstrable experiences enable invitations to the spaces where decisions, albeit often small ones, occur. Despite our concerns about building a system based on neoliberal common-sense, acknowledgement of the presence of good-sense helps foster the relationships necessary for dialogue. The concepts act as a buffer to too-easily otherizing those involved in directly building this system.

For instance, a good-sense aspect of this initiative is that more attention and support is being brought to the field of early childhood in an ECE-resistant state. While not the single solution that advocates (e.g., Heckman, 2011) suggest it to be, this can be meaningful for promoting poor children's rights to nurturance and their individual capacities. Further evidence of good-sense can be found within First Things First 2012 annual report, which includes a section entitled "Growing the Community Conversation" (p. 19). There is reason for skepticism about this sentiment, as using the phrase "community" might be indicative of a desire to build a universalized system of care and education within the state that imposes dominant views and exclusionary practices (FTF asserts that "early childhood impacts everyone" [p. 19], yet there is no mention about it *involving everyone*); however, we maintain that it also suggests small spaces of opportunity.

Publicly raising questions such as what is "the community" exactly, who are the members of this community, and how can we engage with them, may seem like a small act but it's a way to begin to deconstruct common-sense assumptions. While we acknowledge that many may continue to have doubts about the ability to work with(in) systems such as these, our position is that critiques from outside must be paired with those from within in order to mobilize good-sense counternarratives, and that hope lies in engaging with parents, practitioners, children, policymakers, and other scholars to challenge unreflected-upon common-sense, build on the good-sense that can be found within dominant discourse, and work to address unintended consequences that are inherent in policy implementation.

What we are discussing here are only some of many possible strategies and ways of being active in a reconceptualist movement whose future explorations must involve reinvigorating the concept of praxis within neoliberal common-sense and the unquestioned dominance of commodified care (Hochschild, 2003). This involves continuing the movement's troubling of unquestioned assumptions in early childhood education, work that has historically focused on issues of inclusion/exclusion and standing for more inclusive practice, by drawing upon critical theory to inform diverse practice wherein theory, research, advocacy, and teaching are alloyed.

References

Adams, D. (2006, April 7). How can states leverage child care quality? Whose quality? Paper presented at the Annual Meeting of the American Educational Research Association, San Francisco, CA.

Annie E. Casey Foundation. (2013). *Kids count data book: State trends in child well-being*. Baltimore, MD: Annie E. Casey Foundation.

Arizona Child Care Association (ACCA). (2013). Status of state subsidy [web page]. Retrieved from http://azcca.org/category/des-news

Arizona Department of Education. (2009). *2009 ECBG funding distribution report*. Phoenix, AZ: Arizona Department of Education.

Arizona University Consortium. (2012). *Final report: Family and Community Case Study, technical report of the First Things First External Evaluation*. Tempe, AZ: Arizona University Consortium.

Ball, S. J. (2005). *Education policy and social class: The selected works of Stephen J. Ball*. World Library of Educational-ists. London: Routledge.

Barbarin, O. A., McCandies, T., Early, D., Clifford, R. M., Bryant, D., Burchinal, M., & Pianta, R. (2006). Quality of prekindergarten: What families are looking for in public sponsored programs. *Early Education and Development, 17*, 619–642.

Barnett, W. S. (1993). New wine in old bottles: Increasing the coherence of early childhood care and education policy. *Early Childhood Research Quarterly, 8*, 519–558.

Bloch, M. N. (1987). Becoming scientific and professional: An historical perspective on the aims and effects of early education. In T. Popkewitz (Ed.), *The formation of school subjects: The struggle for creating an American institution* (pp. 25–62). New York: Falmer Press.

Brauner, J., Gordic, B., & Zigler, E. (2004). Putting the child back into child care: Combining care and education for children ages 3–5. *Social Policy Report, 18*, 1–16.

Burchinal, M. R., Roberts, J. E., Nabors, L. A., & Bryant, D. M. (1996). Quality of center child care and infant cognitive and language development. *Child Development, 67*(2), 606–620.

Campaign for Quality Early Education. (2013, June). *Rejoinder to Teachstone's "Dual language learners and the CLASS measure."* Los Angeles, CA: Alliance for a Better Community.

Cannella, G. S. (1997). *Deconstructing early childhood education: Social justice and revolution*. New York: Peter Lang.

Ceglowski, D., & Bacigalupa, C. (2002). Four perspectives on child care quality. *Early Childhood Education Journal, 30*(2), 87–92.

Chaudry, A., Pedroza, J. M., Sandstrom, H., Danzinger, A., Grosz, M., Scott, M., & Ting, S. (2011). *Child care choices of low-income working families*. Washington, DC: Urban Institute.

Child Trends. (2010). Quality rating and improvement systems for early care and education. *Early Childhood Highlights, 1*(1), 1–4.

Cochran, M. (2007). Caregiver and teacher compensation: A crisis in the making. *Zero to Three, 28*(1), 42–47.

Crehan, K. A. F. (2002). *Gramsci, culture and anthropology*. Berkeley, CA: University of California Press.

Dahlberg, G., & Moss, P. (2005). *Ethics and politics in early childhood education*. London: RoutledgeFarmer.

Dahlberg, G., & Moss, P. (2008). Beyond quality in early childhood education and care: Languages of evaluation. *CESifo DICE Report, 6*(2) 21–26.

Dahlberg, G., Moss, P., & Pence, A. (2007). *Beyond quality in early childhood education and care: Postmodern perspectives* (2nd ed.). New York: Routledge.

da Silva, L., & Wise, S. (2006). Parent perspectives on childcare quality among a culturally diverse sample. *Australian Journal of Early Childhood, 31*(3), 6–14.

de Sousa Santos, B. (2006). Globalizations. *Theory, Culture and Society, 23*(2–3), 393–399.

Education Week. (2002). Quality counts, building blocks for success: State efforts in early-childhood education. *Education Week, 21*(17).

First Things First (FTF). (2010a). How regional councils work [web page]. Retrieved from http://www.azftf.gov/WhoWeAre/HowWeWork/Pages/Strategies.aspx

First Things First (FTF). (2010b). Quality first for your students and families [web page]. Retrieved from http://www.azftf.gov/WhatWeDo/Programs/QualityFirst/Pages/Providers.aspx

First Things First (FTF). (2011a). *Annual report*. Phoenix, AZ: First Things First.

First Things First (FTF). (2011b). *Ready for school, set for life*. Phoenix, AZ: First Things First.

First Things First (FTF). (2011c). Quality First rating packages. Phoenix, AZ: First Things First.

First Things First (FTF). (2012a). *Annual report*. Phoenix, AZ: First Things First.

First Things First (FTF). (2012b). Board agenda item: Quality First update on estimated rating for enrolled providers, providers on the wait list, and age ranges of enrolled children. Phoenix, AZ: First Things First.

Gallagher, J. J., Clifford, R. M., & Maxwell, K. (2004). Getting from here to there: To an ideal early preschool system. *Early Childhood Research and Practice, 6*(1). Retrieved from http://ecrp.uiuc.edu/v6n1/clifford.html

Gomby, D. S., Krantzler, N., Larner, M. B., Stevenson, C. S., Terman, D. L., & Behrman, R. E. (1996). Financing child care: Analysis and recommendations. *The Future of Children, 6*(2), 5–26.

Gramsci, A. (1971). *Prison notebooks: Selections by Antonio Gramsci*, trans. G. N. Smith & Q. Hoare. New York: International Publishers.

Hallam, R., Fouts, H., Bargreen, K., & Caudle, L. (2009). Quality from a toddler's perspective: A bottom-up examination of classroom experiences. *Early Childhood Research and Practice, 11*(2). Retrieved from http://ecrp.uiuc.edu/v11n2/hallam.html

Heckman, J. J. (2011, Spring). The economics of inequality: The value of early childhood education. *American Educator*, 31–47.

Helburn, S. W., & Cost, Quality and Child Outcomes Team. (1995). *Cost, quality and child outcomes in child care centers: Technical report*. Denver, CO: University of Colorado.

Hochschild, A. R. (2003). *The commercialization of intimate life: Notes from home and work.* Berkeley, CA: University of California Press.

Jipson, J. (2001). Developmentally appropriate practice: Culture, curriculum, connections. *Early Education and Development, 2*(2), 120–136.

Jones, S. (2006). *Antonio Gramsci.* New York: Routledge.

Kagan, S. L., & Kauerz, K. (2010). Governance and transition. In S. L. Kagan, & K. Tarrant (Eds.), *Transitions for young children: Creating connections across early childhood systems* (pp. 243–256). Baltimore, MD: Brookes.

Kessler, S. (1991). Alternative perspectives on early childhood education. *Early Childhood Research Quarterly, 6*(2), 183–197.

Lash, M., & McMullen, M. (2008). The childcare trilemma: How moral orientations influence the field. *Contemporary Issues in Early Childhood, 9*(1), 36–48.

López, F. (2011). The nongeneralizability of classroom dynamics as predictors of achievement for Hispanic students in upper elementary grades. *Hispanic Journal of Behavioral Sciences, 33*(3), 350–376.

Lubeck, S. (1998). Is developmentally appropriate practice for everyone? *Childhood Education, 74*(5), 283–292.

Martin, B. (2012). An increased role for the Department of Education in addressing federalism concerns. *Brigham Young University Education & Law Journal, 1*, 79–110.

Marx, K. (1852/1972). Eighteenth Brumaire of Louis Bonaparte. In R.C. Tucker (Ed.), *The Marx-Engels reader* (pp. 436–525). New York: W.W. Norton.

Nagasawa, M. (2010). *The early childhood block grant: A biography of Arizona's early childhood education program* (Doctoral dissertation). Retrieved from UMI/Proquest. (3410775).

National Education Goals Panel. (1991). *The national education goals report.* Washington, DC: National Education Goals Panel.

No Child Left Behind (NCLB) Act of 2001, Pub. L. No. 107–110, § 115, Stat. 1425 (2002).

Peisner-Feinberg, E. S., Burchinal, M. R., Clifford, R. M., Culkin, M. L., Howes, C., Kagan, S. L., & Yazejian, N. (2001). The relation of preschool child-care quality to children's cognitive and social developmental trajectories through second grade. *Child Development, 72*, 1534–1553.

Perkins, D., Nelms, L., & Smyth, P. (2004). Beyond neo-liberalism: The social investment state? *Social Policy Working Paper 3.* Melbourne: Brotherhood of St. Laurence.

Proposition 203: I-16-2006; First Things First for Arizona's Children, 2006.

QRIS National Learning Network. (2013, May). Current status of QRIS in states. Retrieved from http://www.qrisnetwork.org/qris-state-contacts-map

Soto, L. D., & Swadener, B. B. (2002). Toward liberatory early childhood, theory, research and praxis: Decolonizing a field. *Contemporary Issues in Early Childhood, 3*(1), 38–65.

Swadener, B. B. (2003). "This is what democracy looks like!" Strengthening advocacy in neoliberal times. *Journal of Early Childhood Teacher Education, 24*(2), 135–141.

The White House. (2013). Fact sheet President Obama's plan for early education for all Americans. Washington, DC: Office of the Press Secretary. Retrieved from http://www.whitehouse.gov/the-press-office/2013/02/13/fact-sheet-president-obama-s-plan-early-education-all-americans

Tobin, J. J. (2005). Quality in early childhood education: An anthropologist's perspective. *Early Education and Development, 16*, 421–434.

United Nations. (1989, November 20). Convention on the Rights of the Child. Retrieved from http://untreaty.un.org/cod/avl/ha/crc/crc.html

Vitiello, V. E. (2013, February). *Dual language learners and the CLASS measure.* Charlottesville, VA: Teachstone Training.

Wilgoren, J. (1999, October 22). Quality day care, early, is tied to achievements as an adult. *New York Times,* A16.

TWENTY-THREE

Social Activism: The Risky Business of Early Childhood Educators in Neoliberal Australian Classrooms

Kylie Smith and Sheralyn Campbell

Australia is a nation that has eight states and territories. Each of these is further divided into smaller areas of local government. Early childhood services that sit outside of formal schooling reflect the wide diversity of the social, political, historical, economic, and geographical landscape of Australia. They are both publicly and privately owned and operated. They vary from state to state in size, funding, statutory governance, hours and cost of operation, locations, staff ratios, and staff qualifications. The types of early childhood services used by Australian families include long daycare, preschool/kindergarten, home-based care, outside-school-hours care, occasional/informal care, mobile services, and extended family. During the Australian federal election campaign of 2007, we (Sheralyn and Kylie) watched and listened with great excitement and anticipation, as a call and promise of an investment in the early years was made by the Australian Labor Party. With the subsequent successful election of the Labor government, the Council of Australian Governments (COAG) brought together government ministers and key stakeholders from all states and territories to approve the National Quality Framework (NQF). The NQF comprises an integrated set of laws, regulations, quality standards, and approved early childhood curriculum known as the *Early Years Learning Framework: Belonging, Being, Becoming* (Commonwealth of Australia, 2009). Other changes included increased staff-to-child ratios, the introduction of a national Early Years workforce strategy with resultant up-skilling of educators, and universal access to preschool, to name a few. These changes addressed state-by-state diversity in early childhood services and were justified as a long-term investment in the economic and social future of Australia.

For many early childhood educators, the NQF finally acknowledged years of activism and lobbying for national recognition of the importance of the early years of learning to Australia's future. We strongly supported the need for quality early childhood environments and communities.

However, somewhat naively, we did not anticipate the effects of neoliberal policies that frame the NQF. Now, having lived with this investment in the everyday as early childhood educators and managers of early childhood services, we have begun to ask ourselves the question: investment in what and whom in the early years?

This chapter will examine how we make sense of the hegemony of neoliberalism: standards and outcomes that exclude children, families, and educators from diverse economic, linguistic, and cultural backgrounds. Using concepts of relations of power/knowledge (Foucault, 1994; Gore, 2002) and rhizomes (Deleuze & Guattari, 1987), we will explore some risks for early childhood communities that openly challenge and resist the neoliberal practices within the NQF. We will reflect on opportunities for challenging neoliberalism and navigating more socially just spaces and practices in the everyday classroom.

Neoliberalisms in the NQF

We have been colleagues, mentors, critical friends, supporters, and learners together for more than 20 years. In the past ten years, we have lived in different states in Australia approximately 554 kilometers apart. Phone calls, email, cards/letters, visits, and conferences have supported our continued reflections, dialogue, and debate with each other. This is a space where we are able to critique, query, question, and theorize out loud in a safe space without threat of censor or rebuke. The beauty of our phone conversations is that they are spaces where we can deconstruct what is going on, dream how we might reconstruct things, and go away energized and with questions that help us to transform our dreamings into realities of the everyday. Most recently we have talked about the effects of the national investment in the early years of education on our everyday classrooms.

Alongside the positive changes from the NQF, including more funding for staff, we saw educators increasingly focused on compliance with NQF documents. Rather than improving outcomes for children, we saw educators prioritizing production, assessment, and documentation of learning outcomes. This often took them away from spending time with children and celebrating "moments" that are important in children's lives. There were fewer opportunities for critical reflection among educators on how political forces, including gender, "race," and "class," were part of our classrooms, or how our different subjectivities were part of our pedagogy.

We also talked about how we spent more time on management and administrative tasks and less time engaging with the children or co-educators. We discussed our frustrations with the often rushed and interrupted moments that we had for reflection, debate, or exploring ideas. We found the new directions of the NQF increasingly a process of alienation (from children, families, and colleagues) and production (of compliance practices, systems, and structures). The external pressures to comply with and then be assessed on whether we had got the NQF "right" averted our attention from the increasing political silences in our work.

Our questions included:

- Why am I not coping with the increased demands?
- Why am I not able to juggle NQS and everyday practice?
- Why am I spending more time working?
- Why am I spending less time with children and families?

- Why am I spending less time reflecting and in dialogue with co-educators?
- Why am I feeling like I am failing and not "getting it right"?
- Why am I losing my passion for teaching in a time when I was being told that the investments and new initiatives were creating opportunities for new innovation in early childhood?

Like good neoliberal subjects, we initially placed the blame on ourselves as individuals and used terms like "tired" or "burnout." However, hearing the echoes of "alienation" and "production" in our work and in conversations with other educators helped us to explore the underlying, strong, and explicit connections between the NQF and neoliberalism.

The NQF guides promote consistency across all types of education and care services and argue for the NQF as a means of lifting national productivity, providing evidence-based changes, and embedding universal quality standards. The Department of Education, Employment and Workplace Relations (DEEWR) national website states: "Investing in the health, education, development and care of our children benefits children and their families, our communities and the economy, and is critical to lifting workforce participation and delivering the Government's productivity agenda" (DEEWR, 2012). Education and care services are rated by officers from the state compliance agency against quality indicators. The rating outcomes are publicly available. They are intended as a guide for families to help them make informed decisions about their preferred education and care service. Services are encouraged to use the ratings as a marketing tool. This approach promotes further free-market competition.

Educators are responsible for complying with the NQF and ensuring children and learning programs are evaluated and assessed against universal outcomes. Assessment is described in two ways. First, assessment involves a cycle of gathering and analyzing information to substantiate and inform how programs are designed to reflect the individual child. Second, assessment makes learning visible by examining "the learning strategies that children use and reflect ways in which learning is co-constructed through interactions between the educator and each child" (Early Years Learning Framework [EYLF], 2013, p. 17).

In a neoliberal world, success is the responsibility of the individual and each person has the opportunity to succeed if he or she works hard. That means "I" can be a successful educator if I up-skill, go to the right training, read the right professional development books, develop and use the right observation and assessment template, have better time management, work harder.... Notions of individualism, commodification, and market have meant that where children, families, and/or educators are "failing," disconnected, or struggling, it is a reflection of the service or individual—the inadequacy of the program, service, teaching, parenting, or child rather than a socioeconomic, cultural, or political effect (Angus, 2012; Comber & Nixon, 2009). These ideas began to resonate in our conversations, and in our reflections with co-educators, we saw neoliberalisms seeping through the changes to our practices.

(Un)Realities in the Everyday

I (Sheralyn) work with colleagues in a group of rural education and care services in the Australian state of New South Wales (four services in a local government region, providing centre-based and mobile preschool, long daycare, outside-school-hours care, and occasional care, with around 350 families using these services each week). The families who use our services are not only the people whom we work with but also at times our neighbors, our friends, and our relatives. These intimate insights and experiences of ourselves within our community shape, and sometimes blur, what we do daily with families and children.

We are a diverse and complex group of people with varied histories, knowledges, desires, and passions. Each person has different early childhood perspectives. Our differences inform our conversations about what quality looks like and draw from feminist poststructuralist ideas, sociocultural theory, developmental knowledge, and critical perspectives. The collisions and contradictions among our views are many. Consensus is not guaranteed in our work, nor is compliance with institutionally recognized and endorsed practices. However, we use our multiple views to take action and make educational decisions based on our questions about who is advantaged and disadvantaged by what we do. We have at times found that our decisions about our teaching have located us in a space between compliance with dominant practices and resistance.

The Borderlines of Compliance and Resistance

Prior to the NQF, the New South Wales state law required all children's services to maintain development records of each child using an education and care service. In our region of NSW, this meant good educators were commonly expected to complete an observation "portfolio" for each child in their group. A portfolio comprised developmental observations, digitally recorded and individualized "learning stories," photos, and samples of art work. Educators spent hours of their own time and work time collating these varied snapshots of the individual child. These were inspected by visiting state Children's Services officers once every year or so, and an edited copy was given to parents at the end of the calendar year. Portfolios were both a family keepsake but also evidence of the "good" educator.

Good educators were constituted within this circulating discourse as experts who had special insights into the true picture of who each child was, the child's interests, his or her development, friendships, and so on. The child was both transparent and malleable. There were many silences within portfolios. In particular, children's forays into racisms, classisms, and sexisms were not part of the records of the child or group. Nor were the gendered politics of how these demands impacted the mainly female educators. Although many educators spoke privately about how the time spent on portfolios diminished their pleasure in their work, few risked their status or institutional authorization as a good educator by opting out of the practices.

Cannella (1997) wrote:

> The discourses and actions associated with professional institutions and practices have generated disciplinary powers over educators (who are mostly women) and children. Standards have been created through which individuals judge and limit themselves, through which they construct a desire to be "good," "normal" or both. (p. 121)

Michel Foucault (1977) described disciplinary power over the site of the individual as the "docile body": "A body is docile that may be subjected, used, transformed, and improved" (p. 136).

The introduction of the NQF transformed portfolios into a new language of assessment and evaluation. The portfolio practices associated with NQF assessment and evaluation were not substantially altered because they continued to locate the individual child as transparent, knowable, and primarily developmental. The educator continued to be positioned as the objective expert or apprentice who is responsible for the child's achievement of universal learning outcomes. The emphasis on assessment and evaluation as products of good teaching has added to the ways portfolio documentation practices govern educators and their teaching.

With a feminized workforce in Australian early childhood education and care, we need to find points of resistance, rather than being docile bodies and implementing the NQF without question. Points of resistance enable us to be politically active by questioning and challenging how others decide we are used, transformed, and improved. There are contradictions within the EYLF that offer opportunities to plot borders of resistance where politics and identity are acknowledged.

Borders of Resistance

Prior to the NQF, our group of educators resisted individualizing and sanitizing portfolio practices continued by the NQF and expanded into evaluation and assessment of children's learning outcomes. Rather, we decided to use the time that we were with children to engage with them and with each other in the messiness of learning and relationships. We made commitments to think about what was happening for and among people in our classroom, to pursue our passions and interests, and to share this in a collective way through a single journal. We adopted a stance of collective uncertainty and identified ourselves as skeptics who, as educators, could not "know" a child. Our journal focused on what was happening for and among children, what we thought about it, how our teaching might have been involved in political struggles, and what we would like to explore in response to this. We also prioritized spending our time with families in meaningful conversation. We found ways to comply with state law and regulations about requests for individual developmental child records. Our approach was not perfect. Not every educator wrote in the journal. Not every educator wrote about gendered, racialized, or classist politics. Some educators felt disadvantaged because there was no portfolio to show off the work that they had contributed to the program in the year. Sometimes educators wrote things that appeared tokenistic or unfair to others.

- In 2012, our commitment to resisting dominant practices of documentation continued in our discussions of what the NQF meant for our knowledges and practices. We used the emphasis on critical reflection in the EYLF, Belonging, Being, Becoming, to authorize our spaces for social activism. This emphasis is captured in the questions: What are my understandings of each child?
- What theories, philosophies, and understandings shape and assist my work?
- Who is advantaged when I work in this way? Who is disadvantaged?
- What questions do I have about my work? What am I challenged by? What am I curious about? What am I confronted by?
- What aspects of my work are not helped by the theories and guidance that I usually draw on to make sense of what I do?
- Are there other theories or knowledge that could help me to understand better what I have observed or experienced? What are they? How might those theories and that knowledge affect my practice? (Early Years Learning Framework, EYLF, 2013, p. 13)

Our discussions and journaling were not simply an internal act for the group. We spoke regionally at network meetings about how our practices differed from portfolio documentation and how we would continue our collective approach within the NQF requirement to assess and evaluate learning. We used the emphasis on critical reflection within the EYLF to frame and justify continuing our collective and political journaling. We organized workshops for our region that were given by presenters chosen for challenging dominant practices of child observation and record keeping. We understood this to be "risky," but did not recognize how the effects of our actions would spread across time, and result in a clash between the neoliberal and critical constitution of good educator in the NQF. Power is tricky.

How Regimes of Truth Disrupted Our Resistance

Relations of power circulate within competing educational discourses and authorize some ways of understanding and practicing the positions of educator, and not others. These relations of power/knowledge are recognizable at their disciplinary points of effect. However, power is not simply oppressive, but also a productive web of discursive actions (Foucault, 1994). We came to acknowledge this when we opened our collective journaling to quality compliance and assessment within the NQF. Two state Children's Services officers arrived to undertake their assessment and quality review of our service. They had been part of a workshop that we had organized on alternative and critical methods of documenting, assessing, and evaluating learning. The quality review visit by the Children's Service officers resulted in the following assessment:

> Indicator 1.2.3: Each child's learning and development is assessed as part of an ongoing cycle of planning, documenting and evaluation.
>
> Assessment/ Rating: Not Met.
>
> Comment: Educators document some aspects of the daily program in a format used across the centre and each child's learning and development is tracked with a code. However, there is little evidence that children's development is evaluated to determine how they are achieving learning outcomes.
>
> While educators are active and reflective in designing and delivering the program, evaluation of children's learning and development is not consistent across the program. Therefore the Standard for 1.2 is Working Towards National Quality Standard. (Australian Children's Education & Care Quality Authority, 2012, p. 6)

In conversations with each other after the visit, our team discussed the effects of how the Children's Services officers applied the NQF to assessment and evaluation practices in our service. We examined the operation of relations of power/knowledge (Foucault, 1994) as it was signified by the tactics and strategies of surveillance, normalization, exclusion, distribution, classification, individualization, totalization, and regulation (Gore, 2002). Our conversations mapped how even as power circulates, there are possibilities for resistance (MacNaughton, 2005).

Surveillance:

Dianne: I was very aware of being observed—it's just part of the process. I knew they were watching me and routines. That's [the Children's Services officers'] job.

Catherine: I felt like someone was watching me—it keeps you on your game. It was like they were outside looking in and didn't get involved. One of [the Children's Services officers] sat behind the wall so children couldn't see her but she could hear everything.

Normalization, Classification, Exclusion, Regulation:

Jane: I'm assuming we're not doing the right thing because we're doing it differently. So [to be good educators], we have to change what we are doing.

Sally: I felt I was in the firing line when asked what is my role as an educational leader because I did not give the words: comply with regulation; abide by the Code of Conduct; meet the terms of my employment; be consistent with policies and procedures; conform with the EYLF; understand the operations of management; apply communication skills—it's like making a pledge!

Pat [our cook, whom we consider an educator]: Did they think I'm not really part of [the NQF]? The Children's Services officers made me feel my contribution to the service is insignificant. Our centre is a little different to what they are used to I think. The children here really need what we provide [food and nutrition] so what I do is worked into the program. The questioning was not about how what I do fits in with the EYLF or our philosophy. I might just be the cook, but I'm part of what everyone does here.

Classification, Individualization, Totalization:

Sally: The assessors suggested using a colour-coding system to track children's development and their links to the learning outcomes. Do people really do that? Where does it say we need to be doing it? It's a scary thought that other centres are doing it and the assessors have picked up the idea and are suggesting we all do the same.

The review of our work by the Children's Services officers suggests, within a neoliberal frame, we are "working towards" being good educators. Accepting this construction of our teaching produces silences and carries risks. Our ways of teaching and learning can be subverted, shifted, and colonized by the dominant discourses:

Sally: When I showed [the Children's Services officers] the stories that parents and I had written together about what it's like to leave your child for the first time, I was thought of as being incapable of thinking of this idea without the EYLF. What makes them think we have been sitting on our hands and waiting for a magic framework to come along and say this is the way you need to practice? They took a copy of these stories and the weekly program. I wonder what they will use them for? I wonder in what way they will use them? Will it be to support the EYLF and claim [these stories] as their own?

As agentic subjects of competing discourses, we can refuse this positioning of ourselves as "educators in need of instruction and more work." There are alternative positions that we can take, perhaps found in the unstable spaces constituted by the contradictions between neoliberal and critical discourses of the NQF. Rhizoanalysis is a way of creating ruptures in dominant discourses and opening spaces in which to work differently.

Rhizoanalysis—Exploring Alternative Positions and Unstable Spaces

Rhizoanalysis is a process for exploring what a text "does and how it connects with other things (including its reader, its author, its literary and non-literary context)" (Grosz, 1994, p. 199). The intent of a rhizoanalysis is to produce new meanings by using tactically chosen text to "cast a shadow" over another text and in doing so to disrupt and change the politics of the initial text. For Deleuze and Guattari (1987), as for Foucault (1977), meanings connect to each other, to systems of knowledge, and to how power is organized, produced, and struggled over: "A rhizome ceaselessly establishes connections between semiotic chains, organisation of power, and circumstances relative to the arts, sciences and social struggle" (Deleuze & Guattari, 1987, p. 7).

Gilles Deleuze and Félix Guattari suggest that a rhizomatic analysis draw on six principles: connection, heterogeneity, multiplicity, asignifying rupture, cartography, and decalcomania (Deleuze & Guattari, 1987).

Sheralyn and her colleagues have mapped the effects of the application of NQF neoliberalisms by compliance officers on their practices of documentation, assessment, and evaluation. These effects include the production of a homogenous and de-politicized child and educator, who exist in disconnected spaces of development and individualization. Rhizoanalysis offers ways of creating ruptures for new lines of flight. We have drawn on feminist texts to create ruptures to homogenous and de-politicized spaces where educators position themselves or are positioned as not coping with change, not working hard enough, not managing time, and not being organized. In doing this, we begin to see new lines of flight to resist practices that universalize ways of engaging with children, families, and communities.

Decal text 1. Creating Ruptures for New Lines of Flight: Naming Regimes of Truth
Jennifer Gore (1993) writes:

> As subjects of knowledge, we have constituted ourselves more often as bearers or holders of knowledge, as pedagogues or intellectuals able to use knowledge as revenge, than agents subjected to knowledge, caught up in various regimes. As subjects acting on others we have constituted ourselves particular (modernist) concepts of the role and function of the intellectual. As moral agents, we have constituted ourselves primarily in relation to the ways in which we act on ourselves. (p. 131)

These "regimes" circulate to establish and support rules and regulations that define and depict the truth about how the individual should act, feel, think, and speak. Naming the authorizing neoliberal basis for knowledges and practices of the NQF also provides opportunities for educators to reconstitute themselves in alternative ways and explore critical spaces of pedagogy within the EYLF.

Decal text 2. Creating Ruptures for New Lines of Flight: Identify Discourses That Universalize and Oppress Women Through White Patriarchal Strategies
Joan Cocks (1984) writes:

> What, one can ask, are the dominant culture's basic classifications and assignments of identity, its range of conceivable practices, its encouraged sensibilities, and its prohibited trains of

thought? That is, what is the nature of the order of things both dominant and subordinate populations [educators and students (and theorists)] inhabit? What are the stances toward that order it is possible to take? Which of these stances are most likely to lead the way out, and which populations are most likely to be led, not to some free zone of thought and action, but from the hegemonic set of specifications through their subversion into some other, different sort? How is the dominant culture kept alive, reproduced, and expanded? To what extent is instrumentalism correct when it claims that it is the subordinate population that must be, in the normal times, most thoroughly captivated by hegemonic ideas, or that it is the dominant group that always plays the pre-eminent part in keeping the given order intact? (pp. 189–190)

Cocks questions how dominant cultures like the NQF normalize and capture hegemonic ideas. This creates ruptures for me (Kylie) when I trace this text over our comments and need for answers to support the "right" way or best way to implement the NQF.

Gaile Cannella (1997) wrote:

The discourses and actions associated with professional institutions and practices have generated disciplinary powers over teachers (who are mostly women) and children. Standards have been created through which individuals judge and limit themselves, through which they construct a desire to be "good" or "normal" or both. (p. 121)

Are issues of alienation from children, families, and co-educators and emphasis on producing systems, structures, and practices of compliance with the NQF attempts to be the good or the normal teacher?

As Audre Lorde (1979) observed:

As women we have been taught either to ignore our difference or to view them as causes for separation and suspicion rather than as forces for change. Without community there is no liberation only the most vulnerable and temporary armistice between an individual and her oppression. But community must not mean a shedding of our difference, nor the pathetic pretense that these differences do not exist. (p. 99)

Rather than the individualizing practices of neoliberalism, collectivity, heterogeneity, and community offer spaces in which to reconstitute what pedagogy and NQS looks like.

Ien Ang (2003) further asserts:

The so-called politics of difference recognises the need to go beyond the notion of an encompassing sisterhood and acknowledges that feminism needs to take account of the fact that not all women are white, Western and middle class and take into consideration the experiences of "other" women as well. (p. 191)

The alternative positions and unstable spaces of education are not guaranteed but shifting and entangled in the operation of webs of power.

Jane Flax (1990) comments that:

Feminist theories, like other forms of postmodernism, should encourage us to tolerate and interpret ambivalence, ambiguity, and multiplicity as well as expose the roots of our needs for imposing order and structure no matter how arbitrary and oppressive these needs may be. If we do our work well, reality will appear even more unstable, complex and disorderly than it does now. (pp. 56–57)

When we take the text from these writers and the questions we had been asking ourselves, it creates opportunities to explore the circulation of power and neoliberal policy discourse, to begin to imagine alternative spaces.

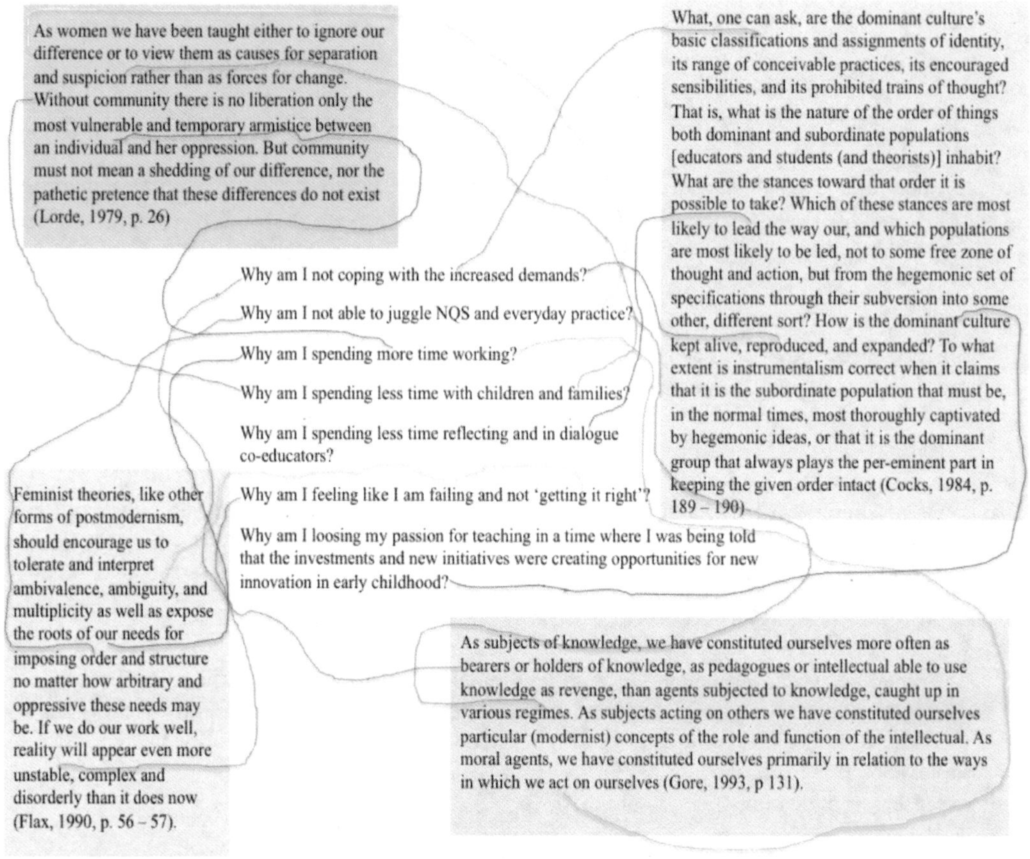

As women we have been taught either to ignore our difference or to view them as causes for separation and suspicion rather than as forces for change. Without community there is no liberation only the most vulnerable and temporary armistice between an individual and her oppression. But community must not mean a shedding of our difference, nor the pathetic pretence that these differences do not exist (Lorde, 1979, p. 26)

What, one can ask, are the dominant culture's basic classifications and assignments of identity, its range of conceivable practices, its encouraged sensibilities, and its prohibited trains of thought? That is, what is the nature of the order of things both dominant and subordinate populations [educators and students (and theorists)] inhabit? What are the stances toward that order it is possible to take? Which of these stances are most likely to lead the way our, and which populations are most likely to be led, not to some free zone of thought and action, but from the hegemonic set of specifications through their subversion into some other, different sort? How is the dominant culture kept alive, reproduced, and expanded? To what extent is instrumentalism correct when it claims that it is the subordinate population that must be, in the normal times, most thoroughly captivated by hegemonic ideas, or that it is the dominant group that always plays the per-eminent part in keeping the given order intact (Cocks, 1984, p. 189 – 190)

Why am I not coping with the increased demands?

Why am I not able to juggle NQS and everyday practice?

Why am I spending more time working?

Why am I spending less time with children and families?

Why am I spending less time reflecting and in dialogue co-educators?

Feminist theories, like other forms of postmodernism, should encourage us to tolerate and interpret ambivalence, ambiguity, and multiplicity as well as expose the roots of our needs for imposing order and structure no matter how arbitrary and oppressive these needs may be. If we do our work well, reality will appear even more unstable, complex and disorderly than it does now (Flax, 1990, p. 56 – 57).

Why am I feeling like I am failing and not 'getting it right'?

Why am I loosing my passion for teaching in a time where I was being told that the investments and new initiatives were creating opportunities for new innovation in early childhood?

As subjects of knowledge, we have constituted ourselves more often as bearers or holders of knowledge, as pedagogues or intellectual able to use knowledge as revenge, than agents subjected to knowledge, caught up in various regimes. As subjects acting on others we have constituted ourselves particular (modernist) concepts of the role and function of the intellectual. As moral agents, we have constituted ourselves primarily in relation to the ways in which we act on ourselves (Gore, 1993, p 131).

Figure 1. Smith & Campbell, selected quotations.

Conclusion

Political activism in the classroom should be contextual. To be politically active for change it is important to have critical friends, time to reflect and enter into dialogue, and to have access to different ways of knowing. For us, understandings of neoliberalism and understandings of power have helped to open journeys for resistance to current understandings of quality and evidence in our Australian early childhood classrooms. But there is more work to do and further questions to explore. We ask what might it look like to rub against the grain of neoliberalisms and constitute ourselves as good educators and agents of change.

Could we:

- Name the regimes of truth by seeking out and transforming the homogenizing and marginalizing practices of neoliberalism within the NQF?
- Resist these practices by continuing to prioritize the political aspects of identities and their racist, sexist, heterosexist, classist effects in what we reflect on and engage with?
- Reconstitute the spaces of our professional knowledge as uncertain and shifting, using questions to explore and reconstruct early childhood pedagogy?
- Reject individualizing spaces for shared community stories in which we rewrite and reauthorize neoliberal NQF practices?
- Explore alternative theories to create new ways of understanding ourselves and support new language and ideas for political activism in early childhood classrooms and communities?

References

Ang, I. (2003). "I'm a feminist but…": "Other" women and postnational feminism. In R. Lewis & S. Mills (Eds.), *Feminist postcolonial theory* (pp. 190–206). Edinburgh: Edinburgh University Press.

Angus, L. (2012). Teaching within and against the circle of privilege: Reforming teachers, reforming schools. *Journal of Educational Policy, 27*(2), 231–251.

Australian Children's Education & Care Quality Authority. (2012, April). National Quality Standard and Assessment Rating Instrument. Retrieved from http://www.acecqa.gov.au/Uploads/files/Assessment%20and%20 Rating/1-NQS_Assessment%20and%20Rating%20Instrument_120522_%20FINAL-1.pdf

Cannella, G. (1997). *Deconstructing early childhood education: Social justice and revolution.* New York: Peter Lang.

Cocks, J. (1984). *The oppositional imagination: Feminism, critique and political theory.* New York: Routledge.

Comber, B., & Nixon, H. (2009). Teachers' work and pedagogy in an era of accountability. *Discourse: Studies in the Cultural Politics of Education, 30*(3), 333–345.

Commonwealth of Australia. (2009). *Early Years Learning Framework: Being, belonging, becoming.* Retrieved from http://www.education.nt.gov.au/__data/assets/pdf_file/0018/20538/BelongingBeing-Becoming.pdf

Deleuze, G., & Guattari, F. (1987). *A thousand plateaus: Capitalism and schizophrenia.* London: Athlone Press.

Department of Education, Employment and Workplace Relations (DEEWR). (2012). Retrieved from http://www.imvc.com.au/broaden-your-horizons/government-departments-programs/federal-government/department-of-education-employment-and-workplace-relations-deewr/

Early Years Learning Framework (EYLF). (2013, 9 July). Retrieved from http://education.gov.au/early-years-learning-framework

Flax, J. (1990). Postmodernism and gender relations in feminist theory. In L. Nicholson (Ed.), *Feminism/postmodernism* (pp. 39–62). New York: Routledge.

Foucault, M. (1977). *Discipline and punish: The birth of the prison.* London: Penguin.

Foucault, M. (1994). Truth and power. In J. D. Faubion (Ed.), *Power: The essential works of Foucault 1954–1984.* London: Penguin, pp. 111–133.

Gore, J. M. (1993). *The struggles for pedagogies: Critical and feminist discourses as regimes of truth.* New York: Routledge.

Gore, J. M. (2002). Some certainties in the uncertain world of classroom practice: An outline of a theory or power relations in pedagogy. Paper prepared for presentation at the Annual Meeting of the Australian Association for Research in Education, Brisbane, December 2–5, 2002. Retrieved from http://publications.aare.edu.au/02pap/gor02317.htm

Grosz, E. (1994). *Volatile bodies: Toward a corporeal feminism.* Bloomington, IN: Indiana University Press.

Grosz, E. (1995). *Sexy bodies: The strange carnalities of feminism.* New York: Routledge.

Lorde, A. (1979). The master's tools will never dismantle the master's house. In C. Moraga & G. Anzaldua (Eds.), *This bridge called my back: Writings by radical women of color* (pp. 98–101). New York: Kitchen Table/Women of Color Press.

MacNaughton, G. (2005). *Doing Foucault in early childhood studies: Applying poststructural ideas.* Abingdon, Oxon: Routledge.

TWENTY-FOUR

[Im]possibilities of Reinvention of Palestinian Early Childhood Education

Janette Habashi

Palestinian non-governmental organizations (NGOs) have been instrumental in spearheading the establishment and development of social welfare services, agriculture cooperatives, health provisions, as well as education and early childhood programs. Non-governmental organizations are the pulse of the community, as they tend to recognize community challenges prior to any governmental body. In fact, NGOs identify community needs and initiate services that form the collective narrative and shape the government's response. Palestinian NGOs are fundamental to national ethos and their existence is considered a form of resistance to Israeli occupation as well as a sign of community resilience (Challand, 2009; Sullivan, 1996). The strength and the meaning of this relationship between Palestinian NGOs and the community facilitate the implementation of early childhood care and education, as opposed to formal educational programs in schools. It is in this spirit that the NGO A Child's Cup Full (ACCF)[1] is imagining and planning an early childhood education project in the Jenin area in the West Bank.

This chapter articulates the progress and the steps taken to understand the role of NGOs in early childhood education in the occupied Palestinian Territories (oPT) and the lessons learned while conceptualizing ACCF's plan for Palestinian early childhood education in Jenin Refugee Camp. To facilitate the achievement of such a dream, it is essential to scrutinize the Palestinian historical, structural, and political context that might or might not make it possible to realize this path, especially as it relates to the challenges of NGOs' external/internal funding and early childhood curricula. The contextualization and interrelation of these elements are the cornerstones for ACCF to envision an example of the reinvention of early childhood education in the oPT, whereby the community is not contingent on external funding and therefore has a voice in the discussion of the curricula and local programming.

Development of ECE in Palestine

With the first political uprising (Intifada) in the occupied Palestinian Territories in the 1980s, the Palestinian NGOs galvanized the enterprise of early childhood education. During this political era, unemployment was high and the Israeli military and government killed, imprisoned, and disabled Palestinians, particularly men, which impacted the social fabric of the society (Nicolai, 2007). Women sought jobs outside the home and became breadwinners while the NGOs, specifically NGOs targeted to women, filled the vacuum of children's care and education (Christina, 2004). The consistent efforts of these organizations planted the seeds for early childhood education, shaped by the political uncertainty in the region. It became apparent that there was a need to care for and educate children that was not merely contingent on political stability. The continuation of needs and the community effort of NGOs and their funders formed the current Palestinian political players and framed the discussion of early childhood education.

The Palestinian NGOs' commitment to early childhood education continues to persist, even though the political landscape has changed drastically since the first Intifada (Christina, 2006). In 1993, the Palestinian Liberation Organization (PLO) signed the Oslo Accord. The premise of the Oslo Accord is to serve as a transitional stage for the creation of a sovereign Palestinian state. The accord was only partially implemented (Ben-Porat & Mizrahi, 2005), creating the Palestinian Authority (PA) that aimed to establish laws, institutions, and governing bodies for statehood while Palestinian territories were still under Israeli occupation (Shikaki, 2002). In fact, the transitional phase is now the status quo, as the oPT remain under Israeli control, which adds layers of difficulties for the development of early childhood education. The reality of this situation is that the Palestinian people and local NGOs have to engage with two political obstacles, the PA and the Israeli occupation, and in many cases the PA is perceived to serve the Israeli agenda (Challand, 2009; Lind, 2010). The Israeli government controls every aspect of Palestinians' lives, yet at the same time the Palestinian Authority is encouraged by the international community to govern through establishing institutions and laws that are constantly reviewed and controlled by the Israeli government (Qarmout & Béland, 2012). The Oslo Accord failed to establish a sovereign Palestine and further enabled the Israeli occupation to continue violating the rights of Palestinian people. Lack of freedom to govern is manifested in the development of a national independent education structure, as the Palestinian people are not able to create their own education policies (Roy, 1999; Sayigh, 2006). The fundamental challenges of the Palestinian education system, including early childhood education and care, are curricula and funding. As Palestine remains stateless, the Palestinian Authority depends heavily on external funding to support educational institutions and programs. This dependence on external funding makes it difficult for the PA to create educational policies that accurately reflect the Palestinian experience and culture, which is contrary to other nation-states that have independently designed their curricula to echo the national narrative. Seemingly, the dependence on funding bodies to shape the curricula is the case in Palestine, as most of the funding sources and organizations perpetuate a political agenda that minimizes national Palestinian curricula. Funding sources use the fact that the PA is dependent on them as leverage to shape the curricula of Palestinian textbooks, oftentimes focusing on a "global" design and rejecting anything that speaks to the Palestinian narrative (Christina, 2006). In addition, much of the donors' agenda is tilted toward Israeli interests (Nicolai, 2007), meaning that the PA is oftentimes having to comply with the agenda of an entity that is controlling the Palestinian people. Also, as education becomes more and more globalized, international NGOs and other donors push a globalized educational curriculum while neglecting the Palestinian voice, effectively controlling Palestinian educational policies and acting as a colonizing force. This globalized educational curriculum advances a neoliberal agenda of western economic importance in order for the West to effectively control their economic and political interests (Christina, 2004, 2006). The implication of the interconnectedness of funding and curricula in Palestine is even more problematic in early childhood education, as NGOs are currently the major provider for early childhood education centers and programs, rather than the Palestinian Authority (Nicolai, 2007). This affects early childhood education more than primary or secondary education as NGOs depend *solely* on international funding.

Players in the Palestinian Early Childhood Story

Religious charitable bodies, women's organizations, and other forms of NGOs have provided and are continuing to deliver childhood care and education. Prior to the Oslo Accord, Palestinian NGOs established preschool centers and developed an early childhood model that spoke to the child's experiences as well as crafted a pre-service program for early childhood teachers. Some of the training program and the curricula were focused on children's environment and incorporated the home as an equal setting for early childhood education and development as early childhood centers. This was executed through teachers' home visitation, in which parents were guided in utilizing the home setting as an educational environment (Christina, 2006). This model reflected the local experience, culture, and resources. The variety of focuses of different local NGOs in early childhood education allowed for the inclusion of the entire spectrum of Palestinian children's education and care, as well as early childhood education staff's professional development. However, this work of NGOs is no longer the case due to the international donors' approach in obligating the PA to regulate national policies and oversee institutions, including all educational institutions and curricula, in a way that mirrors a globalized agenda (Christina, 2004, 2006). From any government's perspective, not having the authority to oversee educational policies jeopardizes the overall state ethos and opens the door to undermine the government's power. For this reason, the role of Palestinian NGOs in early childhood education deviates from its traditional model as the PA and the international donors are aiming to frame the influence of local NGOs in this sector through funding that dictates policy (Challand, 2009). Currently, the overall control of the PA is not explicitly implemented since early childhood education is on the periphery of the Palestinian Ministry of Education and the policy is still in progress. The current work of the Ministry of Education is processing early childhood licenseship that is also completed by the Social Affairs Ministry, depending on the age level of the educational center (UNESCO, 2006). In addition, early childhood centers are supervised by numerous bodies including the Ministries of Education, Social Affairs, Health, Youth and Sport, and Culture (Christina, 2004). The requirement of licenseship is primarily based on health and safety standards.

Licenseship is one strategy of the PA to oversee the discourse on early childhood education in Palestine as it is still mostly administrated by the local NGOs. A national early childhood education is currently on the periphery due to the fact that there are several obstacles to creating a national education policy, including a lack of funding from the PA, external funders' agendas, and the lack of qualified professionals in the field (Christina, 2006; Nicolai, 2007). It seems even though there are multiple ministries that are responsible for supervision of early childhood centers, these national bodies do not provide funding. Rather, external donors provide funding that has stipulations based on a globalized "neo-colonial agenda" (Christina, 2004, p. 143) leading to a lack of cohesive early childhood policy. This external neo-colonial agenda permeates international aid that Palestine receives, especially since the Oslo Accord of 1993, and reflects a globalized, or Western, view of education rather than taking into context the living reality of the Palestinian people. The Western agenda oftentimes perpetuates the dependence of Palestine on international donors by stressing the importance of economic interests of the West rather than trying to actively find solutions to issues in the area (Christina, 2004). According to the Organization for Economic Cooperation and Development (OECD), donors should "take the local context as a starting point; do not harm; align with local priorities in different ways in different contexts; and avoid pockets of exclusion within each context" (Qarmout & Béland, 2012, p. 34). However, international aid to the oPT does not operate in this manner and perpetuates the neo-colonial agenda that promotes Western interests and the West's alliance with Israel (Challand, 2009; Lind, 2010). In a way, this international aid is not neutral as it perpetuates conflict in the region by pushing one interest over another while it promotes Western society's definition of education, health, and social services. Seemingly, this aid creates a "new humanitarianism" that aims to democratize the NGO's efforts and address the educational and social needs of the community from a Western standpoint (Gordon, 2010). Therefore, it is problematic to assume that international donors are neutral in their funding because it conceals their agenda in early childhood education, which fails to consider the community effort in previously developed models of early childhood education in the oPT. The new agenda is to socialize children in early years to endorse Western views of the world and the region through designing curricula that speak to such notions while ignoring the political reality of the Palestinian people.

International donors and organizations such as UNICEF, UNDP, and Save the Children have been facilitating the cooperation between the PA and the Palestinian NGOs in establishing a clear national early childhood policy (Nicolai, 2007), yet such involvement is not without any far-reaching consequences. Since international donors are the bridge between the PA, the NGOs, and early childhood education, they have influential power over policies through their funding, and in a way, policies should comply with the funders' agenda. Hence, a national policy is essential in delivering care and education for all children; however, to craft a partnership in the process does not ensure that the PA and local NGOs have a strong voice in creating a Palestinian early childhood education policy since both entities have to comply with the agenda of the international donor community (Christina, 2004).

The PA and the Palestinian NGOs are virtually dependent on external funding from these international organizations, which at times perpetuate a political agenda that supports the Israeli view of a future Palestine and includes a globalized education for Palestinian children whereby it marginalizes the Palestinian culture, reality, experience, and narrative (Haklai, 2008; Moughrabi, 2001). Therefore, the PA and NGOs are in an impossible situation, as they have no freedom to design a national early childhood curricula that reflects the Palestinian experience and culture. The expected curricula might include cultural symbols but does not always reflect the Palestinian experience or environment. An example of this would be teaching children in a refugee camp that childhood is a violence-free life stage while incorporating Palestinian images of home, garden, and clothing. The paradox is that children recognize through personal experience or through local narrative that for generations they and their families have been living in humiliation due to Israeli occupation (Habashi, 2012). The dilemma in this context is how the PA and local NGOs are going to respond to the globalized educational agenda that is associated with external funds while the alternative is to implement the cultural curricula that was developed by the local NGOs and has no support from the international donor community. This challenge is associated with the enormous need in early childhood education and the lack of local funding in this area. The Ministry of Education is not expected to voice any objection to the globalized educational agenda, as was the case for the primary and secondary school curricula. In addition, most of the staff in the PA ministries are hired according to political party lines and are not based on expertise in the field (Christina, 2006). Apparently, the PA has no control over its educational policies as it is constantly scrutinized by the international community and Israeli government (Nicolai, 2007). However, the main question in this context is whether or not local NGOs have the ability to reinvent the early childhood education curricula and funding in Palestine while engaging with the community.

[Im]possibilities of NGOs in Early Childhood Education

Palestinian NGOs are considered part of the national narrative. They reflect the different periods of the community's needs and consciousness (Sullivan, 1996). In a way, NGOs are the voice of the community and part of the accountability process of policy and power. Hence, the existence of Palestinian NGOs is explicitly contingent on funding from local and external donors. Prior to the Oslo Accord in 1993, there was a push to establish and fund NGOs since these institutions were the alternative function to the state through providing services, galvanizing support for the community, creating change, and forming resistance to Israeli occupation (Nicolai, 2007). The funding of local NGOs was challenging but came mainly from the Palestinian Liberation Organization (PLO), Arab countries, and some Western donors (Challand, 2009; Sullivan, 1996). However, the function of NGOs after 1993 has been reshaped because the funding sources have changed. International donors wanted the PA to assert control over services, security, and political discourse in the community, which seems to be effective through controlling access to funding (Moughrabi, 2001). This impacted the relationship between the Palestinian NGOs and external funders and in return the evolvement of early childhood education. Moreover, the Palestinian NGOs are faced with a new logistical process as part of the funding award. At times financial assistance to local NGOs is conditioned (Christina, 2004; Qarmout & Béland, 2012), and some international funders require the local NGOs to sign an Antiterrorism Act that condemns Palestinian resistance and the support of political parties (Challand, 2009). This requirement has created a strong rift among the community as it denies the Palestinian people the ability to fight for their rights and freedom and in a way perpetuates the political status quo of Israeli occupation. Some local NGOs refuse to comply with the new policies and endorse the birthright of Palestinian people to resist Israeli occupation. The implication of the Antiterrorism Act on early childhood education is complicated as this new logistic created a virtual hierarchy of who is a human, whereby not all children are treated equally (Christina, 2006; Lind, 2010). The hierarchy is reflected in denying services to children who belong to a family with strong political party affiliation that might not speak to the international political agenda. In a way, in one community, some children are provided services of education and some are not. For some local NGOs, this document was not acceptable at the national level because it condemns the Palestinian right to resist and on a practical level denies Palestinian children's their rights to education and health services. To deny services to children is equally propagating the neo-colonial notion and the practice of Israeli occupation of divide and rule. However, the reluctance of some NGOs to accept this new logistic has led to certain local and international NGOs, including such NGO giants as Human Rights Watch, to be criticized as "attacking" Israel and bolstering anti-Israeli sentiment (Steinberg, 2006). Critics have been quick to claim that the NGOs are at the forefront of gaining international condemnation of Israel; however, this critique is, in reality, converse. Even though a few of the NGOs have refused to utilize this document, the majority of international donors to local NGOs who fund early childhood education have their own political agendas that mirror the globalized/Israeli agenda (Challand, 2009). It seems that early childhood education is polarized in which Palestinians are doomed if they accept the funding as equally as if they did not accept the funding, as there is no opportunity to escape reality until there is a change in the political situation in the Middle East. However, this is not true since professionals, advocates, NGOs, and people in general have always had the ability to reinvent reality.

The Path of Reinvention for ECE

The major challenges of NGOs that fund early childhood education in the occupied Palestinian Territories are funding and curricula. It is difficult for NGOs in Palestine to be self-sustainable and independent of external and internal funding while servicing underprivileged children, meaning that they do not have control over the issue of curricula. Early childhood education is oftentimes not a pressing issue in Palestine since there are major health, unemployment, and food security issues facing the community. Therefore, the community effort is usually focused on securing basic needs before addressing early childhood education. While this is the case in the OPT, one organization that has made early childhood education a priority is A Child's Cup Full (ACCF), a hybrid of a local and an international organization that is working in much the same way as NGOs and non-profit organizations. In the initial stages of this organization, ACCF primarily raised money for educational programs through different fundraising activities; however, it became clear that in order to better assist the deprived community in Palestine, it was not enough to continue fundraising for educational programs or even apply for grants from external funders. By obtaining funds from external donors, ACCF did not have the authority to control the funds how they saw fit. Also, ACCF realized that fundraising and grant activity is not sustainable in the long run and that a different course of action was needed to support early childhood education in the camp. Imagination is the key to overcoming the financial obstacles and planning a sustainable project for early childhood care and education without constantly relying on external support. ACCF's proposal was simple in theory and began with a dream for the development of an economic unit whose profit would support early childhood programs throughout the OPT. The implementation of this idea required extensive effort and a transformative learning curve for those involved.

The seeds of ACCF's dream developed after students in the US made a trip to Palestine to deliver musical instruments to children. The students as well as the founder of ACCF saw the great need throughout several communities, and decided that fundraising efforts were simply not enough to make an impact. ACCF is committed to empowering the underprivileged community in Palestine, even though it does not have an abundance of funds to support large-scale programs. Traditionally, money that ACCF raised was utilized to help out local Palestinian after-school educational programs for children. However, the funds were not sufficient to support a large number of children. It became apparent that the need exceeded the support, which demanded a strategic shift to solve the challenge. This epiphany involved ACCF's idea to fund educational programs in a local, self-sustainable manner and was called "Toys for Hope." The concept was simple and capitalized on creating an economic unit in Palestine in which marginalized women produce educational toys through utilizing local repurposed and surplus materials while ACCF markets and sells the items internationally. The goal of Toys for Hope is that the profit of this economic unit will serve twofold: (1) to empower women by providing job opportunities so that the women will be able to financially support themselves and their families, and (2) to fund educational services including early childhood programs. The implementation of this idea has required several steps that are not necessarily related to education but are essential components of developing and sustaining an early childhood care and education program. An important part of the process has been networking with NGOs who are interested in empowering women and learning about the different models that are in the community for this purpose. Undoubtedly, the economic empowerment of women is a goal that many NGOs have embraced and built strategies to implement. Also, ACCF has built a considerable network with US-based groups with business expertise in order to build both a business plan and create a strong marketing plan. On the practical side of the goal of Toys for Hope, it has been imperative to incorporate and develop women's skills in the production of the educational toys. This presented an opportunity for the project and ACCF, as we embarked on a learning curve in ultimately setting up a sustainable small business to parallel the expectation of most funders interested in empowering women through economic independence. ACCF has worked to identify individuals and businesses in the community to donate the surplus and repurposed materials as well as design the educational toy products and build a strategic business idea. The production of the prototypes of Toys for Hope has enabled us to showcase not only the wonderful work of the women but also the overall aim of the project. The irony is that in order to create the economic unit of Toys of Hope it was necessary to receive external funding from international NGOs at startup so we can achieve the ultimate goal of sustainable funds for an early childhood care and educational model in Palestine. As stated previously, Palestinian NGOs that provide early childhood education are in a difficult position as their international donors often have a Western agenda that does not take into account the Palestinian perspective, which the Palestinian NGOs must parallel in their usage of the funds. This leaves the local NGOs at somewhat of a standstill, as they are not able to best serve the community or early childhood education sector in Palestine. ACCF is attempting to reinvent this reality. Even though Toys for Hope's startup was funded externally, the goal and mission is to build sustainable economic units in which the profit goes back to the community educational programs. To become independent from external funding, Toys for Hope aims to create a model for early childhood that is self-sustainable and engages with the larger community as stakeholders.

While Toys for Hope is in its infancy, the dream is to ensure its profitability for the benefit for the community. It should be noted that to reach profitability, the project must overcome obstacles that are at times out of the control of the community and ACCF. The most important obstacle is the Israeli occupation that determines the difficulty of exporting the toys and obtaining needed equipment for the project, and most significantly, the continuation of Toys for

Hope, as the Israeli military could shut it down at any moment. In spite of these challenges, the dream for the project is for its sustainability. Hence, this requires a constant consultation with individuals with expertise in many business aspects including production, marketing, and networking. Additionally, this phase is also associated with the conceptualization of the creation of the model for an early childhood program. It is apparent that the community, artisans of the unit, and ACCF will be included in the conversation of what the program should look like and how the program will take shape. Round-table discussions will also occur and will include diverse perspectives from experts in the model of community-based early childhood education and the current structure of globalized education. This process would allow for different groups and individuals to hold ownership over the future alternative model and allow for the reinvention of the local vision of early childhood education in the oPT in which the neo-colonial agenda is not the objective. While this conceptual model is in its pilot phase and the implementation has not yet been fully realized, this is one option for bridging the challenges of funding and curricula in early childhood education in the occupied Palestinian Territories.

The Dilemma of This Reinvention

ACCF has provided a possibility for local Palestinian NGOs and other organizations to have a voice in the process of creating a national early childhood education policy through the development of sustainable projects. At the surface, this might be true but it does not capture the entire picture. To establish economic units that employ women, local NGOs and other organizations such as ACCF must rely on funding from international NGOs that may have stipulations of signing the Antiterrorism Act or endorse the neo-colonial agenda. In a way, the process to assume a voice in early childhood is not guaranteed. The local NGOs who are interested in early childhood education are in a Catch-22 situation, because they might have to endorse the neo-colonial agenda for the development of economic units to ensure funds or the globalized educational agenda for early childhood education. It is the continuation of the interconnectedness of international donors, the PA, and the local NGOs that make the reinvention limited. However, the navigation of this process might be possible and reinvention achieved through the satiability of local economic units and independence from the international donors.

References

Ben-Porat, G., & Mizrahi, S. (2005). Political culture, alternative politics and foreign policy: The case of Israel. *Policy Sciences, 38*, 177–194.

Challand, B. (2009). *Palestinian civil society: Foreign donors and the power to promote and exclude.* New York: Routledge.

Christina, R. (2004). Contingency, complexity, possibility: Palestinian NGOs and the negotiation of local control in educational development. In M. Sutton & R. F. Arnove (Eds.), *Civil society or shadow state? State/NGO relations in education* (pp. 133–158). Greenwich, CT: Information Age.

Christina, R. (2006). *Tend the olive, water the vine: Globalization and the negotiation of early childhood in Palestine.* Greenwich, CT: Information Age.

Gordon, S. (2010). Civil society, the "new humanitarianism," and the stabilization debate: Judging the impact of the Afghan war. In J. Howell & J. Lind (Eds.), *Civil society under strain: Counter-terrorism policy, civil society, and aid post-9/11* (pp. 109–126). Sterling, VA: Kumarian Press.

Habashi, J. (2012). Palestinian children: Authors of collective memory. *Children and Society*, doi: 10.1111/j.1099-0860.2011.00417.x.

Haklai, O. (2008). Helping the enemy? Why transnational Jewish philanthropic foundations donate to Palestine NGOs in Israel. *Nations and Nationalism, 14*(3), 581–599.

Lind, J. (2010). The changing dynamics of civil society and aid in the Israel–Palestine conflict post-9/11. In J. Howell & J. Lind (Eds.), *Civil society under strain: Counter-terrorism policy, civil society, and aid post-9/11* (pp. 171–190). Sterling, VA: Kumarian Press.

Moughrabi, F. (2001). The politics of Palestinian textbooks. *Journal of Palestine Studies, 31*(1), 5–19.

Nicolai, S. (2007). *Fragmented foundations: Education and chronic crisis in the Occupied Palestinian Territory*. Paris & London: International Institute for Educational Planning & U.K. Save the Children.

Qarmout, T., &, Béland, D. (2012). The politics of international aid to the Gaza Strip. *Journal of Palestine Studies, XLI*(4), 32–47.

Roy, S. (1999). De-development revisited: Palestinian economy and society since Oslo. *Journal of Palestine Studies, XXVIII*(3), 64–82.

Sayigh, R. (2006). Back to the center: Post-Oslo revival of the refugee issue. In J. Beinin & R. L. Stein (Eds.), *The struggle for sovereignty: Palestine and Israel 1993–2005* (pp. 130–139). Stanford, CA: Stanford University Press.

Shikaki, K. (2002). Palestinians divided. *Foreign Affairs, 81*(1), 89–105.

Steinberg, G. M. (2006). Soft powers play hardball: NGOs wage war against Israel. *Israel Affairs, 12*(4), 748–768.

Sullivan, D. (1996). NGOs in Palestine: Agents of development and foundation of civil society. *Journal of Palestine Studies, XXV*(3), 93–100.

UNESCO International Bureau of Education (2006). *Palestinian Authority: Early childhood care and education (ECCE) programmes*. Geneva, Switzerland: UNESCO.

Note

1.   Please see ACCF's website: www.childscupfull.org

The Global Childhoods Project: Complexities of Learning and Living With a Biliterate and Trilingual Literacy Policy

I-Fang Lee and Nicola Yelland

The rise of Asia has made headline news both globally and locally in the 21st century. In particular, the growth of Asian economies and the competitiveness of Asian students' academic performances in international assessment tests such as the Programme for International Student Achievement (PISA), Trends in International Mathematics and Science Study (TIMSS), and Progress in International Reading Literacy Survey (PIRLS) are frequently lauded. For example, in the PISA 2009 assessment results, students in Korea; Hong Kong and Shanghai, China; Singapore; Japan; and Taiwan have been placed in the top five performing countries or economies (OECD, 2011). The dominance of Asian students' high academic performances in such high-stakes tests has not only made international education headline news but also opened up new debates concerning the "effectiveness" of Asian schooling systems and Asian pedagogical practices. Many "Western" countries have indicated that they want to emulate the trend of Asian students' superior academic performances. For examples, mass media reports with titles such as "How China Is Winning the School Race" (Sharma, 2011) and "Top Test Scores from Shanghai Stun Educators" (Dillon, 2010), as well as heated debates following Amy Chua's (2011) controversial publication of *Battle Hymn of the Tiger Mother*, have all come together to highlight the perceived success in the context of Asian cultural practices and contemporary schooling systems as "models" that promise excellence in learning outcomes.

At the end of 2012 the Australian Government released a white paper entitled *Australia in the Asian Century*. This document provides a roadmap for Australia with a strategic plan to engage with Asia in a number of sectors including education. As stated in the document:

> During the Asian century, the importance of education to Australia's economic performance will continue to grow. We can only remain a world-beating economy if we also deliver world-class education. (Australian Government, 2012, p. 164)

The white paper highlights the phenomenon of the Western romanticization of Asian students' academic performance as being the ultimate objective of learning outcomes for contemporary Asian schooling systems. However, while Western systems look at Asian schools and students' academic performances as being systems with "better" learning outcomes, most Asian countries continue to look at the Western education systems as "advanced" progressive models that need to be emulated, especially in terms of students' abilities to be creative, innovative, and imaginative. Education policy "borrowing" from the West to the East seems to be somewhat typical for many Asian countries (Lee & Tseng, 2008; Park, Lee, & Jun, 2013). For example, highlighting Korea:

> Korea is one of the countries that successfully adopted the Western system and achieved modernization in a relatively short period of time. On the surface, its social systems, including education, resemble those of the West. But Confucian tradition remains, as it is deeply rooted in individual life as well as in the nation's guiding philosophy. Confucianism in this context, which often replace "traditional Korean values," include filial piety, respect for the aged, loyalty, and the mutual assistance and cooperation, as opposed to Western individualism. (Park, Lee, & Jun, 2013, p. 41)

While the divide between Eastern and Western cultures is evident, it is nonetheless important not to be trapped in a binary logic of West and East in order to understand the differences between education systems and children's varied learning experiences in their schooling systems in multiple cultures. Such binaries gloss over the complexity of the education systems prevalent in each location and reduce the features to generalizations that do not provide insights into what is going on. Seeking to understand contemporary Asian childhoods and children's lifeworlds (both learning and living experiences), it is important for us to move beyond the simple dichotomies of Western/non-Western binary constructions of childhoods and appropriate/inappropriate pedagogical practices to reconceptualize the notion of childhoods in the era of globalization.

In this chapter, we reflect our work in the collaborative research project entitled Global Childhoods: Portraits of Learning and Living in Asia in the 21st Century. The purpose of this research project was to explore and understand the experiences of childhoods in Asia. In order not to over-simplify the multiplicities of global childhoods to a singular globalized childhood, we seek to reconceptualize children's lived experiences in multiple lifeworlds including homes, schools, and communities.

The Global Childhoods Project

The Global Childhoods Project emerged from a set of shared interests and concerns about the ways in which childhood is constructed, configured, and experienced at the intersection of global forces and local contexts. Additionally, we were interested in how childhoods were currently researched in the Asia Pacific region. Despite a diversity of disciplinary backgrounds and theoretical orientations, collaborators on the project (from Hong Kong, Malaysia, Thailand, Taiwan, Korea, and Japan) maintain a shared interest in education as a key site in which childhood is at once an object of policy formation, a benchmark of national progress, and an expression of cultural imaginaries (Saltmarsh, 2011). This renders education as a focal point for exploring global childhoods in an era in which dominant narratives of globalization, concerned as they are with what Sassen refers to as "upper circuits of capital," and in particular, the "hypermobility of capital" (Sassen, 2008, p. 289), are juxtaposed against issues of a pragmatic and relational, as well as disciplinary and theoretical nature encountered in everyday research practice. Thus for Sassen, and us, critical to understanding the dynamics of globalization "are questions of place and scale because the global is generally conceptualized as overriding or neutralizing place and as operating at a self-evident global scale" (Sassen, 2008, p. 287).

Stronach (2010) maintains that globalizing discourses bring about a need to relocate both education and research practice. This, in turn, indicates "a need to revolutionize qualitative inquiry, particularly in addressing a more performative rather than representational ideal" (Stronach, 2010, p. 1). To that end, we set out a framework for conducting a multi-sited ethnography (Marcus, 1995, 1998) that would enable us to move beyond macro-narratives of global capitalism and its effects in various regions. While not negating these, our interest is instead to explore the nuanced ways in which childhood is experienced at the intersection of education and culture with the range of global flows—of people, capital, technology, media, and ideologies—described by Appadurai (1996). Yet, as Ong highlights, "an approach that views political economy as separate from human agency cannot be corrected by a theory of practice that views political-economic forces as external to everyday meanings and action" (Ong, 1999, p. 5). Instead, she argues, we must take into account the "reciprocal construction" between global processes and everyday practices.

Ethnographic studies generally culminate in rich detailed accounts that are the result of sustained time being spent with participants, learning what happens in their lives, asking questions, and listening to what is said. This approach enables us to explore multiple layers of the meanings of schooling and the effects of education for children across different cultural settings, as well as to probe the nuances of meanings and practices shaped by, and in turn shaping, global processes. An important dimension of this collaboration is our determination to avoid a Western-centric gaze that conscripts local specificities into the service of epistemological rationalities that may bear little relation to the contexts and lifeworlds of participants. It became evident that, over time, educational research in the region was dominated by positivist studies that incorporated quantitative techniques of analysis. Studies funded by local and national funding agencies and publications in both Asian and international journals generally revealed short-term, tightly controlled studies of specific phenomena[1] and surveys of overt behaviors. This could have been due to a variety of factors, yet a major influence seemed to be related to the structure of the schooling systems in which observations of classrooms and working in partnerships with teachers was not common, as well as the fact that many local researchers had experienced working overseas with people who reflected a similar perspective on research methods. Thus, they returned to Asia with a ready-made "toolkit" of positivist approaches and quantitative techniques that would constitute investigations but cause minimal disruption to intact classrooms and orderly lives. Further, this type of research was endorsed by the neoliberal agenda of "evidence-based research" and supported by publications in select journals that showed a preference for traditional research methodologies and forms of dissemination.

Indeed, Chong argues that this is a key problematic within Southeast Asian studies that have "adopted Western-centric theories to illuminate local phenomena [and] has yielded studies and analyses that are prized for their compatibility and comparability to Western experiences" (Chong, 2007, p. 213). According to Chong, "this has come at the expense of local narratives and voices that may not be neatly located in the accepted spectrum of cultural identities" (2007, p. 213). Collaborations that involve international groups are one way of addressing concerns "that there is a western bias in topics, methodologies and data gathering methods" (Shordike et al., 2010, p. 337, see also Harkness, Van de Vijver, & Mohler, 2001). We incorporated the concept of inter-culturality as a means by which research practice brings locally situated researchers within the collective into meaningful dialogues concerning education and global childhoods as they are experienced in each participating country. Thus, we are reminded that differences between the approaches and perspectives of scholars writing from vastly different locally situated contexts should be seen as "not a question of quality, but rather of gaze" (Beazley, Bessell, Ennew, & Waterson, 2009, p. 367).

Living and Learning in Contemporary Hong Kong

Contemporary living and learning in Hong Kong has had varying impacts on children. The Hong Kong government has adopted and implemented a "biliterate and trilingual" policy since 1997. This policy stresses the importance of being biliterate in traditional written Chinese and (British) English, as well as being fluent in Cantonese, Putonghua (also known as Mandarin Chinese), and in spoken English. Such a multilanguage policy inevitably has major implications for children's learning and living experiences, from a very young age. For example, whether to use English or Cantonese as the medium of instruction in classrooms and schools has become a critical educational issue across all education levels.

Currently, all non-profit-making kindergartens offer English and Putonghua lessons to children, in addition to maintaining Cantonese as their daily form of communication language in classrooms. This biliterate and trilingual policy has been creating layers of complexity in children's learning and living experiences (for example, see Poon, 2004). At first glance, while this multilanguage policy appears to pay equal attention to the three languages, with its colonial history, Hong Kong society has come to construct English as the language associated with higher economic, social, and cultural status. Moreover, while the idea of becoming polyglot is desirable, the unequal political, social, educational, and cultural constructions of the three languages in Hong Kong have created noticeable paradoxical conditions in everyday life as well as in teaching and learning contexts. For example, should there be any discrepancies between English and Chinese versions of legal documents, the English version is deemed as the "correct" one. Another example is found in the unequal emphasis on the instructional hours between English and Putonghua classes. In the project reported here, the curriculum and the "instructional" hours, as indicated on the timetable, privileged English over Putonghua. Thus, although the biliterate and trilingual education policy acknowledges all three languages as being equally important, most schools place a greater emphasis on English-language learning over Putonghua and struggle to maintain Cantonese as the primary medium of instruction on a daily basis.

In addition to the effects of the biliterate and trilingual policy in relation to children's learning experiences, the current trend of low-birth rate in Hong Kong over the last decade has generated a new sociological phenomenon, that of the one-child family. This low birth rate has changed children's lived experiences dramatically and can be further understood with a closer examination of contemporary childrearing practices in Hong Kong. Culturally speaking, the responsibility for childrearing in Hong Kong has traditionally been with the mother. However, in recent years, due to the increased female participation in the labor force, many families have two working parents.

Official government statistics, of the 25 to 44 age group, reveal that more than 70% of Hong Kong women are in paid employment. With such a high percentage of female participation in the labor force, most mothers would more than likely be working mothers and thus the need for childcare is imperative. However, due to the lack of any childcare provision, particularly for children under 3 years old in Hong Kong, families in which both parents work are left with few options but to hire foreign domestic helpers from the Philippines or Indonesia to act as nannies or maids for their children. Having a foreign domestic helper as a nanny who lives in the home to take care of a child has complicated contemporary childrearing practices in Hong Kong.[2] Coupled with the low birth rate, these changes in childrearing practices have created a new sociological phenomenon called the "Hong Kong Kid." It refers, rather negatively, to children who have difficulty taking care of themselves, who have low emotional intelligence, and who are weak when faced with adversity.

Here these contemporary learning and living conditions in Hong Kong are viewed as ecological factors that shape children's lifeworlds and their experiences of childhoods.

Hong Kong Childhoods

Perceiving childhood as a significant starting point for learning, we wanted to explore contemporary childhoods in Hong Kong. According to official statistics from the Bureau of Education, about 99.5% of 5-year-old children are in kindergarten. They most commonly attend half-day kindergarten programs, particularly since the implementation of the pre-primary voucher scheme in 2006, which provided financial assistance to families so that their child could attend kindergarten. The majority of children attend a half-day program (either for a morning or afternoon session). What follows are snapshots of two girls who were in their final year of kindergarten. First, we consider who they are and then we explore their lived experiences in literacy in their kindergarten classroom.

Amy: The Only Child

Amy is 5 years old and she is the only child in her nuclear family. Amy lives with her parents in a Hong Kong public housing estate. Amy's father is a professional cook in a local Western-style restaurant, and her mother is not in paid employment and stays at home. Amy's first language is Cantonese. Every morning at 8:15 a.m., Amy's mother walks her to school. Her mother collects her at around 11:45 a.m. for lunch and takes her home. Ms. Wong (the teacher) describes Amy as an outgoing 5-year-old who is willing to cooperate and collaborate with her classmates. However, she also reported that Amy consistently seeks to be the center of attention and attributes this to the fact that she is the only child in the family. The teacher indicated that if Amy does not get everything going her way, she becomes frustrated and withdraws from activities. This was apparent in one of the scheduled classroom observations during a music session; Amy had an outburst when Ms. Wong did not immediately respond to her request for a particular song. Amy turned to face the wall and subsequently did not cooperate or react to Ms. Wong's pre-planned activity for ten minutes. While doing this, Amy missed out on approximately half of the music session, which was only of 20 minutes duration. Ms. Wong indicated that this incident was a "classic example" of Amy's tendency to react as if she is the "center of the universe." And Ms. Wong went on to say:

I am not surprised by Amy's behavior and reaction in this morning's music session.... I see this often in my class.... This kind of behavior is somewhat common among the children. Sometimes it's Amy, another time it could be others. This is what we would describe as the "Hong Kong Kid." (Translated from a casual conversation with Ms. Wong, May 23, 2011)

As discussed earlier, the comment, with reference to the Hong Kong Kid, seems to be a cultural reference point for describing children's immature emotional reactions and their inappropriate behaviors in communal settings.

Sara: A New Chinese Immigrant

Sara is 5 years old and is also the only child in her nuclear family and lives in a public housing estate. Sara's mother migrated to Hong Kong from Mainland China about six years ago after her marriage to a Hong Kong citizen. Therefore, Sara's home languages include both Putonghua and Cantonese. Sara's father works for a small local business and her mother is the primary caregiver. Sara's teacher describes her as a shy and obedient girl who respects and listens to her teachers at all times. According to Ms. Wong, Sara is often very quiet in the classroom and does not have any specific behavioral problems. Since Sara speaks Putonghua at home with her mother, Ms. Wong often calls on Sara as a reference when it comes to Putonghua sessions.

Both Amy and Sara attend the half-day program for the morning session and then return home with their mothers. The two girls' families both live in the same public housing estate where the non-profit kindergarten is located.[3] For Amy, Cantonese is her home language, whereas Mandarin Chinese (Putonghua) is Sara's. The differences in their home languages became a key factor in shaping the children's different learning experiences in the classroom and varied childhoods in Hong Kong society.

Learning: The Challenges of Becoming Biliterate

The classroom literacy learning experiences of Amy and Sara are based on the dual principles of biliteracy and trilingualism. In the classroom, teaching the traditional Chinese literacy texts and spoken Cantonese are Ms. Wong's responsibility. The teaching of Putonghua is organized and presented using a series of educational DVD programs. English literacy and spoken English-language teaching is the responsibility of an English teacher.

It is important to note that Ms. Wong and the children use Cantonese as the daily working and instructional language in the classroom. For example, when Ms. Wong is leading the class for learning activities, she speaks in Cantonese and the children respond to her in Cantonese only. Cantonese as a medium of instruction for children's early literacy learning also highlights a layer of complexity in early literacy learning due to some discrepancies in the oral and written format. This was noted by Poon (2004) who stated:

Modern Standard Chinese and Cantonese are considerably different in lexis, syntax, pronunciation and phonology. Hong Kong students think in their mother tongue Cantonese, the written form of which is not recognised as standard written Chinese. They have to learn to write in Modern Standard Chinese, the spoken form of which (Putonghua) they do not speak. Therefore, they cannot write what they think and say. (p. 56)

This means that the gap between oral and written languages is significant. Thus, Cantonese is used as an oral language but when it comes to formal literacy learning (reading and writing in Chinese), children are required to become fluent in "code-switching" from Cantonese to written Chinese (traditional, not simplified Chinese).

In addition to daily uses of the Cantonese language, each week Ms. Wong gathers the children together in front of a computer and plays the Putonghua DVD program, which last approximately 15 minutes. The contents of the programs are mainly rhymes and songs in Putonghua. The English teacher is scheduled to come into the classroom three days a week for half-hour lessons with the whole class. The planned experiences in English basically include studying phonics, singing English songs, and listening to a story told by the teacher.

It is in this environment that the children are expected to start to become biliterate and fluent in the three languages. What is challenging for the teachers in terms of their pedagogical practices and the desired outcomes for children's learning is that each of these languages and literacies is taught as an independent subject in their early-years curriculum. In other words, the curricula for the three languages and the two forms of literacy are not integrated. The teaching and learning contexts are compartmentalized and disconnected from their living experiences outside of the classroom. For example, while the school curriculum provides opportunities for being exposed to learning English, with lessons to teach the basics of phonics, word recognition, stories, and by singing and learning traditional rhymes, there is very little real-life opportunity to *use* English in Amy's and Sara's daily lifeworlds of the local public housing estate and its environs.

For Amy and Sara, English is a school subject that has very little relevance in their daily lifeworlds. However, in a casual conversation with Amy's mom (Mrs. Tam), she stressed the importance of having English lessons at school while admitting that she can do very little to support her daughter's English learning. She said:

> English class is a must-have for children in Hong Kong. Since I cannot support Amy's English learning at home, it is important that the school is providing this for her. Although we don't need to use English in our everyday life, I do believe that English is important for her success in school. If she can do well in school, maybe she would have a better opportunity than I did when she grows up. (Translated from a casual conversation with Amy's mom, May 26, 2011)

Pre-primary learning experiences for young children in Hong Kong are very different from those of Western cultures. In particular, the pressure of academic performance in the early years is never absent. A Confucius construction of meritocracy is embedded in teachers' and parents' expectations of children's academic performance and reflected in classroom practices. For example, it is expected that students of all ages should study hard and the core responsibility for this rests with the child. A cultural construction of "with effort" and "practice" as "good and obedient students" is ubiquitous. Thus, a strong emphasis on academic outcomes at the pre-primary level is prevalent in everyday pedagogical practice and is strongly emphasized in parental expectations.

Accordingly, classroom observations highlight that children's learning often entails drill and practice of basic skills in multiple workbooks. In Ms. Wong's classroom, the morning learning routine begins with a list of the work for the day. This includes learning Chinese and English vocabulary words, short sentences, as well as basic arithmetic problems that are written on the whiteboard. The learning of the traditional Chinese written forms, English literacy, and arithmetic are regarded as the three core academic subjects. They are taught in parallel, and written exercises are organized in three different workbooks. For example, on a typical Thursday morning, Ms. Wong listed the following items of work to do on the board for the children to copy:

> Chinese traditional literacy: 我會刷牙 (I can brush my teeth.)
> Chinese vocabularies: 刷牙, 穿衣, 洗面 (brush teeth, put on clothes, wash face)
> English literacy: This is a car.
> Arithmetic: combinations of 1–15 (practice addition) and combinations of 1–10 (practice subtraction).

This example of the work illustrates the degree of complexity of children's learning in Hong Kong in enacting the policy of biliteracy and trilingualism into everyday pedagogical practices in the classroom. Literacy learning, in particular, learning to read and write in English and traditional Chinese in the early years, is a fundamental cultural and academic expectation. The pressure on academic outcomes for young children is further exemplified by the existence of the three different workbooks for Chinese, English, and arithmetic assignments through which children learn to write and read in traditional Chinese and English as well as mastering basic arithmetic skills through a daily routine of repetitive practice.

Multiplicities of Childhood Experiences

As previously stated, Cantonese is the daily communication language in Hong Kong and is the first language of the majority of children. However, since the British colonial period, English has been a dominant official language with the associated legal status. For example, in all legal and official documents, if there is any controversy and ambiguity between English and the Chinese translation, English is privileged. This different legal and official status among the languages remains today. In the field of education, debates about which languages should become the medium of instruction are never absent. While Cantonese is the primary language at the pre-primary sector, most parents have a strong desire to enhance their children's English language ability. For example, Amy's parents noted that they have purchased educational DVDs to facilitate their children's English learning at home. Although Sara's mother stated that they cannot afford to buy additional English learning materials for her, they ensure that Sara has the opportunity to watch some cartoons broadcast in English to promote her interests in learning English.

Children's lifeworlds outside of school often vary considerably, even if they live in the same neighborhood of the same public housing estate. As a child of new immigrants in Hong Kong, Sara's family often stays home on weekends and watching TV shows is a favorite pastime. A consideration of the children's families, as well as their community networks, helps to broaden discussions regarding the dimensions of learning for young children in Hong Kong. Thus, a closer look at the families can shed new light on the children's different cultural capital

(Bourdieu, 1984; Lareau, 2000) and their families' social networks. Sara's story provides new insights into the complexities and multiplicities of childhoods in contemporary Hong Kong.

When trying to understand the ways in which children become literate under the implementation of the language policy in Hong Kong, it is important to acknowledge that the diversity of children's home languages plays a key role in shaping their early literacy learning experiences. Children like Sara, whose mothers come to Hong Kong by marriage, are officially categorized and labeled as children of new immigrants by the Hong Kong government. This label of "new immigrants" is used to describe immigrants from Mainland China only. Children like Sara often bear the stigma of being different and face sociocultural and class discrimination when being compared with the mainstream Cantonese-speaking population in Hong Kong.[4] During the observations for this study, we noted Sara's limited Cantonese speaking ability but also observed and heard her perfect Mandarin/Putonghua as she participated in the Putonghua (DVD) lessons. Her identity as a "new immigrant" from (Mainland) China shaped her behavior in school as docile but she was very different in her home context. Ms. Wong described Sara as a "shy and obedient" student in the classroom. However, it became apparent that she demonstrated very different personality traits in her home. This was documented in our fieldnotes, which shows her animated conversations begin as soon as her mother collects her from the kindergarten:

> Sara smiles at her mom as her mom takes Sara's schoolbag from her shoulders. As soon as Sara sees her mom, she switches to speaking in Putonghua. As they walk away from the kindergarten through the marketplace towards the McDonald's, Sara talks non-stop to her mother. During the five-minute walk from school to the marketplace, she continues to share with her mother about her day at school in Putonghua but sings a few songs in Cantonese. The whole conversation is led by Sara in Putonghua with some responses from her mother. Sara even tells two quick jokes to her mother. (Fieldnotes on May 27, 2011)

It was reiterated by Sara's mother, Ms. Chen, who described Sara to us:

> Sara likes to talk. She talks to me a lot and shares with me about her day at school. My Cantonese is not too good...even though I have been in Hong Kong for a few years...thus we would still speak in Putonghua most of the time. Sara has a lot to talk about with me.... So much so that I think she talks too much! She talks about her day at school, about what her teacher said at school, what she did with her friends in class, and she even told me what she had for a snack. Sometimes, I think she may be too talkative and I wonder if that's because she doesn't talk too much in class?... as you can see from our lunch hours at McDonald's, Sara does like to talk, but that's cute and we have a strong mother – daughter bond. As I don't have many friends in Hong Kong, Sara really keeps me entertained with her childish jokes. (Translated from a casual interview with Sara's mom, May 27, 2011)

This description of Sara presents a very different image from the teacher's view of her. Nonetheless, these different images of Sara in home and school help to broaden our understandings about Sara's fluid and shifting identities as a student and as a daughter/child. It provides a unique opportunity for us to rethink the (dis)connections of children's lifeworlds and the multiplicities of childhoods in different contexts as children are thought of as students and/or children.

Conclusion

In this chapter we have located our Hong Kong study in the context of a larger collaborative partnership that aims to interrogate Asian childhoods in a global context. We resonate with what Chen (2010) has called "Asia as method" as a different approach to understanding lifeworlds in the Asia Pacific region. Chen views Asia as method as an extension of China as method, which grew out of the work of Mizoguchi (quoted in Chen, 2010, p. 245) in the 1980s. It requires an inter-referencing of elements in different base-entities to describe and derive meaning from studying phenomena. Recognizing local histories and locating studies in regions that have different, as well as common, experiences is an important element in this process. As Chen states: "We must return to the transformations and trajectories of the base-entity, and to the operating logic driving its interaction with outside forces, to fully understand the characteristics of the changing base-entity" (p. 250).

This method of understanding from the inside out is coupled with inter-referencing with different parts of Asia. In this way the aims are to understand different parts of Asia more deeply, to explore the intra-relationships and connections within Asia, and thus to gain greater insights into oneself and each context. Chen maintains that "the agenda of a transformed self is to transcend existing understandings of Asia and thereby change the world" (2010, p. 254). Therefore, Asia as method is a critical inquiry to facilitate a self-reflexive reflection. As Chen stipulates:

> The goal of Asia as method is to enable Asian societies to be more informed about the ways in which others in their own locale shape their own experiences from their own base-entity and how they might learn from these. It proposes a way forward grounded in critical discourses concerned with Asia, rather than the West, is positioned as interlocutor, so that alternative positions can be imagined from within. (2010, pp. 212–213)

In this chapter, we have outlined an initial investigation in the Global Childhoods project that interrogates the ways in which young children in Hong Kong become literate. Our work has uncovered how policy imperatives are enacted in practice and the (im)possibilities of this reality in the context of the lives of two 5-year-old children. While policy statements maintain a biliterate and trilingual imperative for literacy, it becomes apparent that much of the experiences beyond becoming literate in the "mother tongue" (Cantonese) are minimal and in fact might be described as "tokenistic" since they are infrequent in nature and not linked to lived experiences in any way at all. Nor are they able to be practiced in any context outside of the "official lesson," which in the case of Putonghua is only presented in a DVD lesson.

Contemporary childhoods in Hong Kong cannot be generalized into a singular image of childhood. The varying images of the children across different learning contexts (i.e., home and school) elucidate the multiplicities of childhoods, learning, and living experiences. Our work in the Global Childhoods project offers us a unique opportunity to shift toward critical reconceptualization of what contemporary Asian childhoods as well as studenthoods might look like. Our intention is not to provide a summary of what Asian childhoods are, as a new grand narrative. Rather, our joint efforts in understanding children's literacy experiences in their cultural contexts are to re-narrate, de-colonize, and de-imperialize the notion of childhoods. It is through such critical reconceptualization that we will be able to create new ways of understanding our work with children, as well as opening windows to understand children's lifeworlds.

References

Appadurai, A. (1996). *Modernity at large: Cultural dimensions of globalization*. Minneapolis: University of Minnesota Press.

Australian Government. (2012). *Australia in the Asian century*. Retrieved from http://pandora.nla.gov.au/pan/133850/20130914-0122/asiancentury.dpmc.gov.au/white-paper.html.

Beazley, H., Bessell, S., Ennew, J., & Waterson, R. (2009). The right to be properly researched: Research with children in a messy, real world. *Children's Geographies, 7*(4), 365–378.

Bourdieu, P. (1984). *Distinction: A social critique of the judgement of taste*. Cambridge, MA: Harvard University Press.

Chen, K. H. (2010). *Asia as method: Towards deimperialization*. London: Duke University Press.

Chong, T. (2007). Practising global ethnography in Southeast Asia: Reconciling area studies with globalisation theory. *Asian Studies Review, 31*(3), 211–226.

Chua, A. (2011). *Battle hymn of the tiger mother*. New York: Penguin.

Curriculum Development Council. (2006). *Guide to pre-primary curriculum*. Retrieved from http://www.edb.gov.hk/FileManager/EN/Content_2405/pre-primaryguide-net_en.pdf

Dillon, S. (2010, December 7). Top test scores from Shanghai stun educators. *New York Times*, A1. Retrieved from http://www.nytimes.com/2010/12/07/education/07education.html?pagewanted=all&_r=0

Harkness, J. A., Van de Vijver, F. J. R., & Mohler, P. P. (2001). *Cross-cultural survey methods*. New York: Wiley.

Lareau, A. (2000). *Home advantage: Social class and parental intervention in elementary education*. Lanham, MD: Rowman & Littlefield.

Lee, I. F., & Tseng, C. L. (2008). Cultural conflicts of the child-centered approach to early childhood education in Taiwan. *Early Years, 28*(2), 183–196.

Marcus, G. (1995). Ethnography in/of the world system: The emergence of multi-sited ethnography. *Annual Review of Anthropology, 25*, 95–177.

Marcus, G. (1998). *Ethnography through thick and thin*. Princeton, NJ: Princeton University Press.

OECD (Organisation for Economic Co-operation and Development). (2001). *Starting strong: Early childhood education and care*. Paris: OECD.

OECD (Organisation for Economic Co-operation and Development). (2006). *Starting strong II: Early childhood education and care*. Paris: OECD.

OECD (Organisation for Economic Co-operation and Development). (2011). *PISA 3 in focus*. Paris: OECD.

Ong, A. (1999). *Flexible citizenship: The cultural logics of transnationality*. Durham, NC: Duke University Press.

Park, E., Lee, J., & Jun, H. J. (2013). Making use of old and new: Korean early childhood education in the global context. *Global Studies of Childhoods, 3*(1), 40–52.

Poon, A. Y. K. (2004). Language policy of Hong Kong: Its impact on language education and language use in post-handover Hong Kong. *Humanities & Social Sciences* (Journal of Taiwan Normal University), *49*(1), 53–74.

Saltmarsh, S. (2011). Bus ride to the future: Cultural imaginaries of Australian childhood in the education landscape. *Global Studies of Childhood, 1*(1), 26–35.

Sassen, S. (2008). Theoretical and empirical elements in the study of globalization. In I. Rossi (Ed.), *Frontiers of globalization research: Theoretical and methodological approaches*, (pp. 287–306). New York: Springer Science + Business Media.

Sharma, Y. (2011, October 11). How China is winning the school race. *BBC News*. Retrieved from http://www.bbc.co.uk/news/business-14812822

Shordike, A., Hocking, C., Pierce, D., Wright-St. Clair, V., Vittayakorn, S., & Rattakorn, P. (2010). Respecting regional culture in an international multi-site study: A derived etic method. *Qualitative Research, 10*(3), 333–355.

Stronach, I. (2010). *Globalizing education, educating the local: How method made us Mad*. Abingdon, U.K.: Routledge.

Notes

1. E.g., General Research Fund, "Developing a Framework of Item Response Models for Multifaceted Data," 2011.
2. The importation of foreign domestic helpers as nannies and maids is legal and common in Hong Kong but can be problematic for many families. Foreign domestic helpers as nannies and maids in Hong Kong may not be well respected in many contexts. In extreme cases, children are thought of as the "owners" of their maids who are in fact their primary caregivers. According to the Immigration Department Annual Report, it stated that foreign domestic helpers are allowed to work in Hong Kong to relieve many families of household chores. The domestic helpers' employment is on a two-year contract basis and they

are not allowed to work as full-time chauffeurs. In 2010, the population of foreign domestic helpers was 273,609 (and the total population in Hong Kong was about 7.03 million). For details, please see the official report at http://www.immd.gov.hk/a_report_09-10/eng/ch1/index.htm (note: link no longer able to be accessed October 29, 2013; accessed initially February, 2013.)

3. In Hong Kong, about 30% of the population lives in public housing estates (also known as public rental housing). To be eligible for public rental housing application, single persons and families must meet income and total net asset limits set by the Hong Kong government. For example, for a family of three persons, such as Amy's and Sara's in our study, their parents' maximum monthly income shall not be over $17,060 HKD (for detail public information about public housing policy, please see http://www.housingauthority.gov.hk/en/flat-application/income-and-asset-limits/index.html). It is also important to note that according to the official statistic, the median monthly domestic household income for 2010 was $18,000 HKD (for more details, please see an official report entitled "Hong Kong: The Facts" at http://www.gov.hk/en/about/abouthk/factsheets/docs/population.pdf). These figures could imply that both children's families may be categorized as low-income families. In 2012, for the first time in history, the current chief executive Leung Chun-Ying has promised to appoint a taskforce to define a poverty line that will help to shape governmental policies concerning poverty.

4. It is also important to note that immigrants from locations and cultures other than Mainland China, such as Southeast Asian countries, are categorized as "minorities" in Hong Kong.

About the Authors

Alejandro Azocar is currently an Assistant Professor of English as a Second Language at the University of West Alabama – Livingston. Originally from Chile, his academic interest is the analysis of language ideologies in monolingual societies that co-exist with minority languages and peoples. In particular, his academic work centers on the formation of pedagogical subjectivities among teachers who teach foreign languages as non-native speakers of such languages, for example American teachers of Spanish, or Chilean teachers of English. His dissertation at the University of Wisconsin – Madison examined how subjectivity formation among pre-service Spanish teachers affected curricular decisions in Spanish lessons aimed at children in K-3 classrooms. He has presented his research at several Reconceptualizing Early Childhood Education conferences.

Chelsea Bailey began her career in early childhood education as a young child and continued her career in the field as a preschool teacher and university professor. She has gone on to work as an independent scholar and consultant across various aspects of the field. She has worked extensively in the areas of teacher professional development, school and curriculum design, and early childhood program development in the United States and abroad. Her program development work in the U.S. is focused on strengthening the spiritual aspects of early learning settings. In China, she is working in collaboration with Chinese and U.S.-based educators to design, develop, and launch early childhood programs relevant to China's changing social context. Drawing heavily on systems theory, organization design theory, and radical theories of love, she looks forward to helping rethink how education will look next in the U.S.

Cynthia à Beckett is an experienced early childhood teacher and academic, currently a Senior Lecturer in Early Childhood Education at the University of Notre Dame Australia, Sydney Campus. Her research interests explore new views of social relations through a concept entitled 'Playing in the In-between'. This work employs sociological theories to understand more about young children and families with implications for early childhood education. She is also engaged in research about culturally responsive approaches in teaching and in an interdisciplinary project entitled 'States of Play: Birth and Beyond'.

Marianne (Mimi) Bloch is Professor Emerita in Curriculum and Instruction and in Gender and Women's Studies at the University of Wisconsin – Madison. She, with others, hosted the first Reconceptualizing Early Childhood Education (RECE) conference at the University of Wisconsin – Madison in 1991, 1996, and 2005. In 2012, she received the first annual Bloch Distinguished Career Award for Reconceptualizing Early Childhood Education. Her work focuses on international issues, childcare policy in and out of the U.S., gender and work, and draws on poststructural and feminist cultural history to think about early education and childcare in the U.S. and elsewhere (e.g., West Africa, Europe, Central America). Recent co-edited publications include: *Gender and Education in Sub-Saharan Africa* (Bloch, M., Beoku-Betts, J., & Tabachnick, B. R.); *Governing Children, Families, and Education: Restructuring the Welfare State* (Bloch, M., Holmlund, K., Moqvist, I., & Popkewitz, T. S.); and *The Child in the World/The World in the Child* (Bloch, M., Kennedy, D., Lightfoot, T., & Weyenberg, D.). She is series co-editor, with Beth Swadener, of Palgrave Macmillan's series Critical Cultural Studies of Childhood, and co-edits, with Gaile S. Cannella, *International Critical Childhood Policy Studies*.

Gail Boldt is Associate Professor and Program Coordinator for the PhD program in Language, Culture and Society at Penn State University. Working primarily through feminist, queer, poststructural, and psychoanalytic theories at intersections of early childhood, literacy, childhood studies, and recently, disabilities studies, Boldt uses narrative research to examine how children experience success and failure constituted in school through expectations for normative forms of participation.

Sheralyn Campbell is an educator and manager of children's services in the shire of Bega Valley in New South Wales, Australia. She has worked for 38 years in a range of Australian children's services and completed her doctoral studies with the University of Melbourne Centre for Equity and Innovation in Early Childhood. Her research and practice have focused on equity and diversity in early childhood education and care.

Gaile S. Cannella is currently Research Professor at Arizona State University and the series editor for *Rethinking Childhoods and Critical Qualitative Research*, Peter Lang. She held the Velma E. Schmidt Endowed Chair in Early Childhood Studies at the University of North Texas and was a tenured professor at Arizona State University – Tempe and Texas A&M University – College Station. Published in English, Korean, and Spanish, her books include: *Deconstructing Early Childhood Education* (Peter Lang, 1997); *Kidworld* (with Joe Kincheloe, Peter Lang, 2002), *Childhood and Postcolonization* (with Radhika Viruru, RoutledgeFalmer, 2004); and *Childhoods: A Handbook* (with Lourdes Diaz Soto, Peter Lang, 2010). Her most recent book, *Critical Qualitative Research Reader* (with Shirley Steinberg, Peter Lang, 2012), was awarded an American Education Studies Association Critics Choice Book Award for 2012. Dr. Cannella has published in a range of journals including *Qualitative Inquiry* and *Cultural Studies<=>Cultural Methodologies*. She is currently a founding member of the Coalition for Critical Qualitative Inquiry, an affiliated group with the International Congress of Qualitative Inquiry.

Susan Grieshaber is Chair Professor and head of the Department of Early Childhood Education, Hong Kong Institute of Education. Her research interests include early childhood curriculum, policy, pedagogy, and assessment; families; and women in the academy, all of which have a focus on equity and diversity. She draws on a range of theoretical perspectives to inform her work and is interested in theoretical and methodological innovations that enable alternative ways of seeing, doing, understanding, and being in the world. Sue is foundation co-editor of the internationally known journal *Contemporary Issues in Early Childhood* and has published widely, including five books.

Janette Habashi, an Associate Professor in the Department of Human Relations at the University of Oklahoma, teaches graduate- and undergraduate-level courses with concentrations in the areas of local and global human diversity issues and educational developmental theories. She is committed to advocating for social policy, reflecting her passion for children and the betterment of the community. Her research with children and Indigenous populations examine socialization, national identity, political participation/resistance, and children's rights-based approaches in policy and research. Janette has published several peer-reviewed articles in prestigious social science, cultural, and childhood journals, as well as contributed book chapters and refereed conference papers to the academic community. Janette is also the founder of A Child Cup Full organization that empowers women and children's educational opportunity (www.childscupfull.org).

J. Amos Hatch is Professor of Theory and Practice in Teacher Education at the University of Tennessee. He has published widely in the areas of early childhood education, qualitative research, and teacher education. He served as co-executive editor of *Qualitative Studies in Education* from 1991 to 1996 and the *Journal of Early Childhood Teacher Education* from 2008 to 2012. He has written or edited a number of books, including *Teaching in the New Kindergarten* (Thompson, 2005), *Early Childhood Qualitative Research* (Routledge, 2007), and (with Susan Groenke) *Critical Pedagogy and Teacher Education in the Neoliberal Era* (Springer, 2009).

Richard T. Johnson is Professor at the University of Hawaii at Manoa where he is on the faculty of Curriculum Studies in the College of Education. His recent research and field-based work includes no-touch policies in education, risk, childhood subjectivity, and visual culture. He has taught and served extensively in various field-based preservice early childhood/elementary teacher education programs for over 20 years. He earned his EdD at Vanderbilt University.

Shirley A. Kessler earned a BA in The Teaching of English (1964) and MEd in Special Education for the Gifted (1970) at the University of Illinois where she was introduced to early childhood education by Bernard Spodek and taught under his supervision in a demonstration preschool/kindergarten. Shirley earned her PhD at the University of Wisconsin in 1987, where she studied with Mimi Bloch, Michael Apple, and Herbart Kliebard. Research for her dissertation was conducted in two kindergarten classrooms, which began her lifelong interest in and fascination with attempts to describe the curriculum as practiced. Her essay titled "Alternative Perspectives on Early Childhood Education" was highly controversial and contributed to the formation of the Reconceptualists, where she played a leadership role for several years. Her research includes curriculum theorizing in particular classroom settings and the relationship between historical and contemporary views of early childhood education, all from the standpoint of critical theory. In 1992, she co-edited (Kessler, S., & Swadener, E. B.) *Reconceptualizing the Early Childhood Curriculum: Beginning the Dialogue.* New York: Teachers College Press.

I-Fang Lee is Senior Lecturer in Early Childhood Education at the University of Newcastle, Australia. Her research trajectories focus on contemporary issues relating to changes and reforms in early childhood education and care, constructions of Asian childhoods, and global knowledge on appropriate pedagogical practices in the early years. Dr. Lee draws on critical theories and poststructural theoretical frameworks to reconceptualize and challenge mainstream sociopolitical rhetoric on reforms and policies through which a dominant construction of a desirable cosmopolitan childhood is fabricated. More recently, she investigates the making of quality early childhood education and care in reform policies to deconstruct constructions of social inclusion and exclusion as well as to rethink issues concerning equity in the early years.

Felicity McArdle is Associate Professor, Charles Stuart University, and is also affiliated with QUT School of Early Childhood as Adjunct Associate Professor. Her research and teaching interests are in creativity, curriculum, play and the arts, and in teacher education and social justice goals. Before her university work, she had more than 14 years' experience as a classroom teacher, in before-school settings, and primary schooling. She is a member of the Excellence in Research in the Early Years Collaborative Research Network (CRN), which is a group of 60 researchers across three states in Australia. Her current interests are in the embedding of Indigenous perspectives and knowledges in the curriculum, and inquiring into teachers' work.

Liane Mozère was Professor Emerita in Sociology at the University of Metz in France. Born in China, she lived and worked in Paris and France the majority of her life. Her research focus had been on early childhood, informal work, and women's work. Throughout her career, her work had been influenced by the thinking of Gilles Deleuze and Félix Guattari. She participated in the Psychiatric Clinic "La Borde" from 1965, was active in the feminist movement during the 1960s, and was a member of the Centre d'études, de recherches et de formation institutionnelles (CERFI) organized by Félix Guattari. Her many publications include *Le Printemps des Crèches: Histoire et Analyze d'un Movement* (L'Harmattan, 1992); *Gilles Deleuze et Félix Guattari: Territoires et Devenirs*, volume 20 of *Le Portique*, 2007; and other recent books. She wrote the preface to Félix Guattari's (2011) book *Lignes de Fuite: Pour un Autre Monde de Possibles* (Paris: L'Aube). She had been an active participant in the Reconceptualizing Early Childhood Education conferences. She died in October, 2013.

Mark Nagasawa is Assistant Professor of Child Development at the Erikson Institute. His research applies a critical cultural studies lens to education policymaking to examine how policies unequally affect people in local communities. These inquiries are informed by a professional background that includes experiences as a preschool teacher/social worker and preschool director for an urban school district, as a policy analyst in the Arizona governor's office, and as an early childhood special education specialist with the Arizona Department of Education.

Fikile Nxumalo is a doctoral candidate in the School of Child and Youth Care, University of Victoria, and a sessional instructor in the Early Years Specialization. Fikile holds a doctoral SSHRC (Social Sciences and Humanities Research Council) fellowship for her doctoral research, which brings posthumanist theories, Indigenous relationalities, and postcolonial perspectives into conversation with a focus on possibilities for anticolonial and antiracist responses to everyday encounters in settler-colonial early childhood spaces. Fikile was an early childhood educator for several years. She is currently working as a pedagogical facilitator in a pilot project funded by the British Columbia Ministry of Children and Family Development. Her role in this project involves supporting early childhood educators in her community in critically reflecting and experimenting with theories and practices that serve the well-being of children from diverse backgrounds and settings in British Columbia.

Liselott Mariett Olsson is Senior Lecturer at the Stockholm University, Department of Child and Youth Studies. Special interests include early childhood literacy didactics, literacy, and French philosophy. She is a member of the research group "The Aesthetics and Ethics of Learning" and served as project leader for the government-funded research project "The Magic of Language" (2010–2012). She is author of *Movement and Experimentation in Young Children's Learning: Deleuze and Guattari in Early Childhood Education* (Routledge, 2009).

Michael O'Loughlin is Professor in the School of Education and Clinical and Research Supervisor in the PhD program in Clinical Psychology at Adelphi University. He wrote *The Subject of Childhood* (Peter Lang, 2009) and edited *Imagining Children Otherwise: Theoretical and Critical Perspectives on Childhood Subjectivity* with Richard Johnson (Peter Lang, 2010). He is co-editor of *Psychodynamic Psychotherapy in Contemporary South Africa: Contexts, Theories, and Applications* (Jason Aronson, 2013), and in 2013 he also edited two books on children's emotions: *The Uses of Psychoanalysis in Working With Children's Emotional Lives* (Jason Aronson) and *Psychodynamic Perspectives on Working With Children, Families and School* (Jason Aronson). He is co-chair of the Association for the Psychoanalysis of Culture & Society. His latest edited book projects are: *The Ethics of Remembering and the Consequences of Forgetting: Essays on Trauma, History and Memory* and *Fragments of Trauma and the Social Production of Suffering*, forthcoming from Rowman & Littlefield.

Veronica Pacini-Ketchabaw is Professor of Childhood Studies in the School of Child and Youth Care at the University of Victoria in Canada, where she is also the Coordinator of the Early Years Specialization. She has worked professionally in the field of early childhood education for more than 20 years. Her work focuses on rethinking and reimagining early childhood education from theoretically and philosophically informed standpoints rooted in feminist, postcolonial, anti-racist, and posthumanist perspectives. She is editor of the journal *Canadian Children*; editor of the book *Flows, Rhythms and Intensities of Early Childhood Education Curriculum* (Peter Lang, 2010); and co-editor of *Re-situating Canadian Early Childhood Education* (Peter Lang, 2013). She currently holds a SSHRC (Social Sciences and Humanities Research Council) grant for her ethnographic study entitled "Encounters with Materials in Early Childhood Education" that focuses on educators' and young children's engagement with materials as events.

Michelle Salazar Pèrez is Assistant Professor of Early Childhood at New Mexico State University. She has worked as a practitioner in a variety of early childhood settings and has participated in a range of university- and community-based activist organizations in New Orleans, St. Louis, southern Illinois, and Texas. Her scholarship interests include using situational analysis and marginalized feminist epistemologies to unveil enactments of neoliberalism through the examination of childhood public policy and early education and care discourses.

Lacey Peters is Assistant Professor of Early Childhood Education in the Department of Curriculum and Teaching at Hunter College, CUNY. She earned her PhD from the Arizona State University Mary Lou Fulton Teachers College. In addition, she has been a preschool teacher, working primarily with children aged 3 to 5 years old. Her time in the classroom served as a catalyst for becoming an advocate for children's rights and participation. Lacey uses research to promote the voices and perspectives of members of the early childhood community that are often subverted or excluded from research and policy in the United States, including children, parents (or other family members), and early childhood care and education professionals. Her current interests are primarily focused on examining children and parents' perspectives on their experiences during the pre-kindergarten to kindergarten transition.

Valerie Polakow is Professor of Educational Psychology and Early Childhood, and teaches in the Educational Studies Doctoral Program in the Department of Teacher Education at Eastern Michigan University. Her scholarship encompasses the impact of public policies on children in poverty, women and welfare, and access to childcare and post-secondary education in national and international contexts. In her writings she has attempted to document the lived realities of those who have been shut out—from early childhood education, from K-12 education, and from post-secondary education; and to give voice to those whose rights have been violated by poverty, race, and gender discrimination. She was a Fulbright scholar in Denmark, and is the recipient of several awards for scholarship including the 2010 Distinguished Contributions to Gender Equity in Education Research by the American Educational Research Association. She is the author/editor of seven books including *Lives on the Edge: Single Mothers and Their Children in the Other America* (which won the Kappa Delta Pi book of the year award in 1994, published by University of Chicago Press), and *Who Cares for Our Children?: The Child Care Crisis in the Other America* (Teachers College Press, 2007).

Denise Proud is an Aboriginal woman born and raised in Wakka Wakka country in Cherbourg, Queensland. Denise is a respected elder, teacher, and facilitator. She is a strong social justice advocate, tirelessly promoting the rights of her people and community. She works in partnership with a wide variety of organizations on projects and new initiatives aimed at improving awareness and understanding of Aboriginal and Torres Strait Islander cultures. She was an early childhood educator for many years and is a popular international speaker in this field. Denise has also worked in correctional centres, youth detention centres, and women's centres. Her parents along with many brothers and sisters were major influences in her life and more than a few of the "Chambers" family are well-known artists. Denise has lived for many years with her husband David at The Gap Queensland, where she has set up a studio and likes to paint into the small hours of the morning. She continually supports her family, her community, and her country.

Cheryl Rau is of Tainui, Kahungungu, and Rangitane descent and is currently the central regional manager for Te Tari Puna Ora o Aotearoa/New Zealand Childcare Association. Her educational and research focus has centered on Te Tiriti o Waitangi partnerships in Aotearoa, with Māori educators articulating strategies that nurture tamariki '*Māori potentiality across the early childhood community and support.*' Indigenous children's rights to quality early childhood education. Cheryl's 30-year background in education has been across sector, including primary, secondary, tertiary, and community, and she was previously involved in early childhood professional learning programmes as the coordinator/director of Ngāhihi.

Jenny Ritchie has a background as a childcare educator and kindergarten teacher, followed by 23 years' experience in early childhood teacher education. She is Associate Professor in Early Childhood Teacher Education at Te Whare Wānanga o Wairaka–Unitec Institute of Technology, Auckland, New Zealand. Her teaching, research, and writing has focused on supporting early childhood educators and teacher educators to enhance their praxis in terms of cultural, environmental, and social justice issues. She has recently led three consecutive two-year studies funded by the New Zealand Teaching and Learning Research Initiative. Her recent publications include: "Early Childhood Education as a Site of Ecocentric Counter-Colonial Endeavor in Aotearoa New Zealand" (2012) in the journal *Contemporary Issues in Early Childhood*; and "Titiro Whakamuri, Hoki Whakamua: Respectful Integration of Māori Perspectives Within Early Childhood Environmental Education" in the *Canadian Journal of Environmental Education* (2012).

Cinthya M. Saavedra is an Assistant Professor of ESL and Diversity Education at Utah State University. She has taught bilingual pre-kindergarten and third grade. Her research interests, rooted in her own transnational experiences, include Chicana/Latina and transnational feminist, de/post/colonial investigations of childhood studies and immigrant education. She has published in the *Journal of Early Childhood Research, Journal of Latinos and Education, Equity & Excellence, Urban Education, Language Arts, International Journal of Qualitative Studies in Education*, and in the *Handbook of Critical and Indigenous Methodologies* (Denzin, Lincoln, & Smith [eds.], Sage, 2008) and in *Childhoods: A Handbook* (Cannella & Soto [eds.], Peter Lang, 2010).

Jonathan Silin is a Fellow at the Mark S. Bonham Centre for Sexual Diversity Studies, University of Toronto. Previously a member of the graduate faculty at Bank Street College of Education, he continues as Editor of Bank Street's Occasional Papers series. He is the author of *Sex, Death, and the Education of Children: Our Passion for Ignorance in the Age of AIDS* (Teachers College Press, 1995), and *My Father's Keeper: The Story of a Gay Son and His Aging Parents* (Beacon, 2007). He is also co-editor (with Carol Lippman) of *Putting the Children First: The Changing Face of Newark's Public Schools* (Teachers College Press, 2003) and co-producer of *Children Talk About AIDS*. His numerous scholarly essays have appeared in *Educational Theory, Harvard Educational Review, Reading Research Quarterly*, and *Teachers College Record*. His occasional essays have also appeared in the *Chronicle of Higher Education, Education Week, Newsday*, and *The New York Times*. Most recently his work was the subject of a special issue of *Contemporary Issues in Early Childhood*.

Kylie Smith is a Research Fellow and Senior Lecturer in the Youth Research Centre at the Melbourne Graduate School of Education, Melbourne University. Kylie's research examines how theory and practice can challenge the operation of equity in the early childhood classroom and she has worked with children, parents, and teachers to build safe and respectful communities. Kylie's research is also informed by 25 years of experience working in early childhood services.

Beth Blue Swadener is Professor of Justice and Social Inquiry and Associate Director of the School of Social Transformation at Arizona State University. Her research focuses on internationally comparative social policy, with focus on sub-Saharan Africa, and children's rights and voices. She has published ten books, including *Reconceptualizing the Early Childhood Curriculum* (Teachers College Press, 1992); *Children and Families "At Promise"* (SUNY Press, 1995);

Does the Village Still Raise the Child? (SUNY Press, 2000); *Decolonizing Research in Cross-Cultural Context* (SUNY Press, 2011); and *Children's Rights and Education: International Perspectives* (Peter Lang, 2013). She is a Co-Founder of the Jirani Project (www.jiraniproject.org), serving children in Kenya, and is a Founder of Reconceptualizing Early Childhood Education (RECE; www.receinternational.org). She received the Reconceptualizing Early Childhood Education Bloch Distinguished Career Award in 2013.

Affrica Taylor is Associate Professor in the Geographies of Education and Childhood at the University of Canberra. She has a PhD in Cultural Geography and has worked for many years in Aboriginal education. These experiences have shaped her interest in the relations between children, place, and nonhuman animals. Affrica draws upon more-than-human geographies and alternative knowledge systems to reconceptualize childhood, nature, and pedagogy in challenging ecological times. She is part of an international research collective that brings decolonizing, material, and ecological feminist perspectives to early childhood education. Pursuing the potential for fashioning more liveable worlds, Affrica's recent research traces the ways in which children's lives are discursively and materially entangled with others—human and more-than-human. Her 2013 book, *Reconfiguring the Natures of Childhood* (Routledge), considers the ethical and political concerns and pedagogical affordances of children's common world relations, including relations between cohabiting children and animals.

Ebba Theorell practiced and studied the pedagogic/aesthetic philosophy of Reggio Emilia in Italy (1999–2000) and has since then been working with children and teachers in different projects in schools and preschools. Her basic training is in art and she studied aesthetics at the Södertörn University and documentary film at the Stockholm Academy of Dramatic Arts. She is active as a course leader, supervisor, artist, and she is also a Guest Lecturer at the Stockholm University. In the project presented in this book, Ebba Theorell was Research Assistant and Artistic/Empirical Consultant. In relation to the theoretical basis created by Liselott Olsson and Gunilla Dahlberg, she designed situations for children in preschools that encouraged them to experiment with reading and writing. Her documentation of the children's work consists of films, notes, and photos. The collected material was analyzed in close collaboration with Liselott Olsson and Gunilla Dahlberg.

Mathias Urban is Professor of Early Childhood at the University of Roehampton, London. His research interests unfold around questions of diversity and equality, participatory evaluation, and professionalism in working with young children, families, and communities in diverse sociocultural contexts. Mathias has recently directed a pan-European study on competence requirements in early childhood and care (Urban, Vandenbroeck, Van Laere, Lazzari, & Peeters, 2011, 2012). He currently directs studies on early childhood professionalism in Colombia (Perfiles de Talento Humano para la Atención Integral a la Primera Infancia: Exploración de Requisitos en Colombia) and on early childhood provision for Romani children in Central and Eastern Europe (Roma Early Childhood Inclusion [RECI+]). His recent work includes international case-based comparisons on change processes in early childhood systems ("Strategies for Change," in Hayes & Bradley, *A Decade of Reflection, Centre for Social and Educational Research*, Dublin, 2007), and on professional epistemologies and habitus (*A Day in the Life of an Early Years Practitioner*, Dalli, Miller, Urban, 2011). He has published extensively on professionalism and diversity in early childhood.

Joseph Michael Valente is an Assistant Professor of Early Childhood Education at Pennsylvania State University. He is also the Co-Director of the Center for Disability Studies and core faculty in the Comparative and International Education program. Dr. Valente is the Co-Principal Investigator of the video ethnographic study "Kindergartens for the Deaf in Three Countries: Japan, France, and the United States" funded by the Spencer Foundation, and author of the research-novel *d/Deaf and d/Dumb: A Portrait of a Deaf Kid as a Young Superhero* (Peter Lang). To learn more about Dr. Valente's work, you can visit his website: www.joevalente.net.

Travis Wright is Assistant Professor of Early Childhood Education in the Department of Curriculum and Instruction at the University of Wisconsin – Madison. His research interests focus primarily on four interconnected areas: (1) elucidating how young children, their teachers, and parents experience schools and other early childhood educational settings; (2) strengthening the capacity of early learning environments to serve young children with social-emotional and behavioral challenges; (3) the impact of poverty, trauma, and other forms of toxic stress on the resilience of young children and their families; and (4) qualitative research methodologies. Dr. Wright previously worked as a school-based mental health counselor and public school teacher in Washington, DC and Boston Public Schools.

Nicola Yelland is a Research Professor in the School of Education at Victoria University in Melbourne Australia. Her multidisciplinary research focus has enabled her to work with early childhood, primary, and middle school teachers to enhance the ways in which ICT can be incorporated into learning contexts to make them more interesting and motivating for students, so that educational outcomes are improved. Some recent publications are *Contemporary Perspectives on Early Childhood Education* (OUP) and *Rethinking Learning in Early Childhood Education* (OUP). She is the author of *Shift to the Future: Rethinking Learning With New Technologies in Education* (Routledge, New York). Professor Yelland is the Founding Editor of two journals *Contemporary Issues in Early Childhood* and *Global Studies of Childhood*. She has extensive experience in research projects. Most recently she has been the Co-Convenor (with Lee) of researchers from Malaysia, Thailand, Korea, Taiwan, Hong Kong, and Japan from anthropology, sociology, information and communications technologies, health sciences, and education which will research aspects of *Global Childhoods* (e.g., migration, health and welfare, literacy, popular culture) in the region.

RETHINKING CHILDHOOD

GAILE S. CANNELLA, *General Editor*

Researchers in a range of fields have acknowledged that childhood is a construct emerging from modernist perspectives that have not always benefited those who are younger. The purpose of the Rethinking Childhood Series is to provide a critical location for scholarship that challenges the universalization of childhood and introduces new, reconceptualized, and critical spaces from which opportunities and possibilities are generated for children. Diverse histories and cultures are considered of major importance as well as issues of critical social justice.

We are particularly interested in manuscripts that provide insight into the contemporary neoliberal conditions experienced by those who are labeled "children" as well as authored and edited volumes that illustrate life and educational experiences that challenge present conditions. Rethinking childhood work related to critical education and care, childhood public policy, family and community voices, and critical social activism is encouraged.

For more information about this series or for submission of manuscripts, please contact:

> Gaile S. Cannella
> Gaile.Cannella@unt.edu

To order other books in this series, please contact our Customer Service Department at:

> (800) 770-LANG (within the U.S.)
> (212) 647-7706 (outside the U.S.)
> (212) 647-7707 FAX

Or browse online by series at:
> www.peterlang.com